Stimulus Generalization

Stimulus Generalization

Edited by David I. Mostofsky

Stanford University Press, Stanford, California   1965

Preface

The papers that follow have been prepared by authorities in their respective fields, each in its own way related to stimulus generalization. The collection has not been designed to present the reader with a comprehensive detailed review, though fortuitously it may well come rather close. Neither does it parade as a definitive catalogue of theoretical arguments or empirical studies, although it has the hallmarks of representative sampling from these areas. In a sense, it is an outgrowth of the concern for the confusion attending stimulus generalization experimentation. Never had there been a formal intensive discussion among psychologists sharing a common interest in this field of investigation; certainly never had there been prepared a collection of theoretical and empirical expositions. The sheer volume of activities in this area seemed to warrant convening a meeting. Such a meeting was held at Boston University in June 1963.

From the recommendations of a number of interested psychologists, the final format was molded. At the outset, however, it became necessary to restrict the focus of the conference to those interests that have been primarily pursued in the traditional learning framework of stimulus generalization. To have included such areas as verbal generalization and clinical applications would have extended the scope and size of the program. Participants were invited to present a formal paper without restrictions on length, style, or topic. The papers were distributed prior to the meeting in the hope that it would give the participants ample time to digest the contents and enable them to devote the better part of the three-day meeting to frank discussion. Morning and afternoon sessions were held, during which papers converging on a common issue were discussed. Essentially, the chapters of this book mirror the session themes.

All the papers have been revised since their original presentation, and all but three presented at the conference appear in this volume. The three are: "Generalization and discrimination obtained within the same and different environments" by Garry Margolius, "Nature and variety and levels-varieties of conditioned stimulus generalization" by Gregory Razran, and "Primary stimulus generalization" by William Prokasy and John Hall (which can be found in *Psychol. Rev.*, 1963, **70**, 310–22). To these authors, no less than to their colleagues who went to press, we are indebted.

To Boston University go our thanks for providing the necessary facilities for the conference and for assisting in the preprint copy of the papers. The assistance of the university was itself made possible through the support of the conference by a grant from the U.S. Public Health Service (MH-07348-01). Finally, for making these papers available to their interested audience, a sincere thanks is conveyed to the various officers of the Stanford University Press. I would be remiss not to acknowledge a personal debt to Garry Margolius and Donald Shurtleff, who provided the needed wit and wisdom which seems to lighten the unenviable burden of an editor.

This, then, is a product of the efforts and goals of the stimulus generalization conference. Not everything troublesome was discussed, not everything discussed was resolved. But during the three days of deliberations, and the translation of some of those discussions in the succeeding pages, it is hoped that some new generalizations became possible.

D. M.

Contents

Stimulus Generalization

Introduction

David I. Mostofsky, *Boston University*

Stimulus generalization has been variously defined. Hull (1943) called it "the reaction involved in the original conditioning [becoming] connected with a considerable zone of stimuli other than, but adjacent to, the stimulus involved in the original conditioning." Hilgard and Marquis (1940) described it as "the behavioral fact that a conditioned response formed to one stimulus may also be elicited by other stimuli which have not been used in the course of conditioning." And according to Dollard and Miller (1950), "Once a response has been reinforced in one situation, the function of generalization is to increase the probability that the response will occur in other similar situations."

One can readily notice different emphases in the respective definitions, i.e., a stimulus emphasis (the acquisition of behavior control by additional stimuli), a response emphasis (the transfer of the conditioned response to other conditions), and a process emphasis (the role of generalization as mediating response probability). But however defined, stimulus generalization is accepted by contemporary writers as an undeniable characteristic of behavior: "The fact is now so well established in both respondent and operant behavior that we may state it as a principle" (Keller and Schoenfeld, 1950). As a result, there is hardly any serious exposition of behavior that does not attempt to account for the phenomenon.

In introducing their review of the stimulus generalization literature, Mednick and Freedman (1960) declare:

Stimulus generalization is an empirical phenomenon which has, of late, been seeing heavy duty as an explanatory construct in many disparate situations. It has been used in theoretical explanations of discrimination learning . . . transposition . . . verbal learning . . . psychoanalytic displacement . . . the behavior of brain-damaged individuals and schizophrenics . . . cross-cultural research . . . projective techniques . . . and psychotherapy. It seems likely that these explicatory uses of stimulus generalization are only a beginning.

The diversified energies invested in this "beginning" are represented by the 127 references cited by the authors, and if the current rate of publication may be taken as a reliable predictor, we should not be surprised to witness additional surveys and evaluations of this activity.

The concept of stimulus generalization is attributed to Pavlov, who some fifty years ago wrote:

If a tone of 1000 dv is established as a conditioned stimulus, many other tones spontaneously acquire similar properties, such properties diminishing proportionally to the intervals of these tones from the one of 1000 dv. . . . The same is observed with stimulation of other receptor organs. . . . This spontaneous development . . . we have termed . . . generalization of stimuli (Pavlov, 1927, p. 113). . . . The following interpretation [of the mechanism of generalization] seems best to agree with our present knowledge. It may be assumed that each element of the receptor apparatus gains representation in the cortex of the hemispheres through its own proper central neurone, and the peripheral grouping of the receptor organs may be regarded as projecting itself in a definite grouping of nervous elements in the cortex. A nervous impulse reaching the cortex from a definite point from the peripheral receptor does not give rise to an excitation which is limited within the corresponding cortical element, but the excitation irradiates from its point of origin over the cortex, diminishing in intensity the further it spreads from the center of excitation. (Pavlov, 1927, p. 186.)

A careful examination of the above exposition will reveal many of the complex considerations inherent in the phenomenon of stimulus generalization, as well as the status Pavlov had accorded it in his theoretical system. He had (a) noted the operations necessary for demonstrating the phenomenon, (b) described the nature of the orderly decrement to be expected in a gradient of generalization, (c) suggested that the general effect is not unique to an isolated stimulus dimension, and (d) invoked stimulus generalization as relevant to his conception of neural irradiation as an explanation of observed behaviors.

After Pavlov

The experimentation that has since been pursued in the United States has, in course, investigated each of these detailed aspects. But whereas Pavlov's dominant interest was with neurological mechanisms, the prime interest of the later investigators was behavioral. The early work carried out in this country cast serious doubt on the tenability of neural irradiation as an explanation for generalization (Hovland, 1937), and subsequent experimentation has, in the main, continued to focus on the investigation of stimulus generalization sans neuro-philosophy. It has on occasion been possible to demonstrate the phenomenon even in the face of serious departures from the original Pavlovian specifications. Alternately, it has been shown that relatively subtle and reasonable changes in the experimental conditions can prevent a demonstration of empirical generalization.

The work that followed Pavlov's formulation was as diverse as it was intensive. Any one of several organizational schemas can be applied to describe these investigations, e.g., a grouping of the studies concerned with a common physical stimulus dimension, a common method for establishing a conditioned response, etc. These studies can also be categorized in terms of historical continuity. If this criterion is adopted, at least two major departures from the Pavlovian tradition seem evident and warrant mention, because of the respective directions they gave to subsequent investigations.

The first departure may be associated with Hull. It was he who first drew upon stimulus generalization, incorporating it into his theoretical behavior system while rejecting the isomorphic underlying neurological mechanisms postulated by Pavlov. This de-emphasis of the role of neural irradiation was later accompanied by experimentation using instrumental conditioning techniques as opposed to the original (classical conditioning) methodology advocated by Pavlov. The change was indeed a major one, and Hull and his students proceeded to study stimulus generalization under these conditions with a particular interest in the theoretical ramifications that a *concept* of generalization might offer as an explanatory device or construct. Requiring an adequate model to account for many behaviors, independent of any specific stimulus or response, stimulus generalization became especially suited as a key concept in the analyses of behavioral transfer proposed by both Hull and Spence.

Members of the Hull school provided numerous descriptions of parameters of behavior and their relationship to generalization. In general, they sought to provide evidence supporting the existence of a behavioral mechanism of generalization which, akin to the defunct irradiation theory, might account for other observable events, e.g., the summation of habit strengths leading to overt response production.

The second major departure from the Pavlovian position led to an important avenue of research identified largely with Skinner and the problems of stimulus control. Even more than Hull, Skinner (1938) dismissed any notion of underlying neural activity, and any interest in it even if such activity were shown to be present, while employing operant conditioning techniques. In contrast to Hull, Skinner clearly emphasized *empirical* generalization, regarding it as a behavioral phenomenon and attaching no major theoretical status to the term. For him, stimulus generalization was simply an observable datum. As such, it might be regarded as a dependent variable, or as a set of operations to be used as a testing technique. The data collected with the operant technique have commonly been in the form of response rate as opposed to discrete, single-trial responding. The use of the rate measure is worthy of note if only because of our inability at this time to ascertain its importance (Blough, this vol.).

The distinction in interpretive emphasis of stimulus generalization deriving from the cited departures has been previously formulated as distinguishing between the "empirical phenomenon of generalization" and "theories or hypotheses about generalization" (Brown, Bilodeau, and Baron, 1951). Although there is undeniable merit in maintaining this logical distinction between the theoretical and the empirical, there does not seem to be an implication of mutual exclusiveness. Many a study concerned with the one has felt compelled to treat the other, though often to its disadvantage. Perhaps the first major study attempting to seriously unite both objectives in a single design was reported by Guttman and Kalish (1956). In this study, discriminability and generalization, as concept and as datum, were jointly discussed. In many studies the student of the literature will readily detect a theoretical emphasis. Many others, however, he will find extremely difficult to classify as either theoretical or empirical. This may well lead to an unfortunate confusion whereby the term stimulus generalization is applied equally to define experiments approximating a Pavlovian description, to arguments seeking an explanatory concept for behavior, and to various combinations of these objectives.

Notwithstanding these problems, contemporary research continues to be concerned with theoretical relevancies on the one hand, and with utilizing stimulus generalization as a dependent variable or testing technique on the other (e.g., Guttman, 1963). The chapters in this book also bear out this contention. It would seem that demonstrations of stimulus generalization and psychophysical performances (Stevens), mediational behavior (Grice), and the problems of attention (Ganz) and/or response hierarchies (Baron) are more closely aligned with the theoretical issues. The papers by Jenkins and Perkins reflect this more obviously. In contrast, the investigations reported by Skinner, the matching-to-sample problem (Cumming and Berryman), the generalization of secondary reinforcement (Thomas), and the use of aversive reinforcement (Hearst; Hoffman) and physiological manipulations (Butter *et al.*; Randall; Thompson) seem to be more concerned with stimulus generalization as a means of assessing relative behavioral control.

Some of the Problems

The preoccupation with stimulus generalization at both the theoretical level and the empirical level has not been restricted to students of Pavlov, Hull, and Skinner. The extent of the interest has already been noted, and there is no apparent indication of a decline in the near future. But in the course of past—and even present—efforts, more than technological or behavioral design problems have been left unanswered. Indeed, fundamental questioning continues. Consider, for example, the meaning of generalization. One could have asked of Pavlov, as indeed Klüver did (1933), the rationale for introducing generalization in the face of an already accepted verbal descriptor of differentiation (or discrimination). The proper defense rests on demonstrating the need for a new term to explain an event not accountable for in the existing language of differentiation. Klüver, for one, summarized his objection to retaining such a distinction between the two terms as follows: "Nothing seems to be gained by classifying certain forms of responses as 'generalizations' and others as 'differentiations.' Every 'generalization' is at the same time a 'differentiation' and vice versa." This view of stimulus generalization differs dramatically from both Hull's and Skinner's. In fact, it asserts that the use of the stimulus generalization label is at best redundant and at worst confounding. If accepted, this argument destroys the logical basis of studies designed to relate discrimination to generalization. No doubt the reader will appreciate echoes of this sentiment in the papers in this volume, especially Brown's.

One may also question whether it is valid to assume as invariant, a generalization gradient having a non-zero slope. Although the majority of scientists probably tend to be more surprised at an outcome not exhibiting a "typical" gradient, there is little evidence to indicate that such surprise is inspired by anything other than simple faith. To be sure, there exists a documentation of *some* of the operations that can bring about a change in the slope or symmetry of a gradient (Guttman; Friedman and Guttman; this vol.). But the basic issue revolves around the specification of conditions that can guarantee the invariant result of a gradient having definable slope, i.e., the necessary *and sufficient* conditions. It is known, for example, that the very existence of a gradient may depend upon the physical continuum used or the type of data derived from the experimental situation, i.e., frequency, latency, rate. Yet the problems of measurement arising in stimulus generalization research have only recently been attacked. And only recently has attention been paid to the metric—subjective as well as objective—in the stimulus spacings of the stimulus generalization test. The recognition of the multivariate nature of the situation is relatively new, and the measurement schemes accompanying it are only now being subjected to more sophisticated analyses (Cross; Shepard; this vol.).

A host of problems remains. One hears with greater frequency the challenge that studies conducted under the general heading of stimulus generalization research are not, *de facto*, comparable. Specifically, the validity of comparisons between a study using positive reinforcement and one using negative (or aversive) reinforcement is questionable. Similarly, doubt is raised on the merits of relating the findings of a stimulus generalization study preceded by prior differential discrimination training to one employing single-stimulus training. Equally troublesome is the disparity existing between an experiment in which subjects are given verbal instructions and a study relying solely upon conditioning techniques. As for generalization gradients, the legitimacy of comparing the "true" generalization gradient (obtained in complete extinction) with the discrimination gradient (obtained in a situation that provides for the continued reinforcement of the S⁺) is still suspect.

It would be difficult to attempt an exhaustive listing of the possible variations that can, conceivably, render cross-study comparisons futile. But these variations exist. And although some are subtle (reasonable?) and some are obviously more drastic, the investigator has little information with which to judge or evaluate these differences, or which might enable him to produce the invariant gradient of stimulus generalization, or perhaps to discover the futility of seeking it. These are questions to which few answers have been offered. But in the face of this apparent sea of ignorance stimulus generalization has established itself in the vocabulary of psychology and enthusiasm for going ahead with better controlled and more elaborate experimentation has not waned.

REFERENCES

Brown, J. S., Bilodeau, E. A., and Baron, M. R. "Bidirectional gradients in the strength of a generalized voluntary response to stimuli on a visual spatial dimension." *J. exp. Psychol.*, 1951, **41**, 52–61.

Dollard, J., and Miller, N. E. *Personality and psychotherapy.* New York: McGraw-Hill, 1950.

Guttman, N. "Laws of behavior and facts of perception." In S. Koch (Ed.), *Psychology: A study of a science*, Vol. 5. New York: McGraw-Hill, 1963.

Guttman, N., and Kalish, H. E. "Discriminability and stimulus generalization." *J. exp. Psychol.*, 1956, **51**, 79–88.

Hilgard, E. R., and Marquis, D. G. *Conditioning and learning.* New York: Appleton-Century, 1940.

Hovland, C. I. "The generalization of conditioned responses: I. The sensory generalization of conditioned responses with varying frequencies of tone." *J. gen. Psychol.*, 1937, **17**, 125–148.

Hull, C. L. *Principles of behavior.* New York: Appleton-Century-Crofts, 1943.

Keller, F. S., and Schoenfeld, W. N. *Principles of Psychology.* New York: Appleton-Century-Crofts, 1950.

Klüver, H. *Behavioral mechanisms in monkeys.* Chicago: Univer. of Chicago Press, 1933.

Mednick, S. A., and Freedman, J. L. "Stimulus generalization." *Psychol. Bull.*, 1960, **57**, 169–200.

Pavlov, I. P. *Conditioned reflexes,* translated by G. V. Anrep. London: Oxford Univer. Press, 1927.

Skinner, B. F. *The behavior of organisms.* New York: Appleton-Century, 1938.

Spence, K. W. "The differential response in animals to stimuli varying within a single dimension." *Psychol. Rev.*, 1937, **44**, 430–444.

1. Generalization and Discrimination

Judson S. Brown, *University of Oregon Medical School*

The aim of this paper is to provide an analysis of some of the semantic and theoretical problems arising from the diverse ways in which experimenters and theorists use, misuse, and confuse the terms generalization and discrimination. That each of these terms has meant and continues to mean quite different things to different writers is trivially obvious. But the fact that few attempts are made, in practice, to explain the meanings of these terms is not so trivial. Regrettably, our psychological culture permits us to be highly secretive with respect to the meanings we assign to certain terms, and it is upon such vaguenesses that controversy thrives. Surely the time is ripe for a careful reappraisal of these terminological matters.

Two Kinds of Stimulus Generalization

From an examination of the extant literature on stimulus generalization it seems fair to say that, in general, those who use the term mean by it either (1) a simple, concrete empirical phenomenon or (2) some rather abstract process that underlies, mediates, and allegedly *explains* the empirical phenomenon. We consider these two conceptions in turn.

Probably the least controversial view of stimulus generalization is the one that equates it to an empirical phenomenon. To adopt this position one asserts, by definition, that a subject exhibits generalization if, after he has learned to respond to a conditioned stimulus (CS), he reacts in an identical or similar way to a non-conditioned (generalized) stimulus (GS), even in the absence of specific training to the GS. Defined in this manner, the concept of stimulus generalization means simply that *transfer of training has in fact occurred,* and nothing more. Hereafter, this will be called a Type 1 definition, and generalization of this sort will frequently be des-

The expenses incurred in the preparation of this manuscript have been defrayed, in part, by Grant MH 06900-02 (National Institute of Mental Health) and Grant HE 06336 (National Heart Institute), United States Public Health Service. The author is indebted to R. F. Thompson, R. D. Fitzgerald, and H. D. Kimmel for their critically careful readings of the manuscript.

TABLE 1

THE TWO MAIN CLASSES OF DEFINITION PROVIDED FOR THE TERMS GENERALIZATION
AND DISCRIMINATION IN PSYCHOLOGICAL WRITINGS

	Generalization	*Discrimination*
Type 2 Definitions	Variously defined as: spread of cortical excitation, spread of habit strength, excitation of common sets of neural elements, etc.	Variously defined as: conscious awareness of differences, perception of similarities, a process preventing empirical generalization, etc.

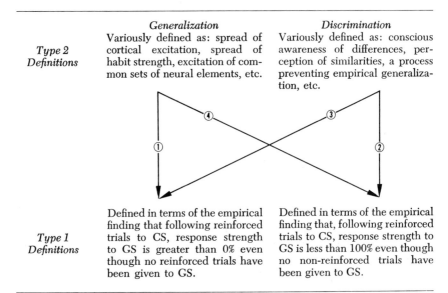

	Generalization	*Discrimination*
Type 1 Definitions	Defined in terms of the empirical finding that following reinforced trials to CS, response strength to GS is greater than 0% even though no reinforced trials have been given to GS.	Defined in terms of the empirical finding that, following reinforced trials to CS, response strength to GS is less than 100% even though no non-reinforced trials have been given to GS.

ignated by a subscript, thus: *generalization*$_1$. One possible form of such a definition is presented for summary and reference purposes in the lower left-hand corner of Table 1. Although incomplete, it is essentially a "definition in use," being likewise operational—at least in principle, if not in detail—since it indicates generally the conditions that must be fulfilled for the intended meaning to be conveyed to the listener.

It is with reference to the detailed nature of these boundary conditions that writers differ considerably, even though all may still use stimulus generalization in this empirical sense. Some might thus insist that one or more of the following conditions must be met if the obtained experimental data are to be regarded as legitimate instances of stimulus generalization: (1) the original learning must be produced by classical conditioning; (2) differential reinforcement must be scrupulously avoided; (3) the distance between the CS and the GS must be expressed in subjectively equal units; and (4) the subjects must not have been exposed to either of the stimuli prior to the experiment. These qualifying variations require comment, to be sure, but I shall defer that task for the moment.

The second major way in which stimulus generalization (or just generalization) has been used is as *a name for some kind of covert process or mechanism conceived to underlie or determine overt transfer.* To be specific, those who use generalization to mean a spread of habit strength, or a postulated spread of cortical excitation (irradiation), or the presence and associative consequences of identical stimulus elements, are using the term in this second sense. Several Type 2 usages are listed in the upper left-hand corner of Table 1. The No. 1 arrow denotes the common assumption that a spread of habit strength, for example, "explains" or permits one to deduce the empirical phenomenon of transfer. The other arrows likewise designate assumptions that have been made regarding explanatory roles purportedly served by Type 2 mechanisms with respect to Type 1 phenomena. As components of a behavior system, generalization$_1$ occupies the position of a dependent variable, whereas a Type 2 conception (generalization$_2$) fulfills the function of an intermediary construct.

That these two meanings have often been confounded is evident to any student of relevant writings. To take a single example, very nearly at random, we exhibit the opening sentence of a recent summary of the generalization literature, which reads: "Stimulus generalization (SG) is an empirical phenomenon which has, of late, been seeing heavy duty as an explanatory construct in many disparate situations" (Mednick and Freedman, 1960, p. 169). Manifestly, generalization is being used in a Type 1 sense in the first part of this sentence and in a Type 2 sense in the latter portion. If generalization is consistently treated as an empirical phenomenon, as a dependent variable, as the fact of transfer of training, it makes little sense to speak of it in the same breath as an "explanatory concept." For example, the observation that a dog exhibits generalized salivary reactions to a non-conditioned test stimulus on odd-numbered trials does not, in any important way, explain the appearance of similar generalized reactions on even-numbered trials. Neither does the dog's behavior on *any* set of trials explain the appearance of intrusion errors in human verbal learning. Two purely empirical concepts cannot play significant explanatory roles with respect to one another.

Two Types of Discrimination

Now let us examine the two principal ways in which the term discrimination has been used. As with generalization, discrimination may be taken to mean nothing more than a parcel of empirical facts. By this definition a subject is discriminating (i.e., reacting differentially) if, after he has been trained to respond to a CS, he does *not* react with comparable vigor to a GS, even though no non-reinforced trials (and no reinforced trials either, of course) with that GS have been administered. Used thus, discrimination is simply *a failure (complete or partial) of training to transfer from one stimulus to another*. A formal definition reflecting this usage would be of the conventional "if and only if" form, with discrimination emerging as a behavioral measure having the status of a dependent variable. We shall usually refer to this meaning as "discrimination$_1$," and have added a partial Type 1 definition of it to our collection in the lower right-hand corner of Table 1. Incidentally, identical conditions of training and testing are assumed to have been involved in gathering the empirical data that define both generalization$_1$ and discrimination$_1$. Up to this point, therefore, the two terms carry no implied references to different experimental procedures.

One additional comment is necessary. If we cling to an empirical, Type 1 meaning of discrimination, we cannot appeal to that kind of discrimination for explanations of differential responding, since the two are indistinguishable. This parallels the point made earlier in connection with Type 1 definitions of generalization.

The second meanings of discrimination (upper right-hand corner of Table 1) include much more than just the empirical phenomenon of differential reactivity. Discrimination structured in this way denotes, rather vaguely, *a kind of conscious awareness or a perceptual-judgmental activity that is treated as the precursor to, and immanent determinant of, overt activity of one sort or another.* While discrimination couched in this perceptual-cognitive language can, in principle, be given an acceptable *formal* definition, this has rarely been done by those who find such terms congenial.

Inevitably, discrimination in this sense (discrimination$_2$) is frequently advanced as an *explanation* of discrimination$_1$. This relation is symbolized by the No. 2 arrow in Table 1. Discrimination$_2$ thus stands in the same relation to differential reactivity as does, say, generalized habit strength to empirical generalization. One might be said to react differentially (discrimination$_1$) *because* he discriminates (Type 2) the difference between the conditioned and non-conditioned (generalized) stimuli.

The Relation of Generalization$_1$ to Discrimination$_1$

Given the Type 1 meanings of our two key terms, and limiting the discussion to that level for the moment, what can now be said about the possible interrelations of generalization and discrimination? As we shall see, the answers turn on whether one is concerned with just a single data point or with a gradient, and on the kinds of variables one manipulates and evaluates in his studies. To make this unequivocally clear, at the risk of becoming pedantic, we consider the fictitious data plotted in Fig. 1. The curve in this graph simulates the outcome of a conventional study of stimulus generalization in which conditioning methods have been used to build up response strength to the CS, and responses to GS-1 and GS-2 have been measured without the prior introduction of differential reinforcement.

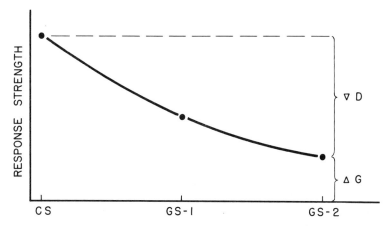

FIG. 1. Results of a fictitious study of stimulus generalization in which subjects have been trained to respond to the CS and are then tested by the presentation of GS-1 and GS-2.

The response-strength value plotted at GS-2 is singled out for consideration, and our attention is focused on the finding that the subjects did indeed respond to GS-2, i.e., upon the fact that the value at GS-2 is significantly greater than zero (denoted by Δ G in the figure). This datum signifies that *transfer of training from CS to GS-2 did take place, or that generalization occurred, or both.* But the same point is also some appreciable distance *below* (symbolized by ∇ D) the value corresponding to the CS. This conveys the information that the subjects were *reacting differentially* to GS-2 as compared with CS, and this as we have seen, constitutes or defines discrimination$_1$. Evidently, *when we deal with but a single data-point from a single experiment, generalization$_1$ and discrimination$_1$ turn out to be nothing more than two different ways of reporting the same experimental result.* It is as though a spot on a wall were to be described as either 5 feet from the floor or 3 feet from the ceiling. Generalization$_1$ is the complement of discrimination$_1$, and either way of specifying the location of the point is as complete, accurate, and objective, as the other.

Suppose further that some variable is manipulated which will elevate the value plotted at GS-2. Such an outcome would mean that *generalization (Δ G) has increased while discrimination (∇ D) has decreased.* Conversely, if a change in the variable lowers the same point, one could say that discrimination has improved while generalization has declined. *This is one perfectly clear sense in which generalization$_1$ and discrimination$_1$ can be said to be inversely related.* Given our limiting assumptions, then, the conclusion is unavoidable that generalization$_1$ and discrimination$_1$ are simply two sides of the same coin. Neither term explains the other, neither is logically or systematically preferable, and neither is theoretically more immaculate than the other.

But now imagine that a different variable is manipulated, e.g., the number of conditioning trials, and that this elevates and steepens our gradient. Figure 2 shows a pair of curves that might be obtained with two values of such a variable. Notice that as the gradient becomes higher and steeper, generalization$_1$ and discrimination$_1$ both increase. That is $\Delta G_2 > \Delta G_1$ and $\nabla D_2 > \nabla D_1$. In this case then, *generalization$_1$ and discrimination$_1$ are seen to be directly, rather than inversely, related!* This one reason why I insisted at an earlier point that the relations of the two concepts are unique to the kinds of data one selects to integrate into one's concept as well as to one's choice of definition.

Furthermore, if a manipulated variable raises (or lowers) the gradient without altering its slope (as in Fig. 3), generalization$_1$ may increase (or decrease) without in any way affecting discrimination$_1$. An inverse relation between generalization and discrimination can be demonstrated across transformations induced by altering some variable, if the gradient becomes flatter as it becomes higher (or steeper as it becomes lower).

Whether one uses an absolute generalization index, as in all of our previous examples, or a relative index must also be considered. Thus, if the magnitude of response to a GS is expressed as a percentage of response to a CS, yielding the customary relative generalization score, identical percentage figures can be obtained, as a variable is altered, even though

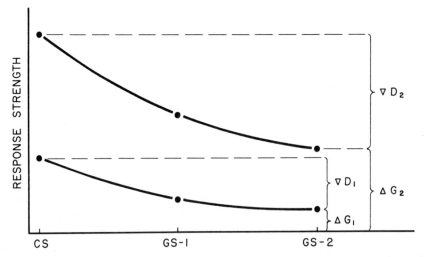

FIG. 2. The upper curve is presumed to represent a generalization gradient obtained following extensive training in responding to the CS. The lower curve suggests the outcome with fewer training trials.

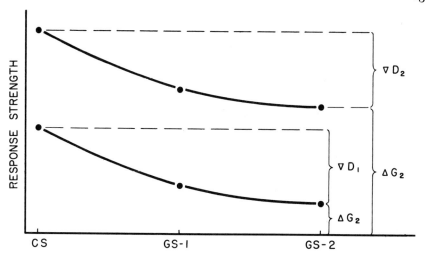

FIG. 3. Fictitious generalization gradients that are parallel throughout, though different in height.

the absolute difference between the magnitude of response to CS and to GS is multi-valued. And since the absolute difference may be taken as reflecting discrimination, we are provided with still another instance in which generalization (relative in this case) remains constant across certain transformations while discrimination does not.

From the foregoing, then, we conclude that so long as the analysis is limited to a single static data-point derived from a single experimental task, our two concepts do indeed turn out to be inversely related, but in such a trivial fashion that the use of the two concepts seems redundant. Moreover, when changes are produced by the manipulation of certain variables, the two constructs can be shown to be directly or inversely related or even quite unrelated, depending on the kinds of variables and measures that have been chosen.

Failure to Discriminate as the Cause of Generalization

The preceding analysis reveals some unsuspected complexities attending the unelaborated assertion that generalization and discrimination are inversely related even when both are explicitly defined as empirical phenomena. However, the conclusion that generalization$_1$ and discrimination$_1$ may be related in several ways or even unrelated permits us to dismiss, as without uniform meaning, the assertion that generalization$_1$ stems from a failure of discrimination$_1$. The conclusion is restricted, naturally, to cases in which the data have been gathered from a single reference task.

To be perfectly fair, however, to those who have sought to interpret generalization in terms of discrimination and to those who have tried experimentally to illuminate the relations of the two concepts, it must be noted that they have not confined themselves to our Type 1 meanings. Instead, they seem rather generally to have adopted a Type 2 meaning of discrimination along with a Type 1 definition of generalization. For example, Kimble (1961, p. 361) asserts "There must be an influence which restricts the range of generalization and restrains the organism from making the same response to all physically similar stimuli. This influence is called *discrimination*." Adopting a Type 2 definition of discrimination in this manner readily leads to the assertion that "generalization occurs to the extent that the organism fails to discriminate" (Kalish, 1958, p. 637), or to the statement that "the generalization function is the result of a failure to discriminate." This, it will be seen, is essentially the conception of generalization favored by Lashley and Wade (1946), Schlosberg and Solomon (1943), Philip (1947), and in some measure by Mednick and Freedman (1960). The No. 3 arrow in Table 1 schematizes this view.

To evaluate this idea in all of its various ramifications would take us far beyond the intended scope of this paper. Some new light may be shed on this problem, however, if it is re-examined in terms of the distinctions that have been made above. Consider, for instance, that generalization$_1$ and discrimination$_1$ can be shown to be inversely related in some one of the several ways in which we have found this to be possible. If it can now be alleged that discrimination$_2$ is *directly* related to discrimination$_1$ (our No. 2 arrow), then generalization$_1$ and discrimination$_2$ *must* be inversely related. In other words, if reacting differentially can justifiably be put down to a perception of a difference between one stimulus and another, then not reacting differentially (generalizing) may, with equal reason, be ascribed to a failure to perceive differences. This conclusion is invalid, naturally, for all instances in which generalization$_1$ and discrimination$_1$ are not inversely related. Since there are evidently many circumstances under which this is true, this stipulation severely limits the generality and utility of the proposition under consideration.

A major problem in this connection is that of achieving definitions of discrimination$_2$ that are sufficiently independent of the process being interpreted. If only a single generalization experiment has been performed and the results are as shown in Fig. 1, we have no basis for saying that the subjects' perceptions served to determine either their generalizations or their differential reactions. The single set of differential responses available to us cannot be used to define both a Type 2 process and the differential reactivity being explained by the process thus defined.

Escape from this vertiginous circularity can be achieved by one or another stratagem, but considerable uncertainty remains about whether the results justify the effort. We illustrate with a specific example from the generalization literature. In an experiment by Brown, Bilodeau, and Baron (1951) subjects were presented with seven small lamp bulbs arranged in a horizontal row at about eye level in a dimly illuminated room. Since the bulbs were white against a black background and were separated by an inter-lamp distance of about eight inches, they could be clearly seen even when unlighted. Moreover, the central light was marked off by a nearby green fixation lamp. The subjects were instructed to react with a manual response as quickly as possible to the lighting of the middle lamp, but to refrain from reacting to other lamps. In spite of these instructions, they exhibited clear-cut tendencies to make "generalized" reactions to the peripheral lamps. Had the subjects been interrogated prior to the experiment, they would not have hesitated to say that they could "tell the difference" between the central and adjacent lamps. Had such a pretest been given, the outcome would have been used as the basis for declaring that the observers could perceive (discrimination$_2$) the differences between and among the lamps. But if so, it would make no sense to say that their generalized responses were due to a "failure to discriminate." Kimble (1961) has emphasized this same point.

The previous example was deliberately selected because the interrogation task that could have been used to define discrimination$_2$ differed markedly from the generalization task. Among other things, the latter involved repeated admonitions to perform the manual (key release) response as quickly as possible, whereas the comparison task would have been administered in a leisurely manner and would have involved verbal reactions. Hence, writers favoring the "failure of discrimination" interpretation could argue that it is not cricket to define a subject's capacity to discriminate in terms of a task that differs so substantially from the to-be-explained task. At first blush this seems like a cogent point, but further consideration brings one face to face with the question of just how similar or how different the two tasks and their respective responses should be. Task similarity could be increased considerably by declaring that performance on the odd-numbered trials of a generalization-test sequence constitutes Task 1 and defines discrimination$_2$. Generalization$_1$, revealed on even-numbered trials, which would be called Task 2, could then be interpreted in terms of discrimination$_2$.

Alternatively, one might take generalization-task performance on Day 1 as defining discrimination$_2$, which is then invoked to explain generalized responses in the same task on Day 2. These examples, while admittedly extreme, make it abundantly clear that as the similarity of the two tasks is increased, it becomes progressively simpler to avoid the accusation of having used an irrelevant or inappropriate task in defining discrimination$_2$. But at the same time there is a concomitant decrease in the probability that the defined concept will add appreciably to our understanding of generalization. As the similarity of the two tasks becomes greater, the appropriateness of the definition increases, while its degree of independence decreases. But at high levels of similarity the explanation may become too trivial to be useful.

Psychophysical Methods and Studies of Stimulus Generalization

In some circles it is often assumed that it is uniquely appropriate as well as illuminating to define discrimination in terms of psychophysical data and then to seek evidence supporting the inverse-relation hypothesis of discrimination and generalization. Guttman and Kalish (1956), for example, have presented various arguments to justify this hypothesis, and have tried to test it by comparing psychophysical discriminability functions with generalization gradients. Although the gradients they obtained through the use of operant conditioning methods with pigeons constitute a landmark in the field, their theoretical expectations were not supported by the data. Subsequently, however, Kalish (1958), in a study with human subjects, obtained better but hardly definitive evidence for the validity of the inverse-relation concept. We comment on these studies in the light of the distinctions made above.

Initially, it is not clear from the report of the Guttman-Kalish experiment whether, in speaking of discrimination, they were referring to discrimination$_1$ or discrimination$_2$. If discrimination$_1$ was what they meant—and this seems likely at times, since they specified discriminability in terms of difference limens based on psychophysical experiments—then they were comparing discrimination$_1$ and generalization$_1$. But even this characterization is misleading. In evaluating the bearing of their results on the inverse hypothesis, they used the *slopes* of the generalization gradients as their basic data, ignoring the absolute amounts of generalization (i.e., generalization$_1$). They were working, therefore, with differences between responses to the CS and the GS, and since a difference score defines our concept of discrimination$_1$, it may be argued that Guttman and Kalish were studying the relation between two different estimates of discrimination$_1$.

Alternatively, if they intended to use the pigeon's difference limens to specify discrimination$_2$—and this jibes with their statement that generalization occurs only to the extent that the organism fails to discriminate— then they were relating discrimination$_2$ to discrimination$_1$. In any case, their own operant–conditioning-derived estimates of differential reactivity were being compared with measures of differential responsiveness drawn from work completed some 30 years earlier, in a different laboratory, and by different methods. In view of the marked dissimilarities of the two tasks, it is hardly surprising that the expectation of an inverse relation was not confirmed. This emphasizes our earlier point that when two tasks differ extensively, concepts based on scores derived from those tasks may not be related in ways that are consistent with one's expectations.

In his 1958 study with human subjects, Kalish used the classic psycho-physical Method of Single Stimuli. But the data obtained by this method were not used to describe discriminability, as one might suppose on first thought, but to define generalization. Further complications arise because the resulting "generalization" data, as in the Guttman-Kalish study, were *slopes* of gradients (psychophysical functions) rather than amounts of absolute generalization. The dependent variable was thus discrimination$_1$ after all, whereupon this experiment also reduces to a comparison of two indices of discrimination$_1$.

The foregoing comments are not intended to be disparaging. They are presented simply to highlight the pitfalls that beset any efforts to draw a sharp line between psychophysical and generalization studies. It must be stressed repeatedly that both methods yield evidence of how well subjects react differentially, or fail thus to react, at the time of the test. Typically, and as a matter of historical fact, the psychophysical methods have pro-duced smaller difference limens than would be obtained from appropriate transformations of generalization data. But this is not a sufficient reason to maintain that these methods alone define the discrimination (whether of Type 1 or 2) which is to be related to generalization. Those wishing to study the relation of our two key concepts thus have considerable freedom in choosing their methods and definitions. Unfortunately, whatever the choice, it will be difficult to avoid the comment that the research involves little more than a comparison of two measures of the same thing.

The blurring of the lines of demarcation between psychophysics and generalization is further underscored by noting that the boundary condi-tions of generalization experiments have changed considerably over the years. At first such studies were uniquely described by the classical Pav-lovian conditioning procedures, but instrumental and operant-conditioning methods are now frequently used. Further departures from the master blueprint are exemplified by studies with human subjects in which volun-tary (instructed) manual reactions and even probability estimations have been employed. Finally, some investigators currently violate tradition still more by applying the label "generalization" to experiments in which differ-ential reinforcement has been explicitly introduced. Differential reinforce-ment procedures are, of course, basic to psychophysical studies of the dis-criminatory capacities of animals, and Kalish (1958, p. 642), for one, has argued that "the use of differential reinforcement during training appears to be the essential difference between studies of generalization and dis-crimination."

Even when differential reinforcement has not been deliberately intro-duced, comparable processes may nevertheless be involved in many gen-eralization studies. Thus, as Perkins (1953) has observed, even the most immaculate classical conditioning procedure may introduce unnoticed dif-ferential reinforcement, since conditioned responses evoked during the intertrial intervals by environmental cues will not be reinforced and will tend to become extinguished. Covert differential reinforcement may likewise be an inherent part of those generalization studies that utilize resistance to extinction as an index of amount of generalization, since reactions to the GSs are not reinforced following consistent reinforcement of responses to the CS.

From these facts it becomes clear that the procedures used in various so-called generalization experiments overlap to such a degree with the techniques employed in studies of psychophysical functions and of discriminatory capacity that no hard and fast distinctions can be defended. Perhaps it is still useful, therefore, as Brown *et al.* (1951) once suggested, to regard generalization and psychophysical studies as members of the same continuum. Both methods yield evidence for differential reactivity and for failures to react differentially. One must view with some caution, therefore, the assertion that generalization and discrimination, not otherwise defined, are related in just one particular way, and that this relation can be appraised by comparing performance on certain tasks alleged to reflect the processes in question.

Failure to Generalize as the Cause of Discrimination

Our final point, requiring but little elaboration, completes the symmetry of the diagrammatic arrangement in Table 1. By reasoning much as before, we arrive at the conclusion that whenever generalization$_1$ and discrimination$_1$ are known to be inversely related, it is meaningful to say that generalization$_2$ must be inversely related to discrimination$_1$. To translate: differential responding may be "explained" by assuming that generalization of habit strength, to pick only one of the various generalization$_2$ possibilities, has failed to occur. The No. 4 arrow in Table 1 mirrors this suggested relation. Thus one may hold that *it is just as meaningful to ascribe differential responding to insufficient habit-strength generalization (or to variation in some comparable Type 2 factor or process) as it is to attribute empirical generalization to a failure to perceive a difference.* Stated this way and in this context, this assertion may appear rather bizarre at first. A moment's reflection reveals, however, that an assumption of this general kind underlies the influential discrimination-learning theory proposed by Spence (1936) and adopted by Hull (1952). These writers, at least, have apparently found it useful to suppose that differential responding (or a lack thereof) is a function of relative amounts of generalized positive or negative (inhibitory) tendencies, or both. Most of the fundamental problems, such as that of definitional independence, which must be faced by the "failure to discriminate" theorist, must also, of course, be considered and resolved by those who hold to the "failure of generalization" theory of discrimination.

Summary

The foregoing analysis points to the need for meticulous care in specifying precisely what is meant by the terms generalization and discrimination. Although usage cannot be legislated, it is painfully evident that useless controversy might be avoided if, at the very least, clear distinctions were typically drawn between what we have called the Type 1 and Type 2 meanings of these terms. Perhaps "empirical generalization" and "differential responding" would be acceptable ways of designating "generalization₁" and "discrimination₁," respectively. When dealing with Type 2 concepts, specifically descriptive terms (e.g., generalized habit strength, awareness of differences, etc.) could be chosen to denote the particular mechanism or process under consideration.

Our analysis has also shown that generalization₁ and discrimination₁ are by no means always inversely related. They may be seen as directly related and even quite unrelated, depending on which variables one manipulates and on the definitions and dependent measures that are adopted. Those who have sought to support the inverse-relation hypothesis have often failed to distinguish between Type 1 and Type 2 meanings, and it is therefore unclear whether the hypotheses under study involve generalization₁ and discrimination₁ or generalization₁ and discrimination₂. Moreover, in some of these cases the data, though used to indicate generalization, might more aptly be said to reflect discrimination₁. Where this seems to hold it would appear that the investigator is actually studying the relation between two different measures of discrimination₁, not the relation of generalization to discrimination.

Finally, while the outcome of psychophysical experiments clearly reveals the capacity of subjects to respond differentially, generalization procedures also tell us something about differential reactivity. Neither procedure, therefore, can be regarded as the only suitable basis for defining discrimination₁. This, taken with the fact that certain procedures such as differential reinforcement, once uniquely appropriate to psychophysical studies with animals, are now employed in "generalization" experiments, adds weight to the conclusion that no sharp dividing line can be drawn between the two kinds of studies. Further doubts are thereby raised about the probable utility of exploring the inverse-relation hypothesis in greater detail, since this is commonly accomplished by using psychophysical data as the sole basis for defining the discrimination (Type 1 or Type 2) that is then compared with generalization, this being variously defined, sometimes by the use of "psychophysical" methods.

Epilogue

The papers comprising this volume provide substantial evidence for the viability of the area of stimulus generalization. New methods are being developed and tested, established concepts are being challenged, and reams of data are being accumulated on cumulative recorder paper and elsewhere. Research on generalization is patently moving, though like any human activity, not always in a forward direction. For example, the papers in this volume clearly show that the terms generalization and discrimination are still used in widely different ways by different writers. Moreover, the label "stimulus generalization" is applied without hesitation, perhaps without cogitation, and without apology to studies employing remarkably dissimilar programs and procedures. Even investigations in which the occurrence of the response is completely uncorrelated with the presentation of the training stimulus, and hence does not vary with changes in some property of that stimulus, are included in the "generalization" group. This happens, of course, when the so-called "discriminative" stimulus is not "discriminated" and consequently does not come to "control" the response. If stimulus generalization denotes something that happens *after* associative connections have been formed between a stimulus and a response, then the generalization designation is inappropriate unless such associations have indeed been established. How can transfer of training be studied until training has produced significant modification in performance?

A further point, closely related to the foregoing, bears on the issue of the role of experience in studies of generalization. Harking back to the classical Pavlovian methods, it is evident that, at an absolute minimum, subjects whose salivary responses have been conditioned successfully to a tone have had experience with both tone and no tone. In fact, since the reinforcing UCS has been presented only with the tone, such subjects have also been differentially reinforced, adventitiously to be sure, but quite inexorably, simply because they have been exposed to classical conditioning procedures. An investigator cannot keep within the boundaries of the procedures defining classical conditioning without exposing his subjects to differential reinforcement of this particular kind.

Similarly, if an instrumental or operant response is to become successfully associated with a stimulus (is to be brought under stimulus control), reinforcement must be provided for responses occurring to that stimulus but not for responses appearing in its absence. As Jenkins and Harrison (1960) have shown, when a differential reinforcement program of this sort is followed, stimulus control is in fact achieved. Response strength to the controlling stimulus is high, and sharply sloping gradients are found along dimensions orthogonal to that formed by the stimulus–non-stimulus axis.

It is inappropriate, therefore, to ask what generalization gradients will be like in the absence of differential reinforcement along the stimulus–non-stimulus dimension. Lacking such experience, a subject cannot have learned what he *must* learn if transfer to other stimuli is to be studied. Exposure to the stimulus–non-stimulus continuum, along with differential reinforcement thereto, seems to be a necessary condition both for effecting the growth of associative strength, whether to conditioned or discriminative stimuli, and for demonstrating generalization gradients. Differentially reinforced exposure to two or more members of the stimulus series used for generalization testing is not, however, a necessary requirement, and as Jenkins and Harrison (1960) have noted, this finding does not agree with one interpretation of the views of Lashley and Wade (1946).

Further evidence against the Lashley-Wade position has rather recently been presented by Ganz and Riesen (1962). In their experiment, the gradients of response strength to visual stimuli varying in hue were steeper, generally, for macaque monkeys that had had no prior exposure to lights of different wavelengths than for normal subjects. This finding was said to be supported by, and predicted from, several different stimulus-deprivation studies. The authors concluded that exposure to the members of the stimulus series was *not* a necessary precondition for the observation of generalization gradients. They also rejected the idea that differential reinforcement is needed to make the dimension "relevant" for the subject. Indeed, they stated that "generalization in some cases simply follows automatically from the physiological properties of the receptor system involved and does not require previous experience" (p. 97).

Hull (1943, p. 183) has said that primary stimulus generalization comes about because the reinforced response "becomes connected with a considerable zone of stimuli other than, but adjacent to, the stimulus conventionally involved in the original conditioning." Although he used the phrase "becomes connected," he could hardly have meant, literally, that an organism can form associative connections between a response and a stimulus that it has never experienced. What he doubtless did mean is that after conditioning to a CS an organism *acts as though* some conditioning had also taken place between a new test stimulus and the response.

Prokasy and Hall (1963), in expressing concern over the concept of stimulus generalization, clearly imply that all who use the term necessarily believe in something that goes far beyond an *as if* interpretation of this kind. Even those of us who have suggested that generalization can be treated simply as an empirical phenomenon (Brown *et al.*, 1951) are accused by Prokasy and Hall of confusing the issue by "implicitly" believing that generalization is an irradiationlike, organic process.

Prokasy and Hall evidently do not see that those who say that "the response has generalized from the CS to the test stimulus" are not saying that something within the organism has moved or spread from one place to another. Nor do the users of the word "generalize" mean that something shifts from one stimulus to another, save in the sense that graphic points can be moved on the paper on which gradients are plotted. What is meant is just that conditioning changes the organism, and hence that even when conventional conditioning procedures have not been used with novel test stimuli, the subject may react as though they had.

Having created, in this wise, their straw man, Prokasy and Hall seek to destroy it by urging that the concept of stimulus generalization, which they themselves do not define, be abandoned as useless. In its place we are urged to use the time-worn clichés of "discrimination" and "perception" operating in conjunction with "specific past training, sets, motivations, etc." Unfortunately, these substitute concepts are themselves incredibly vague, a state of affairs that Prokasy and Hall do nothing to correct. It is hard to believe, therefore, that the perceptual-cognitive terms which they ask us to embrace will reduce rather than increase the conceptual burdens we have shouldered while stumbling along with the term generalization.

Finally, it is of some interest to observe that theories of stimulus generalization occupy relatively little space in this volume. The writer's own preference in this regard is for a view, now under development and elaboration, that equates generalization with transfer of training and attributes transfer to the presence of stimulus components or dimensions common to both conditioned and test stimuli. It is also assumed that the degree of transfer will increase directly with the number of shared components.

A theory of this sort, traceable directly to suggestions by Thorndike (1913), Hull (1920, 1943), Guthrie (1930), and others, seems to offer many advantages. Some of these are (1) it can encompass instances in which transfer ranges from zero to 100 per cent and even exceeds 100 per cent; (2) it may provide solutions to the persistent problem of stimulus similarity; (3) it can be reconciled with molar concepts such as Hull's generalized habit strength and with views as neurologically molecular as Thompson's (this vol., pp. 154–178); and (4) it involves no gratuitous assumptions concerning the subject's capacity to "discriminate" or "perceive."

In brief, such a theory would hold, in the final analysis, that one stimulus can produce the same behavioral results as another only when both stimuli lead to the same neural events just prior to the final common path. At the behavioral level, two stimuli evoke the same reaction if both contain elements or components that are identical and if the reference response has been conditioned to at least one of those elements. Transfer and similarity thus reduce to stimulus-component identity. If a response occurs to a stimulus complex that has never, as an organized assembly of elements, been presented to the subject, our task is to identify the elements of the complex that have previously been experienced elsewhere. And if the reaction to the new aggregate is weaker than to the old, the problem is to itemize components present in the old but missing from the new, or to identify new components to which competing reactions have been conditioned.

REFERENCES

Brown, J. S., Bilodeau, E. A., and Baron, M. R. Bidirectional gradients in the strength of a generalized voluntary response to stimuli on a visual-spatial dimension. *J. exp. Psychol.*, 1951, **41**, 52–61.

Ganz, L., and Riesen, A. H. Stimulus generalization to hue in the dark-reared macaque. *J. comp. physiol. Psychol.*, 1962, **55**, 92–99.

Guthrie, E. R. Conditioning as a principle of learning. *Psychol. Rev.*, 1930, **37**, 412–428.

Guttman, N., and Kalish, H. I. Discriminability and stimulus generalization. *J. exp. Psychol.*, 1956, **51**, 79–88.

Hull, C. L. Quantitative aspects of the evolution of concepts. *Psychol. Monogr.*, 1920, **28**, No. 123.

Hull, C. L. *Principles of behavior*. New York: Appleton-Century-Crofts, 1943.

Hull, C. L. *A behavior system*. New Haven: Yale Univer. Press, 1952.

Jenkins, H. M., and Harrison, R. H. Effect of discrimination training on auditory generalization. *J. exp. Psychol.*, 1960, **59**, 246–253.

Kalish, H. I. The relationship between discriminability and generalization: a reevaluation. *J. exp. Psychol.*, 1958, **55**, 637–644.

Kimble, G. A. *Hilgard and Marquis' conditioning and learning*. New York: Appleton-Century-Crofts, 1961.

Lashley, K. S., and Wade, M. The Pavlovian theory of generalization. *Psychol. Rev.*, 1946, **53**, 72–87.

Mednick, S. A., and Freedman, J. L. Stimulus generalization. *Psychol. Bull.*, 1960, **57**, 169–200.

Perkins, C. C., Jr. The relation between conditioned stimulus intensity and response strength. *J. exp. Psychol.*, 1953, **46**, 225–231.

Philip, B. R. Generalization and central tendency in the discrimination of a series of stimuli. *Canad. J. Psychol.*, 1947, **1**, 196–204.

Prokasy, W. F., and Hall, J. F. Primary stimulus generalization. *Psychol. Rev.*, 1963, **70**, 310–322.

Schlosberg, H., and Solomon, R. L. Latency of response in the choice of discrimination. *J. exp. Psychol.*, 1943, **33**, 22–39.

Spence, K. W. The nature of discrimination learning in animals. *Psychol. Rev.*, 1936, **43**, 427–449.

Thorndike, E. L. *Educational psychology. II. The psychology of learning*. New York: Teachers College, Columbia Univer., 1913.

2. On the Uses of Poikilitic Functions

S. S. Stevens, *Harvard University*

A recurrent topic at the conference was a nagging semantic question: how should we construe the term *generalization?* Many speakers voiced concern about the issue and the paradoxes engendered by recent usages.

To generalize, in a scientific sense, has typically meant to forge a broadened conception of some law or principle. This time-honored usage is consonant with the view, ably spelled out by Prokasy and Hall (1963), that a rat's failure to note a change in the wavelength of light does not mean that the rat has generalized in any constructive sense. The rat has simply failed to react differentially. The imputation of generalization to what may sometimes prove to be mere inattention seems somehow to turn matters bottom end up.

The Question of Symmetry

These two terms, discrimination and generalization, often parade as simple opposites, like the obverse and reverse of a coin. They seem to pertain to the same phenomenon, however much they may suggest differences in detail or point of view. Generalization is failure to discriminate. When discrimination fails, in whole or in part, we seem to need a word for it, and that word has come to be generalization—regrettable as it may seem. The use of the two words in this complementary fashion suggests a degree of symmetry that may prove deceptive.

The ability to react differentially and the process called generalization do not stand on equal footing. Differential reaction, the distinguishing of this from that, constitutes a hallmark of the sentient organism. When differential reaction ceases sufficiently, we usually bury the remains. Not so with generalizing reactions—"generalizing" in the meaning of this volume. We seldom discard organisms because they have ceased to generalize, i.e., because their gradients are too steep or too narrow.

Consider the vast arrays of energetic impingements, such as radio waves, that we habitually ignore. Radio waves pass through my head, but the commercial does not annoy me. I generalize. I make no differential response, even when the music changes. The flatness of my generalization gradient, despite the rich offerings of this electromagnetic bombardment, is hardly of scientific interest. But let it happen, as Frey (1962) has recently claimed, that a differential auditory reaction can be elicited by intense RF flux directed at the temporal area of the head. Scientific interest then becomes alerted, for generalization has declined.

There is a sense, therefore, in which differential response is primary. For certain purposes we may be interested in circumstances that lead to confusions of one kind or another, but it seems plain that if all we ever had were confusions, we would soon turn our attention to some other investigation, one in which discriminations were made.

The Poikilitic Function

The generalization gradient of the animal trainers is the psychometric function of the weight lifters. In both arenas we plot graphs that show, at various stimulus values, the number of responses that fall into certain categories. These graphs are useful devices, so useful in fact that they need a name. The term poikilitic function is proposed. It is a term already used to describe the data in a visual matching experiment (Stevens and Stevens, 1963). The term poikilitic refers to scatter or variation, which, of course, is precisely the matter before us. We instruct the pigeon to peck at a blue key, and then we test to see how widely its responses scatter up and down the spectrum. Or we present an observer with a standard weight and then determine what other weights he will call equal to it or place in some other category. In both kinds of experiments the slope (gradient) of the poikilitic function tells how discriminative or how promiscuous the reactive system proved to be under the circumstances in question.

Poikilitic functions have their obvious uses, but why displace the long-used term psychometric? This term, introduced by Urban in 1908, has served very generally to describe poikilitic gradients of the kind obtained when observers are asked to sort stimuli into categories of one kind or another, e.g., greater or less. Urban's reasoning followed the line laid down by Fechner. It ran as follows: The gradient of the scatter function determines the size of the just-noticeable difference (JND). The JND serves as a unit for the measurement of sensation. Functions whose gradients make possible psychological measurement are therefore *psychometric*.

It has lately become clear that on prothetic continua the JND does not meet our need for a psychological unit (Stevens, 1961a). Now that we know how to measure sensation with reasonable precision, it is evident that, instead of remaining constant as a proper measure should, the subjective size of the JND grows larger almost in direct proportion to the increase of the psychological magnitude (Stevens, 1957). Urban's rationale for associating *psycho* plus *metric* with the gradient of the plot used to determine a JND has therefore lost its force.

Admittedly, the assumptions made at the time of a christening need not bind forever the use of a name. A new look in psychophysics does not necessarily proscribe the word psychometric. But another difficulty arises, namely, a confusion of the psychometric function with what is called the psychophysical function.

The Fechnerian philosophy held that we may use the slope or gradient of the psychometric function to determine the JND, with which we may in turn measure the psychophysical function—the relation between stimulus and sensory magnitude. Although psychophysics has largely abandoned that two-stage process, the term psychophysical function is still with us, and is continually confused with psychometric function. As a matter of fact, speakers at the conference proved this point by saying psychophysical function when they presumably meant psychometric function. The distinction is too subtle and the names are too similar.

Perhaps the most compelling reason for abandoning the term psychometric, with its built-in etymological confusion, lies in the possibility that the adoption of a more neutral term may generate a useful name for the large class of functions that relate number of responses to stimulus value. It will then turn out that the poikilitic function in one context may serve to determine a JND, and in another may provide a similarity ordering. Or as Shepard (this vol., pp. 94–110) has shown, families of poikilitic functions may furnish a unique indication of stimulus relations in a psychological space. It is not merely that generalization gradient means the same as the psychometric gradient, but that both gradients tell us how responses scatter when stimuli are varied. It is this fact of scatter that is given explicit designation by the term poikilitic function.

System Resolving Power

If a poikilitic function turned out to exhibit no degree of flatness, no spread whatsoever, we would have a difficult time explaining the fact. For nowhere in nature do we encounter infinitely fine resolving power, much though the Bureau of Standards may wish that such unlimited precision could be achieved. Noise and perturbations intrude whenever a system is required to respond with fine gradations, or whenever an attempt is made to repeat a measurement with ever greater exactitude. The power to discriminate, whether in plants, animals, or machines, is not infinite, nor do we expect it to be. When a test shows 100 per cent differentiation, we assume that our measure was too coarse to test the true resolving power.

At the other extreme, if the system gives back a perfectly flat poikilitic function, with no gradient whatsoever, we are not particularly alarmed. The psychologist has long been familiar with the color-blind cat. The creature may have puzzled its trainers by its stubborn refusal to be taught the hues, but in the laboratory the cat has remained serenely indifferent to changes in wavelength, or so I am told. Our semantics seem somehow out of joint if on this account we must credit the cat with an outstanding ability to generalize. All systems show insensitivity to wide ranges of inputs of one kind or another.

Between the foregoing extremes lie the phenomena that interest us—the poikilitic gradients that fall at neither zero nor infinity. The gradient can mean many things, because living systems enter into many different states. Brown (this vol., p. 15) tells of an experiment in which an observer was presented with seven lamp bulbs and asked to respond as quickly as possible to the lighting of the *middle* lamp only. In that taut state the observer did not differentiate perfectly. Given time for deliberate inspection, however, the observer would be in a different state, and could easily differentiate among the lamps.

In a typical experiment described in this volume, the experimenter undertakes to put an organism into a desired state by means of instructions, training, deprivation, drugs, or combinations thereof. With the organism thus properly disposed, a test is made of its resolving power along one or another stimulus continuum. The resulting picture of resolving power, as portrayed by the poikilitic function, applies to the state in question, but not necessarily to any other state. In some altered state, the resolving power may prove to be different, often vastly different. It should occasion no surprise, then, that an experiment designed, let us say, to measure reaction time to a light should show less resolution of differences in wavelength than an experiment designed to measure a JND. Poikilitic functions lend themselves, as I have said, to many and varied uses. They may provide the tool whereby one experimenter traces the acquisition of a pigeon's matching response, and another experimenter gauges the size of the neural quantum, which is probably the limiting case of a poikilitic gradient.

Neural Step Functions

Ever since Boring (1926) suggested its possibility and Békésy (1960) demonstrated its reality, evidence for a step function in the action of the sensory systems has been growing stronger. The evidence takes the form of a rectilinear poikilitic function whose slope is predictable and whose intercepts determine the size of a neural quantum (NQ). Sample functions from Stevens, Morgan, and Volkmann (1941) are shown in Fig. 1. An increment lasting 0.3 second was added every 3 seconds to a steady, continuous reference stimulus (1000 cps). Each point is the average of 100 judgments. The lines were drawn to fit the points and at the same time to satisfy the slope requirement that the intercepts at 100 and 0 per cent should stand in the ratio of 2 : 1. The size of the NQ, measured in stimulus terms, is the intercept at 0 per cent. For the six observers these poikilitic gradients probably represent the limits of resolving power imposed by the all-or-none action of a neural process somewhere in the sensory system.

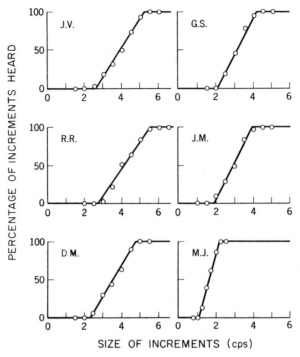

FIG. 1. Poikilitic functions relating percentage of increment heard to the size of the increment in cycles per second for six different observers.

To obtain limiting poikilitic gradients like those in Fig. 1 requires special care. The record seems to show that most experimenters have obtained similar functions, but some have failed. The problem in such a discrimination experiment is to reduce the noise to a level so low that the "grain" in the sensory "continuum" makes itself manifest. It seems to be necessary to make the observer's task as easy as possible, and to pick observers who can maintain a state of acute attention for a relatively long period of time. Not everyone can do it. Monkeys, I imagine, would surely fail. Indeed, it is idle to expect that such a state of unwavering attention would be within the capacity of many organisms, regardless of species.

The simple model (cf. Stevens, 1961b, p. 816) that predicts results like those in Fig. 1 can be regarded as signal-detection theory for the quiet state. Well known to modern psychophysics is a related conception, signal-detection theory for the noisy state, which is a more elaborate model that derives from statistical decision theory (Swets, 1964). Under the experimental paradigm of this theory, an observer tries to detect a tonal signal immersed in a white noise. There is a wayward notion abroad that the quiet theory is incompatible with the noisy theory, a notion fostered no doubt by the claim that the noisy theory disproves the existence of a threshold. Actually, the threshold is banished in much the way that Jastrow tried to banish it in 1888. Since the typical detection experiment with a noise for background gives a poikilitic function that is smooth and ogival, with no obvious break to indicate a threshold, there is said to be no threshold.

Admittedly, the existence of a step-like threshold is difficult, perhaps even impossible, to detect when the experimenter deliberately shrouds the signal with a white noise, but there is still no necessary conflict between the quiet and the noisy theories. Indeed, Luce (1963) presents a threshold theory that may serve as a model for the detection of signals in noise. It suffices here to say that, since the quiet and the noisy theories apply to different circumstances, their poikilitic functions call for different interpretations. One poikilitic function may help to gauge the size of the NQ, the other may serve to compare the human detector with a statistical ideal.

REFERENCES

Békésy, G. von. *Experiments in hearing.* New York: McGraw-Hill, 1960.

Boring, E. G. Auditory theory with special reference to intensity, volume and localization. *Amer. J. Psychol.,* 1926, **37**, 157–188.

Frey, A. H. Human auditory system response to modulated electromagnetic energy. *J. appl. Physiol.,* 1962, **17**, 689–692.

Jastrow, J. A critique of psycho-physic methods. *Amer. J. Psychol.,* 1888, **1**, 271–309.

Luce, R. D. A threshold theory for simple detection experiments. *Psychol. Rev.,* 1963, **70**, 61–79.

Prokasy, W. F., and Hall, J. F. Primary stimulus generalization. *Psychol. Rev.,* 1963, **70**, 310–322.

Stevens, J. C., and Stevens, S. S. Brightness function: effects of adaptation. *J. opt. Soc. Amer.,* 1963, **53**, 375–385.

Stevens, S. S. On the psychophysical law. *Psychol. Rev.,* 1957, **64**, 153–181.

Stevens, S. S. To honor Fechner and repeal his law. *Science,* 1961, **133**, 80–86. (a).

Stevens, S. S. Is there a quantal threshold? In W. A. Rosenblith (Ed.), *Sensory communication.* New York: M.I.T. Press and Wiley, 1961. (b).

Stevens, S. S., Morgan, C. T., and Volkmann, J. Theory of the neural quantum in the discrimination of loudness and pitch. *Amer. J. Psychol.,* 1941, **54**, 315–335.

Swets, J. A. (Ed.) *Signal detection and recognition by human observers: Contemporary readings.* New York: Wiley, 1964.

Urban, F. M. *The application of statistical method to the problems of psychophysics.* Philadelphia: Psychological Clinic Press, 1908.

3. Definition and Measurement in Generalization Research

Donald S. Blough, *Brown University*

The analysis of stimulus generalization has been pressed at two levels in the past few years. Researchers have demonstrated an impressive variety of empirical relations between the response rates that constitute the "gradient" in operant studies and such independent variables as training stimulus, range of stimuli, and deprivation. Here and there, in addition, second-order relations have been suggested. These seek to tie together two or more sets of data, in the manner suggested by Table 1. They attempt to show how functions such as those on one side (B) of this table might be predicted from the corresponding functions on the other side (A).

TABLE 1

Function A	Function B
1. Generalization gradients along a single stimulus dimension	1. "Discriminability" ("JND") functions along the same dimension
2. "Positive" generalization gradient on a stimulus dimension	2. "Gradient of extinction" along the same dimension
3. Several "positive" gradients on the the same dimension	3. "Summation" gradients on the same dimension
4. A "positive" and a "negative" gradient (or more) on the same dimension	4. "Post-discrimination" gradients on the same dimension
5. "Positive" gradients along different dimensions of a stimulus	5. "Bidimensional gradients" found by simultaneous changes along the dimensions
6. Intensity gradients produced by "scaling" procedures	6. Human psychophysical data

It is tempting to seek these second-order relations, for they seem to be the best way to understand generalization phenomena. Yet their pursuit entails serious difficulties, for the functions, being interrelated, must be stated in an unambiguous and quantitative manner. In particular, the response and stimulus variables must be clearly defined and measured. Most of the relationships suggested in Table 1 arose from learning theory, which, though quantitative in form, never clearly stated how to measure the quantities involved. Can the variables be defined and measured well enough that higher-order predictions become feasible? Let us separate this question into response and stimulus components.

The Dependent Variable: "Response Rate"

Comparisons such as those in Table 1 imply certain things about the measure of response, here the rate of emission of a free-operant. Consider, for example, relation 1. It suggests, essentially, that in regions along the stimulus dimension where the gradient is relatively flat, just-noticeable differences (JND's) should be relatively large, and where the gradient is steep, JND's should be small. Now, *if* comparisons of flatness and steepness on a gradient are restricted to the same absolute range of response rate (see Fig. 1), we need not assume too much about the rate scale. Perhaps the assumption that it is ordinal—that increases in rate always mean "more"—will do.

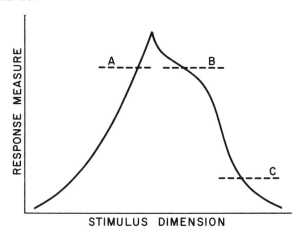

FIG. 1. Lacking information about the response scale (but having a satisfactory stimulus scale), it is meaningful to compare slopes at A and B, but not at B and C. If a stimulus scale is lacking, all the comparisons are questionable.

However, the flatness of a low point on the function cannot be compared with the flatness of a high point, unless we assume that equal changes toward the bottom of the ordinate mean the same thing as equal changes higher up. All pairs except 1 in Table 1 require at least this assumption. They all involve comparisons of shape or algebraic manipulations that need a response scale meeting "interval" or "ratio" requirements. Figure 2 illustrates what happens to "shapes," for example, when the response scale is transformed so as to stretch certain parts of the scale more than others. Here, "positive" and "negative" gradients (Table 1, relation 2) are plotted with the same shape on a linear rate ordinate. The shapes become quite different when a log rate is used instead.

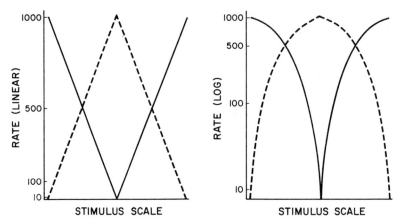

FIG. 2. The same hypothetical generalization data, plotted with a linear (left) ordinate and a logarithmic (right) ordinate. The "inhibition" gradient (solid line) and the "excitation" gradient (dashed line) have the same "shape" at left, very different "shapes" at right.

How, then, can we hit upon the "right" measure? One source for an answer will be attempts, such as those in Table 1, to achieve greater generality. The "right" way to measure responses is that way which shows invariances most clearly. If "log rate" yielded positive and negative gradients of the same shape under various circumstances, and if "log rate" could be added to predict gradient summation, and so on, then "log rate" would be the measure to use.

However, the probability that response rate or any simple transformation of it can be used successfully for these purposes seems low. For one thing, one would think that for "rate" to be so well behaved, the responses that went into it should be interchangeable. That is, each response should (statistically speaking) be controlled by the same variables. This is patently not the case.

First, most generalization experiments are run in extinction. "Rate" is compounded of "rapidity of response in the presence of the stimulus" and "number of responses to extinction in the presence of the stimulus." "Rapidity of response" has, in turn, a "latency-following-stimulus-onset" component and a "response-probability, having-once-responded" component. Experiments that tease apart these various components seem necessary. A unitary component would have a much better chance of behaving in a neat, manipulable manner than the conglomerate "rate" usually used. "Steady-state" rather than "extinction" types of generalization experiment might, for example, be a step in the direction of more meaningful "rates."

Second, most functions that are subjected to comparison as in Table 1 are average functions, despite clear-cut evidence (Guttman and Kalish, 1956; Blough, 1961) that individual subjects produce consistently different curves. Whatever is determining response emission in one case may not be determining it in another, and to average rates obtained under these circumstances is not likely to give us a scale with the metric properties we require.

Third, in individual birds, some responses seem to be emitted under the control of the stimulus and some not. I have suggested (Blough, 1963) that the occurrence of previous responses may almost completely determine the subsequent emission of responses after short inter-response times (IRT's). Thus, these short IRT responses may only be indirectly controlled by the stimulus—yet they are added into "rate."

Can "rate" based on such a hodgepodge be expected to constitute a ratio, or even an interval, scale and respond docilely to algebraic manipulation? Perhaps not, but then, theoreticians are said to have proved that bees cannot fly. We may find that rate flies, despite these dire, somewhat a priori pronouncements. I can hear the empirical voice within me saying, "If rate works, use it!" Does it work? Is "rate" in generalization studies empirically stable enough to enter into general, quantitative relations? There is a fair amount of data in the negative. For example, Thomas and Lopez (1962) found that delaying a generalization test by 24 hours has such an effect on the gradient that the "peak-shift" prediction based on these data is completely different from that based on data collected immediately after training.

For other evidence against the general reproducibility of wavelength-generalization gradients, one can compare all the "control" gradients around 550 mμ, published in various papers. These differ substantially—from the point of view of precise predictive value—yet many were obtained under essentially the same conditions. Haber and Kalish (1963) report that the longer the variable-interval (VI) schedule used in training, the flatter the gradient gets. Friedman and Guttman (this vol., pp. 255–267) explore other factors that appear to control gradient shape. Until we understand and can control the causes of gradient-shape changes, we are unlikely to be able to make accurate predictions such as those suggested by Table 1.

Some of the things we try to do with gradients run counter to what we already know about the control of rate. Take the summation experiments (e.g., Kalish and Guttman, 1959). Here, the general idea is to train animals at two or three stimulus values and see if the "response strengths" will add up in one way or another. "Response strength" here means that composite "rate" we have already dissected. But suppose one trains a pigeon, not for 5 hr. on 550 mμ and 5 hr. on 570 mμ, but instead for 5 hr. on 550 mμ and 5 hr. on 550 mμ—that is, for 10 hours on the same stimulus. Surely this should give the ultimate in "addition," for the response strengths are right on top of each other. No one has tried this, so far as I know, but it is known that doubling training time after an animal is well established on a VI schedule may increase its rate but little.

These arguments are not a council of despair. They suggest, rather, redoubled efforts to understand rate and its determiners before including it in equations that correspond to experimental operations.

The Independent Variable: Stimuli and Their Use

Just as the shape of any gradient is a function of the particular response measure or transformation plotted on the ordinate, so it is a function of the particular stimulus measure or transformation on the abscissa. This has been widely recognized. Guttman and Kalish, in their initial paper (1956), suggested by implication a stimulus scaled in terms of discriminability units, though they rejected this transformation on the available evidence. Shepard (this vol., pp. 94–110) presents a very promising way to determine the most appropriate stimulus scale, based on finding the transformation that gives the most invariant gradient shape. His graphs illustrate how rescaling the stimulus may change the shape of gradients, just as Fig. 2 shows how rescaling the response may change their shape.

Both the discriminability criterion and Shepard's invariance criterion are essentially psychophysical. They require that the stimulus be defined on the basis of the subject's responses. It is evident to many modern researchers that this must be so, yet the problem often seems to be misunderstood or ignored. For example, in the study of wavelength generalization, the "brightness problem" came up. This has long been of concern in color work with animals, and has tripped up many a researcher who was out to determine, for example, "Can the mudminnow see colors?" I recall that the issue was raised once at a meeting, whereupon an authoritative source is said to have expressed surprise at any talk of equating wavelengths for brightness. "What's all this about 'brightness'?" seemed to be the feeling. "You control the stimulus, you record the responses, you observe the regularities, and that's that." This sounds like good, empiricist sense, but it misses the point. The point is, of course, that one of the regularities which investigators teased out of human data long ago is something they labeled "luminance" or "brightness." This varies with both stimulus intensity and wavelength. With this regularity taken into account, relevant human psychophysical data make sense. Statements of great generality can be formulated. Without it, the data would be utterly bewildering.

We can expect the same thing to be true for animals. However much we wish it were not so, we shall not be able to make sense out of data in animal psychophysics (this includes generalization) without taking account of functions that are usually attributed to the "sensory systems."

The transformations imposed by the sensory system must be "subtracted out," as it were, before other regularities will become clear.

It is a bad mistake to think that things like "brightness" are "subjective" or "mentalistic." They are quite well defined, being completely specified by functions that involve physical stimulus measures and behavior. Since this is true, we could, theoretically, bypass such "psychological dimensions" and work with the physical stimuli only. It is to avoid fantastic, needless complexity that we do not do this; "intensity" enters into very complex relations with behavior; "brightness" is much more closely and understandably related to it. We have enough complexity as it is, without borrowing more because of unfounded prejudice.

It might be argued that researchers in generalization have accepted this line of reasoning. The wavelength-generalization people hold brightness constant, or they try to, or at least they apologize for not doing so. But, to be consistent, those of us in this area should be varying *hue*, not wavelength, and we should be holding *brightness* and *saturation* constant. I would not call this hair-splitting, if one is trying, for example, to relate "generalization" to the "JND." In the human case, changing wavelength changes saturation as well as hue. The "yellow" from a monochromator looks almost white, while the "red" is richly saturated. It is quite possible that the pigeon, knowing no better, is responding in "wavelength"-generalization experiments to both "hue" and "saturation" changes—assuming that it operates like a human observer. However, in a JND study it might be pushed below the saturation threshold and respond to hue alone. (This is just a guess, of course, but the names and particulars are not important.) The practical result might be that we will search in vain for order in our data so long as we think that "wavelength" is the dimension we are using.

If pigeons see different dimensions than we do, so much the worse for us. We can probably find out what the dimensions are, in the manner employed with human subjects, but it might take a long time. It may turn out that pigeons are controlled only by dimensions that they are "trained to see," but this seems unlikely to me.

Along with the general problem of stimulus "dimensions," we have to take into account anything else we know about sensory processes. Adaptation is a good case in point. It illustrates unequivocally the necessity for taking the animal into account when defining the stimulus. Prolonged exposure to a visual stimulus may change hue, brightness, and saturation, but particularly the latter two. Let us consider the implications of brightness changes first. My own intensity-generalization experiments (Blough, 1959) were undoubtedly affected by adaption. During training, the birds were exposed for a long time to one intensity. Because of adaptation, they might in effect have been trained at a fairly wide range of brightnesses. The test stimuli were presented more briefly. The rounded, distorted shape

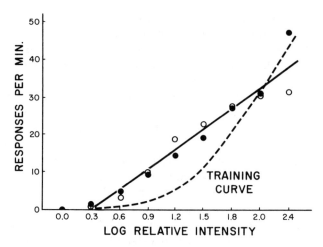

FIG. 3. Intensity scaling data of Herrnstein and van Sommers (1962) replotted with a linear ordinate. Data from two birds appear. The training curve shows the rate of responding prescribed by the differential reinforcement of low rate (DRL) contingency.

of the curves I obtained might well be due largely to adaptation. Had I used a "constant" training stimulus, something else might have appeared in the tests.

Herrnstein and van Sommers (1962) reinforced birds for pecking five stimulus intensities, presented randomly, in such a way that they would peck more rapidly to high intensities. They reinforced particular inter-response times, such that if the birds did just what they were being reinforced for, the logarithm of their response rate would be a linear function of log I. Stevens' power law (1957) was thus "built into" the bird. Herrnstein and van Sommers slipped unreinforced stimulus intensities in amongst the reinforced ones. The birds responded to these stimuli in such a manner as to suggest their adherence to the power law. However, Green (1962) has called attention to the fact that the expected function for eyes adapted to the stimulus light is not the power law at all, but an approximation of the old Fechnerian semilog function. Were Herrnstein and van Sommers' birds adapted to their stimuli? Probably so, most of the time. So let us plot their data in the Fechnerian way (Fig. 3). This shows that the responses rates over-all come close to the expected straight line, despite the "power law" training curve. Whether this interesting relation holds up or not, the moral—consider relevant sensory processes—is clear.

Since adaptation affects saturation, it may be a factor in determining why wavelength-generalization gradients look as they do. The birds stare and stare at 550 mμ, during training, and it becomes desaturated. In testing, when each wavelength appears only briefly, 550 may look quite different.

Desaturated stimuli—such as "yellow" for the human observer—may draw more than their expected share of responses.

Summary

The broad relationships we seek in operant generalization research await (1) the analysis of rate as a quantitative measure and (2) the use of stimulus measures most likely to enter into simple relations with behavior. Working out these measures is essentially a problem in psychophysics. The approach to generalization via learning theory should be very cautious, since learning theorists have failed to deal adequately with these basic issues of measurement.

REFERENCES

Blough, D. S. Generalization and preference on a stimulus intensity continuum. *J. exp. Anal. Behav.*, 1959, **2**, 307–317.

Blough, D. S. The shape of some wavelength generalization gradients. *J. exp. Anal. Behav.*, 1961, **4**, 31–40.

Blough, D. S. Interresponse time as a function of continuous variables: A new method and some data. *J. exp. Anal. Behav.*, 1963, **6**, No. 2, 237–246.

Green, E. E. Correspondence between Stevens' terminal brightness function and the discriminability law. *Science*, 1962, **138**, 1274–1275.

Guttman, N., and Kalish, H. I. Discriminability and stimulus generalization. *J. exp. Psychol.*, 1956, **51**, 79–88.

Haber, Audrey, and Kalish, H. I. Prediction of discrimination from generalization after variations in schedule of reinforcement. *Science*, 1963, **142**, 412–413.

Herrnstein, R. J., and van Sommers, P. Method for sensory scaling with animals. *Science*, 1962, **135**, 40–41.

Kalish, H. I., and Guttman, N. Stimulus generalization after training on three stimuli: A test of the summation hypothesis. *J. exp. Psychol.*, 1959, **57**, 268–272.

Stevens, S. S. On the psychophysical law. *Psychol. Rev.*, 1957, **64**, 153–181.

Thomas, D. R., and Lopez, L. J. The effects of delayed testing on generalization slope. *J. comp. physiol. Psychol.*, 1962, **55**, 541–544.

4. A Conceptual Scheme for Studies of Stimulus Generalization

Charles C. Perkins, Jr., *Emory University*

This volume is but one of many indications that the principle of stimulus generalization in one form or another has come to play a central role in the thinking of many psychologists interested in learning theory. The present paper is designed to clarify the role of generalization in behavior change. The principle of stimulus generalization is employed in the present theoretical frame of reference in a role only slightly different from its role in other theories. The difference is that in the present instance the principle is stated explicitly in more general terms and is used more extensively as a predictive and integrative tool.

The paper will consist of three major parts: (1) a brief presentation of the present theoretical viewpoint including a formulation of the principle of stimulus generalization; (2) examples of how generalization and discrimination are involved in several simple learning situations; and (3) an analysis of the essential features of representative experimental investigations of generalization. This analysis will show that even the most direct empirical investigation of generalization involves a more complex process than is implied by typical definitions of generalization.

Theoretical Frame of Reference

As with other reinforcement theories, it is assumed that whether a stimulus-response (S-R) association will increase or decrease in strength as a result of its occurrence can be predicted only if the conditions that follow the response are known. Nevertheless, the strengthening of S-R associations cannot be predicted from the conditions that follow the response alone. The "same" stimulus situation may act as a positive reinforcer on some occasions and as a negative reinforcer on others. For example, a small amount of food in the right arm of a maze strengthens a hungry rat's tendency to turn right if he has not previously obtained a reward in the maze, but *weakens* his tendency to turn right if he obtained very large

The preparation of this paper was aided by Grant M-4378, National Institute of Health.

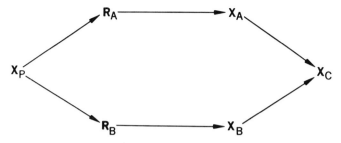

F I G. 1. Diagram of the paradigm used to determine the relative intrinsic attractiveness of two stimulus sequences, X_A and X_B.

food rewards on every one of many occasions on which he had previously turned this way.

Precise analysis of reinforcement effects requires that a distinction be made among several closely related concepts which all too often are lumped together under the single term reinforcement. It is difficult to measure precisely the degree to which antecedent S-R sequences are strengthened or weakened as a result of a single occurrence. It is somewhat easier to specify asymptotic or steady-state S-R strength, which by definition is determined by the *attractiveness* of the stimulus situation that follows the response studied. Detailed specification of the strictly operational concepts of *intrinsic* and *composite* attractiveness will therefore precede further consideration of the concept of reinforcement.

Intrinsic attractiveness. Figure 1 represents the paradigm that may be used to determine the *relative intrinsic attractiveness* of X_A and X_B. To the preceding stimulus situation (X_p), two alternative response classes (e.g., right and left turns in a maze) are available to the organism. X_A and X_B, the two alternative stimulus situations being compared in attractiveness, are of equal duration, and X_C is a stimulus situation that follows both X_A and X_B. If R_A and R_B have each been made to X_P many times and R_A occurs on a clear majority of the trials after many occurrences of each response, then by definition X_A has greater intrinsic attractiveness than X_B.

Additional restrictions are necessary for the paradigm to be strictly appropriate for determination of the relative intrinsic attractiveness of the two stimulus situations. For one thing, the two responses must themselves be equal in intrinsic attractiveness. For example, it would not be appropriate to use biting the tongue as R_A, because it is less attractive (more aversive) than not biting the tongue (R_B). In addition, X_A and X_B must both be distinctive enough so that they will not be "confused" either with each other or with any other stimulus sequences to which the organism is exposed. That is, X_A and X_B, throughout their full duration, must be so different from each other and from all other situations presented to the subject, that by the time the measurement is completed, no changes in

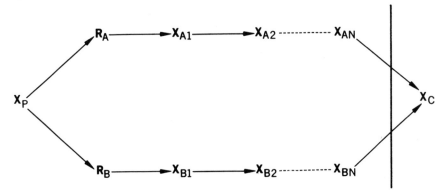

FIG. 2. Diagram of the paradigm used to determine relative composite attractiveness of X_{A1} and X_{A2}.

the attractiveness of any other stimulus situation will generalize to X_A or X_B.

The paradigm is idealized and cannot be perfectly attained in an actual experiment. For one thing, X_C will necessarily differ somewhat depending on whether it has been preceded by X_A or by X_B. That is, the stimulus aftereffect of X_A during X_C is different from the stimulus aftereffect of X_B during X_C.[1] Such a difference based only on the stimulus aftereffect of antecedent events has no important effect because, as implied below, the differential attractiveness of X_C based on these internal stimuli will have been entirely transmitted to X_A and X_B, and stimulus differences during X_C will therefore have no new differential effect on X_A and X_B.

Composite attractiveness. We turn now to composite attractiveness, which, unlike intrinsic attractiveness, may be determined primarily by learning. Figure 2 represents the paradigm for the determination of the *relative composite attractiveness* of X_{A1} and X_{B1}. The same restrictions and conditions that were applied to the paradigm for measurement of intrinsic attractiveness apply here.

If after many presentations of the two stimulus sequences X_{A1} to X_{AN} and X_{B1} to X_{BN}, R_A occurs significantly more often than R_B, then (by definition) X_{A1} is more attractive than X_{B1} at the end of the measurement.[2]

It should be noted that the part of the diagram to the right of the vertical line is the same as the right-hand portion of Fig. 1. Ordinarily we might not speak of the paradigm for measurement of composite attractiveness as involving a common terminal stimulus situation (X_C). However, with any sort of experimental procedure or in any sort of naturalistic setting that

---

[1] The phrase "stimulus aftereffect" refers to the stimulus properties of the aftereffects of some antecedent event.

[2] Attractiveness will refer to composite attractiveness unless the contrary is stated explicitly.

one might reasonably expect to find, stimulus sequences lead to sets of conditions which differ only with respect to the stimulus aftereffects of whatever has preceded them. For example, in many experiments rats are picked up by the experimenter and placed in a transport cage after each trial. In this case, being picked up by the experimenter or being in the transport cage, or both, is X_C.

The two sequences are considered of equal duration. If the two sequences are not equally long, their duration can be "equalized" by adding as much of X_C to the shorter as is needed to equate duration of the sequences. That is, if X_A (or $X_{A1}, \ldots, X_{AN}$) is 5 sec. longer than X_B (or $X_{B1}, \ldots, X_{BN}$), 5 sec. of X_C can be counted as a part of X_B to make X_A and X_B of equal duration.

Relation between intrinsic and composite attractiveness. Stimuli and responses occur as part of a continual process, and a distinction between one stimulus situation and the next, e.g., X_{A1} and X_{A2}, is arbitrary. Thus, Fig. 2 could be "collapsed" so that it would look exactly like Fig. 1. In other words, measuring the relative intrinsic attractiveness of X_A and X_B by the paradigm represented by Fig. 1 cannot be distinguished from measuring the relative composite attractiveness of X_{A1} and X_{B1} as in Fig. 2.

The empirical evidence for "secondary reinforcement" (e.g., Saltzman, 1949) and for "fear" or "acquired aversiveness" (e.g., Miller, 1948) indicates that the composite attractiveness of X_{A1} (Fig. 2) is determined in part by the intrinsic attractiveness of $X_{A2}, X_{A3}, \ldots, X_{AN}$.

Presumably, the separate effects of X_{A2}, X_{A3}, etc., on the composite attractiveness of X_{A1} can be determined. Furthermore, it is convenient to assume (at least as an approximation) that these separate effects can be added, and that additive, equal-unit scales of both intrinsic and composite attractiveness can be constructed.

The arbitrarily divided components of X_A (X_{A1}, X_{A2}, etc.) are each stimulus-situation sequences themselves even when they are quite brief and the external stimuli remain constant. Thus the composite attractiveness of the onset of a stimulus (X) is determined by the intrinsic attractiveness of the briefer components of which it consists. One can consider stimulus situations of finite duration to be sequences of stimuli of infinitesimal duration (x's). Nevertheless, we will continue to use "intrinsic attractiveness" to describe X's of finite duration as well as x's of infinitesimal duration. However, this is merely shorthand for the composite attractiveness of the onset of X.

The term intrinsic attractiveness should be applied to X's only if previous presentations have been of equal duration. In this case, the onset of X will have acquired a composite attractiveness resulting from transmission of the intrinsic attractiveness of the x's into which X can be analyzed (Powell and Perkins, 1957).

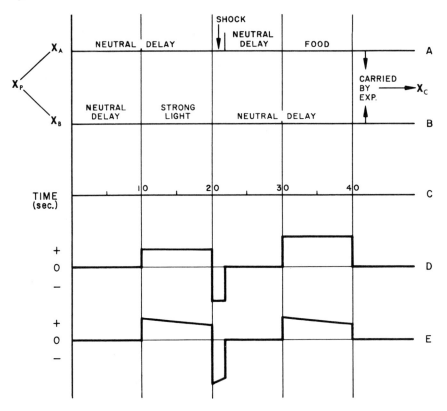

FIG. 3. The relative intrinsic attractiveness of conditions during two sequences of events (A and B) at different times after the response (C).

Transmission of attractiveness. Rather than give a more lengthy and elaborate description of the various ways in which the composite attractiveness of X_{A1} might be determined by the intrinsic attractiveness of $X_{A1}, \ldots, X_{AN}$, we will present a specific hypothesis as an example of the *sort* of principle involved. This hypothesis of 100 per cent transmission of attractiveness can serve as a working hypothesis and as a close approximation to the facts, at least for brief stimulus-situation sequences.

The hypothesis of 100 per cent transmission of attractiveness can be described most easily by means of an hypothetical example. Figure 3 represents the conditions that follow R_A and R_B, alternate responses to X_P, such as right and left turns in a simple T maze. Time relative to response occurrence is indicated by the scale labeled C. The intrinsic attractiveness of the x's that make up the X_A sequence relative to x's within the X_B sequence at the times indicated on the horizontal scale is represented by the vertical position of line D.

The intrinsic attractiveness of the A and B sequences for the first 10 sec.

after choice are equal and thus D is at zero, which represents equal intrinsic attractiveness for the pairs of x's that make up the first 10 sec. of the A and B sequences. During the interval from 10 to 20 seconds after R, conditions in the A sequence have greater intrinsic attractiveness than conditions in the B sequence, which include a strong light. Since strong lights are aversive, line D is above zero. During the period from 20 to 22 sec. after R_A shock is delivered, A has a great deal less intrinsic attractiveness than B. Thus line D drops far below zero. The height of the rest of line D is determined in the same way.

According to the hypothesis of 100 per cent transmission of attractiveness, the difference between the relative composite attractiveness of the onset of sequence A and the onset of sequence B (A minus B) is a linear function of the area above zero on the scale minus the area below zero. In other words, the composite attractiveness of onset of X_A minus the composite attractiveness of X_B equals the difference between the integral of the intrinsic attractiveness of the x's during X_A and the integral of the intrinsic attractiveness of the x's during X_B.

The assumption that differential intrinsic attractiveness is fully transmitted to onset of the sequence, which we have designated the 100 per cent transmission hypothesis, may be unacceptable to some readers. Their views may be incorporated by adding a correction for delay time, the number of intervening stimuli, or some other variable. Such a correction for delay time, if delay is assumed to decrease the effect, would lead to a modification of D in Fig. 3 to something such as E, where the height of the curve represents the effect of differential intrinsic attractiveness on differential composite attractiveness of onset of the two sequences.

Reinforcement and attractiveness. All learnable responses appear to have stimulus properties; i.e., responses can serve as the basis for subsequent differential responding and can affect the level of attractiveness of a stimulus situation of which they are a part. Thus, an increase in the tendency for a response to occur in a particular context may be considered an instance of an increase in the difference between the composite attractiveness of the response in process and this same context without the response.

If a response is followed by a more attractive stimulus situation than prevailed during the response, the attractiveness of the response will increase. Thus a *positive* reinforcer is any stimulus situation that is more attractive than the antecedent stimulus situation, i.e., the one present while the response is in process. Similarly, a *negative* reinforcer is less attractive than the response it follows. The above use of reinforcement will be designated *sequential* reinforcement to distinguish it from *differential* or *relative* reinforcement, which is a difference in the attractiveness of the stimulus situations that follow alternative responses.

For both sequential and relative reinforcement the magnitude of the difference in attractiveness of the pertinent stimuli will be designated the *strength* of reinforcement. Under conditions of 100 per cent reward (ordinarily described as 100 per cent or continuous reinforcement), the strength of sequential reinforcement decreases with successive trials as the attractiveness of X_2, the reinforcing stimulus, is transmitted to X_1, the stimulus situation while the response is in process. The difference between the attractiveness of X_1 and X_2 approaches zero as a limit with increasing trials.

Transmission of attractiveness and stimulus generalization. The tendency for stimulus situations to acquire the attractiveness of the stimulus situations that follow them is assumed to be the basic principle behind *all* learned behavior change. This principle cannot be applied except jointly with the principle of stimulus generalization, which may be stated as follows: *Any change in the attractiveness of a stimulus situation (X_{CS}) resulting from its presentation is accompanied by a comparable but lesser change in the attractiveness of similar situations (X_{GS}), and the greater the similarity, the greater the generalized change in attractiveness of X_{GS}.*

It should be noted that our formulation of the principle of stimulus generalization implies that all changes in the organism resulting from learning generalize, whether they are changes in response tendencies, secondary reinforcing properties (e.g., Bergum, 1960; Thomas, this vol., pp. 268–283), conditioned suppression (e.g., Hoffman, this vol., pp. 356–372), or any other behavioral characteristic of the organism.

Like most definitions of stimulus generalization, whether explicit or implied, ours implies that generalization occurs if (1) a particular response to a certain stimulus situation (CS) is reinforced on one or more occasions; (2) a similar test stimulus (GS) is presented; (3) the response occurs to this GS; and (4) this response would not have occurred as strongly to the GS had there been no reinforced responses to the CS. Such definitions seem to imply that at least from the beginning of training to the end of the test, no other stimulus situations similar to CS or GS have been presented. This, of course, is not the case. There is overwhelming evidence that in all or nearly all stimulus-generalization experiments, the sequence of relevant events is much more complex. Generalization is involved from the beginning of training.

The Role of Generalization in Learning

Instrumental learning. Simple Skinner box learning exemplifies the role of stimulus generalization quite clearly. When the initial bar press occurs and is followed by reinforcement (e.g., click–food), some of the attractiveness is transmitted to the preceding stimulus situation, pressing the bar in the box. As often noted (e.g., Hull, 1943), a stimulus situation cannot be reproduced exactly, and thus the very occurrence of learned behavior change implies generalization. Only through generalization will the attractiveness gained by the stimulus situation at the time of a bar press on one trial have any effect on the attractiveness of a bar press on subsequent trials.

The increase in the strength of the bar-pressing response also implies that there is a greater increment in the attractiveness of pressing the bar in the box than of not pressing the bar in the box. That is, the very acquisition of a bar-pressing response is dependent upon the existence of a positive relation between the size of the generalization decrement and the dissimilarity of the GS from the CS.

It has become almost standard procedure to use the method of successive approximations to get the first bar press. This method, of course, is based upon response generalization, a special case of stimulus generalization. Responses that are somewhat similar to bar pressing are reinforced by click–food. As a result, such responses become more frequent. The class of responses reinforced is gradually restricted so that, to be reinforced, a response must be more and more similar to a bar press. Finally, after a few bar presses have occurred, no other response is reinforced.

I think it is clear that a rather complex process is going on here. We will not try to describe these events in full detail, but will note only that a rather broad class of responses becomes more attractive in the earlier stages of training as a result of positive reinforcement, and that subsequently those responses which are no longer reinforced decrease in attractiveness.

The situation is not a great deal simpler if the experimenter simply waits for the first bar press and then reinforces it. Careful observation of the subject makes it clear that reinforcement of the first few bar presses often strengthens responses similar to bar pressing through generalization. With continued training, however, the attractiveness of these other responses gradually decreases.

In this connection, it should be noted that the criteria for a bar press are somewhat arbitrary and are determined by the experimenter (or the apparatus). Both the pressure on the bar and the distance it must be moved to meet the criterion of a response are determined by the details of the equipment. After a good bit of training the two response classes, bar press and non bar press, become quite well differentiated. It appears that sharply defined response classes result from differential all-or-none reinforcement. In other words, differential training with all-or-none reinforcement seems to be primarily responsible for "isolation" of classes of responses, i.e., all class members approach equivalence at the same time that confusion of members and non-members of the class becomes minimal. Apparently, the development of a well-defined response depends upon differential reinforcement that can be analyzed through a detailed consideration of response generalization, which is a special case of stimulus generalization.

Classical conditioning. Although it does not involve response differentiation to the same extent as instrumental learning, classical conditioning does involve differential reinforcement with context-plus-CS as the positive stimulus and context alone as the negative stimulus. Pavlov (1927, p. 115) reported a conditioned response to the environment (salivation to the experimental situation in the absence of the CS) that dropped out with further training. Apparently, the salivary response generalized from conditioned stimulus to experimental-situation-minus-CS. A classical-conditioning procedure involves generalization and differential conditioning from the beginning of acquisition, not just upon presentation of generalization test trials. Mowrer and Lamoraux (1951) obtained clear evidence of generalization from environment-plus-CS to environment-minus-CS in avoidance learning. Perkins (1953) and Logan (1954) suggested that differential conditioning with a zero intensity CS as the negative stimulus is the basis for the positive relationship between conditioned-stimulus intensity and response strength which Hull had labeled stimulus-intensity dynamism. Champion (1962) has recently summarized much of the evidence for this interpretation, which now seems quite safely established.

Time-dependent stimuli. The further differential conditioning that takes place in delayed classical conditioning is worthy of special attention. Pavlov (1927) showed that after considerable training with a 3-min. CS and a delayed conditioning procedure, dogs salivate during the last 30 to 60 seconds before UCS presentation. Salivation apparently is reinforced only to the stimulus situation present after at least the first two minutes of a 3-min. CS.

Similarly, Boneau (1958) and Ebel and Prokasy (1963) reported different distributions of latencies of the conditioned eye blink with different intervals between onset of CS and onset of UCS. The latencies tended to be such that the response kept the air puff from hitting the subject's eye while it was open. It appears that the blink becomes more attractive, i.e., is reinforced, only if it avoids a puff to the unprotected eye.

There are other time-dependent stimulus characteristics that are differentially reinforced and form the basis for a discrimination in several sorts of learning situations. For example, the length of time since the last reinforced trial is the basis for the discrimination implied by the scalloped curves obtained on a cumulative recorder with a fixed internal reinforcement schedule.

There are also a large number of internal stimuli that one would expect to change systematically with age. Such changes would be expected to occur at a much greater rate while the organism is still maturing. Campbell and Campbell (1962) report that a rat's retention of fear is significantly greater if the fear is acquired when the rat is relatively mature instead of when it is still growing. This is striking confirmation of the interpretation suggested here. The stimulus situation to which fear was learned may be altered so much by stimulus changes resulting from growth that there is a nearly complete generalization decrement resulting from maturation-induced stimulus changes. Further studies of retention at different ages are needed to determine if the rate of forgetting is greatly affected by the rate of change of maturation-dependent stimuli.

Relation between generalization and discrimination. It should be noted that the present treatment is based on an analysis in terms of the effects of single presentations of stimulus situations. Measurement of generalization follows one or more presentations of a single stimulus situation (X_1). A discrimination is measured only after at least two different stimulus situations (a positive and a negative stimulus) have each been presented at least once. It should be noted that Brown's use of the term discrimination in this volume (pp. 7–23) differs from the present usage. An analysis such as the present one, which is in terms of the effects of single presentations of stimulus situations, implies that generalization is a "more primary" process than discrimination, and that discrimination learning can be analyzed into the interaction of generalization effects.

Dissimilarity. The problem of how best to determine distance along stimulus dimensions is extremely complex. It does not seem advisable to attempt an elaborate analysis of stimulus distances here. Nevertheless, some consideration of how to determine distance between stimuli must precede our analysis, since it is partially based on the location of stimulus situations in a conceptual space.

Distance can perhaps be best designated as degree or amount of dissimilarity. The most fruitful measure of dissimilarity between two stimuli, X_{CS} and X_{GS} seems to be in terms of per cent of generalization from X_{CS} to X_{GS}. Precise measurement would, of course, demand standard conditions. Papers in the present volume by Honig (pp. 218–254), Shepard (pp. 94–110), and Cross (pp. 72–93) describe specific techniques that appear quite promising for refined measures of dissimilarity. Such functional definitions of similarity permit us to deal easily with individual and species differences.

A definition of dissimilarity, in terms of per cent generalization, is not circular, although at first it might appear to be. A measure of dissimilarity in terms of generalization of one learned response can be used to predict the per cent generalization of another response. This gets us out of the apparent circularity. A full presentation of this argument would parallel that of Miller and Dollard (1941) and that of Meehl (1950) concerning the circularity of the law of effect.

Explicit analysis of the concept of dissimilarity brings out a point that should be noted. It indicates that the dissimilarity of two stimulus situations may change quite markedly as a result of training. For example, as already noted, the dissimilarity of a bar press and certain other responses may have been small early in training, but after the bar press has become well established, bar press and non bar press are quite dissimilar. It complicates our analysis to have the dissimilarity of two stimuli changed during the course of an experiment. Nevertheless, it appears more fruitful to define dissimilarity in terms of amount of generalization than in any other way.

Since stimuli presented on successive trials differ somewhat from trial to trial, it is hardly precise to speak of repeated presentations of the same stimulus. Nevertheless, for most purposes, we may speak of highly similar stimuli as though they were identical. That is, if the fluctuations from trial to trial are random and non-systematic, we can represent these repeated presentations by the same point in space without seriously detracting from the accuracy of our predictions. The use of a single point for repeated trials implies only that there is no systematic variation, and that *random* variation of "the same stimulus" is not marked enough to produce measurable differences from the behavior that would result from less variation.

Analysis of Generalization Experiments

Let us review the information assumed to be necessary for complete and precise treatment of learned-behavior modification. If our assumptions are correct, nothing more is required to predict the results of generalization experiments. The information required is as follows: (1) the location in a conceptual space of all the stimulus situations (X_1's) to which the subject is exposed that are sufficiently similar to the stimulus situations under study (the CS and the GS) to affect responses to these stimuli; and (2) the order in which these X_1's are presented (actually this may be a secondary effect that can be adequately explained in terms of certain time-related attributes of the stimulus situation such as those already mentioned); and (3) the attractiveness of the stimulus situations (X_2) that follow each presentation of these X_1's. For many purposes, including specification of the factors determining asymptotic (steady state) behavior, we need only consider the mean relative attractiveness (mean relative reinforcing properties) of whatever follows the various stimulus situations rather than the attractiveness of the reinforcing stimulus on each presentation.

The "spatial location" of stimuli as presented in the figures that follow are at best approximations; these figures should not be thought of as representing Euclidean space. Relative distances should be considered only as rather wild guesses. They are sometimes presented as approximately equal merely because we have no rationale for doing anything else. Figure 4 represents the stimulus situations that are involved in operant conditioning studies of "generalization." We are not considering the full course of training here. The analysis starts with the well-established operant. Thus bar pressing and non-bar-pressing are well-differentiated responses. That

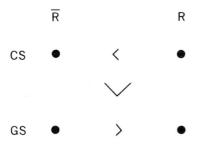

FIG. 4. Location within a conceptual space of the four relevant stimulus situations (X_1's) that occur in an experiment of generalization of a well-differentiated operant response.

is why these responses are represented as spatially separated in Fig. 4. A test for generalization involves presenting a stimulus situation that is altered in one or more respects as in Ferster's study (1951), where conditions of auditory stimulation and level of illumination were changed between training and extinction (test) trials. The $<$ near the top of Fig. 4 stands for "is less attractive than." That is, not pressing the bar under the training conditions is less attractive than responding under these conditions, $(\text{CS} + \bar{\text{R}}) < (\text{CS} + \text{R})$. We should note, however, that since bar presses are discrete responses, such responses cannot occur continuously. The training involves non-reinforced non bar presses as well as reinforced bar presses. That is, $\text{CS} + \bar{\text{R}}$ is presented during training. Both responding and not responding also occur during test trials when not responding is followed by a slightly more attractive stimulus than is responding. This difference in attractiveness is assumed to be dependent upon fatigue, stimulus satiation, or some such factor. Note that responding to the CS makes a greater difference in the attractiveness of the stimulus situations that follow than does responding to the GS. This can be stated in symbols where $\text{R} = $ bar press, $\bar{\text{R}} = $ no bar press, and all relationships ($-$ and $>$) refer to attractiveness. $[(\text{R} + \text{food}) - (\bar{\text{R}} + \overline{\text{food}})] > [(\bar{\text{R}} + \overline{\text{food}}) - (\text{R} + \overline{\text{food}})]$. This is represented in the figure by $\vee$, which indicates that $<$ at the top of Fig. 4 represents a greater difference than $>$ at the bottom.

It is interesting to consider how investigations of generalization following discrete-trial instrumental learning differ from experiments involving a free-operant procedure. Obviously, there are a number of differences, such as the regularity or control of the "inter-trial interval." From the present frame of reference an important difference is that with discrete-trial learning an additional type of differential reinforcement is involved from the beginning of learning. In the case of the bar-pressing response, a discrimination between bar present and bar absent must be formed. Details of the experimental procedure determine what additional cues are provided to serve as the basis for this discrimination. Typically, a discriminative stimulus such as a buzzer or light is presented when the bar is introduced. It should also be noted that discrete-trial instrumental learning in an apparatus such as a straight runway may not involve comparable dif-

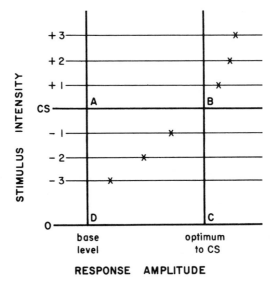

FIG. 5. Stimulus situations presented during an experimental study of generalization of a classically conditioned response along the dimension of stimulus intensity.

ferential reinforcement. Discrete-trial and free-operant procedures also differ in that in the former, $\overline{R}$ does not always occur early in the test series.

Figure 5 represents the various stimulus situations that are presented in the case of a classical-conditioning experiment of generalization along an intensity dimension. The best known such study is probably Hovland's (1937). Two stimulus dimensions are of particular importance in such studies, the intensity of the conditioned stimulus, which is represented by the vertical dimension in Fig. 5, and the response amplitude, which is represented by the horizontal dimension. During training two intensities of the CS are presented: the prescribed intensity of the CS and zero intensity, the stimulus that prevails during the intertrial interval.

The responses typically studied in classical conditioning, e.g., salivation or the galvanic skin response (GSR), vary in amplitude. They are not all-or-none responses like bar-pressing and many other instrumental responses for which there is a single dividing line between R and $\overline{R}$. During an acquisition series, a classical conditioned response varies from the base level of responding to the level that is optimum (i.e., most attractive) immediately before reinforcement, e.g., food presentation. The subject will respond at approximately the base level on early presentations of the CS, but response amplitude will vary somewhat; and the greater the amount of salivation, the more attractive the stimulus situation at the time of UCS presentation. That is, so long as the amount of salivation is below the optimum level, the greater the amount of saliva in the mouth (stimulus aftereffect of the salivary response) and the greater the attractiveness of the stimulus situation at the time of food presentation. As a result of the correlation between the attractiveness of the subsequent stimulus situation and the amplitude of the salivary response, there will be a systematic increase in the amplitude of this response that will eventually stabilize at the optimum level. Early in training, this effect generalizes to some extent to zero intensity of the conditioned stimulus that is present during the intertrial interval. With sufficient training, behavior will stabilize so that only two stimulus situations, B and D, will continue to occur. All the X_1's that will have been presented will fall on the heavy horizontal lines in Fig. 5.

In this kind of experiment, the vertical dimension is controlled by the experimenter, the horizontal dimension by the subject. According to the present interpretation, the subject makes the most attractive response. If the investigator now tests for generalization to stimuli less intense than the CS, responses must be somewhere on the horizontal lines labeled -1, -2, and -3. If the test stimuli are more intense than the CS, responses must be somewhere on lines labeled $+1$, $+2$, and $+3$. The X's in Fig. 5 represent the location of the responses that are typically obtained. It will be noted that they fall in the sort of position that one would expect from the location of the response to the CS and to zero intensity.

Two other factors probably affect the locations in the conceptual space of the responses to test stimuli of less intensity than the training CS: the difference between the attractiveness of A and B as compared with the difference in the attractiveness of C and D, and the relative number of presentations of the CS and of a zero-intensity stimulus or the proportion of the experimental time each is present. Responses to test stimuli probably also depend partly upon the intensity of the CS, the distance between the CS and the negative training stimulus of zero intensity. Typically in studies of stimulus generalization the test trials are non-reinforced. As a result, the responses to test stimuli shift toward the left of Fig. 5 with successive test trials.

In considering generalization along a "qualitative dimension" with a classical-conditioning procedure, it becomes necessary to use a three-dimensional representation as in Fig. 6, where the vertical dimension represents stimulus intensity, the horizontal dimension response amplitude, and the depth dimension stimulus quality. In the case of pure tones, the depth dimension is pitch or frequency. Conditions at the end of training are like those represented in Fig. 5. However, the test stimuli are represented by parallel dimensions in front of and behind the dimension on which the CS falls. These test stimuli are on dimensions labeled $a1$, $a2$, $a3$, and $b1$, $b2$, and $b3$. The X's on these lines indicate where the most attractive responses fall. Since test trials are ordinarily non-reinforced, one would expect these points to shift to the left as testing continues. Typically, they do, and the

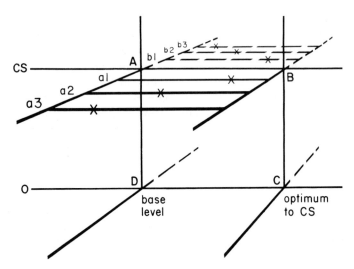

FIG. 6. The stimulus situation that precedes reinforcement and similar stimulus situations (X_i's) occurring in an experimental study of generalization of a classically conditioned response (e.g., salivation) along a qualitative dimension.

points farthest from the CS, e.g., $a3$ and $b3$, shift most rapidly. Apparently, the attractiveness of the more novel or unique stimuli changes more as a result of a single trial.

Direct experimental evidence indicates that the steepness of generalization gradients obtained with the sort of procedures represented by Fig. 6 is increased by the non-reinforced presentations of a stimulus of zero intensity (Reinhold and Perkins, 1955; Perkins, Hershberger, and Weyant, 1959; Jenkins and Harrison, 1960).

Absence of the CR (point D) is more attractive than the response (point C) when CS intensity is zero. Keeping this in mind while examining Fig. 6, one would expect that responses to test stimuli would fall on a steeper gradient (one further to the left) when the unreinforced zero-intensity stimulus situation has been provided during training.

Only a few relatively simple types of experimental procedures have been analyzed above. It is hoped that they will serve as adequate examples of a type of analysis that can also be extended to more involved procedures. For example, the finding that rats trained on low drive will run faster on high drive (Deese and Carpenter, 1951) is just what one would expect from such an analysis of their experiment and of the pre-experimental learning of their subjects. Since such an analysis implies an associative interpretation of motivation, the argument (Brown, 1961) that the results of this experiment strongly favor a motivational over an associative interpretation of motivated behavior is not very convincing.

Summary

We have summarized a general theory of behavior change which is integrated by the assumption that all learning consists of changing the attractiveness of stimulus situations. The major implications of such a formulation for stimulus generalization are as follows. First, the principle of stimulus generalization is required for a precise description of the processes involved in even the simplest instances of learning. Second, since responses are a special class of stimuli, response generalization may be regarded as a special case of stimulus generalization. Third, experimental investigations of stimulus generalization necessarily involve presentation of a number of different stimulus situations, not just a single training stimulus and one or more test stimuli. Fourth, the location of such stimuli within a conceptual space and specification of the attractiveness of the reinforcers that follow them is a useful method for conceptualizing generalization experiments, a method which has implications that seem to conform well with empirical findings.

REFERENCES

Bergum, B. O. Gradients of generalization in secondary reinforcement. *J. exp. Psychol.*, 1960, **59**, 47–53.

Boneau, C. A. The interstimulus interval and the latency of the conditioned eyelid response. *J. exp. Psychol.*, 1958, **56**, 464–472.

Brown, J. S. *The motivation of behavior.* New York: McGraw-Hill, 1961.

Campbell, B. A., and Campbell, E. H. Retention and extinction of learned fear in infant and adult rats. *J. comp. physiol. Psychol.*, 1962, **55**, 1–8.

Champion, R. A. Stimulus-intensity effects in response evocation. *Psychol. Rev.*, 1962, **69**, 428–499.

Deese, J., and Carpenter, J. A. Drive level and reinforcement. *J. exp. Psychol.*, 1951, **42**, 236–238.

Ebel, H. C., and Prokasy, W. F. Classical eyelid conditioning as a function of sustained and shifted inter-stimulus intervals. *J. exp. Psychol.*, 1963, **65**, 52–58.

Ferster, C. B. The effect on extinction responding of stimuli continuously present during extinction. *J. exp. Psychol.*, 1951, **42**, 443–449.

Hovland, C. I. The generalization of conditioned responses. II. The sensory generalization of conditioned responses with varying intensities of tone. *J. genet. Psychol.*, 1937, **51**, 279–291.

Hull, C. L. *Principles of behavior.* New York: Appleton-Century-Crofts, 1943.

Jenkins, H. M., and Harrison, R. H. Effect of discrimination training on auditory generalization. *J. exp. Psychol.*, 1960, **59**, 246–253.

Logan, F. A. A note on stimulus intensity dynamism. (V). *Psychol. Rev.*, 1954, **61**, 77, 80.

Meehl, P. E. On the circularity of the law of effect. *Psychol. Bull.*, 1950, **47**, 52–75.

Miller, N. E. Studies of fear as an acquired drive: I. Fear as motivation and fear-reduction as reinforcement in the learning of new responses. *J. exp. Psychol.*, 1948, **38**, 89–101.

Miller, N. E., and Dollard, J. *Social learning and limitation.* New Haven: Yale Univer. Press, 1941.

Mowrer, O. H., and Lamoraux, R. R. Conditioning and conditionality (discrimination). *Psychol. Rev.*, 1951, **58**, 196–212.

Pavlov, I. P. *Conditioning reflexes.* London: Oxford Univer. Press, 1927.

Perkins, C. C. The relation between conditioned stimulus intensity and response strength. *J. exp. Psychol.*, 1953, **46**, 225–231.

Perkins, C. C., Hershberger, W. A., and Weyant, R. G. Difficulty of a discrimination as a determiner of subsequent generalization along another dimension. *J. exp. Psychol.*, 1959, **57**, 181–186.

Powell, D. R., and Perkins, C. C. Strength of secondary reinforcement as a determiner of the effects of duration of goal response on learning. *J. exp. Psychol.*, 1957, **53**, 104–112.

Reinhold, D. B., and Perkins, C. C. Stimulus generalization following different methods of training. *J. exp. Psychol.*, 1955, **49**, 423–427.

Saltzman, I. J, Maze learning in the absence of primary reinforcement: A study of secondary reinforcement. *J. comp. physiol. Psychol.*, 1949, **42**, 161–173.

5. Generalization Gradients and the Concept of Inhibition

H. M. Jenkins, *McMaster University*

The procedures used to obtain generalization gradients are also the procedures by which the controlling stimuli for a response can be identified. For example, to test for the discriminative or excitatory function of a stimulus that has accompanied the reinforcement of a response, reinforcement is discontinued, the stimulus is varied, and the effects on responding are observed. If responding is unaffected by variation of the stimulus over its full range, the resulting gradient will be indistinguishable from a horizontal line, and it must be concluded that the stimulus has no control or no signaling function. On the other hand, a sloping profile of responding over variations of the stimulus in question provides the evidence for stimulus control.

This paper is a discussion of a parallel use of the generalization test as a method for identifying inhibitory stimulus control in discriminative conditioning. It is concerned with the identification of inhibition at a behavioral or descriptive level. At issue is how to determine that a stimulus is acting as a signal for not responding. Describing such a signal as inhibitory implies no more about the physiology of its effect than does using the term "excitatory" in connection with a signal for responding.

Pavlov on Differential Inhibition

There has been controversy about the need for a concept of inhibition in discriminative conditioning. Pavlov thought that "differential inhibition" was fundamental to an account of discriminative conditioning by the method of contrasts. The most convincing demonstration rested on the transfer of inhibitory control (cessation of response upon presentation of the stimulus) to new stimulus combinations. When a stimulus to which the animal had learned not to respond was added to an excitatory stimulus, the result was a depression of response (Pavlov, 1927, pp. 76ff). Recall that Pavlov's procedure was to reinforce presentations of one stimulus, S_A, and non-reinforce, when S_A was presented with another stimulus, S_B. Thus, S_A

was excitatory, while the combination $S_A S_B$ eventually produced no response. When S_B was now paired with a third stimulus, S_C, which was excitatory when presented alone, the new combination, $S_C S_B$, was found to produce no response. Pavlov assigned the result to the inhibitory effect of S_B.

Skinner (1938) argued that the concept of inhibition was unnecessary in both classical and operant discriminative conditioning. His critique of Pavlov's demonstration of transfer was to note that the extinction of the response to $S_A S_B$ could weaken the same response to a third stimulus, S_C, directly, as the result of generalization of extinction. The factual basis of Skinner's argument is doubtful, since Pavlov presented adequate data to show the inhibitory effect of S_B even when the excitatory effect of S_C alone was ensured through subsequent reinforcement. However, Skinner's discussion brings out clearly the nature of the logical problem of assigning an inhibitory function to a stimulus. The problem is how to distinguish the presence of an inhibitory effect from the absence or reduction of an excitatory effect. We turn now to a discussion of the use of generalization tests as one method of handling the problem.

Identification of Inhibitory Control

The bare fact that an animal has learned a "go/no-go" discrimination with, say, S_1+ and S_2-, does not in itself provide evidence of inhibitory control. One can equally well assume the animal to be operating by any one of the following rules: 1. Respond if S_1; otherwise do not respond. 2. Do not respond if S_2; otherwise respond. 3. Respond if S_1, and do not respond if S_2. The first rule entails only excitatory control, the second, only inhibitory control, the third, a combination of the two.

The results of several experiments in which generalization gradients were obtained following discrimination training allow us to reject the alternative of exclusive inhibitory control (Rule 2). For example, one of the conditions in Newman's experiment as reported by Baron (this vol., p. 63) involved training on a vertical white stripe on a green background as S+, and the green background alone as S−. Variations in the angular orientation of the stripe away from the vertical resulted in substantial response decrements in a subsequent generalization test. Now, since these variations of the former S+ did not bring the stimulus closer to nor move it further from the blank green stimulus which was S−, we can conclude that there was specific control over responding by the positive stimulus. If the animal had simply learned when not to respond (i.e., to a homogeneous green field), all variations of the angular orientation of the stripe would have been equivalent. A statistically flat profile of response over the range of angular orientations would have resulted.

The rejection of Rule 2 will come as a surprise to no one familiar with discriminative operant conditioning. Still, Harlow and Hicks (1957) proposed a "uniprocess" theory of discrimination learning based exclusively on inhibitory stimulus control, a theory that has no place for the present observation.

Consider next Rule 1. It says that no specific inhibitory control by S_2 is acquired as the result of discrimination training. The animal has simply learned to respond to S_1. The particular S_2 stimulus is, by this rule, equivalent to any one of an indefinitely large set of stimuli that are not S_1. The fact that discrimination training narrows the profile of responding around S_1 when compared with single-stimulus training does not in itself, contradict this alternative. Such training may be thought of as removing generalized excitatory effects, or, to use an unpopular metaphor, as disconnecting the S_2 stimulus from the response. Disconnection does not imply a connection to anything else.

In order to demonstrate that training to discriminate S_1+ from S_2- gives S_2 discriminative control over not responding (i.e., connects S_2 to a no-response), we proceed as in the excitatory case. If there is inhibitory control, then a decrease in the tendency to not respond (i.e., an increase in responding) should be found upon varying some property of S_2. We must be careful, however, that the variations of S_2 do *not* change its distance from any property of S_1 that might control responding. Otherwise, an increase in responding could be the result of more closely approximating some value of S_1. Just as in a "pure" test for excitatory control one must keep equidistant from the non-reinforced stimulus while varying S_1, in a pure test for inhibitory control one must keep equidistant from the reinforced stimulus while varying S_2.

An attempt to meet this condition was made by Jenkins and Harrison (1962) in a study of auditory generalization. In different experiments they used no-tone or white noise as S_1+ and a pure tone or tones as S_2-. If it is granted that the absence of a tone or white noise are stimuli without a sensible dimension of tonal frequency, then the effect on responding of variations in the frequency of the tone(s) which served as S_2- in training provides relevant data on inhibitory control. Their results did provide evidence for inhibitory control since variations in S_2- were associated with increased responding although in all cases the gradients were shallow. Honig, Boneau, Burstein, and Pennypacker (1963) attacked the problem along the same lines. The S_1+ was a blank key, while the S_2- was a key showing a line in the vertical orientation. A clear inhibitory gradient was obtained by varying the orientation of the line during the generalization test. Responding increased progressively as the orientation of the line was changed from vertical to horizontal.

It is clear that as a result of at least some forms of discrimination training, animals learn to not respond on signal. There is inhibitory stimulus control. The evidence, which is that variations of the negative stimulus result in more responding, is of the same general form as evidence for positive or excitatory stimulus control. The kind of information given by the stimulus generalization experiment allows us to conclude in favor of Rule 3; both excitatory and inhibitory stimulus controls are developed as the result of at least certain forms of discrimination training.

The Measurement of Excitatory and Inhibitory Control

At first glance one might be impressed with the symmetry of the experimental operations which one uses to obtain an excitatory or an inhibitory gradient. Consider the previously cited experiment by Honig *et al.* (1963). In order to obtain an excitatory gradient, the line stimulus is made S_1+, the blank key S_2-, and a decreasing tendency to respond is observed upon varying S_1 in the test phase. In order to obtain an inhibitory gradient, the blank key is S_1+, the vertical line is S_2-, and an increasing tendency to respond is observed upon varying S_2 in the test phase. In spite of this apparent symmetry a closer look at how these gradients are obtained will, I think, suggest an asymmetry at the behavioral level.

To pursue the question, let us suppose the pigeon's key-peck is being recorded. Designate it R_1. All the pigeon's movements not directly connected with activating the key are designated $\bar{R}_1$. But $\bar{R}_1$ may have some identifiable (even though not recorded) subclasses within it. For example, in work with the discriminated trial procedure (Jenkins, 1961), where there are really three stimuli, S_1+, S_2-, and the between-trial stimulus condition S_3-, we have observed that what the pigeon does on presentation of S_2- is recognizably different from what it does between trials. The pattern of movement initiated by an S_2- presentation in a late stage of training often involves a momentary orientation toward the key, followed immediately by turning away to the side and remaining at some distance from the key until the S_2- trial is terminated by external control. At this point the animal resumes oscillatory pacing in front of the key and continues with these movements until the next trial. Further, the movement pattern on S_2- trials during discrimination can always be distinguished from that obtained late in extinction, where all trials go unreinforced. Late in extinction the animal ceases to orient toward the key, and is often immobile for long periods. For the purpose of the present discussion, however, we need only assume that $\bar{R}_1$ can be separated into two subclasses: the movement pattern associated in the late stages of discrimination-learning with S_2-, which we designate as R_2, and everything else, which we designate as $(\bar{R}_1 \bar{U} \bar{R}_2)$.

Now let us consider the change in the relative frequency of occurrence of these subclasses as we vary stimuli in the generalization test. Consider first the case of the excitatory gradient. As S_1 is varied toward more remote values, a decrease in R_1 is observed. This decrease may reflect an increase in R_2 or in $(\bar{R}_1 \ \bar{U} \ \bar{R}_2)$, or in both. But no matter how the loss in R_1 is distributed between these remaining subclasses, all losses are summed in the determination of the sloping excitatory gradient. In the case of the inhibitory gradient, S_2 is varied, and again there may be losses in R_2 either because of the more frequent occurrence of R_1 or of $(\bar{R}_1 \ \bar{U} \ \bar{R}_2)$, or both. The difference is that in plotting an inhibitory gradient only that part of the loss in R_2 which appears as an increase in R_1 is counted into the gradient since the gradient is plotted as an increase in the occurrence of R_1 . Therefore, losses in R_2 reflected by increases in $(\bar{R}_1 \ \bar{U} \ \bar{R}_2)$ simply lower the overall level of responding. Only if all the transfer out of R_2 is to R_1 will excitatory and inhibitory gradients be equal and opposite. In all other cases the inhibitory gradients will be flatter *even on the assumption that completely symmetrical changes in the probability of occurrence of the sub-classes takes place in each case.*

Talking about the behavioral changes that give rise to gradients in terms of subclasses suggests an identification of inhibition with the development of a response to S_2- which is incompatible with the reinforced response. However, I see no reason why the present view should entail a guess about how this change of movement pattern is developed; whether, for example, it is reinforced indirectly by certain contingencies in discrimination training or reflects an emotional state conditioned to S_2- .

Results that allow a comparison of excitatory and inhibitory gradients seem to reflect something like the hypothetical state here described. Honig *et al.* (1963) found the over-all level of responding in the inhibitory gradient to be less than for the excitatory gradient. When the excitatory and inhibitory gradients were normalized in terms of percentage of total responses to test stimuli (excluding the blank-key test stimulus), the gradients were initially of similar form, but in the course of testing, the inhibitory gradients become flatter than the excitatory gradients. Jenkins and Harrison (1962) obtained inhibitory gradients (taken over an entire test) that showed a far lower level of responding and were far more shallow than excitatory gradients.

Determinants of Inhibitory Stimulus Control

Insufficient data are available on inhibitory gradients obtained by the more direct method described above (i.e., by a method that does not entail an interaction of a gradient on the excitatory stimulus with the inhibitory gradient) to allow us to move very far toward answering the question of what conditions of training give rise to inhibitory control. There are several experiments, on the other hand, in which gradients have been obtained following discrimination training where S_1+ and S_2- lie along the same dimension. If some characteristic shape of the resulting gradients could be accepted as a sure sign of inhibitory control, these experiments would provide relevant information.

In an earlier version of the present paper, the position was taken that the peak-shift, which can be produced by discriminative training with non-reinforcement on S_2, is a symptom of inhibitory control by S_2. On that premise, training conditions leading to a peak-shift would be sufficient conditions for the development of inhibitory control. A review of the evidence then available appeared to support the notion that the development of the shift depended upon the interspersal of reinforced trials on S_1 with the non-reinforced trials on S_2. Thus, it seemed that inhibitory control was present when the animal had learned not to respond to one stimulus while concurrently maintaining a reinforced response to a related stimulus. On the other hand, non-reinforcement on S_2 after all reinforcement on S_1 has been discontinued appeared not to be sufficient to produce the peak-shift. Perhaps it is also not adequate to produce inhibitory control. These conclusions were based primarily on the experiment by Honig, Thomas, and Guttman (1959) in which the peak-shift was found after training with interspersed S_1+ and S_2- trials, but not after a separate extinction on S_2. However, the results of Friedman and Guttman (this vol., pp. 255–267) show that a separate extinction on S_2 can produce a peak-shift if the animal has previously learned a discrimination involving S_1 by means of interspersed non-reinforced trials. Thus it appears that a peak-shift resulting from non-reinforcement in the presence of S_2 may be obtained even though reinforcement is discontinued before non-reinforcement on S_2 is begun. From our assumption that the peak-shift is a symptom of inhibitory control, it would follow that stopping in the presence of concurrent reinforcement is not necessary for the development of inhibitory control.

At present, I am doubtful of the wisdom of my earlier assumption that the peak-shift is a symptom of inhibitory control. Perhaps a better approach is to recognize how little we understand of the causes of the peak-shift, and to pursue that phenomenon and the one of inhibitory stimulus control quite independently. When more is known about each, we shall be able to see how they are related.

It has been shown that inhibitory control does develop when a discrimination is trained with interspersed positive trials on S_1 and negative trials on S_2. Even such an abbreviated statement of the circumstances producing inhibitory control suggests a number of isolable features, the bearing of which on inhibitory control is unknown. For example, is it essential that responses occur to S_2? Perhaps the method of errorless discrimination training developed by Terrace (1963) also produces inhibitory control; perhaps not. Is the maintenance of a response to S_1 through interspersed reinforced trials essential, or would a separate extinction produce inhibitory control? Further, is it essential that the reinforcement and non-reinforcement occur with respect to different stimuli, or does inhibitory control develop when a single stimulus is first reinforced and then non-reinforced until the response to that stimulus is extinguished? Should it turn out that simple extinction does not yield inhibitory control while at least some forms of discriminative training do, the prevalent view that discrimination is simply a case of combined conditioning and extinction would come in for a thoroughgoing revision.

The techniques of generalization testing can be used to identify inhibitory stimulus control in a straightforward way. Their use to learn more about the conditions leading to inhibitory control should give us a clearer view of the fundamental processes in discriminative conditioning.

REFERENCES

Harlow, H. F., and Hicks, L. H. Discrimination learning theory: uniprocess vs. duoprocess. *Psychol. Rev.*, 1957, **64**, 104–109.

Honig, W. K., Boneau, C. A., Burstein, K. R., and Pennypacker, H. S. Positive and negative generalization gradients obtained after equivalent training conditions. *J. comp. physiol. Psychol.*, 1963, **56**, 111–116.

Honig, W. K., Thomas, D. R., and Guttman, N. Differential effects of massed extinction and discrimination training on the generalization gradient. *J. exp. Psychol.*, 1959, **58**, 145–152.

Jenkins, H. M. The effect of discrimination training on extinction. *J. exp. Psychol.*, 1961, **61**, 111–121.

Jenkins, H. M., and Harrison, R. H. Generalization gradients of inhibition following auditory discrimination learning. *J. exp. Anal. Behav.*, 1962, **5**, 435–441.

Pavlov, I. P. *Conditioned reflexes*, translated by G. V. Anrep. London: Oxford Univer. Press, 1927.

Skinner, B. F. *The behavior of organisms*. New York: Appleton-Century, 1938.

Terrace, H. S. Discrimination learning with and without "errors." *J. exp. anal. Behav.*, 1963, **6**, 1–27.

6. The Stimulus, Stimulus Control, and Stimulus Generalization

Martin R. Baron, *Kent State University*

It has been found, in some investigations, that single-stimulus (non-differential) training results in flat generalization gradients, while differential training produces steep gradients. For example, Butter and Guttman (1957), using pigeons, obtained a steep gradient along a dimension of angular orientation (tilt of a white line) only after differential training, and Jenkins and Harrison (1960), also using pigeons, found that similar training was necessary to produce a steep gradient along a dimension of auditory frequency. These findings suggest that the establishment of stimulus control might universally require differential training. There is, however, no universal requirement.

Single-stimulus training does produce control by some stimuli. Guttman and Kalish (1956) established, in pigeons, good behavioral control by wavelength without differential training. Butter and Guttman (1957), using a similar procedure, obtained a relatively flat but reliable gradient along a dimension of angularity of a white line. However, similar training resulted in good control by the angularity of a *green* line (Butter, 1963). Comparable results were obtained by Margolius, who found, following single-stimulus training with albino rats, a steep gradient along a size–brightness dimension but a flat gradient along a light-intensity (brightness) dimension.[1] This occurred despite the fact that the range of light intensities employed (from .01 mL to 1100 mL) was probably wider than the range of brightness in the size-brightness dimension (from 20 to 79 sq. cm.). These findings suggest that all stimuli are not equally capable of acquiring behavioral control. The remainder of this paper will be devoted to a consideration of this possibility.

The Concept of Attending Hierarchy

In conflict with the simple assumption that all stimuli are equally capable of controlling behavior, psychological literature (and the experimental psychologists' folklore) includes statements to the effect that various orga-

[1] Personal communication.

nisms respond more readily or with greater sensitivity to some modalities than others. Rats are considered to be highly proprioceptive, pigeons especially visual, and humans, unless they have suffered early and prolonged visual deprivation (Ganz, this vol., p. 111), more visual than auditory. Harlow notes that investigators of discrimination-learning studies with monkeys have avoided the auditory modality, and suggests that they may have done so because it has been assumed that such training would require a larger number of trials than training in a visual modality.[2] Even within the visual modality, monkeys (and humans) appear to respond more readily to color than to form. What is being suggested is that for any organism presented a complex of stimuli there may be an attending hierarchy, i.e., an ordering of the degree to which each element or dimension of the complex will come to control behavior.

Attending Hierarchies in Discrimination Learning

In a discrimination-learning study with monkeys, Warren (1953), found the effectiveness of cues to be greatest for color, next for form, and least for size. In addition, the combination of form or size, or both, with color cues did not result in better performance than was obtained with color alone. In a cue-reduction study (Warren, 1954), subjects were first trained to discriminate objects distinguishable by a combination of color, form, and size cues, and then retrained following removal of some of the cues from the complex. Cue dominance, measured by mean errors following removal of cues, showed the dominance order, from highest to lowest, to be color and form, color and size, color, size, size and form, and form. Both studies demonstrate the dominance of color cues for these subjects.

Findings showing greater ease of control by color than by angular orientation were obtained in an as yet unpublished study performed by Newman (1963) under the direction of the author. In his study, operant discrimination training was provided three groups of twelve pigeons each. The discriminanda are shown in Table 1. It can be seen that for Group 1

TABLE 1

Discriminanda Employed by Newman

Group	Positive	Negative
1	White vertical line	No line
	Green circular surround	Green circular surround
2	White vertical line	No line
	Green circular surround	Red circular surround
4	White vertical line	White vertical line
	Green circular surround	Red circular surround

[2] Personal communication.

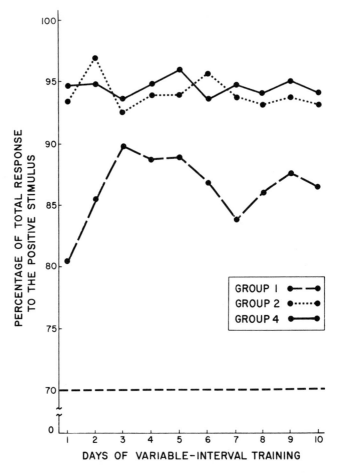

FIG. 1. Percentage of total responses made to the positive stimulus during variable-interval training by three differentially trained groups.

the only difference between positive and negative stimuli was the presence and absence of the white vertical line. For Group 2 the positive and negative stimuli were changed in two ways, i.e., vertical present to vertical absent, and green surround to red surround. For Group 4 the only difference between positive and negative stimuli was the change in color of the surround.[3]

Performance during ten days of differential training is shown in Fig. 1, which indicates the percentage of total responses that each group made to the positive stimulus. Chance performance is indicated by the horizontal

[3] Group 3 was non-differentially trained; performance of this group is relevant only to later discussion.

dashed line; positive and negative stimuli were not presented for equal periods. Learning apparently took place for Groups 2 and 4 early in the first day. For these two groups performance was relatively stable, with the percentage of total responses to the positive stimulus varying between 92.5 and 96.7. For Group 1, differential behavior was closer to chance (70 per cent) and fluctuated between 80.4 and 89.7 per cent; these subjects, it will be recalled, were required to differentiate between positive and negative stimuli that were the same color, but different in regard to presence-absence of the vertical line. Group 2, which differentiated very well (relative to Group 1), had both color change and presence-absence of the line as discriminanda. Group 4, given only color-change cues, performed like Group 2. Clearly, under the reinforcement schedule employed, it was easier for pigeons to differentiate green from red than to differentiate presence of the vertical from absence. Stated another way, the subjects in this study, provided with a stimulus complex of color and vertical line, attended more readily to the element of color than of line; i.e., color was higher in the hierarchy than the line.

Various explanations of Newman's data are possible. One is that the position of each element in the visual attending hierarchy is determined by the relative size of the elements on the retinal image; in this case color took up a larger area than did the vertical. In addition, it is tempting to consider that the green surround, because it was present during reinforcement for Group 1, acted as a secondary reinforcer (Thomas, this vol., p. 268), and maintained responses in the presence of the negative stimulus (line absent, green surround). One might argue that the decrease (following Day 3) in the percentage of total responses made to the positive stimulus indicates the growth of secondary reinforcement to the green surround. To continue with this interpretation, the vertical line, present during reinforcement for Group 4, should have acquired secondary reinforcing value and maintained responses to the negative stimulus (line present, red surround). Such was not the case, however. Whatever the explanation, the pigeons' behavior in this experimental situation was controlled more by color than by the vertical line. Group differences were significant at the .01 level.

Newman's (1963) findings, coupled with those of Warren (1953; 1954), show that stimulus differences are more readily discriminated along some dimensions than along others. This fact is consistent with the notion that there exists, inborn or as a result of prior experience, or both, an attending hierarchy to elements of a stimulus complex, as a result of which behavior control is more readily acquired by some stimulus elements than by others.[4]

---

[4] Recent evidence suggests that prior experience plays a strong role. Peterson (1962) found that for ducklings reared in monochromatic light, a generalization gradient along wavelength following single-stimulus training was flat. The gradient along wavelength was sloped for a second group of ducklings raised in white light, and provided the same single-stimulus training.

This concept suggests a way to reconcile some inconsistent findings described earlier, specifically, that single-stimulus training is effective in establishing control (steep generalization gradients) by some stimulus elements but not by others. It may be that the elements highest in the attending hierarchy quickly acquire good control with non-differential training, while those lower in the hierarchy acquire control less quickly or to a lesser degree. Raising the relative position of the element low in the hierarchy might hasten control acquisition or increase the amount of control obtained. One way to accomplish this might be through differential training in which "paying attention" to changes in an element low in the hierarchy is reinforced while "paying attention" to changes in elements high in the hierarchy is non-reinforced.

Modification of Attending Hierarchies with Differential Training

Evidence regarding the influence of differential training upon the attending hierarchy is found in a portion of Newman's (1963) study, to which reference was made earlier in this paper. It will be recalled (see Table 1) that Newman provided differential training to three groups (Groups 1, 2, and 4). An additional group, Group 3, was given non-differential training; for this group the reinforcement schedule in the presence of the positive stimulus (vertical white line on a green surround) was the same as for the other groups, but no negative stimulus was employed. For all four groups generalization was tested to five degrees of angular orientation (including the vertical) on the day following the tenth day of variable interval training. The stimulus complex during the generalization test consisted of a white line on a green surround. The response frequencies of the four groups to the various test stimuli are presented in Fig. 2.

On the basis of the differential training data described above (see Fig. 1), it seems reasonable to assume that, prior to differential training, the surround color in this experimental situation was higher in the pigeons' attending hierarchy than the white line (and its angular orientation). It would therefore be expected that the behavior of Group 3 (non-differentially trained) would be under greater control of the dominant element (color) than the angular orientation of the white line. The flat gradient for this group is consistent with this expectation. In sharp contrast, Group 1 subjects, for whom presence-absence of the line was differentially reinforced while color was not, were expected to pay less "attention" to color of the surround and "attend" the white line and its angular orientation. The significantly sloped, symmetrical gradient along the angularity dimension for Group 1 is consistent with the expectation that for this group angularity would acquire behavioral control. Thus far, the evidence simply confirms findings obtained by Butter and Guttman (1957), and while consistent with the concept of attending hierarchy, does not rule out any other

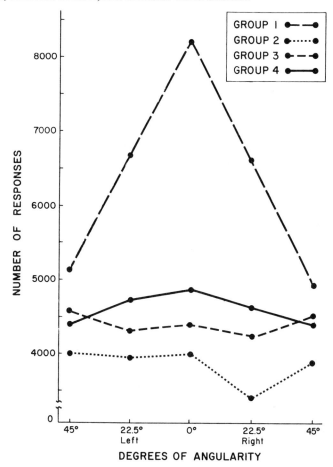

FIG. 2. Total number of responses during two days of generalization testing made to each test stimulus by four groups.

explanation. However, the performance of Groups 2 and 4, where angularity did not gain control, can be more readily explained with this concept than without it.[5]

The differential training given Group 1 subjects was effective in producing control by angularity. It is perhaps instructive to examine the characteristics of this training to determine which of them may have been responsible for the gain in control. The training conditions for Group 1, as noted above, involved two components: color was not relevant to reinforcement, but presence of the vertical was. Thus, for this group, control by verticality

[5] An over-all analysis of variance showed the interaction of angular orientation by groups to be significant at the .001 level. Angular orientation was a significant source of variability only for Group 1.

may have resulted from (a) lowering the position of color in the attending hierarchy, (b) raising the position of line presence, or (c) both of these. The training for Group 2 was provided in an attempt to examine the second possibility, i.e., to see if raising the position of line presence in the hierarchy without lowering the position of color would produce control by angularity. The procedure employed was to provide differential reinforcement for both color and line presence-absence. If angularity had gained control for Group 1 simply because line presence had been raised in the hierarchy (i.e., because presence-absence of the line had been differentially reinforced), then the generalization gradients along the angularity dimension should have been similar for Groups 1 and 2. However, Fig. 2 shows that while the gradient for Group 1 was steep, the gradient for Group 2 was flat. Differential reinforcement of both presence-absence of the line and of color was not sufficient to bring behavior under the control of angularity. It further suggests that angularity gained control for Group 1 subjects by lowering the position of color in the attending hierarchy, or by lowering the position of color while raising the position of line presence.

Group 4 was incorporated in Newman's study to determine whether differential reinforcement of color and non-differential reinforcement of line presence would influence the control by angularity of the line. If "calling attention" to color by differential reinforcement would raise color in the attending hierarchy and "distract" the subjects from line presence, control by angularity would be less for Group 4 than for Group 3 (non-differentially trained). The fact that a flat gradient was obtained in Group 3, where "attention" was not called to either stimulus element, does not permit us to check this possibility. If, on the other hand, differential reinforcement of color in Group 4 would serve to increase "attention" to all aspects of the stimulus complex, then the gradient along the dimension of angular orientation should have been steeper for Group 4 than for Group 3. It is clear from Fig. 2 that differential reinforcement of color alone did not, in Group 4, increase control by angularity.

In summary, Newman's study provides evidence that may be interpreted to suggest the following: (a) the position of an element low in the hierarchy may be raised by differentially reinforcing its presence and providing non-differential reinforcement for presence of an element high in the hierarchy; (b) differential reinforcement of two elements, one low in the hierarchy and the other high, is not likely to produce control by the low element; and (c) differential reinforcement of an element high in the hierarchy, with non-differential reinforcement of the presence of an element low in the hierarchy, is not likely to increase control by the lower element. To restate the last two points more empirically, Newman found, in the case of Group 4, that differential training in regard to color, with non-differential reinforcement of the presence of the line, did not produce a sloped gradient along the angularity dimension. Even in the case of Group 2, where *both* color and line presence were differentially reinforced, a flat gradient along angularity was obtained. Thus in two groups, differential training along one dimension did not produce a sloped gradient along a second. This evidence, on the surface, appears to be inconsistent with findings reported in the literature.

Reinhold and Perkins (1955) and Hoving (1963) report that differential training along one dimension increases the slope of the gradient along a second dimension. Perkins, Hershberger, and Weyant (1959) observed that the greater the difficulty of the discrimination along the first dimension, the steeper the slope of the gradient along the second dimension. It has been pointed out above that in the situation employed by Newman, color (Dimension I, along which differential training was provided) was probably high in the hierarchy, and verticality of the white line (Dimension II, along which generalization was tested) was low.

At what points on the attending hierarchy were the stimulus elements located in the three studies just mentioned? In two of the three studies, they were probably reversed, i.e., Dimension I was probably low in the hierarchy and Dimension II was high. For Reinhold and Perkins (1955), Dimension I was hardware cloth–no hardware cloth; Dimension II was black-white. The fact that the gradient along the black-white dimension, while shallow, was significantly sloped following single-stimulus training provides support for the notion that this dimension was high in the hierarchy at the outset of differential training.

In the Hoving (1963) study, which employed human subjects, Dimension I, along which differential conditioning was provided, was tonal intensity, while Dimension II was pitch. The fact that generalization tests following classical conditioning showed sloped gradients along both pitch and intensity dimensions (Hovland, 1937a; 1937b) suggests that the two dimensions are about equally high in the attending hierarchy.

Finally, in the Perkins *et al.* (1959) study, which employed albino-rat subjects, Dimension I was level of illumination and Dimension II was presence-absence of a buzzer. In view of Margolius' findings described above it seems reasonable to suspect that for albino rats, level of illumination is relatively low in the attending hierarchy. On the other hand, it is likely that presence-absence of the buzzer is relatively high; Perkins *et al.* (1959, p. 182) note, "The Behavior of Ss indicated that the buzzer was clearly audible and not markedly aversive." No similar statement was made regarding the light intensities.

An attending-hierarchy interpretation of the results obtained by Newman (1963), Reinhold and Perkins (1955), Perkins *et al.* (1959), and Hoving (1963) suggests that if Dimension I is at the same position or lower in the hierarchy than Dimension II, differential training along Dimension I increases the slope of the generalization gradient along Dimension II. On the other hand, if Dimension I is higher in the hierarchy than Dimension II, differential training along Dimension I does not increase gradient slope along Dimension II. Tests of the adequacy of this interpretation require, first, that for given stimulus complexes, attending hierarchies be ascertained by comparing slopes of generalization gradients for various elements following non-differential training. It would then be possible to determine the effect of differential training in regard to each of the elements upon the slope of the gradients for each other element.

In conclusion, it appears that all stimuli are not equally likely to acquire behavioral control. The concept of "attending hierarchy," as described in this paper, appears to reconcile some inconsistent evidence, and to have predictive power. Further relationships between the position of the stimulus element in the hierarchy, hierarchy modification, and stimulus control (as measured by slope of the generalization gradient) need to be explored.

REFERENCES

Butter, C. M. Stimulus generalization along one and two dimensions in pigeons. *J. exp. Psychol.*, 1963, **65**, 339–346.

Butter, C. M., and Guttman, N. Stimulus generalization and discrimination along the dimension of angular orientation. *Amer. Psychol.*, 1957, **12**, 449. (Abstract)

Guttman, N., and Kalish, H. I. Discriminability and stimulus generalization. *J. exp. Psychol.*, 1956, **51**, 79–88.

Hoving, K. L. Influence of type of discrimination training on generalization. *J. exp. Psychol.*, 1963, **66**, 514–520.

Hovland, C. I. The generalization of conditioned responses. I. The sensory generalization of conditioned responses with varying frequencies of tone. *J. gen. Psychol.*, 1937, **17**, 125–148. (a)

Hovland, C. I. The generalization of conditioned responses. II. Then sensory generalization of conditioned responses with varying intensities of tone. *J. genet. Psychol.*, 1937, **51**, 279–291. (b)

Jenkins, H., and Harrison, R. Effect of discrimination training on auditory generalization. *J. exp. Psychol.*, 1960, **59**, 246–253.

Newman, F. L. Factors affecting the generalization gradient along the dimension of angular orientation with pigeons. Unpublished M.A. thesis, Kent State Univer., 1963.

Perkins, C. C., Hershberger, W. A., and Weyant, R. G. Difficulty of a discrimination as a determiner of subsequent generalization along another dimension. *J. exp. Psychol.*, 1959, **57**, 181–186.

Peterson, N. Effect of monochromatic rearing on the control of responding by wavelength. *Science*, 1962, **136**, 774–775.

Reinhold, D. B., and Perkins, C. C. Stimulus generalization following different methods of training. *J. exp. Psychol.*, 1955, **49**, 423–427.

Warren, J. M. Additivity of cues in visual pattern discriminations by monkeys. *J. comp. physiol. Psychol.*, 1953, **46**, 484–486.

Warren, J. M. Perceptual dominance in discrimination learning by monkeys. *J. comp. physiol. Psychol.*, 1954, **47**, 290–292.

7. Metric Properties of Multidimensional Stimulus Generalization

David V. Cross, *University of Michigan*

Often the stimuli that set the occasion for differential responding differ on two or more physical dimensions and may even involve different sensory modalities. How does the behavior evoked in these situations compare with discriminative behavior that is controlled by stimulus properties which vary along one physical dimension only? What are the rules that govern how the component properties of a complex stimulus combine to exert control over responding? These questions may be raised with regard to a variety of experimental problems: whether we are concerned with the course of development of stimulus control, as in discrimination-learning experiments; with the specificity of stimulus control, as in generalization experiments; or with the relation between specific properties of stimuli and presumptive measures of sensory magnitude, as in psychophysical experiments.

Shepard (1964) has pointed out that these questions correspond to the problem of what metric, if any, behavioral measures impose upon the space of stimulus variables. Unfortunately, very few studies have approached the problem of multidimensional data analysis from the point of view of evaluating the metric, or combination rule, that actually generated the data. It is generally assumed, for mathematical convenience, that "true psychological distance" is Euclidean, and analysis is directed toward appropriate scaling of the stimulus or response variables, or both, in a manner compatible with a Euclidean embedding. Such scaling procedures have been and will continue to be useful techniques for constructing coordinate systems descriptive of stimuli of unknown dimensionality or on which the physical measurements that can be made are not directly related to the behavior under investigation. However, the practice of demanding reference to a Euclidean metric for behavioral data that come equipped with their own metric imposes constraints upon the analysis that may result in an unwanted misrepresentation of the behavior.

Coombs (1964, p. 206) has discussed the advantages of exploring alternative metric representations of behavioral data. In his own words, "One of the most desirable consequences of developing alternative models and their algorithms for data analysis is that *their existence destroys any naïve complacency with any one model and leads to a search for ways of testing and comparing alternative theories."* The point is that the algorithms used in multivariate data analysis and the metric embeddings of multidimensional scaling models are, by their nature, theories about behavior. They are theories about how unidimensionally scaled stimulus effects combine to determine the behavior evoked in multidimensional situations. There is not necessarily just one combination rule to which all behavior conforms but rather alternative rules that may correspond to alternative theories about behavior, or to alternative behaviors, or to behavior under different circumstances or under the control of different kinds of stimuli.

If the properties of discriminative behavior under multidimensional stimulus control can be suitably represented by the mathematical properties of *metric spaces*, they can then be analyzed in terms of the mathematical procedures of the geometries associated with these spaces. This would not only assist us in the practical business of dealing with multidimensional stimulus variables but also provide a basis for important theoretical conclusions and the techniques for comparing and testing alternative theories of behavior.

Metrization of Multidimensional Stimulus Control

The basic concept underlying the notion of a metric space is that of the *distance* between two points. The properties of distance will depend to some extent on the space considered, but certain basic properties are definitive and assumed always to hold. These are (1) the distance between any two points is nonnegative, and only the distance of a point from itself is zero; (2) the distance between any two points is symmetric, that is, the distance from the first point to the second is the same as that from the second to the first; and (3) for any three points the distance between one pair is no greater than the sum of the other two distances, a condition called triangle inequality.

These assumptions can be stated a little more exactly by formulae. We consider a set S such that with each pair x, y of its elements we can associate a nonnegative real number $d(x, y)$, called their *distance*, which satisfies the conditions: (1) $d(x, y) = 0$ if and only if $x = y$; (2) $d(x, y) = d(y, x)$; (3) $d(x, z) \leq d(x, y) + d(y, z)$, for all x, y, z in S. The function $d(x, y)$ is said to be a *metric* for S. Any set (or space) S is said to be *metrizable* if a distance between its elements (or points) can be defined. The ordinary physical space of three dimensions is a metric space with Euclidean distance.

However, the above conditions are quite general, and are also satisfied by the following example. Take a set of color patches. For each pair x, y

define the distance $d(x, y) = 0$ if both members of the pair are labeled with the same color name and define $d(x, y) = 1$ if they are labeled differently. The function $d(x, y)$ could serve as a metric for the color domain, but it does not provide a basis for a very interesting or especially informative model for color perception.

We might ask whether the measures of differential responding obtained in experimental studies of discriminative behavior in which the fact or degree of stimulus control is the primary variable under investigation, and in which the relevant dimensions of control are known and subject to experimental manipulation, provide a basis for defining a metric for the stimulus variables involved. These experiments include studies of stimulus generalization, in which a response is brought under the control of a particular stimulus complex and then tested in the presence of other stimuli that differ from the initial training stimulus with respect to one or more of its properties. Also included are conditioning experiments and discrimination-learning experiments, in which the dependent variable is either the different number of stimulus presentations or trials, required to establish control, or the degree of control established, as measured by differential amounts of conditioning, or the number of correct discriminations obtained.

If these experiments yield measures that satisfy the properties of distance, then the physical coordinates of the stimuli can be transformed into behavioral coordinates (i.e., coordinates scaled in units of behavioral control) of a metric space that may serve both as a multidimensional representation of the stimuli and as a description of the behavior in question. The distance function defined on the transformed coordinates represents how behavioral control is distributed over the several stimulus properties, and represents the combination rule that enables us to predict multidimensional effects from unidimensional quantities.

Evidence from earlier experiments. The results from a variety of experiments indicate that a metric treatment of generalization and discrimination data is feasible, and that the stimulus sets involved are at least locally metrizable. The continuity of the empirical relations that obtain between changes in the controlling stimulus and properties of responding is strongly suggestive of the triangle-inequality property of distances. That is, the total effect of changing a stimulus along two or more dimensions is no less than the largest of the component unidimensional effects.

For example, Miller (1939) found that a combined auditory and visual stimulus (a drop in pitch of a continuous tone and the movement of a pointer), paired with electric shock to the cheek, resulted in faster and stronger conditioning of an eyelid response in humans than did either stimulus property used alone. Similarly, Eninger (1952) found that rats formed a discrimination much more rapidly when auditory and visual cues were combined (tone vs. no-tone and white vs. black) than when either of these sets of cues was presented alone.

In a generalization study, Fink and Patton (1953) controlled certain visual, auditory, and tactile characteristics of the stimulus situation in which rats learned to drink water from a tube. After establishing a stable baseline of drinking rate, the investigators altered one or more of the stimulus properties under their control. They found that any change led to a decrement in drinking: light changes were most effective, sound changes were moderately effective, and tactual changes were least effective in modifying the strength of the learned drinking response. More important, however, they found that a change in any two stimulus properties resulted in a greater response decrement than a change in any single property; when all three stimuli were changed, maximum response decrement occurred.

Using a card of a certain hue and saturation (Munsell 10GY 8/6) as a discriminative stimulus, White (1958) trained children to pull a handle to get marbles. Then, for different groups of subjects, he changed either the hue of the stimulus card, its saturation, or both, in a series of unreinforced test trials. There was greater generalization decrement to test stimuli that differed from the training stimulus in both dimensions than to those that differed in either of the dimensions alone. In other words, the properties of hue and saturation combined to exert more control over differential responding than either property exerted alone. A generalization suggested by these results is that every stimulus property that happens to be correlated with the contingencies of reinforcement requiring differential responding acquires some degree of stimulus control; when stimulus properties are presented in combination, their effects combine in some manner to exert an even greater degree of control.

However, it has been found, in some discrimination experiments, that stimuli differing in two properties are discriminated with no greater ease or efficiency than stimuli differing in *the single one* of these properties which is most readily discriminated. In other words, the degree of behavioral control exerted by the several properties of a compound stimulus is no greater than that exercised by the component property which, alone, is most effective. Harlow (1945) trained monkeys to respond discriminatively to stimuli differing in color only, form only, or both. Stimuli differing in both color and form, or in color alone, were discriminated equally well, although both were discriminated more readily than form.

This result was also obtained by Warren (1953), who tested monkeys on discrimination problems involving stimuli which differed in color, form, size, or in the four combinations of these properties taken two or three at a time. Stimuli that differed in color and some other property were little, if any, more discriminable than those differing in color alone. In a later experiment, Warren (1954) trained monkeys to discriminate pairs of stimuli that differed simultaneously in color, form, and size. After establishing stimulus control, he reduced the number of discriminative cues by eliminating stimulus differences in one or two dimensions. In each instance, performance scores were depressed. Discriminative control was almost completely lost when color differences were eliminated, regardless of which other property or combination of properties remained. Some control was lost when both form and size differences were eliminated, and the smallest decrements in performance occurred when only the form or the size differences were eliminated, size being the least effective.

These findings are also consistent with a metric interpretation, i.e., triangle inequality is not violated, but the class of combination rules suggested differs drastically from those consistent with the preceding experimental findings. The experimental results considered first suggest a distribution of behavioral control over the several stimulus properties, whereas the others suggest that a single dimension, along which the greatest distances are defined, overshadows the rest and is dominant in controlling differential responding.

Metric Models for Multidimensional Stimulus Generalization

There are three major points of view concerning these rules of combination as they pertain to multidimensional stimulus generalization. Two-dimensional models of these views are presented graphically in Fig. 1. The two stimulus dimensions are labeled S_1 and S_2, respectively, and their point of intersection represents the training stimulus. Degree of generalization is depicted as a third dimension, labeled R, orthogonal to the other two. The stimulus dimensions are assumed to be appropriately scaled in units of behavioral control so that the generalization gradients for the separate dimensions are linear and of equal slope. The task of the models is to predict the height of the generalization surface at any point in the four quadrants of the stimulus plane.

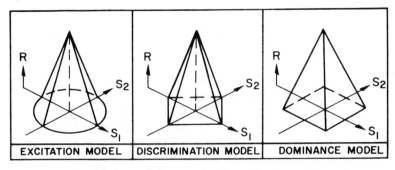

FIG. 1. Possible forms of the generalization surface in two dimensions.

Theoretical justification for the first model, the *excitation* model, comes from Pavlov, and later from Hull, who conceived of generalization as resulting immediately as a spread of excitation in all directions from the training stimulus. According to this view, prior differential training along specific stimulus dimensions is not necessary to obtain gradients of generalization. Thus, for a generalization surface of given dimensionality, one set of dimensions or frame of reference is as good as any other in predicting generalization behavior—there are no preferred dimensions. Although he never stated it explicitly, Hull implies that a generalization surface for two dimensions can be generated by rotating a unidimensional gradient around its peak, resulting in a surface which is conical in shape, as depicted in the first panel of Fig. 1 (Guttman, 1956; Jones, 1962).

A contrasting view, proposed by Lashley and Wade (1946) and by Guttman (1956), is that generalization is a performance phenomenon reflecting only the discriminative control exercised by stimuli varying along dimensions previously established for the organism by differential training. This view predicts that the generalization decrement for any stimulus varying in two dimensions is the sum of the decrements to stimuli changed in each dimension alone. The generalization surface has the appearance of a pyramid with its four corners on the stimulus axes. This *discrimination* model is depicted in the second panel of Fig. 1.

The *dominance* model, depicted in the third panel of Fig. 1, is suggested by the results of the experiments, discussed earlier in this paper, in which some one stimulus property appeared to be "dominant" in exerting behavioral control. The dominance model states that stimulus control is selective—i.e., it is exerted only by the dimension along which the most discriminable stimulus change occurred. The theoretical background for this model may be found in Lashley's "principle of dominant organization." Lashley (1942) maintains that the mechanism of nervous integration is such that, when any complex of stimuli arouses nervous activity, that activity is immediately organized, and certain stimulus properties become dominant for reaction while others become ineffective. The generalization surface predicted by the dimensional dominance model is also a pyramid with its corners at 45° to the stimulus axes.

If we look at successive sections through the generalization surfaces depicted in Fig. 1, sections taken horizontal to the respective stimulus planes, sets of concentric contours are revealed. These have been called isosimilarity contours by Shepard (1960, 1964). The contours are circular for the excitation model, diamond-shaped (rotated squares) for the discrimination model, and square for the dominance model. Each contour corresponds to a prescribed amount of generalization decrement and describes a locus of equally effective stimuli. That is, all stimuli on a contour are equivalent with respect to the amount of control exercised over differential responding, and thus equally substitutable one for another to produce a given generalization decrement.

The question of the shape of these contours turns out to be equivalent to the question of just what metric is appropriate for a given set of measures (see Shepard, 1964). The shape of the contours uniquely determines, and is determined by, the structure of the underlying metric space. Thus, the assumption of the excitation model that all contours are circular is equivalent to the very special assumption that distances, i.e., the amount of generalization decrement, or the separation between the training stimulus and the test stimulus on the underlying scale, are Euclidean. In Euclidean space, the distance between two points is given by the Pythagorean formula, i.e., the distance between two points is equal to the square root of the sum of squared differences between the projections of the two points on each of their coordinate axes. This is the basic assumption underlying most multidimensional scaling models.

Multidimensional scaling models based on the Euclidean metric have been used in several studies involving color stimuli. In general, the model fits the behavioral data well. Shepard (1958) constructed a model of this kind applicable to stimulus-response confusion data, typically obtained in paired-associate (identification learning) experiments. The model is based on the assumption that stimulus generalization, in terms of probability of a correct identification, is an exponential decay function of distance in Euclidean space. The model was applied to a matrix of confusion probabilities obtained from subjects required to identify each of nine Munsell colors varying in brightness (value) and saturation (chroma). Approximately 99 per cent of the original variance in the data was accounted for by the model.

In certain experimental settings, however, a model of stimulus generalization based on a non-Euclidean metric has proved to be a more appropriate description of the findings. The non-Euclidean metric associated with the discrimination model provides a particularly simple rule for combining distances—namely, the distance between two points is equal to the sum of the differences between the projections of the two points on each of their coordinate axes. Theoretical arguments for this rule of combination have been proposed by Landahl (Householder and Landahl, 1945, p. 76; Landahl, 1945) and by Restle (1959). This rule is often called the "city-block" metric because the distance between two points is the total distance that must be traversed in a north-south direction plus the distance that must be traversed along the east-west direction. Attneave (1950) found that measures of both judged similarity and frequency of confusion among simple geometrical figures (triangles or parallelograms), varying along the dimensions of size and either brightness or shape (tilt), conformed more to the city-block metric than to the Euclidean metric.

In an attempt to discover what rule of combination applies in multi-dimensional stimulus generalization, Butter (1963) trained pigeons to peck at a key illuminated by a narrow vertical strip of monochromatic (550 mμ) light. The birds were tested under extinction conditions for generalization to stimuli varied in the wavelength dimension, in the angular orientation (tilt) dimension, and in both dimensions. There was greater generalization decrement to stimuli changed in both dimensions than to stimuli changed in either dimension alone.

Analysis of variance performed on the generalization measures revealed a significant interaction between the two stimulus dimensions. The source of this interaction was revealed in a graph depicting generalization as a function of stimulus changes along one dimension, with levels of the other dimension as the parameter. The gradients in the family of curves thus described were not parallel but appeared to be multiples of each other. This suggested that relative generalization to a stimulus that is changed in two dimensions simultaneously equals the product of the values of relative generalization obtained when the two changes are made independently, i.e., along single dimensions alone. If we denote by $R(i, j)$ the number of responses emitted in the presence of a stimulus different from the training stimulus by i units along one dimension and by j units along the second dimension, then

$$\frac{R(i, j)}{R(0, 0)} = \frac{R(0, j)}{R(0, 0)} \cdot \frac{R(i, 0)}{R(0, 0)},$$

where $R(0, 0)$ denotes the number of responses evoked by the training stimulus. This "multiplicative rule" was tested against the obtained data and was found to predict the number of responses to generalized stimuli with a remarkably high degree of accuracy. The investigator concluded that this result was not consistent with the discrimination model.

It is proper to point out, however, that when ratios multiply, logarithmic differences summate. The multiplicative rule generates isosimilarity contours that vary in shape as a function of distance from the origin. The multiplicative rule is not a distance function in an affine space, because it violates homogeneity. However, the measures can be represented by an affine geometry, in particular the "city-block" space, by a logarithmic transformation on response measures. The appropriateness of a logarithmic transformation on these data is evidenced by the observed dependence of response variability on response magnitude; scaling the dependent variable to render measurement equally precise at all levels of the scale (the achievement of variance homogeneity) meets a desirable measurement criterion. Thus, Butter's results may be interpreted as favoring the discrimination model.

Jones (1962) also found evidence for a multiplicative rule of combination in generalization along the dimensions of length and angular orientation, and also in generalization along the combined dimensions of hue, saturation, and brightness. A scaling of the response measures obtained in both of these experiments by a logarithmic transformation renders these results consistent with the discrimination hypothesis that predicts generalization in two or more dimensions as the sum of the generalization decrements along component dimensions. No comparable transformation would make these results consistent with the excitation hypothesis that is based on the notion of Euclidean distance and a rule of combination given by the Pythagorean formula. These results are consistent with the notion that generalization is an exponential decay function of psychological distance.

The metric for the dominance model requires that the distance between two points be simply the greatest of the distances separating their projections on each of the coordinate axes. This metric has never been formally employed in any multidimensional scaling model, although the rule of combination inducing the metric was indirectly employed by Eriksen and Hake (1955) to predict the discriminability of stimuli varying along only one dimension at a time. Their subjects were trained to identify each stimulus, in series of up to 20 stimuli varying in either size, hue, brightness, or the four combinations of these taken two or three at a time, by assigning different numbers to each stimulus. The probability of assigning a particular number, during testing, to a stimulus varying in two or three dimensions, was predicted from the response probabilities obtained from the unidimensional series. The predictions were based on the assumption that a stimulus of a given hue, size, and brightness evokes either response i under the control of hue, response j under the control of size, or response k under the control of brightness. *The response with the greatest probability was assumed to be the response that would be emitted.* Predictions of response probabilities were based on the assumption of independence of events, and involved computation of the joint probability associated with each event. The probability that a particular response i would be emitted to a compound stimulus was predicted by summing the joint probabilities of all events in which response i was most probable. The predictions fit the empirical probabilities notably well.

The Minkowski distance function. Each of the metrics just discussed has different implications for interpreting the quantitative properties of behavior under complex stimulus control. These do not exhaust all the possible metric spaces of potential psychological interest. In fact, consistent geometries have been developed for more general classes of metric spaces, of which the three described are only special cases. In all cases in which the obtained contours are centrally symmetric, convex, and of the same shape, there exists a distance function that will map the underlying measures into a metric space.

Of particular interest is the class of metric spaces generated by the Minkowski distance function, which defines the *distance* between any two points $x = (x_1, x_2, \cdots, x_n)$ and $y = (y_1, y_2, \cdots, y_n)$, where x_i and y_i ($i = 1, 2, \cdots, n$) are the coordinates of the points in n-dimensional space, as

$$d\,[(x_1, x_2, \cdots, x_n)\,(y_1, y_2, \cdots, y_n)] = [\sum_{i=1}^{n} d_i^r (x_i, y_i)]^{1/r}, r \geq 1,$$

where $d_i(x_i, y_i)$ is the distance between the coordinate projections of x and y on the ith dimension. In application to two-dimensional stimulus generalization, the training stimulus may be identified as the origin of the space, a test stimulus as the point P, and x and y as the amount of generalization decrement along the respective stimulus dimensions with respect to which P may vary. The "unit circles," i.e., the locus of stimulus points at a distance 1 from the origin is given by

$$|x|^r + |y|^r = 1.$$

The shape of the "unit circle" when graphed relative to cartesian coordinates depends on the value of r (Fig. 2). When $r = 1$, we have the city-block "unit circle"; for $r = 2$, we have the Euclidean "unit circle"; and as r approaches infinity, $d_r(OP)$ approaches the distance

$$\lim_{r \to \infty} d_r(OP) = \max\,\{|x|, |y|\},$$

and the "unit circle" for $\max\,\{|x|, |y|\} = 1$ is given by the square with sides

$$|x| = 1, \qquad 0 \leq |y| \leq 1,$$
$$|y| = 1, \qquad 0 \leq |x| \leq 1.$$

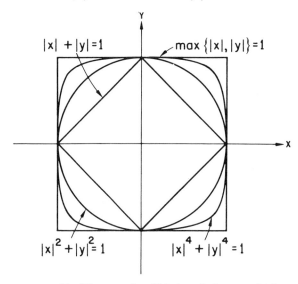

FIG. 2. Euclidean graphs of Minkowski "unit circles."

This is the metric implied by the dominance model discussed above. It can be shown (Beckenbach and Bellman, 1961, pp. 103–106) that Minkowski distance satisfies the metric axioms described earlier as well as certain properties deduced from them; it is translation invariant, symmetric, always positive, and it satisfies the conditions of triangle inequality and homogeneity.

Shepard (1964) performed four experiments to determine the particular Minkowski metric that describes how differences in size and angular orientation combine to exert control over differential responding in various tasks. The stimuli employed were circles with single radial lines (spokes) drawn at different angles. Shepard analyzed the frequencies with which stimuli varying in size, inclination, or both, were matched with a standard stimulus, and the frequencies with which stimuli were actually confused during identification learning. The implied isosimilarity contours were concave, indicating a violation of the condition of triangle inequality.

Shepard concluded that this anomalous result was due to the indiscriminate pooling of data from subjects who were attending to different aspects of the stimuli. Therefore, the subjects were divided into two groups; the data from subjects whose behavior appeared to be under the control of both stimulus properties were analyzed separately from the data of subjects whose behavior appeared to be dominantly under the control of one or the other stimulus property. The subjects in the latter group were described as adopting a "matching strategy" which essentially involved "finding the best match along one of the two dimensions." Data from the former group, presumed to have attended both dimensions, suggested that the isosimilarity contours were roughly four-cornered, indicating the appropriateness of a Minkowski metric somewhere between the Euclidean and the "city-block" varieties.

Attention and the Metrization of Behavioral Data

In general, we must allow that the different properties of a complex stimulus may be selectively effective in controlling differential responding. The fact that the controlling relations between a stimulus and responding may be different from one instance to the next, and that every aspect of the stimulus situation present when a reinforced response occurs may not subsequently be an occasion for the emission of that response, has been interpreted as meaning that subjects can selectively "attend" different aspects of the stimulus situation (Lashley, 1938; Reynolds, 1961).

The possibility of different controlling relations between the stimulus and response upon different presentations of the same physical stimulus raises an important question with respect to the use of behavioral data for the metrization of stimulus control. Shepard (1964) asserts that a static metric solution, or combination rule, to multidimensional data is not possible when a subject's attention shifts from one stimulus property to another upon different presentations of the same physical stimulus, or when data are indiscriminately pooled over subjects who are attending different properties of the same stimulus.

On the basis of an a priori analysis of multidimensional discrimination situations, it can be deduced that the combination rule implied by the discrimination hypothesis should apply when a subject's responding is under the exclusive control of one or another property of the stimulus upon any one stimulus presentation and never under simultaneous control of two or more properties. Consider two stimuli differing with respect to properties X and Y. One stimulus might be the training stimulus in a generalization experiment, and the other might be a particular test stimulus. If both stimuli evoke the same response—that is, if the response generalizes—then neither X nor Y exercises differential control. If the stimuli evoke differential responding, however, it can be attributed to the fact that discriminative control is exercised by either the difference with respect to property X alone, or to Y alone, or to both.

These obviously comprise four mutually exclusive and exhaustive events with respect to the controlling relations that can obtain between a response and two-dimensional stimuli. The probabilities of these joint events must sum to 1; that is,

$$(1) \qquad P(XY) + P(X\bar{Y}) + P(\bar{X}Y) + P(\bar{X}\bar{Y}) = 1.00 ,$$

where

$P(XY) \equiv$ the probability that no differential control is exerted,
$P(X\bar{Y}) \equiv$ the probability that differential control is exerted only by Y,
$P(\bar{X}Y) \equiv$ the probability that differential control is exerted only by X,
$P(\bar{X}\bar{Y}) \equiv$ the probability that differential control is exerted by both X and Y simultaneously.

The probability $P(XY)$ that a stimulus changed with respect to both X and Y will evoke the response appropriate to the training stimulus is given by

$$(2) \qquad P(XY) \equiv 1 - [P(\bar{X}) + P(\bar{Y}) - P(\bar{X}\bar{Y})] ,$$

where

$P(\bar{X}) \equiv$ the marginal probability that X will exert differential control,
$P(\bar{Y}) \equiv$ the marginal probability that Y will exert differential control.

If it is assumed that differential responding is never under the control of both properties simultaneously, then

$$P(\overline{XY}) \equiv 0 \rightleftarrows P(\overline{X}|\overline{Y}) = P(\overline{Y}|\overline{X}) = 0 \,,$$

i.e., the probability that both X and Y exercise differential control is zero, which implies that the conditional probability that one property exercises control given that the other does is zero. From this it follows that

(3) $$1 - P(XY) = [1 - P(X)] + [1 - P(Y)].$$

In other words, the generalization decrement to a stimulus changed with respect to two properties equals the sum of the decrements to either property alone—the prediction made by the discrimination hypothesis. However, if the controlling relations are such that one of the stimulus properties is dominant in exerting control, i.e., $P(X\overline{Y}) = 0$ when $P(\overline{X}) > P(\overline{Y})$, then $P(\overline{X}|\overline{Y}) = 1$ and

$$P(XY) = 1 - [P(\overline{X}) + P(\overline{Y}) - P(\overline{X}|\overline{Y}) \, P(\overline{Y})] \,,$$
$$P(XY) = 1 - P(\overline{X}) = P(X) \,,$$

or

(4) $$1 - P(XY) = \max \, [P(\overline{X}), P(\overline{Y})] \,,$$

which is the prediction made by the dominance model discussed above.

Although this analysis was based on the possible controlling relations between responding and two-dimensional stimuli, the results easily generalize to stimuli of greater dimensionality. Equations (3) and (4) with the corresponding assumptions represent two cases with respect to the role played by "attention" in multidimensional stimulus control. It is suggestive in the latter case, the dominance model, to consider that the property attended by a subject upon presentation of a complex stimulus is controlled by certain discriminability characteristics of the component dimensions. That is, a subject attends or observes only the dimension along which greatest change occurred, or which is easiest to discriminate.

The discrimination model, on the other hand, suggests that attention or observing responses are independent of these discriminability relations but are, instead, a function of extraneous factors—for example, a subject's prior reinforcement history with respect to the dimensions involved and consequent predisposition on sensitization to changes along selected dimensions, a condition which might differ among subjects. Fluctuating sensory processes such as those underlying the perception of reversible visual figures, like the Necker cube, might also account for differential observing or attending responses on separate occasions. Another possibility that is particularly amenable to experimental investigation is the influence of contextual cues in the discrimination situation. That is, some aspects of the stimulus situation may set the occasion for attending to different properties of a discriminative stimulus. These may be interpreted as higher-order discriminations that control subordinate discriminative behavior.

AN EXPERIMENTAL STUDY OF ATTENTION AND STIMULUS GENERALIZATION[1]

The present study was designed to examine multidimensional stimulus control of responding when the dominance of the stimulus dimensions was under experimental control. The pattern of reinforcement for discriminative responding by the subject to members of the two-dimensional array of auditory stimuli was contingent on a higher-order visual discrimination. For one value of the visual cue, differential responding with respect to one dimension of the stimulus array was reinforced; for a second value of this cue, differential responding with respect to the orthogonal auditory dimension was reinforced. In generalization testing, the two values of the visual cue were presented both singly and in combination. Under these conditions, we examine the metric properties of stimulus generalization. In particular, we consider the appropriateness of the city-block metric when differential responding to one or the other stimulus dimension is independently controlled.

Method

Subjects

Twenty male undergraduate students who had had no previous experience in generalization or discrimination experiments served as subjects.

Stimuli and Apparatus

The stimuli were sinusoidal tones varying in both fundamental frequency and the rate at which they were frequency-modulated $\pm$ 20 cps. The tones were generated by a beat frequency oscillator (Bruel and Kjaer 1014) and prerecorded on magnetic tape (Ampex 351-2U) at four different levels of fundamental frequency, 500, 600, 750, and 900 cps, and of modulation rate, 2, 4, 8, and 16 sweeps/sec (sps). All combinations of fundamental frequency with modulation rate were used, yielding a set of 16 stimuli.

The experimental space was a sound-attenuating room containing a rack-mounted panel and shelf. On the front of the panel were two pilot lamps of different colors, amber and blue, and a tray for receiving pennies. An electrically operated coin dispenser, obtained from a vending machine and modified for experimental use, was mounted behind the panel. A response key (Poucel Electronics) that could be pressed either to the left or

[1] This study was performed pursuant to contract with the Language Development Section, United States Office of Education, Contract No. SAE-9265.

to the right was mounted on the shelf. The chamber was dark except when one or both of the pilot lamps was lit. The control equipment was in an adjoining room.

The stimuli were reproduced by the tape recorder and presented to the subject through calibrated earphones (Grason-Stadler TDH-39). Interposed between the tape recorder and the earphones was an electronic switch (Grason-Stadler 829D) that closed upon presentation of the stimulus and opened when the response key was pressed thus terminating the stimulus. The electronic switch, as well as occasions for reinforcement and other experimental events, was controlled by voice-operated relays (Miratel), which were operated, in turn, by coding tones synchronized with the stimuli and prerecorded on a second track of the magnetic tape. Response latencies were measured by recording, on a seccnd tape recorder (Ampex 601), 1,000 cps tones passed through a second channel of the electronic switch. The duration of these tones corresponded exactly to the time interval from the onset of the stimulus to its termination by a response. On subsequent playback, these durations were measured by a frequency counter (Hewlett-Packard) and automatically punched on IBM cards for analysis.

Procedure

The subjects were seated individually in the experimental chamber and the following instructions were read:

You can earn money in this experiment if you can learn to respond to certain properties of sounds that you will hear in these earphones. You will respond by pressing this key either to the left or to the right. If your response is correct, a penny will be dispensed to you; if it is not, you will get nothing. In either case, the response you make, right or wrong, will terminate the stimulus. The basis for a correct discrimination will depend upon which of these two lights is on at the time. The faster you learn and the fewer errors you make, the more money you will earn.

Discrimination training. Three stimuli were presented five times each in 10 randomized sequences, for a total of 150 stimulus presentations. During five sequences the amber light was on, and during the other five sequences the blue light was one. (The order was randomized.) Under either light condition, a 500 cps/2 sps signal was an S^D for the response of pressing the key to the left, R_1. A 500 cps/16 sps signal was also an S^D for R_1 when the amber light was on, but it was an S^D for a key press to the right, R_2, when the blue light was on. A 900 cps/2 sps signal was an S^D for R_2 when the amber light was on, and for R_1 when the blue light was on. The stimuli were presented at 10-sec. intervals for a maximum of 5 sec. on each presentation. If at the end of 5 sec. the subject did not respond, the stimulus terminated and the reinforcement mechanism was inoperative.

Otherwise the stimulus was terminated by the response, whether it was correct or not. If correct, a penny was dispensed and a bell, with a sound similar to that of a cash register, was rung. There was a 30-sec. time out between each stimulus sequence.

Generalization testing. At the completion of training, the experimenter re-entered the chamber and told the subject that, for the remainder of the experiment, the coin dispenser and bell would be disconnected. In addition, he instructed the subject to respond to each stimulus. All subjects were presented with 10 random permutations of the 16 stimuli in sequence, with a 30-sec. time out between each sequence. For ten subjects the amber light was on for half of the sequences and the blue light was on for the other half. For the other ten subjects, two of the first four stimulus sequences were presented with the amber light on and the other two with the blue light on. For the remaining six stimulus sequences, both the lights were on.

Results

Formation of a correct discrimination was rapid for all subjects. Very few errors were made after the fourth stimulus sequence. Figure 3 shows that discriminative control was established over differential responding to one or the other of the dimensions of the auditory stimuli. Only the R_1 gradients are represented because the R_2 gradients are complementary

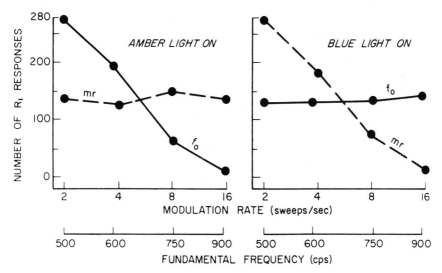

FIG. 3. Auditory generalization under visual control. Each point represents the total number of R_1 responses emitted (of a possible 280) at each level of a given dimension, summed over levels of the orthogonal dimension, as a function of color of the visual stimulus. During training, the amber light was a discriminative stimulus controlling differential responding to differences in fundamental frequency, and the blue light a discriminative stimulus controlling differential responding to differences in modulation rate.

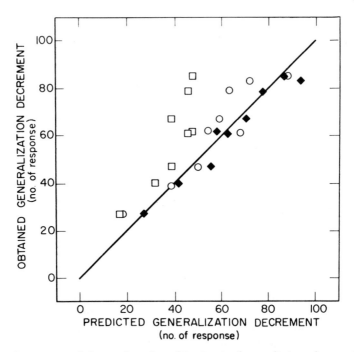

FIG. 4. Comparison of three rules of combination in the prediction of generalization decrements. Predictions based on the city-block rule of combination are represented by diamonds, the dominance rule by squares, and the multiplicative rule by circles.

functions. The functions depicted represent the over-all discriminative control exercised by each dimension under the two light conditions. When the amber light was on, discriminations were clearly based on changes in fundamental frequency only, and when the blue light was on, modulation rate exercised exclusive control. There was virtually no interaction between the levels of either dimension under the two conditions. The generalization gradients for the controlling dimensions in both conditions coincided at all levels of the irrelevant dimension, and the generalization gradients along the irrelevant dimension, for different levels of the dominant dimension were parallel.

Having established the fact of selective stimulus control, we may pool the results obtained under the two light conditions and compare the city-block rule of combination with the multiplicative and dominance rules of combinations in describing the generalization gradients. The primary gradients along the dimension of fundamental frequency, with modulation rate fixed at 2 sps, and along the dimension of modulation rate, with fundamental frequency set at 500 cps, were used to predict the decrement in the number of R_1 responses (relative to the number of responses emitted to the training stimulus) at each of the other nine stimuli. Figure 4 pre-

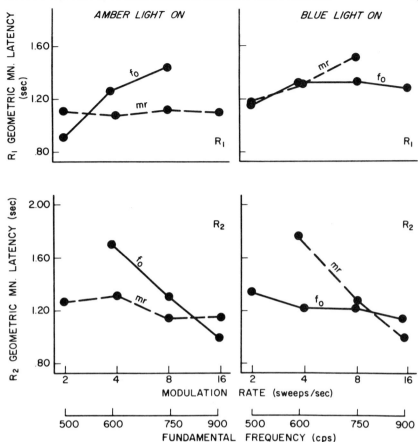

F I G. 5. Generalization gradients of response latency. Both R_1 latency gradients (top graphs) and R_2 latency gradients (bottom graphs) are shown as a function of light condition during testing. Each point represents the geometric mean latency of all responses to a single level of a given dimension. Points were not plotted if the corresponding latencies were based on too small a sample size (two or less determinations).

sents a plot of obtained vs. predicted decrements for the city-block rule (diamonds), the dominance rule (squares), and the multiplicative rule (circles). The straight line drawn at 45° to the axes represents perfect agreement between obtained and predicted generalization decrements. It will be seen that, of the three, the city-block rule is the best predictor. Only two of the nine city-block predictions deviate from the ideal line by more than three responses, as compared with six out of nine for the multiplicative rule and all nine out of nine for the dominance rule.

Response latency provides a second and highly sensitive index of discriminative control (Fig. 5). Latencies were not plotted for four stimuli,

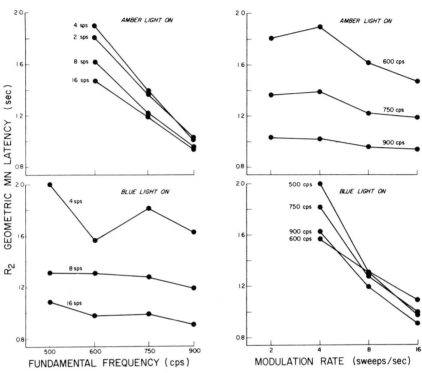

F IG. 6. Generalization gradients of response latency. The geometric mean latency of all R_2 responses to a single stimulus are represented as a function of one dimension with levels of the other as parameters, and as a function of the color of the controlling visual stimulus.

because either no responses or only one or two responses were emitted. The latency gradients along the dominant dimension under each light condition tend to be steeper than the latency gradients along the irrelevant dimension. This shows up particularly well for the R_2 latencies.

Figure 6 permits a more detailed examination of the R_2 latency gradients. The gradients in Fig. 6 represent response latencies at each level of one dimension with levels of the other dimensions as parameters. These gradients show surprising uniformity.

Figure 7 presents the results of testing with both the amber and the blue lights on simultaneously. It is apparent that both dimensions exercise behavioral control with respect to over-all results. Latencies show a general decreasing trend which, except at three data points, is fairly systematic. The unfilled circles in the latency gradients (top graphs) indicate that these latencies are based on less than five responses and thus unreliably estimated. The number of responses entering into latency estimates for all the points is given directly by the gradients in the lower half of Fig. 7. The

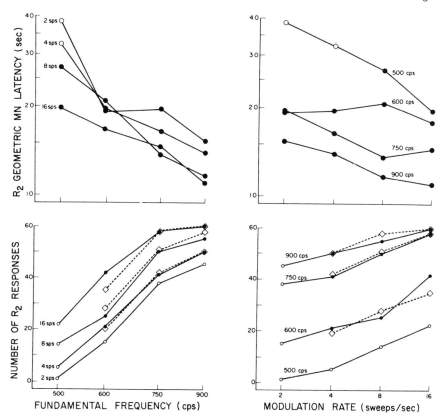

FIG. 7. Generalization under the combined light conditions. Both R_2 latency (top graphs) and frequency (bottom graphs) gradients for each dimension, with levels of the other dimension as parameters, are shown as a function of both visual stimuli presented together. The unfilled circles in the top graphs represent geometric mean latencies computed on five responses or less. The unfilled circles in the lower graphs represent the number of responses emitted to stimuli on the primary dimensions. These quantities were used to predict generalized responding to the other stimuli, represented by filled circles. The predictions for each family of gradients are depicted by the diamonds connected by broken lines.

diamonds in this figure, appropriately enough, represent the number of responses predicted by the city-block rule of combination. The prediction was based on the number of responses to those stimuli identified by the unfilled circles (bottom graphs). This set of data points corresponds to the R_2 generalization gradient with respect to the common S^D (500 cps/2 sps). Except for one point (at 600 cps/16 sps), the predicted amounts of generalization decrement accord with those obtained rather well, indicating the appropriateness of the metric for these data.

Summary

Twenty human subjects were employed in a study of multidimensional stimulus generalization. The pattern of reinforcement for discriminative responding (key-press) by a subject to the 16 members of a two-dimensional array of auditory stimuli, varying in center frequency and modulation rate, depended on a higher-order visual discrimination. Differential responding along each dimension during discrimination training came under the control of the correlated light condition (amber or blue). In generalization testing, either or both of the lights was presented during the several series of auditory stimuli, and the conditional frequency and latency of responding was observed.

Generalization gradients of response frequency and latency were found to be steep along the dimension correlated with the concurrent visual cue, and flat along the orthogonal dimension. When both visual cues were presented concurrently, both dimensions of the auditory stimuli exercised control over differential responding.

Among the possible Minkowski metrics that may be employed to predict the shape of the generalization surface, based on the pair of gradients obtained for the two dimensions at the levels which intersect at the training stimulus, the "city-block" metric, which corresponds to the "discrimination model" of multidimensional stimulus generalization, was found to be most accurate.

REFERENCES

Attneave, F. Dimensions of similarity. *Amer. J. Psychol.*, 1950, **63**, 516–556.

Beckenbach, E., and Bellman, R. *An introduction to inequalities.* New York: Random House, 1961.

Butter, C. M. Stimulus generalization along one and two dimensions in pigeons. *J. exp. Psychol.*, 1963, **65**, 339–346.

Coombs, C. H. *A theory of data.* New York: Wiley, 1964.

Eninger, M. U. Habit summation in a selective learning problem. *J. comp. physiol. Psychol.*, 1952, **45**, 604–608.

Eriksen, C. W., and Hake, H. W. Multidimensional stimulus differences and accuracy of discrimination. *J. exp. Psychol.*, 1955, **50**, 153–160.

Fink, J. B., and Patton, R. M. Decrement of a learned drinking response accompanying changes in several stimulus characteristics. *J. comp. physiol. Psychol.*, 1953, **46**, 23–27.

Guttman, N. The pigeon and the spectrum and other perplexities. *Psychol. Rep.*, 1956, **2**, 449–460.

Harlow, H. F. Studies in discrimination learning by monkeys: VI. Discrimination between stimuli differing in both color and form, only in color, and only in form. *J. gen. Psychol.*, 1945, **33**, 225–235.

Householder, A. S., and Landahl, H. D. *Mathematical biophysics of the central nervous system.* Bloomington, Ind.: Principia Press, 1945.

Jones, J. E. Stimulus generalization in two and three dimensions. *Canad. J. Psychol.*, 1962, **16**, 23–36.

Landahl, H. D. Neural mechanisms for the concepts of difference and similarity. *Bull. math. Biophysics*, 1945, **7**, 83–88.

Lashley, K. S. The mechanism of vision: XV. Preliminary studies of the rat's capacity for detail vision. *J. gen. Psychol.*, 1938, **18**, 123–193.

Lashley, K. S. An examination of the "continuity theory" as applied to discriminative learning. *J. gen. Psychol.*, 1942, **26**, 241–265.

Lashley, K. S., and Wade, M. The Pavlovian theory of generalization. *Psychol. Rev.*, 1946, **53**, 72–87.

Miller, J. The rate of conditioning of human subjects to single and multiple conditioned stimuli. *J. gen. Psychol.*, 1939, **20**, 399–408.

Restle, F. A metric and an ordering on sets. *Psychometrika*, 1959, **24**, 207–220.

Reynolds, G. S. Attention in the pigeon. *J. exp. Anal. Behav.*, 1961, **4**, 203–208.

Shepard, R. N. Stimulus and response generalization: Tests of a model relating generalization to distance in psychological space. *J. exp. Psychol.*, 1958, **55**, 509–523.

Shepard, R. N. Similarity of stimuli and metric properties of behavioral data. In H. Gulliksen and S. Hessick (Eds.), *Psychological scaling: theory and application*. New York: Wiley, 1960.

Shepard, R. N. Attention and the metric structure of the stimulus space. *J. math. Psychol.*, 1964, **1**, 54–87.

Warren, J. M. Additivity of cues in a visual pattern discrimination by monkeys. *J. comp. physiol. Psychol.*, 1953, **46**, 484–486.

Warren, J. M. Perceptual dominance in discrimination learning by monkeys. *J. comp. physiol. Physiol.*, 1954, **47**, 290–293.

White, S. W. Generalization of an instrumental response with variations in two attributes of the CS. *J. exp. Psychol.*, 1958, **56**, 339–343.

8. Approximation to Uniform Gradients of Generalization by Monotone Transformations of Scale

R. N. Shepard, *Bell Telephone Laboratories, Inc.*

Apparent Arbitrariness of the Gradient

Just as there has been a lively interest in the mathematical form of curves of acquisition, extinction, and forgetting (see, e.g., Hovland, 1951, pp. 677–679; Bush and Mosteller, 1955), there was, for a while, a similar interest in the precise shape of curves of stimulus generalization (Hovland, 1937; Hull, 1943; Plotkin, 1943; Schlosberg and Solomon, 1943; Spence, 1937). However, in recent years the extension and refinement of mathematical accounts for empirical curves of the former type has not been paralleled by similar developments with respect to curves of the latter type. Indeed, with the exception of my own single attempt in this direction (Shepard, 1958b), nothing in the way of a quantitative characterization of "gradients of generalization" seems to have appeared since the early 1940's.

The difference in the extent to which learning curves and generalization gradients have invited precise mathematical accounts cannot, I think, be attributed to any difference with respect to the dependent variables involved. In either case the probability (or relative frequency) of a specified response, for example, seems to be a particularly natural choice. Perhaps then the difference is traceable, rather, to a difference in the nature of the independent variables. In particular, for the purpose of constructing gradients of generalization, there does not appear to be any one measure of the dissimilarity between stimuli that has the kind of uniqueness or fundamental status that number of trials (or reinforcements) has for the construction of curves of acquisition. Purely physical measures of the degree of difference between stimuli are certainly inappropriate, and the once-held hope that cumulated just-noticeable differences (JND's) would yield the desired kind of invariances now appears overly optimistic in the light of both empirical results (Guttman and Kalish, 1956; Guttman, 1956) and theoretical arguments (Shepard, 1957, p. 334).

I am indebted to Miss Maureen Sheenan for her assistance in preparing the figures for the present paper.

On the other hand, if arbitrary transformations are to be permitted on the independent variable, then, as has been generally recognized, a gradient of generalization can be made to assume any of an uncomfortably wide variety of shapes—including linear, convex, concave, and inflected (cf. Guttman, 1956, p. 454). It is this realization, I imagine, that has discouraged more extensive attempts at quantitative characterization of "the" gradient of generalization. Indeed, such mathematically minded theorists as Bush and Mosteller (1951, pp. 413, 417) have in effect concluded that the question of the shape of the gradient of generalization is meaningless because there is really no independent measure of dissimilarity, or, in other words, because the only reasonable measure of similarity or dissimilarity is generalization itself.

Non-Arbitrariness of Overlapping Gradients

Despite the initially compelling character of these rather discouraging conclusions, they are, I think, based upon an overly simplified view of the actual experimental procedures. For these procedures are often designed to yield not a single gradient of generalization but several gradients originating from separated points along the same underlying continuum. Thus, in a study that has opened up a particularly fruitful area of research, Guttman and Kalish (1956) obtained gradients of generalization around four different training stimuli spaced out along the wavelength continuum cf spectral colors. The important thing to notice here is that gradients that overlap in this way along the same continuum are necessarily highly interdependent. In particular, any transformation of that continuum that is designed to make one gradient concave may have the unavoidable consequence of making another, overlapping gradient convex. Thus, while it is true that any *one* gradient can still be transformed into an essentially arbitrary shape, it clearly is not true that all of these overlapping gradients can simultaneously be transformed into the same arbitrary shape.

As a matter of fact, artificial examples can readily be constructed so that no transformation of the horizontal scale, however complex or nonlinear, will convert all gradients into the same shape, let alone an arbitrarily specified shape. Therefore, it seems all the more significant that, for a considerable number of empirical examples I have examined, it has generally been possible to find an essentially unique transformation that simultaneously converts all gradients into one uniform shape (except, of course, for discrepancies attributable to the unreliability of the original dependent measures). This result is a little weaker than the relation postulated by Hull (1943, p. 199) and subsequently cast into doubt by the experiment of Guttman and Kalish (1956), for we do not require, in addition, that the transformed scale be equivalent to the JND scale. Nevertheless, the fact that there exists a preferred scale with respect to which all gradients assume a uniform shape strongly suggests that this scale has some fundamental psychological significance. At the very least, such a scale can contribute to descriptive parsimony and predictive power; for the one scale together with a single gradient should then provide a sufficient basis for the construction of all other gradients that might be obtained on that same continuum.

Owing to the finding that the required transformation is essentially unique, the discovery of that transformation yields two quite different kinds of information in a single stroke: First, it tells us what the true psychological spacing of the test stimuli is in the underlying continuum or "psychological space." And, second, it tells us what the uniform shape is for all generalization gradients in this underlying space. Or, more precisely, it tells us what this shape is up to a monotone transformation of the dependent variable (or vertical scale).[1] For if all gradients have been rendered uniform in shape, then this uniformity of shape (though not the shape itself) will be preserved under all such "vertical" transformations. This is not of course true for transformations of the horizontal scale—only *linear* transformations will preserve uniformity there. This is why the desired spacing is essentially unique. The problem, obviously, is to discover the one transformation that does yield this unique spacing. However, before I go more deeply into this problem, let me illustrate the preceding ideas a little more concretely by reference, primarily, to the well-known data of Guttman and Kalish (1956).

Illustration with Published Data

Guttman and Kalish trained each of several pigeons to strike at a translucent key illuminated from behind by monochromatic light of one of four different wavelengths (viz., 530, 550, 580, or 600 mμ). After having been trained on one of these wavelengths, then, each pigeon was tested (in random order) on other wavelengths ranging in 10-mμ steps up and down the wavelength continuum from the original training stimulus. Since the rate of pecking systematically decreased with the difference in millimicrons between the training and test stimulus, orderly gradients of generalization were obtained on the physical continuum of wavelength (Guttman and Kalish, 1956, Fig. 1). Indeed, Guttman and Kalish remark that the gradients were more nearly uniform with respect to this physical continuum than with respect to the JND scale. Even so, the obtained gradients were not entirely uniform. By further adjustments of the interstimulus spacing, one can achieve the still closer approach to uniformity shown in Fig. 1.

Here, as elsewhere in this paper, what is plotted as the ordinate of a

---

[1] Cf. Blough, this vol., p. 31.

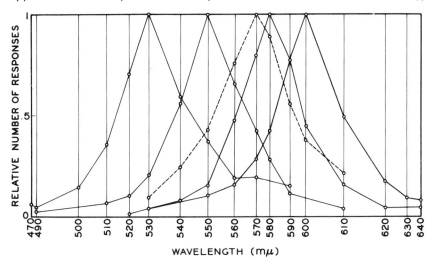

FIG. 1. Modified generalization gradients based upon data from Guttman and Kalish (1956) (solid lines) and from Blough (1961) (broken line). The horizontal spacing of the stimuli has been adjusted to increase the uniformity of the gradients.

gradient for a given test stimulus is the ratio of the number of responses for that test stimulus to the number of responses for the original training stimulus. In effect, then, the vertical axis has been re-scaled for each gradient so that the peak corresponding to the original training stimulus always has unit height. Since there was something of a gap, in the Guttman-Kalish (1956) data, between the two gradients resulting from training at 500 and 580 mμ, I have also included on the same graph a fifth gradient subsequently obtained by Blough (1961, Fig. 5) around an intermediate training stimulus at 570 mμ (dashed curve).

Just how close an approach to uniformity has been achieved can be seen by rigidly translating all curves along the horizontal axis until their peaks exactly coincide as shown in Fig. 2. That the dashed curve for Blough's experiment is perhaps the most deviant of the five may reflect a slight difference in his procedure or somewhat greater variability owing to his smaller number of subjects. Over-all, though, there is, I think, a rather striking uniformity in the shape of the five transformed gradients. Certainly, if the gradients are plotted on the original physical scale of wavelength, the agreement is somewhat less impressive (Fig. 3). Presumably, then, the arrangement of the stimuli as indicated in the horizontal scale of Fig. 1 is a closer approach to the "true" or appropriate psychological spacing than was the original, regular spacing along the physical continuum of wavelength. Possibly, too, the uniform shape of the resulting gradients is of greater psychological significance than the more variable

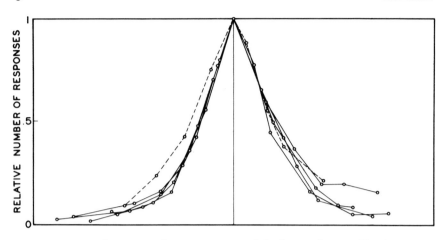

FIG. 2. Comparison, by superposition, of the five gradients in Fig. 1.

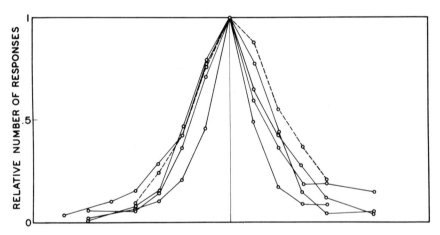

FIG. 3. Superposition of the five gradients in Fig. 1 before the interstimulus spacing had been adjusted.

shapes originally found on the purely physical scale. In any case these resulting gradients (shown in Fig. 2) conform quite closely to the exponential form proposed earlier on the basis of certain theoretical notions (Shepard, 1958b).

Finding the Appropriate Transformation

A close approximation to the interstimulus spacing that yields the greatest uniformity of all generalization gradients can, of course, be found by an iterative trial-and-error process. Such a process might start, say, with the set of test stimuli represented as evenly spaced along their common underlying continuum. In the case of the spectral colors studied by Guttman and Kalish (1956) and Blough (1961), for example, this would amount to the original physical spacing of these stimuli along the continuum of wavelength. The next step, then, would be to construct tentative gradients of generalization that would differ from those shown in Fig. 1 only in the horizontal spacing between the vertical lines. An examination of these tentative gradients will typically reveal that they depart from uniformity in that the segments between a pair of adjacent vertical lines tend to be either too steep or too flat in comparison with the segments between other vertical lines. This immediately indicates that the spacing between the two corresponding test stimuli should be increased, in the former case, or decreased, in the latter case. Adjustments of this kind can be continued until the separate gradients, when superimposed as in Fig. 2, come as nearly as possible into mutual coincidence.

Note that the points at which the several gradients pass through the vertical line corresponding to any one test stimulus are prescribed by the original data. Since these ordinates must therefore remain fixed throughout the entire process of adjustment, I have been able to construct a simple mechanical device that greatly facilitates this process. As shown schematically in Fig. 4, the vertical lines corresponding to the test stimuli are represented, in this device, by the vertical edges on one side of as many rigid rectangular plates or "leaves," all pivoted about their opposite edges as in a book. Different spacings between the various test stimuli can readily be tried, then, by adjusting the angular separations between these rigid "leaves." The fixed ordinates of the separate gradients are represented by small holes drilled at the appropriate heights through the outside edges of the leaves. The gradients themselves, then, are constructed by threading strings through these holes as shown. (In the device actually constructed, heavy-gauge nylon fishing line was found to work quite well for this purpose.) With this device one can immediately assess the effect upon the gradients of any proposed adjustment in the position of any one test stimulus. (Final adjustments can be facilitated by cutting out a paper template and superimposing it over each of the several gradients in turn.)

What one would like, of course, is some way of achieving the same kind of convergence to an optimum spacing automatically or, at least, without recourse to subjective judgment and tedious manipulation. The possibility of such a solution is suggested by a simple modification of the described device. Elastic bands are attached to the ends of each of the threaded nylon lines and the free ends are drawn back in such a way as to place all lines under equally high tension. Since undesirable irregularities tend to increase the lengths of the lines for some of the gradients, these irregularities tend to be corrected as the tension is increased on these lines. The gratifying result is that the rigid leaves appear to position themselves so as to achieve smooth, uniform gradients.

Actually, of course, there are many different ways in which departures

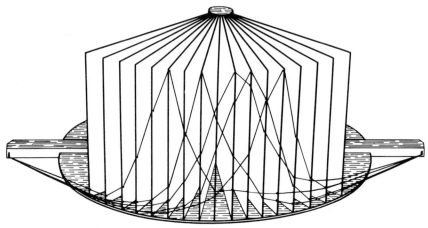

FIG. 4. Perspective drawing of a mechanical device for adjusting the interstimulus spacing.

from uniformity might be measured, and there is no reason to presume that the most appropriate of these measures will be precisely the one that is minimized by the most easily realized mechanical scheme. Indeed, the scheme described above appears to place too much weight on departures from local linearity (or "smoothness") of the gradients and not enough weight on larger-scale departures from over-all superimposability of the separate curves. This shows up particularly in undesirable distortions at the two ends of the horizontal scale (where the gradients do not really over-lap). Then, too, it is difficult to reduce friction to an acceptable level in a physical device of this kind.

Use of a Digital Computer

Fortunately, the minimization of arbitrarily specified measures (as well as the total elimination of friction) can be achieved by substituting, for the construction of an actual physical system, the simulation of an idealized system of this general kind on a digital computer. Such a substitution has the further advantage that the idealized system, as abstractly represented in the computer, can be directly generalized to find optimum spatial con-figurations for stimuli that vary along more than a single dimension. In-deed, a two-dimensional solution that was actually obtained in this way will be presented in a following section. By contrast, the corresponding multidimensional generalization of the purely mechanical device illus-trated in Fig. 4 (confined, as it is, to the three dimensions of physical space) poses design problems of seemingly prohibitive complexity.

The details of the iterative processes that I have been using on the IBM 7090 computer at the Bell Telephone Laboratories have already been described elsewhere (Shepard, 1962a; 1962b; 1963; Kruskal, 1964). For present purposes the following brief statement will perhaps suffice. At the outset each test stimulus is represented by a point in an arbitrary spatial configuration. In the case of stimuli that vary along a single physical dimension, the known physical coordinates (e.g., of wavelength) might be used to define the initial spacing (as explained for the mechanical device described above). Thereafter, during each iteration the separations between all pairs of these points are rank-ordered in size and compared with a similar rank ordering of the observed amounts of generalization between all corresponding pairs of stimuli. The interpoint separations are then slightly readjusted so as to approach that configuration of points for which each of the two rank orders is as nearly as possible the inverse of the other. The iterative process is terminated when the points have converged to a stationary configuration. The relation between observed amount of generalization and interstimulus separation will then approximate (as nearly as possible) the same monotonic function (or "gradient") for all training stimuli.

One limitation of this method, as exemplified both by my original program (Shepard, 1962a; 1962b) and by the improved program developed more recently by my colleague Joseph Kruskal (1964), is that no requirement is imposed that the relation between generalization and interstimulus distance be "smooth" (as well as monotonic). As a consequence, gradients obtained by means of these programs sometimes have an appearance that is somewhat more irregular or "step-like" than ones (like those shown in Figs. 1 and 2) obtained, so to speak, by hand. In a still more recent program, therefore, I have attempted to improve the estimation of gradient shape by fitting a polynomial of low degree (rather than a merely monotonic function) during each iteration. The results of preliminary tests of this program have been quite encouraging.[2] However, the results to be described here were all obtained by means of the original program, and hence, do not benefit from this additional requirement of "smoothness."

Application to Paired-Associate Data

Under certain conditions, the intrusion errors that occur during the learning of paired associates can be regarded as the direct results of stimulus generalization (Shepard 1957; Shepard, 1958a). As an example, consider a paired-associate experiment by McGuire (1961). Each subject learned a fixed random assignment between nine circles varying only in size and the response numbers "one" through "nine." Previous reports

[2] These results have subsequently been reported in a symposium on "Multidimensional Analysis of Similarity Data" at the International Congress of Psychology, August, 1963, Washington, D.C. A fuller report is in preparation for later publication.

have already presented the 9 × 9 matrix of generalization data for all pairs of stimuli in McGuire's experiment (Shepard, 1958a) as well as the details of the original computer analysis of those data (Shepard, 1962b). The results of that analysis will be presented in a different form here, however, to facilitate comparison with Figs. 1 and 2 above. Figure 5, then, presents the overlapping gradients of generalization as determined from this analysis of McGuire's paired-associate data. As before, the spacing between the vertical lines was adjusted so as to maximize the uniformity of these gradients (though the adjustments, this time, were performed entirely by the computer). The ordinates for each curve, again, give the frequencies with which the corresponding response was made to each of the nine stimuli divided by the frequency with which that response was made to its correct stimulus. Note that the modal peak of the gradient for the response assigned to the fifth largest circle actually occurred at the fourth largest circle (and, hence, exceeded unit height). This and other lesser irregularities in these curves may be attributable to the fact that McGuire (1961) used only two different assignments of the responses to the stimuli, and so did not achieve a complete counterbalancing of other factors such as response generalization (Shepard, 1957, p. 331) or more complex stimulus-response interactions (Shepard, 1961). In any case, such irregularities are completely absent in the curves (not shown) based upon another of Mc-Guire's conditions in which the response numbers were assigned to the circles consecutively (in order of size) rather than at random. (The curves for this condition of consecutive assignment are a little difficult to interpret in the present context, however, owing to the complete confounding of stimulus and response factors.)

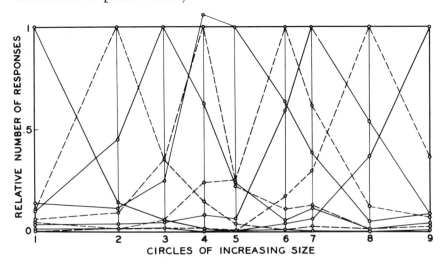

FIG. 5. Modified generalization gradients based upon data from McGuire (1961).

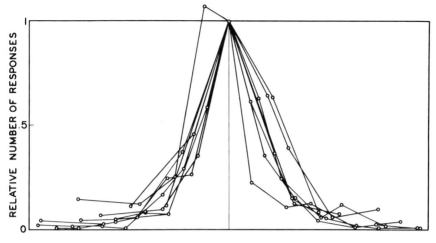

FIG. 6. Superposition of the nine gradients in Fig. 5.

In Figure 6 the nine curves shown in Fig. 5 have been superimposed in the manner previously used for Fig. 2. The degree of uniformity that was achievable here is not as good as that achieved for the data of Guttman and Kalish (1956). Still, with the exception of the one especially deviant point (already discussed), these superimposed curves suggest a general shape that is rather similar to that observed for the Guttman-Kalish data.

I have also broken McGuire's (1961) data down into successive blocks of 126 stimulus presentations each, in order to see how the gradient of stimulus generalization changes during learning. For this purpose, the curves (like those shown in Fig. 6) for each such block of trials were averaged

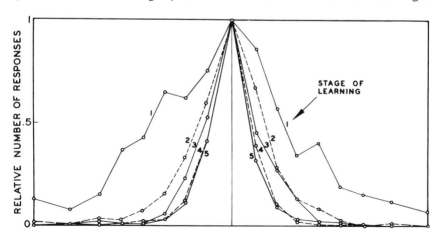

FIG. 7. Shape of the average gradient for five stages of learning in McGuire's (1961) experiment.

together to yield a single gradient. This was done simply by finding the centroid for each set of points on the gradients that were on the same side of the training stimulus and removed from it by the same number of steps (or test stimuli). These centroids were then connected, in order, by line segments to yield a kind of average gradient. The smooth bidirectional gradients thus obtained are plotted together for each successive block of trials in Fig. 7. The result clearly shows how the gradient becomes more and more sharply "tuned" as learning progresses. This process appears to be asymptotic in that the gradients for the last two blocks of trials are almost identical.

Application to the Multidimensional Case

For purposes of dealing with generalization data, a representation of the stimuli as points along a spatial scale is obviously most useful if that scale is so constructed that generalization is invariantly related to the distance between points on that scale. For this is the only circumstance under which the amount of generalization between two stimuli can be inferred solely from the spatial configuration (together, of course, with the fixed gradient of generalization). This is the kind of spatial representation that was achieved above for the spectral colors investigated by Guttman and Kalish and Blough (Fig. 1) and, at least approximately, for McGuire's (1961) nine circles varying in size (Fig. 4). However, such a representation is not always possible within a single linear dimension or scale.

In the case of pure sinusoidal tones varying in frequency, for example, there is some evidence that the generalization between two tones is greater if those tones are exactly an octave apart than if they are somewhat less than an octave apart (Blackwell and Schlosberg, 1943). In order to accommodate such anomalous effects without disrupting the fixed monotonic relation between generalization and distance, the linear scale of pitch might have to be distorted into a more complex spatial configuration— perhaps like the helix illustrated in Fig. 8. As can be seen, this configuration achieves the desired property that any two stimuli (such as S_a and S_b) that differ by just one octave in frequency are closer together than two stimuli that differ by a little less than one octave. Interestingly, this "tonal helix" was proposed by Drobisch and again by Ruckmick long before the octave effect appeared in the generalization literature (see Ruckmick, 1929, p. 173).

The continuum of pure spectral colors also contains a phenomenon of this kind. In particular, the shortest and the longest of the visible wavelengths (viz., violet and red) subjectively resemble each other more than either of these resemble the intermediate wavelengths (e.g., in the vicinity of yellow-green). This, of course, is why the spectral colors are conventionally represented on a "color circle" rather than along a straight line. The

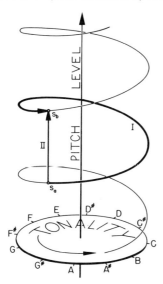

FIG. 8. Representation of sinusoidal tones as points on a helix.

behavorial counterpart of the subjective observation, presumably, is that a gradient of generalization resulting from training on a violet stimulus, instead of decreasing monotonically with increasing wavelength, would first decrease and *then* increase as very long wavelengths were approached. The fact that the gradients obtained by Guttman and Kalish (1956) do not exhibit this kind of non-monotonicity can probably be attributed to the fact that none of their gradients spanned a sufficient fraction of the total range of the visible spectrum.

In any case, if the augmented generalization that is presumed to occur between octaves or between the extremes of the spectrum is to be represented by interpoint distances in a more complex configuration (such as the tonal helix or the color circle), then the iterative process must not confine the points to a single, rectilinear line (or dimension). For this reason the computer program described above provides for solutions in spaces of whatever number of dimensions are required, and hence can handle multidimensional generalization and unidimensional generalization with equal facility. A demonstration of this capability is provided by an analysis of data obtained by Ekman (1954) for 14 spectral colors. What Ekman obtained for each pair of these colors was a direct judgment of the subjective similarity of those two colors. These data are not, of course, measures of generalization in the strict sense. Still, I think they are of some interest in this connection.

The details of the computer analysis of Ekman's (1954) data can be found in an earlier report (Shepard, 1962b). The main point to be noticed here is that for no arrangement of the 14 points on a straight line is judged

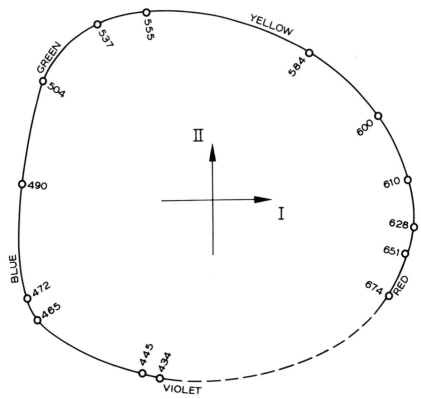

FIG. 9. Two-dimensional computer solution obtained for Ekman's (1954) 14 color stimuli (from Shepard, 1962b).

similarity everywhere related to interpoint separation by the same monotonic function. In two dimensions, however, a unique solution exists that achieves a very close approximation to an invariant relationship of this kind. This solution, shown in Fig. 9, bears a striking resemblance to the conventional color circle. The number attached to each point is the wavelength of the corresponding stimulus (in mμ). The augmented similarity between the two extreme wavelengths (434 and 674 mμ) is accommodated, here, by bending the sequence of colors around in such a way as to bring the two extreme points into closer proximity.

If this sequence is straightened out into a rectilinear line without disturbing the relative spacing between adjacent colors, the resulting gradients (plotted as before) are as shown in Fig. 10. The gradients for the extreme stimuli clearly exhibit the expected departure from monotonicity; that is, they first decrease and then slightly rise again at the other end of the spectrum. Such violations of monotonicity do not, of course, occur when interpoint distance is taken from the quasicircular configuration in two dimensions (see Shepard, 1962b, Fig. 14), rather than from the one-

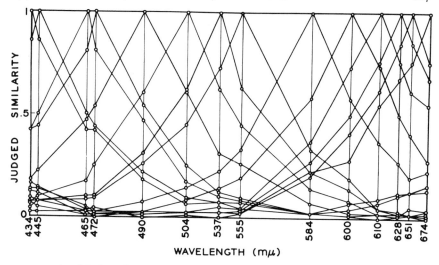

FIG. 10. Modified gradients based upon Ekman's (1954) data. (The spacing between adjacent stimuli is the same as in Fig. 9.)

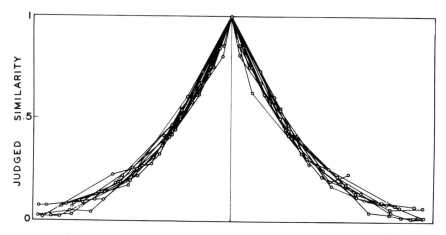

FIG. 11. Superposition of the fourteen gradients in Fig. 10. (The non-monotonic tails evident in Fig. 10 fall outside the horizontal range covered here.)

dimensional representation. Nevertheless, even in one dimension the descending portions of the gradients show a remarkable uniformity of shape. This is illustrated in Fig. 11, where the gradients of Fig. 10 have been horizontally translated into approximate coincidence as before.

Special Aspects of the Multidimensional Case

Certain new considerations arise as soon as we turn from a one-dimensional representation to a representation, like the one shown in Fig. 9, that requires two or more dimensions. Note, first of all, that care must be exercised in attempting to relate data on generalization between stimuli that are psychologically far apart to JND data based on the discriminability of neighboring stimuli. Typically, the number of JND's between two remote stimuli would be estimated by cumulating JND's along the physical continuum between them; i.e., the wavelength continuum for spectral colors or the frequency continuum for sinusoidal tones. But this carries the summation around the perimeter of the color circle (in Fig. 9) and around a curved arc in the tonal helix (e.g., path I in Fig. 8). According to the multidimensional model proposed here, on the other hand, generalization is determined by the direct or shortest distance across the space (e.g., path II in Fig. 8). Indeed, this is the geometrical explanation for the augmented generalization over octaves or between the spectrally extreme colors (red and violet).

Note, too, that stimuli (like spectral colors or sinusoidal tones) that can be specified, physically, in terms of a single variable (wavelength or frequency) may be representable, *psychologically,* only in a multidimensional embedding space. In the case of the spectral colors, of course, points in the implied two-dimensional interior of the "color circle" actually correspond to physically producible stimuli; namely, the desaturated colors obtained by mixing the pure spectral colors around the perimeter. So, at least in this particular case, one might be able to cumulate JND's in a psychologically straight line, directly across the space. Whether this would lead to a more nearly invariant relation between number of JND's and generalization presumably remains a matter for empirical investigation.

The computer methods described here are designed to find the least number of dimensions required for the psychological embedding space. But, in addition, they often can enable us to interpret just what these dimensions are. An example of this is provided by a recent application of these methods to long-standing data on generalization among the dot-and-dash signals of the Morse Code (Shepard, 1963). Two-dimensional solutions were obtained for each of two independent sets of data and, for both sets, one dimension was found to correspond to the number of components in each signal (whether dots or dashes), while the other dimension was found to distinguish between homogeneous signals (composed of all dots or all dashes) and heterogeneous signals (composed of a mixture of dots and dashes).

A final point to be made here is that, although the multidimensional solutions described thus far were all obtained on the assumption of a Euclidean metric, this is not an inherent restriction of this method (see Shepard, 1962b, p. 244). In fact, in Kruskal's (1964) more recent program of this type, the square and square root of the Euclidean distance formula can be replaced by an arbitrary power and root, r. However, when values of r ranging from 1 to 5 were tested against Ekman's (1954) color data, the best-fitting solution was obtained when r was close to its Euclidean value, viz., 2 (Kruskal, 1964). The alternative "city block" metric, which has been proposed by Attneave (1950), by Restle (1959), and now by Cross (this vol., pp. 72–93), led to the poorest fit of all. Indeed, the departure from a perfect fit for this metric (which corresponds to $r = 1$) was nearly three times the departure obtained for the Euclidean metric.

The appropriateness of the Euclidean metric seems to depend upon the psychologically "unanalyzable" character of the stimuli (Shepard, 1964; Shepard and Chang, 1963; Torgerson, 1958, pp. 253, 292). A color, for example, is a relatively homogeneous, unitary stimulus in the sense that it is difficult to look at its saturation without also seeing its hue (and vice versa). For stimuli that are analyzable into perceptually distinct dimensions (of size, shape, brightness, etc.), on the other hand, the emergence of attentional phenomena may well entail a breakdown of the Euclidean metric in the manner considered by Cross (this vol., p. 82) or by Shepard (1964).

Conclusions

A single gradient of generalization can be transformed into an essentially arbitrary shape by monotone transformations of the horizontal scale. The interdependencies between multiple, overlapping gradients, however, are usually sufficiently strong that such gradients cannot all be simultaneously transformed into the *same* arbitrary shape. Indeed, there is usually one relatively unique interstimulus spacing that has the effect of rendering all such gradients essentially uniform in shape. An iterative process, suitable for a digital computer, can be used to find this optimum spacing— whether along a single unidimensional scale or, when necessary, in spaces of a higher number of dimensions. The uniqueness of the interstimulus spacing that produces a uniform shape for all gradients of generalization suggests that this spacing—as well as the shape of the associated gradients —may be of psychological significance.

REFERENCES

Attneave, F. Dimensions of similarity. *Amer. J. Psychol.*, 1950, **63**, 516–556.
Blackwell, H. R., and Schlosberg, H. Octave generalization, pitch discrimination, and loudness thresholds in the white rat. *J. exp. Psychol.*, 1943, **33**, 407–419.
Blough, D. S. The shape of some wavelength generalization gradients. *J. exp. Anal. Behav.*, 1961, **4**, 31–40.
Bush, R. R., and Mosteller, F. A model for stimulus generalization and discrimination, *Psychol. Rev.*, 1951, **58**, 413–423.
Bush, R. R., and Mosteller, F. *Stochastic models for learning.* New York: Wiley, 1955.
Ekman, G. Dimensions of color vision. *J. Psychol.*, 1954, **38**, 467–474.

Guttman, N. The pigeon and the spectrum and other perplexities. *Psychol. Rep.*, 1956, **2**, 449–460.

Guttman, N., and Kalish, H. I. Discriminability and stimulus generalization. *J. exp. Psychol.*, 1956, **51**, 79–88.

Hovland, C. I. The generalization of conditioned responses: I. The sensory generalization of conditioned responses with varying frequencies of tone. *J. gen. Psychol.*, 1937, **17**, 125–148. (a)

Hovland, C. I. Human learning and retention. In S. S. Stevens (Ed.), *Handbook of experimental psychology*. New York: Wiley, 1951, pp. 613–689.

Hull, C. L. *Principles of behavior*. New York: Appleton-Century-Crofts, 1943.

Kruskal, J. B. Multidimensional scaling by optimizing goodness of fit to a nonmetric hypothesis. *Psychometrika*, 1964, **29**, 1–27.

McGuire, W. J. A multiprocess model for paired-associate learning. *J. exp. Psychol.*, 1961, **62**, 335–347.

Plotkin, L. Stimulus generalization in Morse Code learning. *Arch. Psychol.*, 1943, **40**, No. 287. New York.

Restle, F. A metric and an ordering on sets. *Psychometrika*, 1959, **24**, 207–220.

Ruckmick, C. A. A new classification of tonal qualities. *Psychol. Rev.*, 1929, **36**, 172–180.

Schlosberg, H., and Solomon, R. L. Latency of response in a choice discrimination. *J. exp. Psychol.*, 1943, **33**, 22–39.

Shepard, R. N. Stimulus and response generalization: A stochastic model relating generalization to distance in psychological space. *Psychometrika*, 1957, **22**, 325–345.

Shepard, R. N. Stimulus and response generalization: Tests of a model relating generalization to distance in psychological space. *J. exp. Psychol.*, 1958, **55**, 509–523. (a)

Shepard, R. N. Stimulus and response generalization: Deduction of the generalization gradient from a trace model. *Psychol. Rev.*, 1958, **65**, 242–256. (b)

Shepard, R. N. Role of generalization in stimulus-response compatibility. *Percept. mot. Skills*, 1961, **13**, 59–62.

Shepard, R. N. The analysis of proximities: Multidimensional scaling with an unknown distance function. I. *Psychometrika*, 1962, **27**, 125–140. (a)

Shepard, R. N. The analysis of proximities: Multidimensional scaling with an unknown distance function. II. *Psychometrika*, 1962, **27**, 219–246. (b)

Shepard, R. N. Analysis of proximities as a technique for the study of information processing in man. *Human Factors*, 1963, **5**, 33–48.

Shepard, R. N. Attention and the metric structure of the stimulus space. *J. math. Psychol.*, 1964, **1**, 54–87.

Shepard, R. N., and Chang, J. -J. Stimulus generalization in the learning of classifications. *J. exp. Psychol.*, 1963, **65**, 94–102.

Spence, K. W. The differential response in animals to stimuli varying within a single dimension. *Psychol. Rev.*, 1937, **44**, 430–444.

Torgerson, W. S. *Theory and methods of scaling*. New York: Wiley, 1958.

9. The Partial Dissociation of Discrimination and Generalization

Leo Ganz, *University of California, Riverside*

The relation between generalization and discrimination has been clarified by a number of recent experimental studies. It appears that this relation is not fixed but labile, because discrimination training alters theoretical gradients of generalization. It will be recalled that the Hullian (1947) formulation of generalization demands a fixed gradient, altered only in height upward by the development of positive habit strength and downward by the development of negative habit strength. Yet Hanson (1959) found the theoretical gradients, both excitatory and inhibitory, that he extracted from the empirical generalization curves to be somehow altered by discrimination training. Honig, Thomas, and Guttman (1959) have demonstrated changes in the extinction gradient that were the result of changes in the manner of presenting extinction trials (specifically, whether massed or in alternation with reinforcement trials). Friedman and Guttman (this vol., pp. 255–267), have shown how the gradient slope of extinction can be altered by discrimination along an orthogonal dimension. Peterson (1962) and Ganz and Riesen (1962) have shown changes in gradient slope to follow from stimulus deprivation.

Elsewhere, the gradient has been modified by specific demands of the discrimination task, and authors have spoken of observing perceptual differences (Guttman, 1963, p. 159), effects of discrimination *sui generis* (Honig *et al*, 1959), behavioral contrast (Reynolds, 1961), perceptual contrast (Ganz, 1963; Guttman, 1963), series effects (Gewirtz, Jones, and Waerneryd, 1956), and changes in stimulus control (Jenkins and Harrison, 1960). In recent work, Butter, Mishkin, and Rosvold (this vol., pp. 119–133; see especially their Figs. 2, 3, and 4) have shown that it is possible to obtain much flatter generalization gradients *without corresponding changes in discriminatory capacity*. This has been accomplished with visual stimuli in monkeys with inferotemporal lesions. Thompson (this vol., pp. 154–178) has demonstrated the same separation in cats with bilateral removal of auditory neocortex, using auditory stimuli.

We must also recognize that the predicted inverse relationship between generalization and discrimination has often simply not been verified (Guttman and Kalish, 1956; Blough, 1961) *unless* certain discrimination conditions were imposed. This again suggests a looser coupling of the generalization and discrimination concepts than was initially anticipated by the earlier theorists. In a word, the generalization gradient and discrimination capacity can be completely independent, although we know they need not always be (see, e.g., Yarczower and Bitterman, this vol., pp. 179–192).

In this paper, we want to present a simple model of stimulus generalization that makes it possible to dissociate generalization and discrimination under some circumstances but not under others. We make two assumptions. First, not all cues impinging on the organism are necessarily effective on a trial, and this effectiveness is partially determined by the organism. Second, cue effectiveness usually goes up when at least two values of that cue dimension are involved in differential reinforcement (if those two values, S^+ and S^-, are presented in close succession); cue effectiveness diminishes when few or no opportunities of experiencing the cues with differential reinforcement are present. By using these assumptions, we illustrate a statistical learning theory model of stimulus generalization derived partly from previous analyses of the process of discrimination learning (Burke and Estes, 1957; Atkinson, 1961). We then compare some of the properties of the model with the experimental literature.

Suppose a training situation that consists of two sets of stimuli, an S set, which can be manipulated by the experimenter, and a B set made up background stimuli, which are not under the experimenter's control. On some trials, T_1 trials, the experimenter presents the S set and the B set is also present; on the T_2 trials, he presents no stimuli, but the B set is present nevertheless. We will restrict ourselves, for purposes of simplicity, to only the simplest conditions of reinforcement. However, such a restriction is in no way essential. On a T_1 trial, an E_1 event follows. On a T_2 trial, an E_2 event follows. An E_1 event is one that connects all the stimulus elements sampled by the subject to an A_1 response. An E_2 event does the same to an A_2 response. The A_1 and A_2 response classes are mutually exclusive (e.g., A_1 is pressing a manipulandum, and A_2 is all other behavior). Another arbitrary and unessential restriction, which we impose for purposes of illustration, is that T_1 and T_2 trials occur equally often. We suppose the organism can emit a different type of response, R_i, which allows him to sample the cue dimension i. The R_i, R_j ... are mutually exclusive. In our example, when an R_s is emitted, the organism can sample the S stimulus set but not the B set; when an R_b is emitted, the B set is sampled and not the S set. The probability of an R_s and an R_b are given by ω_s and $(1 - \omega_s)$, respectively. If a set is selected, then the probability that any element in it will be sampled equals θ. Thus, the probability that a cue in a set i will be effective on any trial equals $\theta \omega_i$.

The probability that an element in set i is attached to the A_1 response on the nth trial is denoted by $F_{i,n}$. Four recursion formulas define a simple matrix giving the probability that an element in a set will be connected to an A_1 response on trial $n+1$, as a function of the state of the element on trial n:

Set	T_1	T_2
S	$F_{s,n}(1-\theta\omega_s) + \omega\theta$	$F_{s,n}$
B	$F_{b,n}[1-\theta(1-\omega)] + \theta(1-\omega)$	$(1-\theta)F_{b,n}$

Solving the difference equations obtained for equal numbers of T_1 and T_2 trials, we obtain two acquisition curves, one for the probability that an element in set S is connected to A_1 on trial n:

$$(1) \qquad F_{s,n} = 1 - (1 - F_{s,0})\left(1 - \frac{\theta\omega}{2}\right)^n,$$

and one for the probability that an element in set B is connected to A_1 on trial n:

$$(2) \qquad F_{b,n} = \frac{1-\omega}{2-\omega} - \left(\frac{1-\omega}{2-\omega} - F_{b,0}\right)\left(1 - \frac{\theta(2-\omega)}{2}\right)^n.$$

In Eq. (1), the factor $(1 - \theta\omega/2)$ determines the rate of acquisition, the rate of approach to asymptote. Thus, the rate is faster when ω is larger. In Eq. (2), the rate of acquisition is also controlled by the rate of emission of the cue-observing response R_s, but inversely. Acquisition for the elements in B is faster when ω_s is small. The asymptotes are

$$F_{s,\infty} = 1 \text{ and } F_{b,\infty} = \frac{1-\omega}{2-\omega}.$$

If the probability of an A_1 response is directly a function of the proportion of elements selected *and* sampled *and* connected to A_1 to the total selected and sampled, then

$$(3) \qquad P[A_{1,n}] = \omega\left[1 - (1 - F_{s,0})(1 - \frac{\theta\omega}{2})\right]^n$$

$$+ (1-\omega)\left[\frac{1-\omega}{2-\omega} - \left(\frac{1-\omega}{2-\omega} - F_{b,0}\right)\left(1 - \frac{\theta(2-\omega)}{2}\right)^n\right],$$

and at asymptote:

$$(4) \qquad P[A_{1,\infty}] = \frac{1}{2-\omega}.$$

Equation (4) demonstrates an interesting property of the model. It is apparent that the asymptotic probability of the A_1 response can vary from 1.0 to 0.50, as the probability of the organism selecting the set of cues, S, varies from one to zero, during training. The more readily the subject selects the cue, *the higher the rate at which he will respond.* Below we will show how that property is manifested empirically in current generalization studies.

Now we are ready to examine the generalization gradient. During generalization testing, we suppose that the experimenter presents a stimulus made up of a proportion δ of new stimulus elements from a third set G. We suppose none of the elements in G to be connected to A_1. But this is not critical to the argument. At the same time, the experimenter presents a proportion $(1-\delta)$ of the elements from the training set S. The background set, B, not under his control, is, of course, also present. On different generalization tests he chooses different values of δ_i. For any given value, δ_i, the probability of an A_1 response at asymptote is given by

$$(5) \qquad P[A_1, \delta_i, \infty] = \omega(1 - \delta_i) + (1 - \omega)\left(\frac{1 - \omega}{2 - \omega}\right)$$

$$= \frac{1}{2 - \omega} - \omega\delta_i .$$

The slope of the generalization gradient can be obtained by differentiating with respect to δ, assuming δ to be a continuous stimulus dimension:

$$(6) \qquad \frac{dP[A_1]}{d\delta} = -\omega\delta(n = \infty) .$$

Thus the slope of the gradient is inversely proportional to the probability of the cue-selecting response R_S.

To summarize, in this model the three main properties of the cue-selecting response on the generalization gradient are simply these: the more readily the subject selects the cue dimension (high ω) under the experimenter's control, (a) the faster the acquisition rate, (b) the higher the asymptotic level of A_1 responding will be in the presence of S^D, and (c) the steeper the gradient will be. These three effects should covary. It can be shown that very similar effects, (a), (b), and (c), can be obtained if, after the organism has maintained one level of ω_i responding throughout training, he then changes to a higher ω_i level, for one reason or another. We will deal here with (b) and (c) only. The relationship between these two variables is presented graphically in Fig. 1.

In the studies we will review, we will show that when a discrimination procedure is applied to a stimulus continuum under extinction, it *raises the level of responding at* S^+ and *steepens the gradient on both sides of* S^+,

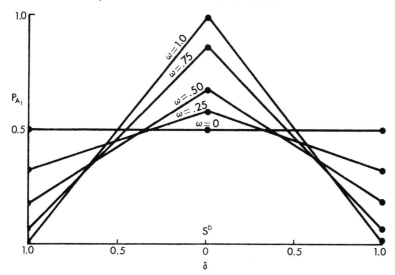

FIG. 1. Theoretical generalization gradients along a stimulus continuum, *i*, as a function of the probability, ω, of the cue-selecting response R_i during training and generalization testing. The gradient is obtained by varying the proportion (δ) of experimenter-controlled training stimuli presented.

near and away from S⁻. The following facts have been puzzling, to say the least, from an excitation-inhibition summation model: (1) administering extinction trials sometimes *raises* response strength, even though there is a generalization of extinction from S⁺ to S⁻; (2) administering extinction sometimes steepens the gradient on both sides of S⁺; and (3) effects (1) and (2) are not dependent on the position of S⁻ on the stimulus continuum. This is also discussed in the paper by Friedman and Guttman (this vol., pp. 255–267), where these effects are termed *symmetrical effects*.

Turning to some experimental results, in Newman's study cited by Baron (this vol., pp. 62–71, and especially results for Group 1), it was found that a group of pigeons that was trained to discriminate the presence from the absence of a line generalized much more steeply along the line-orientation continuum, as might be expected. Groups that did not appear to select the line-orientation cue (i.e., groups that generalized in a shallow gradient on this dimension) also showed lower response levels, as our model predicts. As Baron discusses in his description of cue-attending hierarchies, it seems possible for the pigeons to be under the control of color cues and be almost totally insensitive to cues such as line orientation presented in almost identical geographical loci. The obvious insensitivity of the line-cue to the contingencies of reinforcement, even though the cue must have impinged on the subjects' receptors, suggests the need for a cue-selection parameter such as the one described here.

Hanson (1959) probably gives us the first indication that after operant responding in the presence of S^+ has been brought to almost asymptotic levels, the introduction of S^- *raises* responding at S^+ quite powerfully. Concurrently, it steepens the gradient. Pavlov (1927) had called attention to such an effect, which he called positive induction, although in his work this might have been confounded with temporal conditioning. Additional evidence comes from Jenkins and Harrison (1960), from Reynolds (1961), from Ganz (1963), and from Friedman and Guttman (this vol., pp. 255–267, and especially Fig. 1). In all of these studies, when extinction was introduced, the gradient about S^+ steepened symmetrically and S^+ responding increased. In Jenkins and Harrison's (1960) experiment, the pigeons who were not given differential reinforcement not only responded with an essentially horizontal gradient, but also showed low S^+ response levels *and* responded quite as readily in the total absence of any tone. Both would follow if $\omega \cong 0$ (see Fig. 1).

Similar findings have been obtained in two very different studies on stimulus-deprived organisms. In a study on the wavelength generalization gradients of color-deprived monkeys, the gradient was found to be very flat on the initial test days (Ganz and Riesen, 1962; Ganz, 1962). When extinction trials were introduced along the wave length continuum, not only did the gradient steepen, but S^+ responding doubled. Very similar results have been obtained in an experiment by Peterson (1962). Pigeons reared and trained exclusively under sodium-light illumination (589 mμ) showed a gradient that was flatter and a level of S^+ responding that was lower than shown by normally reared subjects. In both of these deprivation experiments, although the subjects were acting as if they were not selecting the color cue (their behavior was not under its control), they were clearly receiving the stimuli at their receptor organs.

It might be suggested that there is a simpler explanation for the association of steep generalization gradients with higher response levels on the one hand and shallow generalization gradients with lower response levels on the other. When discrimination training is administered, perhaps there is a shift in a number of responses from S^- to S^+. Thus, the area under the generalization gradient may remain roughly constant. As the gradient steepens, S^+ responding would necessarily rise. "Reflex reserve" would remain roughly constant. This is quite possibly sometimes the case. But a glance at Baron's Fig. 2 (this vol., p. 67) shows that the area is not always equal. More decisively, Reynolds (1961) has proven this could not be the explanation in his studies. He controlled response levels by differential reinforcement of low response levels. Responding to a red lit key on the first component of a two-component multiple schedule was not increased by reinforcing not-pressing when a green lit key was presented during the second component. In other words, low key-pressing rates were induced during the presence of green and did not raise response levels during presentation of red.

We can now return to the question of coupling and uncoupling generalization-discriminability. Figure 1 indicates how a gradient may change its slope, without any concomitant changes in discriminability (of the cue once it is selected). Thus, when ω is high in value, the coupling between generalization and discriminability is tight. When ω is low, the relationship of these two variables can become vanishingly low, especially in the presence of the high noise levels we know are associated with generalization measurement. That generalization and discriminability can in fact be dissociated is clearly indicated by the results of Butter et al. (this vol., pp. 119–133) and of Thompson (this vol., pp. 154–178). Following cortical lesions, they obtained shallower gradients in subjects without any concomitant loss in discriminability. In our model, this would be the result of low ω values. For whatever reason, lesioned animals were no longer selecting as readily the cue dimension the experimenter chose to manipulate during generalization testing. On the other hand, high levels of ω are usually associated with explicit discrimination training procedures. Thus, it is discrimination training that assures a tight coupling of discriminability to generalization. It is interesting, then, to remember Kalish's (1958) conclusion that the generalization-discriminability inverse relationship could only be clearly demonstrated where discrimination procedures were employed.

REFERENCES

Atkinson, R. C. The observing response in discrimination learning. *J. exp. Psychol.*, 1961, **62**, 253–262.

Blough, D. S. The shape of some wavelength generalization gradients. *J. exp. Anal. Behav.*, 1961, **4**, 31–40.

Burke, C. J., and Estes, W. K. A component model for stimulus variables in discrimination learning. *Psychometrika*, 1957, **22**, 133–145.

Ganz, L. The effect of an anchor stimulus on the stimulus generalization gradient. *J. exp. Psychol.*, 1963, **65**, 270–279.

Ganz, L., and Riesen, A. H. Stimulus generalization to hue in the dark-reared macaque. *J. comp. physiol. Psychol.*, 1962, **55**, 92–99.

Gewirtz, J. L., Jones, L. V., and Waerneryd, K. Stimulus units and range of experienced stimuli as determinants of generalization-discrimination gradients. *J. exp. Psychol.*, 1956, **52**, 51–57.

Guttman, N. Laws of behavior and facts of perception. In S. Koch (Ed.), *Psychology: A study of a science*. Vol. 5. New York: McGraw-Hill, 1962, pp. 114–178.

Guttman, N., and Kalish. H. I. Discriminability and stimulus generalization. *J. exp. Psychol.*, 1956, **51**, 79–88.

Hanson, H. M. Effects of discrimination training on stimulus generalization. *J. exp. Psychol.*, 1959, **58**, 321–333.

Honig, W., Thomas, D. R., and Guttman, N. Differential effects of continuous extinction and discrimination training on the generalization gradient. *J. exp. Psychol.*, 1959, **58**, 145–152.

Hull, C. L. The problem of primary stimulus generalization. *Psychol. Rev.*, 1947, **54**, 120–134.

Jenkins, H. M., and Harrison, R. H. Effect of discrimination training on auditory generalization. *J. exp. Psychol.*, 1960, **59**, 246–253.

Kalish, H. I. The relationship between discriminability and generalization: A re-evaluation. *J. exp. Psychol.*, 1958, **55**, 638–644.

Pavlov, I. P. *Conditioned reflexes,* translated by G. V. Anrep. London: Oxford Univer. Press, 1927.

Peterson, N. Effect of monochromatic rearing on the control of responding by wavelength. *Science*, 1962, **136**, 774–795.

Reynolds, G. S. Behavioral contrast. *J. exp. anal. Behav.*, 1961, **4**, 57–71.

10. Stimulus Generalization in Monkeys with Inferotemporal and Lateral Occipital Lesions

Charles M. Butter, *University of Michigan*

Mortimer Mishkin and H. Enger Rosvold
National Institute of Mental Health

Inferotemporal lesions in monkeys produce a marked discrimination impairment that appears to be selectively related to the visual modality (Brown, 1963; Weiskrantz and Mishkin, 1958; Wilson, 1957), and yet seems not to be attributable to visual-field or visual-acuity defects (Cowey and Weiskrantz, 1963; Weiskrantz and Cowey, 1963; Wilson and Mishkin, 1959). This impairment in vision is usually reflected as a retardation in the rate at which inferotemporal animals can master particular discrimination problems. The question to which the present study is directed concerns the nature of this final learning. Specifically, we asked whether the trained inferotemporal animal is responding to the same features of the stimulus as those to which the normal animal has learned to respond.

To investigate this problem, inferotemporal animals and their control animals were first trained to respond to a compound visual stimulus consisting of a particular hue and a particular pattern. They were then tested in extinction for generalization along each of these two dimensions separately, according to the method described by Guttman and Kalish (1956). If the inferotemporal animals were to show a flat gradient along the wavelength dimension, it would suggest that they had failed either to attend to the specific hue used in training or to associate this stimulus feature with the reward. A similar interpretation could be advanced with regard to the specific pattern used in training if the generalization test were to reveal a flat gradient along this dimension. Thus, an analysis of the inferotemporal animals' performance in generalization testing might indicate whether, and in what way, the effective stimulus for the learned response of these animals differed from the effective stimulus for the control animals.

This study was conducted while the senior author held a U.S.P.H.S. Postdoctoral Fellowship MF-9588-C1, at the Section on Neuropsychology, National Institute of Mental Health.

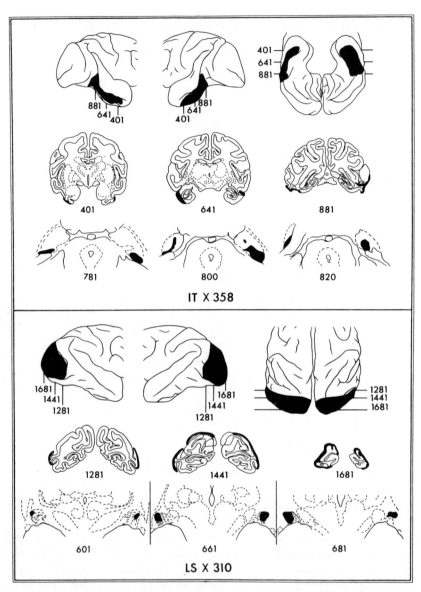

FIG. 1. Reconstructions of representative inferotemporal (top panel) and lateral striate (bottom panel) lesions and cross sections through the lesions and the thalami.

Experiment I

Method

Subjects. The subjects were eighteen experimentally naïve monkeys (*Macaca mulatta*), ranging in weight from 3.5 to 5 kg. Four monkeys with bilateral lesions of the inferotemporal cortex constituted the experimental group; ten unoperated monkeys and four monkeys with bilateral lateral striate lesions served as controls. The animals with subtotal striate lesions were included in order to determine what type of generalization impairment, if any, is associated with visual-field and visual-acuity defects, and to permit a better assessment of the impairment in visual generalization that may be due specifically to ablation of the inferotemporal cortex.

Lesions. Animals were anesthetized with Nembutal (40 mg/kg),[1] and surgery was performed under aseptic conditions. One-stage bilateral lesions were made by aspiration with a small-gauge sucker through openings in the temporal or occipital bone. Wounds were closed with silk sutures.

On completion of testing, the operated animals were perfused under anesthesia, and their brains were removed and prepared for embedding in celloidin. Frontal sections were cut at 25 μ, and every twentieth section was stained with thionine for use in examining the lesions. Figure 1 shows reconstructions of representative inferotemporal and lateral striate lesions, together with cross sections through the cortex and thalamus. The inferotemporal lesions included the middle and inferior temporal gyri and varying portions of the fusiform gyrus. The cortex on the temporal pole was spared, and the posterior boundary of the lesions was approximately ½ cm. in front of and parallel to the ascending inferior occipital sulcus. These lesions produced retrograde degeneration in the medial portion of the pulvinar. The occipital lesions included all striate cortex on the lateral surface of the occipital lobe, extending from the pole forward to the lunate sulcus and down to the inferior occipital sulcus. Retrograde degeneration was present in the intermediate portion of the lateral geniculate nuclei.

Apparatus. Animals were trained in a noise-shielded enclosure containing a 40-watt lamp and a speaker, both mounted on the ceiling, and a translucent response panel (4.25 in. square) located on one wall 11 in. above the floor. An automatic dispenser delivered pellets to a food-well located directly below the response panel. A circular area (3.5 in. in diameter) in the middle of the panel contained a pattern of 13 bars, which were alternately black and colored (see Fig. 2). This colored pattern was produced by a film-strip projector and a series of filters located outside the enclosure. The angular orientation of the bars was varied by projecting different images on the film strip, and the color of the bars was varied by

---

[1] *Nembutal is the trademarked name of pentobarbital sodium, supplied by Abbott Laboratories, N. Chicago, Illinois.*

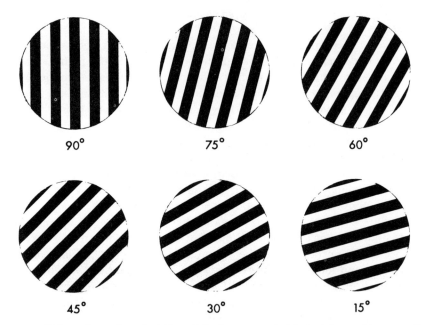

FIG. 2. Values of angular orientation of the bars presented in training and in generalization testing.

placing different second-order interference filters in the light path. These monochromatic filters (Bausch & Lomb Co.) had bandwidths of 7 to 9 mμ at half-height. In order to exclude wavelengths in the first-order spectrum, a Wratten K-2 filter (Eastman Kodak Co.) was used in conjunction with interference filters having peak transmission values above 550 mμ. Constant luminance of the projection lamp was maintained by use of a circuit that delivered constant current. A circular optical wedge (Eastman Kodak Co.) was used to vary the brightness of the various monochromatic hues. The entire projection pathway was enclosed within a light-tight housing.

Procedure. Beginning ten to fourteen days after surgery, the animals were trained to press the panel for food reward. During this initial stage of training, white masking noise was delivered through the speaker, the overhead light was on, and the stimulus area on the response panel was illuminated with bars of blue light (479 mμ) oriented vertically (90°). After this initial training, which required from one to four days, the animals were given continuous reinforcement for 30 responses on each of two successive days. During this second stage of training, stimulus conditions were the same as before except that there was no overhead light. In the final stage of training, the subjects were reinforced on a variable-interval (VI) schedule with a mean inter-reinforcement interval of 1 min. (VI 1′). Daily sessions consisted of 30 stimulus periods, each 50 sec. in duration, during which the panel was illuminated with the blue, vertical bars, and responses were reinforced on the VI schedule; these stimulus periods alternated with 15-sec. blackouts, during which responses were extinguished. In these final training sessions, the blue, vertical bars were presented at three levels of brightness—2.6, 5.5 and 13.2 ml—in a random sequence. Training was continued beyond eight sessions until all subjects made at least 1,000 responses to the stimulus compound on each of three consecutive days.

On the day following the completion of training, the animals were tested in extinction for generalization along both the wavelength and angular-orientation dimensions. Immediately prior to generalization testing, the training stimulus compound was presented during six 30-sec. periods, which alternated with 15-sec. blackouts, and the animals were reinforced for responding once during the first, third, and sixth stimulus periods. After this initial "warmup," the animals were presented in extinction with five new wavelengths—510, 543, 570, 598, and 634 mμ—each combined with the vertical (90°) bars, and five new values of angular orientation of the bars—75, 60, 45, 30, and 15°—each combined with blue (479 mμ) light (see Fig. 2). Each hue was presented at three brightness levels, matched by an observer to the three brightness levels used in training, and presented in a mixed order. The ten new stimulus compounds, together with the training stimulus compound, were presented in eight different random sequences. The durations of the stimulus and blackout periods were the same as those in the initial warmup.

Results

VI training. Figure 3 shows the mean ratios of responses in blackout periods to responses in stimulus periods for each group on the first eleven days of VI training. On the first eight days, the inferotemporal group tended to show less discrimination between light on the panel and blackout than the lateral striate group, which, in turn, tended to discriminate less than the unoperated group. However, after the eighth day the mean scores of the operated groups did not appear to differ from those of the normal group, and over all eleven days there were no significant group differences. Furthermore, there were no reliable group differences in the number of VI training sessions required to meet the criterion, or in the response rates finally attained.

Generalization testing. Mean total responses to each of the stimuli presented in the generalization test are shown in Fig. 4. Whereas the inferotemporal group did not differ from the others in the total number of responses it emitted during this extinction session, it did differ in the manner in which its responses were distributed. Thus, the wavelength generalization gradient of the inferotemporal group is flatter than those of the other

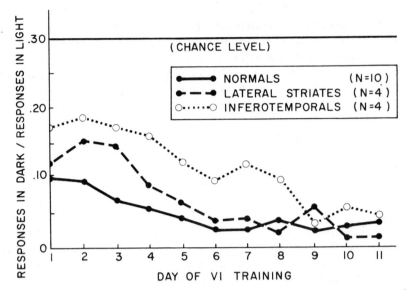

FIG. 3. Mean ratios of total responses in blackout periods to total responses in stimulus periods for the three groups on the first eleven days of VI training (Exp. I).

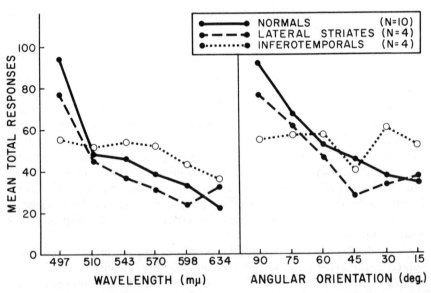

FIG. 4. Mean total responses of the three groups to wavelength and angular-orientation stimuli presented in generalization testing following single-stimulus training (Exp. I).

two groups (see left panel of Fig. 4). This difference is reflected in the analysis of variance as a significant Groups × Wavelength interaction ($P < .001$). A similar result appears in the responses to angular-orientation stimuli (see right panel of Fig. 4), and is reflected in the analysis as a significant Groups × Angular-orientation interaction ($P < .001$). By contrast, the slopes of the lateral striate and unoperated control groups do not appear to differ along either dimension (the lateral striate group's increase in responses from 30° to 15° of angular orientation is not statistically reliable).

Experiment II

Although at the end of VI training the inferotemporal animals performed as well as the control animals in differentiating stimulus periods from blackouts, they behaved in generalization testing as though they had failed to perceive the specific hue and the specific pattern of the training stimulus compound. That is, it appears that the inferotemporal animals had learned to respond at most to "colored bars" on the panel and not to "blue, vertical bars." A second experiment was undertaken in order to determine whether the specific hue and pattern of the training stimulus compound would become effective stimuli after the inferotemporal animals had been trained to discriminate this compound from another differing in both wavelength and angular orientation.

Method

Subjects and apparatus. The subjects and apparatus were the same as those used in Experiment I, except that the unoperated group was reduced from ten animals to four.

Procedure. The subjects were trained to discriminate the original stimulus compound, 479 mμ–90° (positive), from another stimulus compound, 570 mμ–45° (negative). The two stimulus compounds were presented successively at the three brightness levels that had been used with each in Experiment I. The duration of both the stimulus and the blackout periods was the same as in the VI training sessions in the previous experiment. Responses to the positive stimulus compound were reinforced on a VI 1′ schedule, but responses to the negative stimulus compound were never reinforced. Daily sessions consisted of 15 presentations of each stimulus compound in an order determined by a Gellerman (1933) series. Discrimination training was continued until the animals completely suppressed responses to the negative stimulus compound and maintained responses to the positive stimulus compound in 27 out of 30 consecutive stimulus periods. The animals were then tested for wavelength and angular-orientation generalization in the same manner as in Experiment I. In addition, the negative stimulus compound was presented within each random sequence of generalization stimuli.

Results

Discrimination training. Figure 5 shows the mean number of stimulus periods required by each of the three groups to reach the discrimination criterion. The inferotemporal group was significantly retarded in learning the discrimination compared with both the lateral striate and the unoperated groups ($P < .05$ for both, Dunnett's t-test, one-tail [Dunnett, 1955]). The latter two groups did not differ significantly from each other.

Generalization testing. Although the inferotemporal subjects had difficulty in learning, once they achieved the criterion they were able to maintain a high level of discrimination performance; like the control subjects, they showed nearly complete suppression (range, 0–6 responses) to the negative stimulus compound (570 mμ–45°) when it was presented in generalization testing. However, separating the wavelength and angular-orientation aspects of the negative stimulus compound revealed that the inferotemporal animals, unlike the control animals, had not utilized both cues in the discrimination problem.

Considering first the wavelength dimension, it is clear that at all stimulus values the inferotemporal group showed generalization decrements that were at least as large as those shown by the two control groups (see

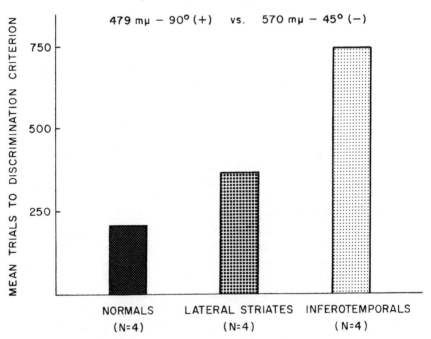

FIG. 5. Mean number of stimulus periods required by the three groups to discriminate between 479 mμ–90° and 570 mμ–45° (Exp. II).

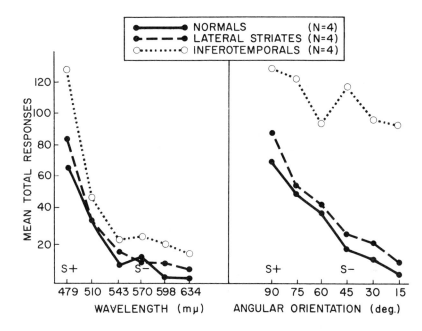

FIG. 6. Mean total responses of the three groups to wavelength and angular-orientation stimuli presented in generalization testing following discrimination training between 479 mμ–90° (positive) and 570 mμ–45° (negative). S+ and S- refer to the positive and negative aspects of the stimulus compounds presented in prior discrimination training (Exp. II).

left panel of Fig. 6). In fact, it may be seen from the figure that the initial portion of the inferotemporal group's gradient was somewhat steeper than that of the control groups. By contrast, on the angular-orientation dimension, the gradient of the inferotemporal group was much broader than that of the other groups (see right panel of Fig. 6); this is reflected in the analysis of variance as a significant Groups × Angular-orientation interaction ($P < .05$).

Further evidence that the inferotemporal subjects were neglecting differences in angular orientation is indicated by their abnormally high rate of responding to stimuli along the entire dimension ($P < .025$); presumably this was due to the fact that each value of angular orientation was combined with the positive hue, and the inferotemporal subjects were responding primarily to this aspect of the stimulus compound.

Experiment III

Comparison of the angular-orientation gradients obtained in Experiments I and II suggests that, with respect to this stimulus dimension, the inferotemporal animals benefited surprisingly little from the extensive discrimination training they received between the two generalization sessions. It seems that the primary effect of discrimination training on the inferotemporal subjects was to convert the effective stimulus from "colored bars" to "blue bars," irrespective of their angular orientation. The purpose of the following experiment was to establish that inferotemporal animals could be trained to distinguish vertical from oblique bars when these were the only cues available, and then to ascertain by generalization testing how *specific* the effective stimulus had now become.

Procedure. The same animals that were used in the previous experiment were trained to discriminate vertical bars (positive) from bars oriented at 45° (negative) with wavelength held constant at 479 mμ. The discrimination procedure was as follows. Responses to the positive stimulus were reinforced on a VI 27″ schedule, whereas responses to the negative stimulus were extinguished. The animals were required to make 80 per cent of their responses to the positive stimulus in one session. Following discrimination learning, the animals were tested for generalization to the

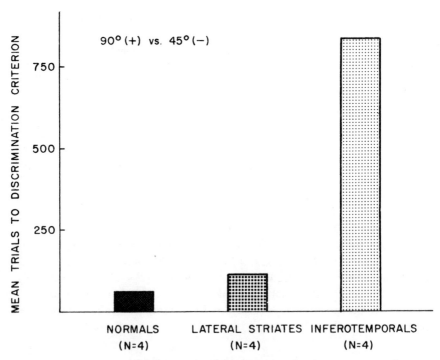

FIG. 7. Mean number of stimulus periods required by the three groups to discriminate between bars oriented at 90° and bars oriented at 15° (Exp. III).

same values of angular orientation that were presented in the first two experiments, with the wavelength of the light maintained at 479 mμ. The six orientation stimuli were presented in ten different random sequences. In all other respects, discrimination training and generalization testing were conducted in the same manner in this experiment as they were in Experiment II.

Results

Discrimination training. As may be seen in Fig. 7, the inferotemporal group was severely retarded in learning the angular-orientation discrimination compared with the two control groups ($P < .01$ for both comparisons, Dunnett's *t*-test). Nevertheless, by the end of training the inferotemporal group attained a level of performance (83 per cent) only slightly lower than that attained by the normal and lateral striate groups (87 and 88 per cent respectively).

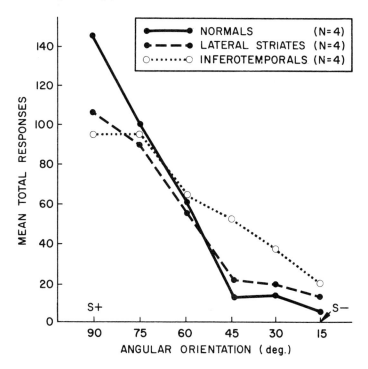

FIG. 8. Mean total responses of the three groups to angular-orientation stimuli presented in generalization testing following discrimination training between bars oriented at 90° and bars oriented at 15°. S⁺ and S⁻ refer to the positive and negative values of angular orientation presented in prior discrimination training (Exp. III).

Generalization testing. The data presented in Fig. 8 indicate that the inferotemporal subjects were now showing clear-cut generalization decrements to stimuli on the pattern dimension. However, inspection of the figure suggests that they still had a small (though non-significant) residual impairment. Thus, their apparent failure to differentiate 90° from 75°, together with their relatively broad gradient beyond 60°, suggests that the effective pattern stimulus for this group was still not as specific as it was for the control groups.

Experiment IV

The results of Experiments II and III imply that inferotemporal animals are more severely impaired in differentiating values on a pattern dimension than on the wavelength dimension. This difference could have resulted simply from the use of non-equivalent scales along the two dimensions. If this were the case, a residual impairment on the wavelength dimension might be detected in the inferotemporal subjects by testing for generalization to wavelength values much closer together than those used in the earlier experiments. The final experiment was undertaken in order to investigate this possibility.

Procedure. The same animals were retrained to discriminate 479 from 570 mμ, with the angular orientation of the bars held constant at 90°. Otherwise, the discrimination-training procedure was the same as that used in Experiment II. Following discrimination learning, the animals were presented in generalization testing with wavelengths of 479, 488, 494, 498, 505, and 510 mμ, all matched for brightness by two observers. These seven stimuli were presented in ten different random sequences. In all other respects, the procedure was the same as the one used in Experiment II.

Results

All the animals quickly reattained the criterion on the wavelength discrimination, and there were no reliable group differences in rate of relearning. Furthermore, in subsequent generalization testing, the inferotemporal monkeys, like the others, showed distinct gradients (see Fig. 9), and an analysis of variance failed to reveal any significant Groups × Wavelengths interaction. However, examination of the gradients indicates that the experimental subjects did show abnormally broad generalization from 479 to 482 mμ and from 505 to 510 mμ, suggesting that the inferotemporal subjects had a small residual impairment along the wavelength dimension, just as along the pattern dimension.

The failure to find equivalent defects in discriminating small wavelength differences in the animals with lateral striate lesions is surprising

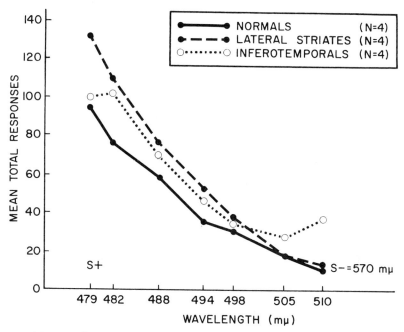

FIG. 9. Mean total responses of the three groups to wavelength stimuli presented in generalization testing following wavelength discrimination relearning. S⁺ and S⁻ refer to the positive and negative wavelength values presented in discrimination retraining (Exp. IV).

in view of the results of previous studies indicating a variety of sensory losses in such animals (Cowey and Weiskrantz, 1963; Mishkin and Weiskrantz, 1959; Weiskrantz and Cowey, 1963; Wilson and Mishkin, 1959). Presumably, the stimulus differences employed in the present experiment were not sufficiently small to detect a sensory impairment.

Discussion

The finding in Experiment I that the inferotemporal animals had abnormally broad gradients along both the wavelength and the angular-orientation dimensions suggests that they had learned little about either the specific hue or the specific pattern of the stimulus compound during single-stimulus training. Only after they had learned to discriminate first between wavelengths in Experiment II, and then between values of angular orientation in Experiment III, did they give evidence of responding selectively to these stimulus features by showing clear-cut generalization decrements along the two dimensions. Thus, over the course of the study, the specificity of the effective stimulus for the inferotemporal animals appears to have increased in a step-wise fashion from "colored bars" (Exp. I) to "blue bars" (Exp. II) and finally, to "blue, vertical bars" (Exp. III).

This gradual evolution of the effective stimulus suggests that the performance of the inferotemporal animals, as opposed to that of the control animals, was governed at first only by the most salient or distinctive features of the training stimulus compound, and not until they had received the appropriate discrimination training did the less distinctive characteristics of the stimulus begin to exert control. However, even at the end of discrimination training, the less salient features of the stimulus compound were still not quite so specific for the inferotemporal animals as for the control subjects.

These results point directly to the possibility that the animals with inferotemporal lesions were impaired in some process—referred to as the acquisition of cue distinctiveness by Lawrence (1949, 1950) and the learning of stimulus identity by Hebb (1949)—by which particular features of repeatedly presented, complex stimuli become more and more readily identified. Such an interpretation would help to account not only for the present findings concerning stimulus generalization but also for the most commonly described defect after inferotemporal lesions, namely, a retardation in visual discrimination learning.

REFERENCES

Brown, T. S. Olfactory and visual discrimination in the monkey after selective lesions of the temporal lobe. *J. comp. physiol. Psychol.*, 1963, **56**, 764–768.

Cowey, A., and Weiskrantz, L. A perimetric study of visual field defects in monkeys. *Quart. J. exp. Psychol.*, 1963, **15**, 91–115.

Dunnett, C. W. A multiple comparison procedure for comparing several treatments with a control. *J. Amer. Statist. Ass.*, 1955, **50**, 1096–1121.

Gellerman, L. W. Chance orders of alternating stimuli in visual discrimination experiments. *J. genet. Psychol.*, 1933, **42**, 207–208.

Guttman, N., and Kalish, H. I. Discriminability and stimulus generalization. *J. exp. Psychol.*, 1956, **51**, 79–88.

Hebb, D. O. *The organization of behavior.* New York: Wiley, 1949.

Lawrence, D. H. Acquired distinctiveness of cues: I. Transfer between discriminations on the basis of familiarity with the stimulus. *J. exp. Psychol.*, 1949, **39**, 770–784.

Lawrence, D. H. Acquired distinctiveness of cues: II. Selective association in a constant stimulus situation. *J. exp. Psychol.*, 1950, **40**, 175–188.

Mishkin, M., and Weiskrantz, L. Effects of cortical lesions in monkeys on critical flicker fusion. *J. comp. physiol. Psychol.*, 1959, **52**, 660–666.

Weiskrantz, L., and Cowey, A. Striate cortex lesions and visual acuity of the rhesus monkey. *J. comp. physiol. Psychol.*, 1963, **56**, 225–231.

Weiskrantz, L., and Mishkin, M. Effects of temporal and frontal cortical lesions on auditory discrimination in monkeys. *Brain*, 1958, **81**, 406–414.

Wilson, M. Effects of circumscribed cortical lesions upon somesthetic and visual discrimination in the monkey. *J. comp. physiol. Psychol.*, 1957, **50**, 630–635.
Wilson, W. A., Jr., and Mishkin, M. Comparison of the effects of inferotemporal and lateral occipital lesions on visually guided behavior in monkeys. *J. comp. physiol. Psychol.*, 1959, **52**, 10–17.

11. Generalization after Frequency Discrimination in Cats with Central Nervous System Lesions

Walter L. Randall, *Duke University*

In this study, a generalization procedure was applied to the conditioned-avoidance behavior of cats after central nervous system lesions. The cats were trained to a frequency discrimination, and then generalization testing was conducted with tones varying in both frequency and intensity.

A number of ablation studies on the frequency-discriminatory behavior of the cat in a conditioned-avoidance situation have been performed (Butler, Diamond, and Neff, 1957; Goldberg and Neff, 1961; Meyer and Woolsey, 1952; Thompson, 1960), and these results have been summarized and integrated with other findings (Diamond and Chow, 1962; Neff, 1960; Neff, 1961; Neff and Diamond, 1958; Rose and Woolsey, 1958; Thompson, this vol., pp. 154–178). These studies have reported different amounts of behavioral deficit on frequency-discrimination problems as a result of ablation of the auditory cortex: Meyer and Woolsey (1952) found irreversible loss of the frequency-discriminatory behavior, and Butler *et al.* (1957) found reversible loss.

Thompson (1960) has analyzed the differences in these studies and discovered that the manner of presentation of the positive and negative stimuli can account for the different findings. There is an irreversible loss of the frequency discrimination when there are intervals of silence between the presentation of the positive and negative stimuli, and a reversible loss when there are no intervals of silence, i.e., when the negative stimulus is presented continuously except for the aperiodic changes to the positive stimulus.

Thompson's (1960 and this vol., p. 154) interpretation of the irreversible loss of frequency discrimination after cortical ablation is in terms of diffi-

This research was supported by Grant B-801(C4) from the National Institute of Neurological Diseases and Blindness (principal investigator: K. L. Chow) and by Grant M-4849 from the National Institute of Mental Health (principal investigator: I. T. Diamond). Part of this work was submitted to the Biophychology Section, Department of Psychology, University of Chicago, in partial fulfillment of the requirements for the Ph.D. degree. I wish to thank Drs. K. L. Chow and W. D. Neff, whose kind generosities made this study possible.

culty of response inhibition: "Removal of auditory cortex appears to inter-fere with the ability to inhibit response to negative stimuli in frequency discrimination rather than to interfere with frequency discrimination as such." Less or no response inhibition is necessary for the frequency-dis-crimination task when there are no intervals of silence between the nega-tive and positive stimuli, because all that is required here is a "simple re-sponse to change." Goldberg and Neff (1961) think that failure of response inhibition does not explain the irreversible loss of pattern discrimination that occurs after auditory cortex lesion (Diamond and Neff, 1957), and for this reason they do not think that response-inhibition failure is the "primary effect" of the cortical lesion.

As an alternative to Thompson's explanation, a neural theory has been proposed (Diamond, Goldberg, and Neff, 1962; Goldberg and Neff, 1961) to account for the discriminatory behavior of cats with lesions of the audi-tory cortex. To explain the difference between the reversible and irrevers-ible losses of frequency-discriminatory behavior, this theory proposes that cats without auditory cortex make discriminations on the basis of size of neural responses. In the frequency-discrimination situation where there are no intervals of silence separating the positive and negative stimuli, there is habituation to the negative stimulus so that the change from the negative to the positive stimulus results in an increase in the size of the neural response to the positive stimulus. Thus cats without auditory cortex can do this problem. In the frequency-discrimination situation where there are intervals of silence between presentations of the positive and negative stimuli, there is no opportunity for habituation; thus the size of the neural responses to positive and negative stimuli are the same, and cats without auditory cortex cannot do this problem.

Thompson (1962) has supported his ideas on response inhibition with data obtained from generalization tests. Generalization data have been used in ablation studies (e.g., Halstead, 1940; Klüver, 1951; Maier, 1941; Thompson, 1962; Wapner, 1944), and some of these studies suggest that generalization data are sensitive indicators of brain damage. The particu-lar use of generalization testing as applied to ablation studies has varied considerably. Maier (1941), on the basis of generalization data obtained from normal and lesion groups of rats, proposed that two fundamentally different processes may be involved in generalization: either responses to "likenesses" or responses to "differences." Wapner (1944), who found an increase in generalization after brain damage, criticized speculations on generalization as a higher mental process. Halstead (1940) found that hu-mans with frontal-lobe lesions behaved differently from normal subjects on a test that required the grouping of heterogeneous stimulus objects. In an ablation study of the striate cortex, Klüver (1951) demonstrated that the change in behavior after lesion could be attributed to a restriction of the monkey's visual capability to luminous flux differences. Thus the use of generalization testing in ablation studies has generated or supported hypotheses, provided criticisms of important concepts, and specified the stimulus to which the animal is responding before and after central nervous system lesions.

Answers to the question "What is learned (with respect to the stimulus complex)?" may be approached by the use of generalization testing. Since the typical result of central nervous system lesions on learned behavior is loss of the behavior with reacquisition occurring with subsequent retraining, the question "What is learned?" may be extended to "What, if any, are the changes in the effective properties of the stimuli in the preoperative and postoperative situations?"

The present study utilizes a generalization procedure in an attempt to specify the nature of the effective stimuli involved in the frequency-discriminatory behavior of the cat.

Materials and Procedure

Cats with stereotaxic lesions of the midbrain (Figs. 3–8) that involved the auditory pathways were trained on two conditioned-avoidance problems in a double-grill box: first an onset-of-buzzer problem and then a frequency-discrimination problem. Retention tests were conducted on these problems after one month, and then generalization tests were performed. These same cats were then subjected to bilateral ablation of the auditory cortex (Figs. 9 and 10) and retested on the buzzer, frequency-discrimination, and generalization tests.

The double-grill box that was used for the conditioned-avoidance problems was in a sound-treated room that measured 8 by 10 feet with a 6-foot 9-inch ceiling. The box was 18¼ inches wide, 50 inches long, and 25 inches high, and was placed on a table about five feet from the loudspeaker. A microphone was hung from the ceiling and positioned just outside the double-grill box between the speaker and the center of the double-grill box. This microphone was connected to a sound-level meter outside the room (General Radio Company type 759-8 with type 759-P30 cable).

Before the microphone was positioned in this fashion for monitoring the stimuli during the learning sessions, the sound-pressure level was determined at 36 positions inside the double-grill box for the two tones that were used for the frequency discrimination. The two tones were 800 cps and 1,000 cps, and were generated by two Hewlett-Packard audio-oscillators. The intensities of these two oscillators were equated by means of a voltmeter inserted into the circuit on the speaker side of the amplifier. For the 36 positions that were monitored inside the box, the sound-pressure level of the 800-cps tone varied over a 15-db range, and the 1,000-cps tone over a 12-db range. The difference in the sound-pressure level between the

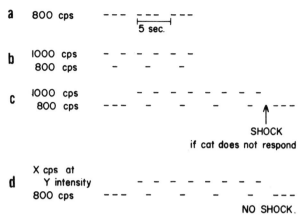

FIG. 1. (*a*) Represents the groups of tones at 800 cps that were used for the negative stimulus. These five second groups were repeated continuously except when the positive stimulus (*b*) was presented; this change is shown in (*c*), which represents all the training trials; (*d*) indicates how the test trials were presented.

800- and 1,000-cps tones at any one position was not as great, averaging 4 db for the 25 positions where the sound-pressure level of the 800-cps tone was greater and 2 db for the 11 positions where the sound-pressure level of the 1,000-cps tone was greater. The sound-pressure level of the 800-cps tone averaged 65.2 for the 36 positions; the 1,000-cps tone averaged 62.6.

The negative stimulus was the 800-cps tone that was presented in groups of three (as illustrated in Fig. 1a). Each tone was of 1-sec. duration with ¼-sec. intervals between tones within groups and 1½-sec. intervals between groups. The positive stimulus (Fig. 1b) differed from the negative stimulus in the first and third tones of each group of three. A switch activated the 1,000-cps oscillator, which then provided the first and third tones of each group of the positive stimulus. A mechanical timer controlled the presentation of the negative and positive stimuli. An electronic switch controlled the rise and fall times of the tones.

Training procedure. At the beginning of each daily session the outputs of the 800- and 1,000-cps oscillators were equated by means of the voltmeter. The training method used was that employed by Butler *et al.* (1957). A *training trial* consisted of switching from the negative stimulus to the positive stimulus and shocking the cat lightly if he did not cross to the opposite side of the double-grill box. As soon as the cat crossed to the opposite side, the positive stimulus was changed back to the negative stimulus (Fig. 1c). For each daily training session, three to twelve trials were presented (the average was five), and the inter-trial interval varied from ½ min. to 7 min. (the average was 2½ min.). Criterion for learning was a high level of performance on three successive days (four avoidance responses in five trials on one of the days and five avoidance responses in five trials on the other two) with a low level of spontaneity (a 15-min. interval where avoidance responses were made on four consecutive trials and where no more than one spontaneous response was made). If there was spontaneity above this criterion level, the cats were simply given additional training sessions until the spontaneity dropped out. During the criterion performance the cat was allowed 20 sec. to respond to the positive stimulus pattern (Fig. 1c) before he was shocked.

After the cats with the midbrain lesions learned the frequency-discrimination problem, tests were conducted to make sure that the conditioned-avoidance responses were due to changes in the stimulus and not to switching artifacts or to differences in oscillator characteristics.

The cats were then rested for one month and then retested to both the buzzer and frequency-discrimination problems.

Generalization procedure. After the retention tests, generalization tests were conducted. A daily generalization session consisted of frequency-discrimination *training trials* and *test trials*. A *test trial* consisted of changing the 1,000-cps oscillator to another frequency and intensity setting, presenting this new stimulus group to the cat for 20 sec., and recording the cat's behavior. The 800-cps oscillator remained the same; that is, all of the negative stimulus and the middle tone of the test stimulus never changed (Fig. 1d). The first and third tones of the positive stimulus were the only tones that changed (i.e., only the intensity and frequency of the "1,000-cps" oscillator of the training procedure were changed), and the first and third tones were always the same for any one test trial. The first and third tones of the positive stimulus pattern were changed to various values on different trials over a range of 40 to 85 db and 200 to 1,600 cps. The intensity changes were made by manipulating the dial on the oscillator, and the intensity was read from the sound-level meter during the presentation of the test trial. The frequency setting was adjusted before the presentation of the trial by use of Lissajous figures, and was either 200, 400, 600, 800, 1,000, 1,200, 1,400, or 1,600 cps.

A generalization session consisted of an average of 7 *test trials* and 5 *training trials*. Each time a cat did not respond to a test trial, he was presented with a training trial. If he did not respond to the training trial, he was shocked, and the test trial was not used in the data tabulation. Thus any effects of extinction were eliminated, and a high performance level was maintained. If spontaneity above the criterion level appeared in the generalization sessions, regular training sessions were given until the spontaneity disappeared. If spontaneous responses never appeared in the generalization sessions, training sessions were given anyway after every fourth or fifth generalization session. In each generalization session, an attempt was made to select test stimuli so as to cover the entire test range. Thus some idea of the stability of the responses from day to day could be obtained.

After the generalization data were obtained, the cats were subjected to ablation of the auditory cortex (Figs. 9 and 10) and then retested on the buzzer, frequency-discrimination, and generalization tests.

Surgical procedure. The coordinates for the placement of the stereotaxic lesions were selected from the atlas of Snider and Niemer (1961). The lesions were made in stages, with complete recovery of the cats permitted before additional stages were attempted. Five milliamperes of direct current were used with a No. 20 hypodermic needle as the anode. Full details of the stereotaxic surgery have been presented elsewhere (Randall, 1964). The removal of the auditory cortex was accomplished by subpial aspiration. For all surgical procedures, sodium pentobarbital was the anesthetic, and atropine sulfate, a tetracycline, and Mikedemide were routinely administered on the day of the surgery; rigorous aseptic procedures were employed.[1]

When retesting on the buzzer, frequency-discrimination, and generalization tasks had been completed, the cats were anesthetized with sodium pentobarbital and perfused first with saline and then with 10 per cent formalin. The brains were embedded in celloidin and sectioned in the transverse plane. Serial transverse sections were prepared with thionin, Weil, Holmes (1947), and Klüver-Barrera (1955) methods so that there were adjacent fiber- and cell-stained sections for every ¼ mm. With the aid of a projection microscope, lateral and sagittal views of the lesions were reconstructed, and transverse views of the lesions were drawn.

Results

Behavior. There were no systematic differences in learning or generalization between cats with different midbrain lesions. Their learning scores are presented in Table 1 and their generalization data in Fig. 2a. After auditory cortical lesions retraining was required for the buzzer and frequency discrimination as indicated in Table 1, and there were changes on the generalization test (Fig. 2b).

The letters "T" (tegmental) and "VL" (ventral-lateral) in Table 1 refer to two different midbrain lesion groups. A description of the changes in instinctive behavior of these two midbrain lesion groups has been made (Randall, 1964). The subsequent lesions of the auditory cortex did not modify the changes in instinctive behavior that resulted from the midbrain lesions. Cats T1 and VL2 (Figs. 2 and 5) are not included in Table 1 or Fig. 2 because they did not complete the procedures. VL2 did not learn to escape shock to the onset of the buzzer. T1 never received a cortical lesion

---

[1] Mikedemide is an antagonist for barbiturates. It is 3,3-methylethyl-glutarimide produced by the Parlam Corp., Englewood, New Jersey.

because he was a retarded learner; when his first generalization tests were completed, it was decided that the study was too far advanced to include him among the cortical lesion group. T1's generalization scores were like those shown in Fig. 2a.

The responses on the generalization test to different test stimuli both before and after cortical lesion were "all or none"; i.e., for any one test stimulus, the cat either consistently responded on each occasion of its presentation or never responded (with the one exception noted below). Thus Fig. 2 is divided into two areas: an area where the cats crossed to the other side of the double-grill box (represented by solid bars), and an area where they did not cross (represented by cross-hatched bars). Occasional responses occurred in the areas of the cross-hatched bars, but the frequency of these responses was not greater than the spontaneity.

The results from the generalization tests before auditory cortex lesions are presented in Fig. 2a in the form of a bar graph that represents an av-

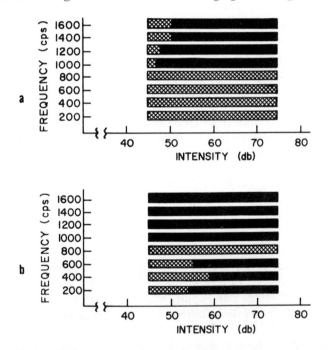

FIG. 2. These bar graphs indicate the stimuli to which the cats responded (solid bars) and the stimuli to which they did not respond (cross-hatched bars) during the generalization procedure. The data are an average derived from four cats, with the original stimulus range reduced somewhat to include more data in the averages. Figure 2a is the condition found before cortical ablation and 2b the condition found after cortical ablation.

TABLE 1

THE NUMBER OF DAILY SESSIONS ON THE CONDITIONED-AVOIDANCE PROBLEM (NOT INCLUDING CRITERION SESSIONS) AND THE SESSIONS OF GENERALIZATION PROCEDURE BEFORE AND AFTER ABLATION OF AUDITORY CORTEX

| | Before Auditory Cortical Ablation | | | | | After Auditory Cortical Ablation | | |
| | Initial Learning | | Retention after 1 mo. | | No. of Gen. | | | No. of Gen. |
Cat	Buz.	Freq.	Buz.	Freq.	Sessions	Buz.	Freq.	Sessions
T4	17	7	0	0	22	12	1	24
T3	11	10	0	0	26	7	2	17
VL7	6	5			26	7	3	6
VL6	11	28	0	2	22	9	6	18

erage of the four cats that subsequently received auditory cortex lesions. The bars in Fig. 2 indicate continuity along the intensity axis because the test stimuli were presented for every three or four db, which is of difference-limen magnitude (Oesterreich and Neff, 1960; Raab and Ades, 1946). The responses of the cat to the various test stimuli were the same from one day to the next throughout all test sessions.

After ablation of the auditory cortex, additional training was required on both the buzzer and frequency-discrimination problems before the criterion performance level was achieved. More training was required for the buzzer than for the frequency problem after auditory cortex lesions, indicating that most of whatever is lost as a result of the surgery is not related to the frequency problem itself. For the buzzer problem, all cats displayed at least one conditioned emotional response in the first postoperative session, and the first appearance of a conditioned-avoidance response to the buzzer was in the second session for three of the cats and in the seventh session for the other (T4). On the frequency problem, which followed re-acquisition of criterion performance on the buzzer problem, complete conditioned-avoidance responses appeared in the first session. Thus the learned behavior appeared earlier (for two of the cats on the first trial), and criterion was reached more quickly for the frequency problem.

The conditioned emotional responses become more and more subtle with experience, and since the cats of this study had considerable experience on the conditioned-avoidance problems, it was not always possible to record these behaviors. However, motion pictures were taken of the conditioned emotional responses before the cortical lesions were made, and the postoperative behavior was compared with these film records. Each individual cat had an idiosyncratic conditioned emotional-response pattern, and this pattern, although completely absent in the initial postoperative trials, was not changed by the cortical ablation. The emotional responses consisted of ear, lip, eye, hair, neck, and head movements in various combinations; pupillary dilation was a part of each individual's response.

The cats also performed the avoidance response in idiosyncratic ways; i.e., they followed superstitious routes or always touched the centerpiece of the double-grill box several times before crossing or carefully positioned themselves "on the mark" to cross in one mighty leap. These idiosyncratic ways of performing the avoidance response were not changed by the cortical lesions.

In short, test stimuli that were reacted to, both before and after ablation of the auditory cortex, in no way elicited different responses, either different conditioned emotional responses or different avoidance responses. The cats, like those described by Guthrie and Horton (1946), had one (or several) ways of performing, and they either responded in these typical fashions or did not respond at all. The one exception to this occurred for all cats at the points on the bar graphs where there is a change in the bar from solid to cross-hatching, i.e., where there is a change from equivalence to non-equivalence. Stimuli in these regions would sometimes produce fragments of the conditioned emotional response. At other times they would produce a complete response (including the avoidance response) or no response at all. Thus the point of change of equivalence on the bar graphs (solid to cross-hatching) is the center of a 5- to 6-db interval in which variable responses were obtained. There could be many reasons for this variability, one of which is that the sound-pressure level varied as much as 5 db as a result of the movements of the cat.

After ablation of the auditory cortex, the generalization tests revealed that the cats made avoidance responses to more stimuli (Fig. 2b). Like the preoperative behavior, this new response pattern was stable. If the conditioned emotional responses had been used as the behavioral indicator in the generalization tests, the generalization data would have been the same except that responses would have been recorded at slightly lower intensities (2 to 5 db).

To control for the general effects of the surgical procedure, one cat (VL6) was subjected to a lesion of non-auditory parts of the neocortex (middle suprasylvian and adjacent lateral gyri). After this lesion (which was somewhat smaller than the lesions of the auditory cortex and therefore does not provide a control for size of lesion), VL6 showed perfect retention on both the buzzer and frequency problems and exhibited no changes on the generalization test. VL6 was then subjected to the lesion of the auditory cortex, after which the generalization changes (Fig. 2) occurred. VL6 was also unique in that she made strong and frequent attempts to bite her way out of the double-grill box during the initial training. This persistence in attempting to escape from the box probably accounts for the large number of sessions required for her to learn the frequency discrimination. VL6 did not learn this discrimination until these attempts to escape stopped. VL7 had no retention test because he was added to the project a month later than the other cats.

The time intervals between the onset of the stimuli and the occurrence of the avoidance responses were recorded for all the training and generalization sessions. An analysis of variance of the latencies was performed to assess the effects of frequency, condition (preoperative versus postoperative), and their interaction. Only the effects of frequency were significant ($F_9{}^3 = 5.52$, P $<$ .05). The average latencies for 1,000, 1,200, 1,400, and 1,600 cps were 10.1, 11.9, 14.0, and 13.8 seconds, respectively.

Anatomy. Figures 3–8 show the midbrain lesions for six of the cats, including the four that subsequently received cortical lesions. Some of the midbrain lesions involve large parts of the lemniscal fibers of the auditory system, but in all cases some of these fibers remained intact. Figures 9 and 10 show the cortical lesions and the retrograde degeneration in the dorsal thalamus for VL7 and T4. There was not much variation in the lesions of the auditory cortex among the four cats, and the extent of the variation in the retrograde degeneration is represented by the differences in VL7 and T4. These differences are not correlated with any aspect of the postoperative behavior.

Discussion

Certain factors may be eliminated as unimportant in the explanation of the changes in equivalence that occurred after ablation of the auditory cortex. Any general effects of the surgical procedure—the drugs that were used or the trauma that occurred—are ruled out by the performance of VL6, who was subjected to surgery of cortex adjacent to the auditory cortex. The behavior of VL6 on the discrimination and generalization tasks was unimpaired by surgery of the adjacent cortical tissue, but changed after the subsequent ablation of auditory cortex. After the cats relearned the frequency discrimination following auditory cortex lesions, there were no changes in the terminal performance level. No more punishment was required to maintain the high performance level after than before the surgery, and this finding is consistent with the performance-level data reported by Goldberg and Neff (1961) for a similar lesion group. There were no differences in the frequency of spontaneous responses in the preoperative and postoperative periods.

Attempts were made to change the generalization behavior of the cats by introducing tetanizing levels of shock. Although this procedure produced obvious changes in the "emotional" state of the cats, it did not change

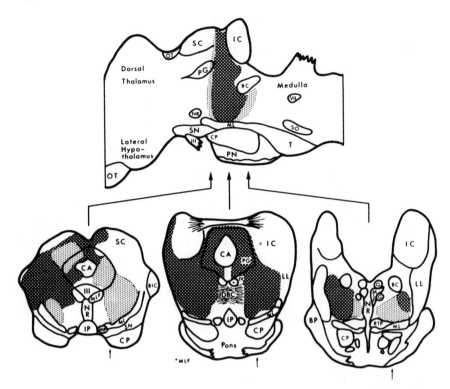

FIG. 3. The midbrain lesion in cat T1. The upper part of the figure is a sagittal reconstruction 2 mm. from the midline. The three lower parts of the figure are transverse sections at the levels indicated by the arrows. Cross-hatching indicates complete absence of neurons; stippling indicates partial absence. Abbreviations for Figs. 3–8: BC, brachium conjunctivum; BIC, brachium of the inferior colliculus; BP, brachium pontis; CA, cerebral aqueduct; CP, cerebral peduncle; DBC, decussation of the brachium conjunctivum; DTD, dorsal tegmental decussation; G, dorsal and ventral tegmental nuclei of Gudden; IC, inferior colliculus; IP, interpeduncular nucleus; LL, lateral lemniscus; MG, medial geniculate; ML, medial lemniscus; MLF, medial longitudinal fasciculus; NR, red nucleus; OT, optic tract; PG, periaqueductal gray; PN, pontile nuclei; RN, raphe nuclei; RTP, nucleus reticularis tegmenti pontis; SC, superior colliculus; SN, substantia nigra; SO, superior olive; T. trapezoid body; III, oculomotor nucleus; IV, trochlear nucleus; VII, facial nucleus.

the responses to the test stimuli. Sidman (1961) and Hearst (this vol., pp. 331–355) did not find any changes in the generalization gradients of monkeys when different amounts of shock were used.

Similar changes in generalization have been obtained after cortical lesions. Diamond (1953) trained cats to a frequency discrimination with 800- and 1,000-cps tones and then presented transposition tests by using different pairs of new frequencies. After ablation of the auditory cortex,

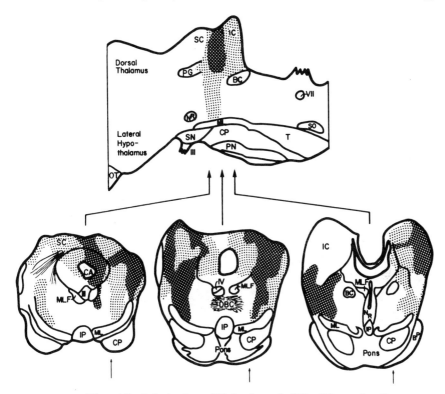

F I G. 4. The midbrain lesion in cat T3. See legend of Fig. 3 for explanation.

Diamond found that the cats performed the avoidance response with pairs of stimuli that were not responded to before the surgery. Thompson (1962) obtained generalization gradients after training normal and lesion groups of cats on an avoidance response to the onset of a 250-cps tone. The cats with lesions of the auditory cortex responded to more test frequencies than normal cats; i.e., there was an increase in equivalence after destruction of the auditory cortex (see Thompson's Fig. 1, this vol., p. 156).

Both Maier (1941) and Wapner (1944) found an increase in equivalent responses after cortical lesions in the rat. Maier and Wapner trained rats on a two-choice visual discrimination and then recorded the rats' responses to new pairs of stimuli. The increase in equivalence after cortical lesions was found to be independent of the locus of lesion by both Maier and Wapner, and Maier found a positive correlation between the size of the lesion and the extent of the increase in equivalence. The present study presents no evidence that size and not locus is the important factor. However, Thompson (1962) obtained data on cats with somatic cortex lesions that indicated normal behavior in generalization tests to tones. And Halstead

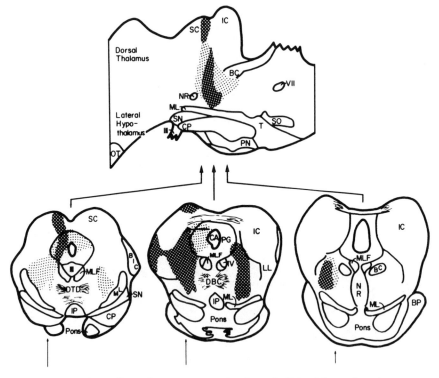

FIG. 5. The midbrain lesion in cat T4. See legend of Fig. 3 for explanation.

(1940) found that the locus of neocortical lesions was of importance in producing generalization changes in humans.

No simple hypothesis that may account for the cat's behavior is provided by the generalization data. An approximation to the condition found before cortical lesion is that the cats respond to any frequency higher than the frequency of the negative stimulus. The cats never responded to the frequency of the negative stimulus or to lower frequencies regardless of intensity, but the exception to the above approximation involves the cat's behavior to high frequencies at very low intensities; the cats did not respond to higher frequencies at low intensities before cortical ablation (Fig. 2a).

After cortical lesion, the situation indicated by the generalization data is similar in that the situation can be described by one rule and one exception: the cats responded to any change in frequency except for the lower frequencies at low intensities. Because this exception occupies only a small area in the test space (Fig. 2b, cross-hatched area), the similar proposals of Thompson (1960) and Diamond et al. (1962) to account for the discriminatory behavior of cats without auditory cortex are good approximations.

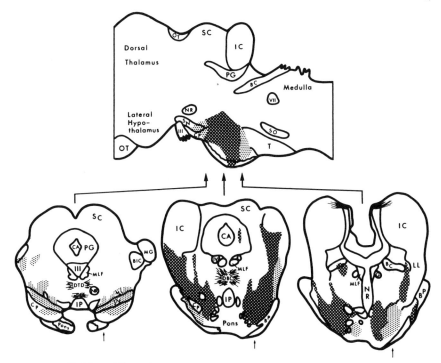

F I G. 6. The midbrain lesion in cat VL2. See legend of Fig. 3 for explanation.

Thompson suggested that auditory operates make "a simple response to change," and Diamond *et al.* suggested that auditory operates respond on the basis of increases in size of neural responses. The fact that auditory operates do not respond to changes to low frequencies at low intensities or to intensity changes of the negative stimulus, and that they respond to different frequencies with different latencies, suggests the requisite complexity that is required for any complete account of this behavior. The specific nature of this requisite complexity is not suggested by the data obtained here.

However, even with consideration of these complexities, the behavior under consideration here seems relatively simple. "Simplicity" has been suggested by Weiskrantz and Mishkin (1958) and discussed by Thompson (1960) as a characteristic of those tasks that are relearned after cortical lesions. "Simplicity" can be defined in two ways. One way is to use learning rate; this definition provides two categories of tasks (easy and difficult) that separate those tasks that are relearned (onset of a sound and the continuous frequency discrimination [Butler *et al.*, 1957] and intensity discrimination [Raab and Ades, 1946]) from those tasks not relearned (the discontinuous frequency discrimination [Meyer *et al.*, 1952], tonal pattern

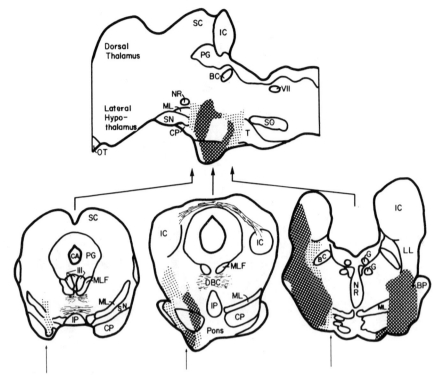

FIG. 7. The midbrain lesion in cat VL6. See legend of Fig. 3 for explanation.

discrimination [Diamond *et al.*, 1957], and the reverse frequency discrimination [Diamond *et al.*, 1962]).

Another way to define simplicity, more anthropomorphic than operational, is in terms of the degree of complexity of the hypothesis that is required of the cat to solve the problem. The data that would permit comparison in these terms are not available. But the nature of the minimum hypothesis suggested for the frequency-discriminatory behavior by the generalization data obtained here (where the "continuous" method of presenting the stimuli was used) is probably toward the simple end of any "simplicity" scale, and intuitively suggests that more complex hypotheses would be required for those tasks that are not learned after ablation of auditory cortex.

Summary

Cats were used in an ablation study with conditioned-avoidance discrimination learning followed by generalization tests as the behavioral indicators. The cats were first subjected to midbrain lesions. These lesions of various size and locus brought about no systematic differences between

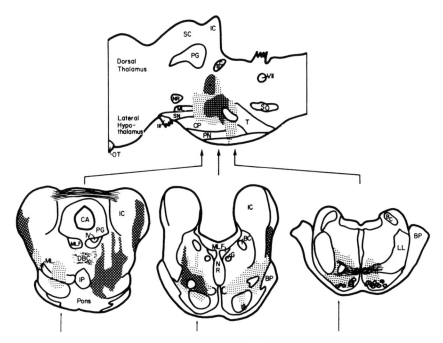

FIG. 8. The midbrain lesion in cat VL7. See legend of Fig. 3 for explanation.

the lesion groups in learning or in generalization. Subsequent ablation of the auditory cortex resulted in changes in generalization.

Addendum

Klüver's monograph on generalization (1933) and the few ablation studies that have used generalization as a behavioral indicator comprise most of the studies where "class" instead of "gradient" data have been systematically considered. With reference to generalization gradients, the two classes of response are those responses greater than the operant level of response and those responses less than the operant level. Thus the points of emphasis in the preceding report are the points where the gradient crosses the operant-response level. Guttman (this vol., pp. 210–217) has found gradients on both sides of the operant rate of response. No multi-dimensional analysis of generalization phenomena, where class and gradient data are both systematically investigated in terms of obtaining a complete specification of the behavioral changes occurring as a result of learning, has been attempted. A complete specification of behavior is highly desirable for ablation studies because of the difficulty of both demonstrating and specifying changes following brain damage. Honig's experiments are among those in this volume that seem to lead in the proper direction.

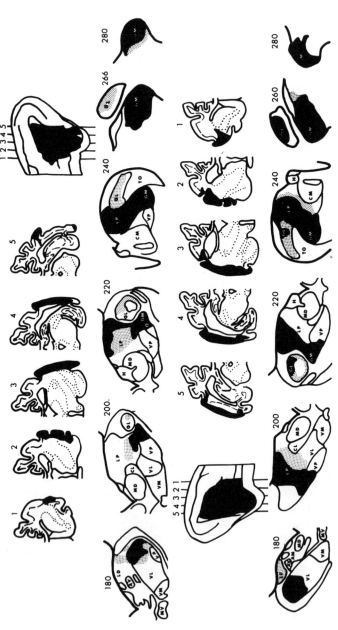

FIG. 9. The cortical lesion and the retrograde thalamic degeneration of cat VL7. The top line shows a lateral view of the left hemisphere together with five frontal sections at the levels indicated by the vertical lines. The lesions are represented by solid black. The second line shows the thalamic degeneration reconstructed from a 50μ coronal series; thus the sections are approximately 1 mm. apart. Solid black indicates severe degeneration, and stippling indicates moderate degeneration. The third and fourth line show the lesion and the degeneration for the right side. The abbreviations are: AM, nucleus antero-medialis; AV, nucleus antero-ventralis; CL, nucleus centralis lateralis; CM, center median; GL, corpus geniculatum laterale; GM, medial geniculate; H, nucleus habenularis; LD, nucleus lateralis dorsalis; LP, nucleus lateralis posterior; MD, nucleus medialis dorsalis; MV, nucleus medialis ventralis; TO, tractus opticus; VL, nucleus ventralis lateralis; VM, nucleus ventralis medialis; VP, nucleus ventralis posterior.

FIG. 10. The cortical lesion and the retrograde thalamic degeneration of cat T4. See legend of Fig. 9 for explanation.

REFERENCES

Butler, R. A., Diamond, I. T., and Neff, W. D. Role of auditory cortex in discriminations of changes in frequency. *J. Neurophysiol.*, 1957, **20**, 108–120.

Diamond, I. T. The function of the auditory cortex: The effect of ablation of the auditory cortex on the discrimination of temporal frequency patterns. Unpublished doctoral dissertation, Univer. of Chicago, 1953.

Diamond, I. T., and Chow, K. L. Biological psychology. In S. Koch (Ed.), *Psychology: A study of a science.* Vol. 4. New York: McGraw-Hill, 1962. Pp. 158–241.

Diamond, I. T., Goldberg, J., and Neff, W. D. Tonal discrimination after ablation of auditory cortex. *J. Neurophysiol.*, 1962, **25**, 223–235.

Diamond, I. T., and Neff, W. D. Ablation of temporal cortex and discrimination of auditory patterns, *J. Neurophysiol.*, 1957, **20**, 300–315.

Goldberg, J., and Neff, W. D. Frequency discrimination after bilateral ablation of cortical auditory areas. *J. Neurophysiol.*, 1961, **24**, 119–128.

Guthrie, E. R., and Horton, G. P. *Cats in a puzzle box.* New York: Rinehart, 1946.

Halstead, W. C. Preliminary analysis of grouping behavior in patients with cerebral injury by the method of equivalent and non-equivalent stimuli. *Amer. J. Psychiat.*, 1940, **96**, 1264–1294.

Holmes, W. The peripheral nerve biopsy. In *Recent advances in clinical pathology.* Philadelphia: Blakiston, ed. 1, 1947.

Klüver, H. *Behavior mechanisms in monkeys.* Chicago: Univer. of Chicago Press, 1933.

Klüver. H. Functional differences between the occipital and temporal lobes with special reference to the interrelations of behavior and extra-cerebral mechanisms. In L. A. Jeffress (Ed.), *Cerebral mechanisms in behavior.* New York: Wiley, 1951. Pp. 147–182.

Klüver, H., and Barrera, E. A method for the combined staining of cells and fibers in the nervous system. *J. Neuropath*, 1955, **12**, 400–403.

Maier, N. The effect of cortical injuries on equivalence reactions in rats. *J. comp. Psychol.*, 1941, **32**, 165–189.

Meyer, D. R., and Woolsey, C. N. Effects of localized cortical destruction upon auditory discriminative conditioning in the cat. *J. Neurophysiol.*, 1952, **15**, 149–162.

Neff, W. D. Role of the auditory cortex in sound discrimination. In G. L. Rasmussen and W. F. Windle (Eds.), *Neural mechanisms of the auditory and vestibular systems.* Springfield, Ill.: Thomas, 1960. Pp. 211–216.

Neff, W. D. Neural mechanisms of auditory discrimination. In W. A. Rosenblith (Ed.), *Sensory communication.* Cambridge, Mass.: M.I.T. Press, 1961. Pp. 259–278.

Neff, W. D., and Diamond, I. T. The neural basis of auditory discrimination. In H. Harlow and C. N. Woolsey (Eds.), *Biological and biochemical bases of behavior.* Madison: Univer. of Wisconsin Press, 1958. Pp. 101–126.

Oesterreich, R., and Neff, W. D. Higher auditory centers and the DL for sound intensities. *Fed. Proc.*, 1960, **19**, 301.

Raab, D. H., and Ades, H. W. Cortical and midbrain mediation of a conditioned discrimination of acoustic intensities. *Amer. J. Psychol.*, 1946, **59**, 59–83.

Randall, W. The behavior of cats (*Felis catus* L.) with lesions in the caudal midbrain region. *Behaviour*, 1964, **23**, 107–139.

Rose, J. E., and Woolsey, C. N. Cortical connections and functional organization of the thalamic auditory system of the cat. In H. Harlow and C. N. Woolsey (Eds.), *Biological and biochemical bases of behavior.* Madison: Univer. of Wisconsin Press, 1958. Pp. 127–150.

Sidman, M. Stimulus generalization in an avoidance situation. *J. exp. Anal. Behav.*, 1961, **4**, 157–169.

Snider, R., and Niemer, W. *A stereotaxic atlas of the cat brain.* Chicago: Univer. of Chicago Press, 1961.

Thompson, R. F. Function of auditory cortex of cat in frequency discrimination. *J. Neurophysiol.*, 1960, **23**, 321–334.

Thompson, R. F. Role of the cerebral cortex in stimulus generalization. *J. comp. physiol. Psychol.*, 1962, **55**, 279–287.

Wapner, S. The differential effects of cortical injury and retesting on equivalence reactions in the rat. *Psychol. Monogr.*, 1944, **57**, 59.

Weiskrantz, L. and Mishkin, M. Effects of temporal and frontal cortical lesions on auditory discrimination in monkeys. *Brain*, 1958, **81**, 406–414.

12. The Neural Basis of Stimulus Generalization

Richard F. Thompson, *University of Oregon Medical School*

Stimulus generalization, the tendency of organisms to respond to stimuli other than the original conditioned stimulus in the absence of differential training, is a basic phenomenon of learning. An adequate neurophysiological theory of stimulus generalization might well facilitate analyses of the more complex processes of learning. General neurophysiological theories of behavior have tended to be global in nature, permitting only qualitative predictions of behavioral events from neurophysiological principles. It may be that a restricted theory dealing with a limited aspect of behavior, in this case stimulus generalization, will permit more quantitative prediction.

A large and elegant literature devoted to precise electrophysiological analyses of cortical and subcortical sensory systems is currently available (see, e.g., Hind *et al.,* 1961; Hubel, 1959; Jung, 1961; Lettvin *et al.,* 1961; Mountcastle, 1957; Mountcastle, Poggio, and Werner, 1963; Woolsey, 1958; Woolsey, 1961). A correspondingly large behavioral literature concerned with the empirical relations of stimulus generalization exists (Mednick and Freedman, 1960). Such parallel data would seem to provide an opportunity for the verification of quantitative predictions relating brain function and behavior. This paper will attempt to demonstrate that a simple theoretical assertion allows precise and quantitative predictions of many behavioral phenomena of stimulus generalization from neurophysiological data.

The first neurophysiological formulation of stimulus generalization was, of course, that of Pavlov, who discovered and characterized the behavioral phenomenon. His familiar concepts of spreading cortical waves of excitation and inhibition became difficult to interpret with the advent of the neuron doctrine in neurophysiology. More recently a network theory, im-

Supported in part by grants from the National Institute of Neurological Diseases and Blindness (B-2161), the National Science Foundation (G-15603), and a Public Health Service research career program award (MH-K3-6650) from the National Institute of Mental Health.

plying the same constructs proposed by Pavlov but in terms of interconnections rather than waves, has been suggested (Wolpe, 1952). Mednick and Freedman (1960) presented a vigorous critique of this approach. Recent developments in neurophysiology permit a much more detailed analysis of potential neural mechanisms underlying generalization behavior than was hitherto possible.

Stimulus generalization is essentially an aspect of learning, in that operational definitions necessitate reference to prior learning. In spite of over 70 years of intensive study, nothing is known today about the neural *mechanisms* of learning (although a great deal is of course known about the general roles of a number of neural structures in various types of learning situations). Consequently, it is unreasonable to expect that current theories can explain in any detail the mechanisms involved in the initial development of generalization gradients through learning, whether this be by failure of discrimination (Lashley and Wade, 1946), development of positive and negative gradients of habit strength (Spence, 1937), or whatever molar constructs are preferred. It would be sufficient if neurophysiological theory could predict the behavioral phenomena of generalization, given a constant level of learning. In brief, can it be demonstrated that an animal is in fact responding to the relative overlap of patterns of neural activity developed in the sensory cortex by the training and test stimuli, given that he has learned to respond to the training stimulus?

Role of the Cerebral Cortex

Before developing the theory in detail, two points must be established: (1) does the cortex play any role in generalization, and (2) can learned and generalized behavior be elicited by electrical activation of sensory cortex? Recent evidence indicates that the sensory cortex is indeed involved in generalization behavior (Thompson, 1962a). Normal cats trained to respond to a tone of 250 cps show a regular decreasing gradient of response to tones of higher frequencies (Thompson, 1958). Animals with prior total bilateral removal of all auditory cortex subsequently trained in the same way respond equally to all test tones up to at least 5 octaves' separation, thus showing total generalization—i.e., no generalization gradient was developed (Thompson, 1962). Figure 1 illustrates these results in terms of both absolute and relative generalization performance. As indicated, animals with ablation of somatic sensory cortex tested at 2,000 cps behaved as did normals (upper graph of Fig. 1), thus suggesting that the effect was specific to auditory cortex.

It is of fundamental importance to note that this finding does not result from a postoperative "failure of discrimination." *Animals with the same cortical lesions can, under appropriate conditions of training, learn frequency discriminations rapidly and with normal preoperative differential*

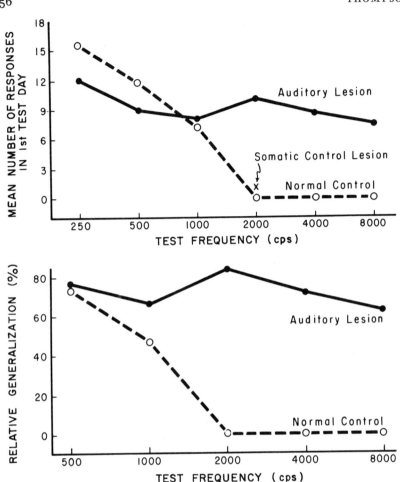

FIG. 1. (Top). Absolute frequency-generalization gradients for normal, auditory lesion and somatic sensory-control lesion cats. (Bottom). Relative generalization gradients for the normal and auditory lesion groups. All animals were trained at 250 cps, and separate subgroups were tested at octave multiples. (Taken from Thompson [1962a].)

frequency thresholds (Butler, Diamond, and Neff, 1957; Thompson, 1960; Goldberg and Neff, 1961). Thus cortical lesions can differentiate between generalization and discrimination behavior. This differentiation deserves emphasis in view of current tendencies to consider either generalization or discrimination the "basic process" and the other an epiphenomenon, even though the respective operational definitions generally differ (Prokasy and Hall 1963). Empirically, generalization and discrimination *may* be considered as two aspects of the same set of operations. If an organism trained to one stimulus responds less to another, this can be labeled as either incomplete generalization or incomplete discrimination (Brown, this vol., pp. 7–23). Viewed in this way, ablation of auditory cortex results in total generalization, or total failure to discriminate, under conditions of generalization (i.e., single-stimulus) training, but results in normal discrimination behavior under other conditions.

The study by Randall (this vol., pp. 134–153) demonstrates the same total generalization behavior in cats following ablation of auditory cortex, using different testing procedures from those of Thompson (1962a). Butter, Mishkin, and Rosvold (this vol., pp. 119–133) also report much increased visual generalization behavior in rhesus monkeys following temporal lesions. Recent studies are thus in agreement in finding marked increases in generalization following cortical ablation.

The other point, whether electrical activation of cortex will of itself elicit learned and generalized responses, was established a number of years ago by the pioneering investigations of Loucks (1938), Culler (1938), Brogden and Gantt (1937), and others. They demonstrated that animals could be trained to respond to electrical stimulation of the cortex, and that a stimulus to the brain could serve as an unconditioned stimulus. More recently, some of these findings have been repeated by Doty, Rutledge, and Larsen (1956). Doty and Rutledge (1959) further demonstrated that animals trained to respond at the 60 per cent level to either peripheral or electrocortical stimulation of one modality showed generalization to stimulation of another modality.

Thompson (1959) has shown that while behavioral generalization across sensory modalities does occur after acquisition training to the 50 per cent level, *no* cross-modal generalization occurs when animals are first trained to the 90 per cent level. This latter condition has not yet been fulfilled for brain stimulation across "modalities," so the extent of parallelism cannot be ascertained. However, a study by Grosser and Harrison (1960) showed that if care was taken to stimulate two entirely separate populations of cells in the visual cortex of rat electrically, no "cross-stimulus" generalization occurred when the animals were first trained to the 90 per cent response level on one stimulus. In any event, it is now well established that electrical activation of the sensory cortex, even of an "unadequate" nature, will elicit learned and generalized responses.

Feasibility of "Connectionistic" Models

The present theory will assume that neurons interact by means of anatomical synaptic interconnections. The diagram of Fig. 2 illustrates the simplest kind of overlap of two stimulus inputs permitting interaction. This diagram is meant to represent a possible synaptic relay at any point in the central nervous system. Consider first the excitatory circuit represented by the curved synaptic endings on the large open-circle neurons. A response

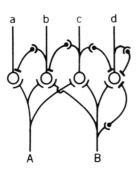

FIG. 2. Possible synaptic mechanisms at a given relay in the central nervous system. Curved endings are excitatory synapses; small filled neurons with bar endings are inhibitory. A and B are input channels or neurons; a, b, c, and d are output neurons.

is learned to the pattern of neuronal excitation resulting from stimulation of channel A. Activation of channel B results in a neural pattern having some elements in common with that of A, and as a consequence a partial response is given.

The real situation is undoubtedly far more complex than this. The small filled-circle neurons in the diagram represent possible inhibitory interconnections between neurons. The various interconnections illustrated have in fact been demonstrated to exist in the spinal cord (Eccles, 1957). Such a system will exhibit differential response not only to A and B inputs, but also to differing intensities of input in A or B, and to simultaneous inputs of differing intensities in A and B. It is even possible to obtain asymmetrical differential response patterns from weak to strong and strong to weak inputs for such a system. Thus suppose a weak stimulus to channel B results in more excitatory than inhibitory activity, producing a moderate amount of activity in channels b, c, and d. With high-intensity stimulation to channel B, channels b and c might increase activity, but inhibitory activity on d might increase to the point that channel d stabilized below discharge threshold. Thus all channels activated by the strong stimulus are also activated by the weak stimulus, but all channels activated by the weak stimulus are not activated by the strong stimulus.

Consequently, in the final common pathway, there would be more generalization response strength with training to the weak stimulus and testing to the strong stimulus than vice versa. It would obviously not be profitable to elaborate such a hypothesized model because of present limited knowledge concerning which mechanisms are operative in the various regions of the central nervous system. The model of Fig. 2 was presented merely to show that such a connectionistic approach is feasible.

Hypothesis

In attempting to make behavioral predictions from neurophysiological data, the following working hypothesis will be used. Assuming that (1) a relatively stable measure of generalization is used, (2) some degree of learning to the training stimulus has occurred, and (3) drive level is held relatively constant, *the amount of behavioral stimulus generalization given by an organism to a test stimulus is a monotonic (linear?) increasing function of the degree of overlap of excitation in the cerebral cortex resulting from the training and test stimuli.* The phrase "overlap of excitation in the cerebral cortex" need not imply that all neural interactions responsible for generalization occur in the cortex. Such stimulus-produced interactions undoubtedly occur at many levels from receptor to cortex. It is only necessary to *know* the patterns of cortical excitation to predict generalization behavior.

Because of an almost total lack of neurophysiological information, it is difficult even to speculate about the "readout" system from cortex to response. The present hypothesis assumes that there is a predictable relationship between pattern of activation in the cortex and response strength. Training to a given stimulus somehow results in a link between the pattern of cortical excitation resulting from the stimulus and the response. The degree of overlap of cortical excitation, or number of common cortical elements activated by the test and training stimuli, determines the probability that the response will occur to the test stimulus. This hypothetical approach has the implicit assumption that the cerebral cortex is the "final common pathway" in the brain for *behavioral* response prediction.

The study by Grosser and Harrison (1960) cited above provides direct evidence concerning the proposed hypothesis. In addition to finding no generalization with electrical stimuli to separate populations of cells in the visual cortex, they found that if the electrical stimuli were increased sufficiently in intensity to activate a common overlap population of cells, behavioral generalization from one stimulus to the other did occur.

In attempting to determine degree of overlap of cortical excitation, at least two types of measures are available: single nerve-cell recordings and gross evoked responses. While single-unit data provide exact information about the stimulus conditions and parameters that will activate a given cell, the sampling problem is difficult. Gross evoked responses, presumably summated graded synaptic potentials, provide a measure of the activity of large populations of neurons, but whether the activity is excitatory, inhibitory, or a combination of these cannot be determined. The relations between the two measures are not always clear. Gross evoked responses can be obtained in the absence of unit discharges. Further, when units are activated there is not always a simple relationship between the latency and pattern of unit activity and the gross evoked response. However, under conditions of moderate anesthesia, the great majority of unit discharges to a synchronous peripheral stimulus do tend to occur with fixed temporal relations to the gross evoked response. In the present discussion, unit data will be taken from studies that have used relatively large samples, and gross evoked responses will be assumed to represent activation of the cortex. It should be pointed out that there is close correspondence of *location* on the cortex for gross and unit activation by a given peripheral stimulus.

An Application of the Hypothesis

Neurophysiological data. Having established that the cortex plays a significant role in generalization, we will give a brief demonstration of the application of neurophysiological data to behavioral generalization. Generalization along the dimensions involving spatial cortical representation of receptors (basilar membrane = auditory frequency; skin surface = local sign; retina = location in space) are obviously the simplest systems where neurophysiological and behavioral results can be compared. Auditory freqency generalization of cats will be used since both types of data are available here.

A brief summary of data from a recent publication by Hind *et al.* (1961) analyzing activity of single neurons in the auditory cortex of cat follows. Extracellular responses of single cells were isolated with a microelectrode, and the frequency-threshold relation for each cell determined. Typically, a cell had a best frequency where the threshold was much lower (e.g., 70 db) than at other frequencies. Examples of response characteristics of a few such cells, taken from Hind *et al.* (1961), are shown in Fig. 3. Each separate graph is the threshold sound-pressure level (SPL) vs. frequency plot for an individual cortical cell. In many cases, cells having differing best frequencies were found in the same penetration of cortex by the microelectrode, but the range of best frequencies was less than 3 octaves for 93 per cent of the penetrations.

The response bandwidths of single cells at best frequencies increased as stimulus intensity was increased above response threshold. At 20 db above best-frequency threshold, 90 per cent had bandwidths less than 3 octaves, and at 40 db above best-frequency threshold, 75 per cent had bandwidths less than 3 octaves. The decrease in number of units with increasing bandwidth is approximately linear for the 40-db condition. Best-frequency thresholds for the units ranged approximately from 0 to 80 db re .0002 dynes/cm^2, and seemed to average about 30 db re .0002 dynes/cm^2. Thus for the 60-db loudness level used in the behavioral data to be given below, the bandwidths of most of the units would be below 4 octaves. Best-frequency points were distributed on the cortex in such a way that a linear relationship obtained between best frequency and distance along the auditory cortex. The equation for the best-fitting straight line was of the form

$$Y = 4.2X - 24 ,$$

where Y is the best frequency in Kc/sec. and X is the distance in mm. from the posterior estosylvian sulcus.

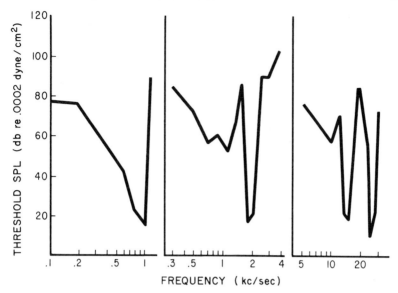

FIG. 3. Examples of threshold vs. frequency plots for three individual cortical auditory neurons. (Taken from Hind *et al.* [1961].)

The above data suggest several predictions of frequency-generalization behavior. First, the total range of generalization should not exceed approximately 3 octaves, this being the extent of overlap of excitation for most of the unit data at the appropriate intensity level. Second, the form of the generalization gradient may well be a linear function of the distance along the cortex separating the training and test tone best-frequency points. By assuming that response strength 3 octaves from the training stimulus is zero, it is possible to write a linear equation predicting generalization performance. In the behavioral data given below, all animals were trained at 250 cps and tested at higher octaves for generalization. From the equation given above for best-frequency points on the cortex, a frequency increase of 3 octaves above 250 cps represents a distance of 0.42 mm. on the auditory cortex. At this distance response strength should be zero. If the equation is of the form

$$Y^1 = BX_T + A ,$$

where Y^1 = response strength and X_T = distance along cortex from the training tone, then A, the intercept constant, will equal the response strength to the training tone, i.e., $Y^1 = B(0) + A$, so that $A = Y^1$. When X is .42 mm., Y^1 will equal zero (see above), and B, the slope constant, will equal $-A/0.42$. Thus the general equation will be

$$Y^1 = \frac{-A}{0.42} X_T + A ,$$

where A, response strength to the training tone, is the only parameter. The derivation and parameters of the equation are thus *completely independent* of generalization-behavior data.

Behavioral data. The data presented here are taken from a previous study (Thompson, 1958). Cats were trained using instrumental shock avoidance in the Brogden-Culler Wheel to respond to a 250-cps tone of approximately 60 db loudness level re .0002 dynes/cm². Different subgroups were tested for generalization at 500, 1,000, 2,000, 4,000, and 8,000 cps. Loudness level was randomly varied over a restricted range to prevent possible loudness cues. The data presented here are for all animals trained initially to respond more than 50 per cent of the time to the training stimulus. Upon completion of training, all animals were extinguished (20 trials/day) to the appropriate test tone. A given animal was tested to only one tone. A control group was extinguished to the 250-cps training tone. The three possible measures of generalization strength, number of responses to first response failure, number of responses in first test day, and number of responses to extinction, were analyzed for stability and reliability, and the number of responses in the first test day (20 trials) measure was found to be the best (Thompson, 1958). However, all measures gave comparable results. The generalization data for this measure are shown in Fig. 4, with frequency plotted on the usual geometric scale. Each point is the mean for 8 animals. There was no generalization to tones higher than 2,000 cps, and essentially none at 2,000 cps.

The first prediction from the neurophysiological data is thus borne out—generalization does not extend beyond 3 octaves. The form of the curve is clearly non-linear, but the geometric frequency scale does not correspond

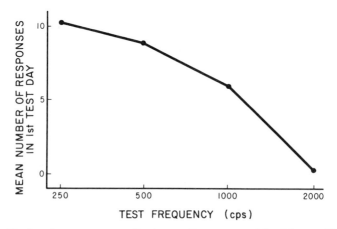

FIG. 4. Absolute frequency-generalization gradient averaged for 32 cats. All animals trained at 250 cps; separated subgroups tested at 250 cps and octave multiples. (Based on data from Thompson [1958].)

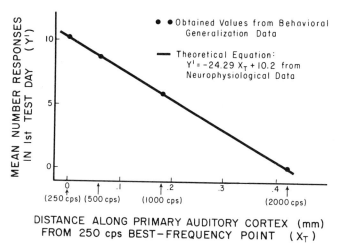

FIG. 5. Dots represent data of Fig. 4 plotted in terms of distance along auditory cortex. Straight line is plot of theoretical equation derived from neurophysiological data.

to distance along the cortex for best-frequency points. In Fig. 5, the data are plotted in terms of distance along the cortex from the training tone. The dots give the behavioral data. The general linear equation derived above from neurophysiological data was

$$Y^1 = \frac{-A}{0.42} X_T + A .$$

The response strength to the training stimulus, A, is here equal to 10.20. Thus

$$Y^1 = \frac{-10.20}{0.42} X_T + 10.20$$

$$= -24.29 X_T + 10.20$$

is the equation relating response strength to distance along the cortex from the training stimulus. The straight line of Fig. 5 is this equation.

The general hypothesis is thus seen to be successful in prediction of auditory frequency-generalization behavior in normal animals. Can it predict the total generalization behavior shown by animals with auditory cortex removed (Thompson, 1962a)? It might seem on a priori grounds that one could equally well predict total frequency generalization or no frequency generalization following the ablation of auditory cortex. The hypothesis requires response to the *cortical* pattern of excitation resulting from test and training tones. When the cortical auditory field is removed, an additional cortical system may be invoked to permit prediction from the hypothesis. Responses can be evoked in "association" areas of the cerebral cortex of cat to click stimulation, using chloralose anesthetic (cf. Figs. 9 and 10) (Buser, Borenstein, and Bruner, 1959; Thompson and Sindberg, 1960). These association-response fields to auditory stimulation, following ablation of auditory cortex with subsequent total degeneration of the medial geniculate body, are identical in appearance and distribution to those seen in the normal anesthetized cat (Thompson and Sindberg, 1960). Thus the auditory association-response system projects to the cortex quite independently of the classical thalamo-cortical auditory system, and remains intact following chronic total removal of the temporal auditory cortex.

According to our generalization hypothesis, animals with prior removal of auditory cortex would thus be expected to respond in terms of the overlap of excitation in the auditory association response fields of the cortex to the training and test stimuli. The distribution of evoked responses in the primary field and the suprasylvian association fields to electrical stimulation of the basal (high frequency) and apical (low frequency) turns of the cochlear nerve were studied (Thompson and Sindberg, 1960). Primary auditory areas I and II exhibited the typical tonotopic organization seen using pentobarbital (Woolsey, 1961), with high frequencies represented in anterior AI and posterior AII, and low frequencies represented in posterior AI and anterior AII. Although there are minor differences in amplitude of response in the suprasylvian association field, the distribution of responses is *identical* for both stimulation sites. There is no tonotopic organization in the auditory association fields; the overlap of excitation is total. Thus our hypothesis would predict 100 per cent generalization to all test frequencies in animals with auditory cortex removed but association cortex intact. This was the obtained result.

Objections to the Hypothesis

The demonstration of behavioral prediction from neurophysiological data given above was relatively successful. However, it can be argued that such success must of necessity result from the uniform layout of frequency representation along the auditory cortex. This, together with the fact that a frequency-generalization gradient averaged for a large number of animals is likely to give a monotonic function, may suggest to some that the approach is of limited value. The predictive utility of the general hypothesis would be more convincing if it could be shown to handle specific contradictions that have been pointed out between neurophysiological and behavioral data. Mednick and Freedman (1960) listed a series of such contradictions: (1) the disproportionate representation of different regions of body surface on cortex does not correspond to obtained generalization gradients on skin; (2) body-surface representation on the cortex is very distorted, but obtained generalization gradients on skin are smooth; (3) the organization of the auditory cortex cannot account for the "octave gen-

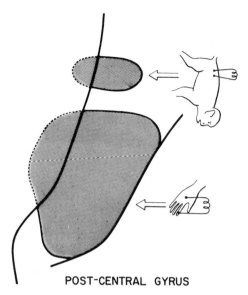

POST-CENTRAL GYRUS

F I G. 6. Areas of cortex excited by identical stimuli to finger and back of *Macaca mulatta.*

eralization" effect; and (4) since there is no neuronal representation of intensity, intensity generalization cannot be accounted for.

The first two objections concern the lack of correspondence between generalization data obtained on the skin surface and the projection of the skin surface on the primary somatic sensory cortex. These objections are telling against any hypothetical wavelike process spreading across the cortex. It will be shown here that they do not contradict the overlap-of-excitation hypothesis. The detailed projection of the skin to the cortex in rhesus monkey has been studied by Woolsey and colleagues (Woolsey, 1958). In brief, the cortical hand area is much expanded relative to the back area, and splits the head area into two separate regions (Woolsey, 1958). The essential relations are comparable to those for man (Penfield and Rasmussen, 1950).

The first specific objection refers to generalization gradients obtained on the hand vs. gradients obtained on the back. Grant and Dittmer (1940) reported that the generalization gradient is steeper for 4-in. steps along the back than it is for 1-in. steps along the finger. It is argued that since the cortical hand area is much larger than the cortical back area, just the opposite effect should result. The argument assumes a point-to-point projection from skin to cortex. In fact, a given stimulus to a point on the hand excites a much wider area of cortex than does the same stimulus to the back. This is illustrated in Fig. 6, where the total evoked-response fields for the same stimulus delivered to the hand and to the back are shown.

The data were taken in 1-mm. steps on the post-central gyrus of an anesthetized rhesus macaque to electrical stimulation by a single pulse of 1 msec. duration delivered through two needles inserted 1 cm. apart on the hand or on the back. Stimulus intensity was the same for both stimulus loci. The total cortical area activated for hand stimulation was approximately 70 sq. mm., and for back stimulation was approximately 10 sq. mm. Thus the overlap of excitation on the hand area of cortex will be considerably greater than on the back area. In fact, equal gradients might be expected only if the ratio of physical distances for hand-to-back stimuli were 7 : 1. For the ratio of 4 : 1 used by Grant and Dittmer (1940), our general hypothesis would predict the back gradient to be steeper than the hand gradient. This was the obtained result.

The other objection concerning the somatic sensory system refers to the fact that smooth generalization gradients are found on skin in spite of distorted projection of the skin surface on the somatic sensory cortex (e.g., Bass and Hull, 1934). A good example of this distortion is found in the projection of the head surface to the cortex. As noted, the hand area has expanded so much in rhesus (and man) that it splits the head into two widely separated areas (Woolsey, 1958). In rodents and carnivores, where the hand area is relatively smaller, this has not occurred (Woolsey, 1958). Since smooth generalization gradients would presumably be obtained across the head, with no "hole" and no intervening spread to the hand, cortical organization contradicts behavior. This argument is valid only in terms of an hypothetical wavelike process irradiating over the surface of the cortex. Such, of course, is not the case. Overlap of excitation is the result

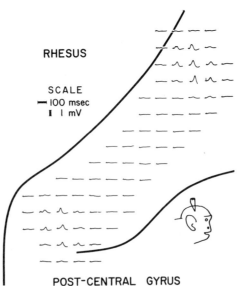

FIG. 7a. One-mm. map of evoked response fields on post-central tactile area of *Macaca mulatta* resulting from stimulation of single point on skin of head (see text).

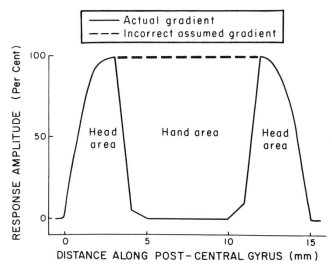

FIG. 7b. Gradient of excitation as a function of distance along post-central tactile area for data of 7a.

of *interconnections* at all levels from the periphery to the cortex. For excitation to "spread" from one portion of the head representation to the other, it is not necessary to activate the intervening hand area. The interconnections are such that the hand area simply is not there.

The evoked-response map shown in Fig. 7a was obtained under the following conditions to illustrate this. A point on the lateral surface of the head of an anesthetized rhesus macaque was stimulated with a single electrical pulse delivered through two needles 1 mm. apart, and the cortical response fields in somatic sensory area I (post-central gyrus) mapped. As seen, there are two entirely separate responsive fields, the intervening hand area being completely silent. A gradient of excitation for this hand field is illustrated in Fig. 7b. The solid line indicates the actual gradient, the dotted line the gradient postulated by the objection cited above. From the actual gradient of excitation our general hypothesis would predict a relatively smooth generalization gradient across the head.

The third objection, dealing with the "octave generalization" effect, appears more serious. The effect was first noted by Humphreys (1939) and subsequently studied carefully by Blackwell and Schlosberg (1943). In the latter study, rats trained to a 10,000-cps tone were tested for generalization at other frequencies. The percentage of responses to the octave tone of 5,000 cps was some 13 per cent higher than that expected on the basis of a smooth decreasing curve drawn through the other points. An effort was made to eliminate overtones as a source of error. Mednick and Freedman (1960) argue very effectively that the smooth and regular representation of frequency along the auditory cortex stands in contradiction to the

behavioral results. This effect has been a considerable barrier to the development of a straightforward neurophysiological theory of stimulus generalization. However, electrophysiological data from the study of Hind
et al. (1961), cited extensively above, make this effect an elegant example
of the correspondence of neurophysiological and behavioral phenomena.
Some cells of the auditory cortex have more than one "best frequency"
(cf. Fig. 3). In most cases, the additional best frequencies are approximately *octave multiples* of the "fundamental" best frequency. In all these
cases acoustic resonance and other possible artifacts were ruled out.

The fundamental best frequency generally corresponds to the best frequency for the particular region of cortex determined by gross evoked-
response mapping, and "other best frequencies" are additional low-thresh-
old frequencies. To determine whether the other best frequencies tended
to be approximately octave multiples of the fundamental, the multiple-
response unit data from Hind *et al.* (1961) were reanalyzed as follows: A
range of frequencies from the fundamental to somewhat less than 2 octaves
higher was subdivided into four equal intervals, with the octave multiple
of the fundamental being the midpoint of one of the intervals. The probability of another best frequency's lying in the octave range by chance is
then ¼. Of twelve multiple response pairings, nine were approximate octave multiples. The probability of nine or more such occurrences in twelve
is 1 in 10,000 by chance. Thus there is a significant tendency for other best
frequencies to be approximate octave multiples of the fundamental best
frequency.

The neurophysiological and behavioral "octave" effects are of the same
general order of magnitude: roughly 10 per cent of the cells studied show
the effect, and, behaviorally, response strength is about 13 per cent higher
than a smooth decreasing generalization gradient would predict. Consequently, the octave-generalization effect can be predicted from neurophysiological data, and is in complete accord with our general hypothesis
that amount of generalization is a direct function of overlap of excitation
in the cortex.

The final objection to a neurophysiological approach to stimulus generalization is concerned with intensity generalization. Mednick and Freedman
(1960, p. 190) argue that since "degree of intensity of a stimulus is not
reflected in the firing of a specific neuron, it is not clear how common pathways can develop in the intensity dimension." To the contrary, there is a
very clear effect of intensity on cell activity. As intensity of stimulus is increased, the bandwidth of frequencies to which a cell will respond increases
(cf. Fig. 3). Consequently, degree of stimulus intensity is very definitely
reflected in the behavior of a given neuron. An additional finding of the
Hind *et al.* (1961) study suggests a possible mechanism for the differential
steepness of high to low vs. low to high intensity generalization gradients.
They noted that some cells tended to stop firing as intensity of tone was

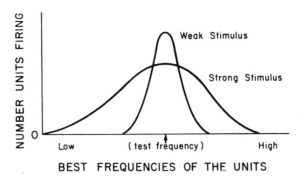

FIG. 8. Hypothetical diagram illustrating effects of stimulus intensity on activity of cortical auditory cells for a given stimulus frequency.

increased above from 20 to 40 db above best-frequency threshold. Both intensity effects are illustrated in the diagram of Fig. 8.

If we limit our considerations to units having best frequencies at the frequency used for testing intensity generalization, it will be seen that the weak stimulus activates all units activated by the strong stimulus, but that the strong stimulus does not activate all units activated by the weak stimulus. In other words, when training is to the weak stimulus, no new elements are activated by the strong test stimulus, but when training is to the strong stimulus, new elements are activated by the weak test stimulus. The strong-to-weak generalization gradient would thus be steeper than the weak-to-strong gradient. Hovland (1937) and Brown (1942) have reported such effects.

Predictions from the Hypothesis

The general hypothesis relating stimulus-generalization behavior to overlap of excitation of training and test stimuli on the cerebral cortex has permitted quantitative prediction of auditory frequency-generalization behavior and resolved a number of apparent contradictions between cortical organization and generalization behavior. It also permits predictions about behavioral studies as yet unperformed. For example, Fig. 8 indicates that strong-intensity stimuli activate cells over a wider range of frequencies than do weak stimuli. Thus it can be predicted that a strong-intensity training tone will result in more frequency generalization than a weak-intensity training tone. Figure 8 also illustrates the fact that the frequency-threshold curves for auditory cells are asymmetric: at higher intensities, cells respond to a wider spread of frequencies below best frequency than above it. Thus animals trained at a given frequency should show a steeper generalization gradient to tones above the training tone than to tones below it.

These predictions are not completely surprising on the basis of other theoretical positions—i.e., Hullian treatment of intensity (Hull, 1949) for the first prediction, and reference to the frequency just noticeable difference (JND) scale for the second. A more unexpected prediction can be made from an electrophysiological study by Tunturi (1952) on the auditory cortex of dog. He found that intensity tended to have an area representation at right angles to frequency on the auditory cortex of the hemisphere contralateral to the ear stimulated, but no differential representation on the ipsilateral hemisphere. Thus animals with the left cochlea and right auditory cortex destroyed should have much steeper intensity generalization gradients than animals with the left cochlea and left auditory cortex destroyed. Clearly, such predictions as this could not be made by other types of theory.

Effect of Acquisition Level on Generalization

The discussion to this point has assumed a relatively fixed level of learning in attempting to predict behavioral generalization from pattern of cortical excitation. However, there is a considerable behavioral literature dealing with effects of acquisition level on stimulus generalization. Because so little is currently known about neural mechanisms and systems involved in learning, any discussion of the possible neural basis for the effect of acquisition level on generalization must of necessity be very speculative. Since generalization and discrimination may be viewed empirically as two aspects of the same behavior (Brown, this vol., pp. 7–23), any model concerned with learning effects on generalization must also be consistent with discrimination-learning data. For brevity the model developed here will be limited to auditory and auditory-visual generalization and discrimination phenomena, and should be looked upon as only a very tentative suggestion.

A number of studies have indicated that relative generalization is greater in the early stages of learning and becomes more restricted with increased training to the training stimulus (Hovland, 1937; Razran, 1949; Littman, 1949; Thompson, 1958; Mednick and Freedman, 1960; etc.). Absolute generalization also becomes more restricted for stimuli relatively unlike the training stimulus (Thompson, 1958; Thompson, 1959), and even for stimuli similar to the training stimulus when overtraining is given (Hoffeld, 1962). Results of the study by Ganz and Riesen (1962), where dark-reared monkeys gave flat hue gradients on first test trials, are consistent with these findings. Thus in the earlier stages of single-stimulus training, an organism tends to respond to a wide variety of stimuli, but in later stages of learning the class of response-eliciting stimuli becomes restricted to the training-stimulus modality. A regular gradient develops that becomes progressively steeper with further training.

A cortical system mediating generalization phenomena characteristic of early stages of training should thus be activated by all varieties of stimuli, but should stop responding, i.e., habituate, during the course of training. For the later stages of training a modality-specific system permitting progressive steepening of the response gradient might be invoked. It is suggested here that in the normal mammal, cortical association-response fields play a special role in the early stages of learning, and that primary sensory areas are more concerned with the subsequent steepening of the response gradient later in learning. The primary auditory cortex, for example, has previously been implicated in the development of response inhibition, at least where auditory frequency is the cue (Thompson, 1960; Thompson, 1962a). Thus, after ablation of auditory cortex, the normal frequency-generalization gradient does not develop; animals respond equally to all test stimuli (Thompson, 1962a; Randall, 1963).

Further, frequency discrimination cannot be relearned following ablation of auditory cortex if any type of training procedure requiring the development of response inhibition to the negative stimulus complex is used (Allen, 1945; Meyer and Woolsey, 1952; Thompson, 1960). Development of response inhibition has been suggested as the fundamental process in discrimination learning (Harlow and Hicks, 1957) and as a basic aspect of conditioning (Konorski, 1948).

Evoked association responses to auditory, visual, and somatic stimuli, obtained using chloralose anesthetic, have been described for several cortical regions of cat (Amassian, 1954; Albe-Fessard and Rougeul, 1958; Buser *et al.*, 1959; Thompson and Sindberg, 1960). Recent evidence indicates that there are four such response fields in cat, two on the suprasylvian gyrus, one on the anterior lateral gyrus, and one on pericruciate cortex, that respond in an equivalent and non-specific fashion to all modalities of stimulation (Thompson, Johnson, and Hoopes, 1963; Thompson, Smith, and Bliss, 1963). An example of such data is shown in Fig. 9, where association responses on the middle suprasylvian gyrus of cat evoked by auditory, visual and somatic stimuli are shown. For all stimuli the regions of cortex activated are identical.

A summary diagram showing the association response fields and their relations to various sensory specific and motor area of the cortex of cat is given in Fig. 10. Current data suggest that this response system may involve the ascending reticular formation (Albe-Fessard, Bowsher, and Mallart, 1962; Thompson, 1962b; Thompson, Johnson, and Hoopes, 1963). The reticular formation in turn plays a major role in EEG activation (Moruzzi and Magoun, 1949). Sharpless and Jasper (1956) have shown that EEG activation, recorded from suprasylvian cortex of cat, habituates to a repeated auditory stimulus. Finally, cortical EEG activation appears to become progressively more restricted as training is continued (Morrell and Jasper, 1956).

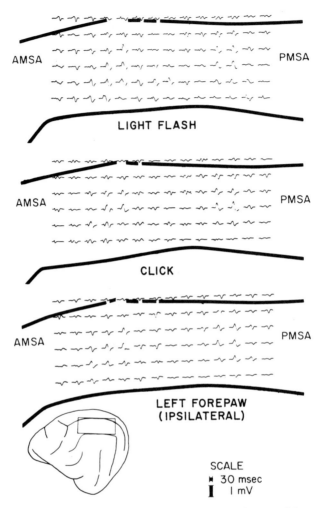

FIG. 9. One-mm. maps of evoked association responses to three modalities of stimulation on the middle suprasylvian gyrus of cat (see inset) under chloralose anesthetic. Taken from Thompson, Johnson, and Hoopes [1963].)

Thus it might be assumed that the cortical association-response fields represent non-specific but localized projection foci of the ascending reticular formation. In the early stages of training many types of stimuli would activate this system and hence have similar probabilities of eliciting a behavioral response. As training proceeds, cortical activation would become limited to modality-specific primary sensory cortical areas, which would then be responsible for the subsequent development of the gradient

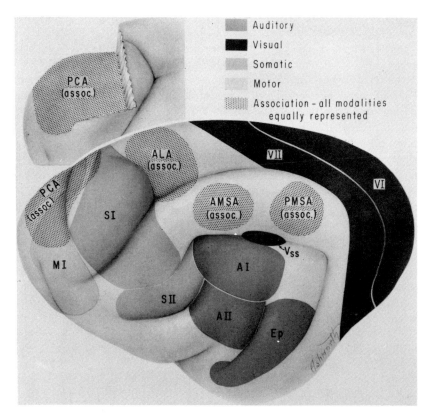

F I G. 10. Summary diagram of cat cerebral cortex showing relation of association evoked response areas to the various sensory specific fields and motor area. (Taken from Thompson, Johnson, and Hoopes [1963].)

of generalization, whose form and characteristics are predictable from the neural organization of primary sensory cortex (see above).

Results of several studies are at least consistent with this tentative view of the behavioral role of cortical association response areas. Generalization across sensory modalities, for example, is characteristically found only in the earlier stages of learning (Pavlov, 1927; Thompson, 1959). After ablation of auditory cortex alone, cats can learn to discriminate frequency only by training procedures involving response to changes from ongoing background stimulation (Butler *et al.*, 1957; Thompson, 1960; Goldberg and Neff, 1961), where habituation of EEG activation in association response areas could occur (Sharpless and Jasper, 1956). After joint ablation of auditory and association areas, animals are unable to discriminate frequency by any training procedure (Thompson, 1964).

A more general statement of the hypothesis developed here concerning association-response areas of the cerebral cortex would be that they play a special role in a variety of behavioral phenomena associated with the earlier stages of learning, phenomena that have often been characterized by the term "attention." If association-evoked responses in fact represent localized cortical projections of the ascending reticular formation, the work of Lindsley and others on the role of the reticular formation in attention (e.g., Lindsley, 1958) adds face validity to our hypothesis.

A number of testable predictions can be developed from this view. The orienting response to novel stimuli shown by normal animals, which can serve as an operational definition of "attention," ought to be much impaired after ablation of association-response areas, as would the related phenomena of "curiosity" behavior. Animals with such lesions should not show cross-modal generalization even in the earlier stages of learning; they ought not to develop auditory-visual sensory preconditioning, and might be expected to have difficulty with auditory-visual conditional learning tasks. Somewhat unexpected is the prediction that animals with these lesions will have great difficulty learning auditory frequency discrimination by the response to change from background stimulation training procedure, *even though the auditory cortex is intact*. Finally, a predictable relation should exist between amplitude of the evoked association response and behavioral state of attention.

Conclusions

In attempting to demonstrate a consistent relationship between cortical activity and behavioral generalization, a number of close parallels were developed. However, it must be admitted that many behavioral observations cannot be predicted accurately at present by the methods of analysis used above. For example, Hebb (1958) has emphasized that the generalization behavior of chimpanzees and rats is very different after training to the same stimulus object. Many of the generalization studies using humans (Mednick and Freedman, 1960), where verbal mediation may play a role, are also difficult to interpret in neurophysiological terms. Such species-specific effects are of course not contradictory with our approach, but rather too complex to handle at present.

A general result of this analysis has been at least partial verification of the assumption that overlapping patterns of excitation on the cortex are predictively related to behavior. The cerebral cortex might well be regarded as the final common pathway determining behavioral response probability. If this view has any general validity, it may be feasible to apply the method of analysis to classes of behavior other than stimulus generalization. Such an approach has of course been utilized quite successfully in psychophysical research. Elegant examples are Bartley's predictions of brightness-enhancement phenomena from patterns of cortical activity (Bartley, 1939; Bartley and Nelson, 1963), and Mountcastle's demonstration (Mountcastle *et al.*, 1963) that discharge frequencies of thalamic neurons are related to intensity of kinesthetic stimulus by the same type of power function that Stevens (1957) has found for the relation between stimulus intensity and psychophysical judgment.

These findings and the results of the present paper can be summarized by paraphrasing a statement from Mountcastle *et al.* (1963): Patterns of neural activity in the cerebral cortex are predictively related to behavioral response tendency in such a way that subsequent neural transformations from cortex to behavior may well occur along linear coordinates.

A final point concerns the relation between neural and behavioral theories of stimulus generalization. In broadest terms, the neurophysiological theory developed above is based on the concept of identical elements, i.e., number of common neurons excited by training and test stimuli. It is compatible with behavioral theories utilizing common stimulus elements as the fundamental explanatory construct. Brown (this vol., p. 7, and personal communication), for example, has proposed a transfer theory of stimulus generalization based on number of identical effective stimulus elements. This type of behavioral theory permits direct translation into neural terms. Further, "effective" stimulus elements can be defined independently of behavior using neurophysiological measures. It would seem that such parallel and interlinear neural and behavioral approaches can provide a much broader foundation for the development of behavior theory.

REFERENCES

Albe-Fessard, D., and Rougeul, A. Activités d'origine, somesthésique evoquées sur le cortex non-specifique du chat anesthesié au chloralose: rôle du centre median du thalamus. *EEG clin. Neurophysiol.*, 1958, **10**, 131–151.

Albe-Fessard, D., Bowsher, D., and Mallart, A. Réponses evoquées dans la formation reticules bulbaires au niveau du noyau *giganto cellularis* d'Olzewski. Rôle de ce noyau dans la transmission vers le centre median du thalamus des afférences somatiques. *J. Physiol.* (Paris), 1962, **54**, 271.

Allen, W. F. Effect of destroying three localized cerebral cortical areas for sound on conditioned differential responses of the dog's foreleg. *Amer. J. Physiol.*, 1945, **144**, 415–428.

Amassian, V. E. Studies on organization of a somesthetic association area, including a single-unit analysis. *J. Neurophysiol.*, 1954, **17**, 39–58.

Bartley, S. H. Some factors in brightness discrimination. *Psychol. Rev.*, 1939, **46**, 337–358.

Bartley, S. H., and Nelson, T. M. Some relations between sensory end results and neural activity in the optic pathway. *J. Psychol.*, 1963, **55**, 121–143.

Bass, M. J., and Hull, C. L. The irradiation of a tactile-conditioned reflex in man. *J. comp. Psychol.*, 1934, **17**, 47–65.

Blackwell, H. R., and Schlosberg, H. Octave generalization, pitch discrimination, and loudness thresholds in the white rat. *J. exp. Psychol.*, 1943, **33**, 407–419.

Brogden, W. J., and Gantt, W. H. Cerebellar conditioned reflexes. *Amer. J. Physiol.*, 1937, **119**, 277–278.

Brown, J. S. The generalization of approach responses as a function of stimulus intensity and strength of motivation. *J. comp. Psychol.*, 1942, **33**, 209–226.

Buser, P., Borenstein, P., and Bruner, J. Etude des systems "associatifs" visuels et auditifs chez le chat anesthesie au chloralose. *EEG clin. Neurophysiol.*, 1959, **11**, 305–324.

Butler, R. A., Diamond, I. T., and Neff, W. D. Role of auditory cortex in discrimination of changes in frequency. *J. Neurophysiol.*, 1957, **20**, 108–120.

Culler, E. A. Observations on direct cortical stimulation in the dog. *Psychol. Bull.*, 1938, **35**, 687–688.

Doty, R. W., and Rutledge, L. T. "Generalization" between cortically and peripherally applied stimuli eliciting conditioned reflexes. *J. Neurophysiol.*, 1959, **22**, 428–435.

Doty, R. W., Rutledge, L. T., and Larsen, R. M. Conditioned reflexes established to electrical stimulation of cat cerebral cortex. *J. Neurophysiol.*, 1956, **19**, 401–415.

Eccles, J. C. *The physiology of nerve cells.* Baltimore: Johns Hopkins Press, 1957.

Ganz, L., and Riesen, A. H. Stimulus generalization to hue in the dark-reared macaque. *J. comp. physiol. Psychol.*, 1962, **55**, 92–99.

Goldberg, J. M., and Neff, W. D. Frequency discrimination after bilateral ablation of cortical auditory areas. *J. Neurophysiol.*, 1961, **24**, 119–128.

Grant, D. A., and Dittmer, D. G. An experimental investigation of Pavlov's cortical irradiation hypothesis. *J. exp. Psychol.*, 1940, **26**, 299–310.

Grosser, G. S., and Harrison, J. M. Behavioral interaction between stimulated cortical points. *J. comp. physiol. Psychol.*, 1960, **53**, 229–233.

Harlow, H. F., and Hicks, L. H. Discrimination learning theory: Uniprocess vs. duoprocess. *Psychol. Rev.*, 1957, **64**, 104–109.

Hebb, D. O. Alice in Wonderland, or Psychology among the biological sciences. In H. F. Harlow and C. N. Woolsey (Eds.), *Biological and biochemical bases of behavior.* Madison: Univer. of Wisconsin Press, 1958. Pp. 451–467.

Hind, J. E., Rose, J. E., Davies, P. W., Woolsey, C. N., Benjamin, R. M., Welker, W. I., and Thompson, R. F. Unit activity in the auditory cortex. In G. L. Rasmussen and W. F. Windle (Eds.), *Neural mechanisms of the auditory and vestibular systems.* Springfield, Ill.: Thomas, 1961. Pp. 201–210.

Hoffeld, D. R. Primary stimulus generalization and secondary extinction as a function of strength of conditioning. *J. comp. physiol. Psychol.*, 1962, **55**, 27–31.

Hovland, C. I. The generalization of conditioned responses: II. The sensory generalization of conditioned responses with varying intensities of tone. *J. genet. Psychol.*, 1937, **51**, 279–291.

Hubel, D. H. Single-unit activity in striate cortex of unrestrained cats. *J. Physiol.*, 1959, **147**, 226–238.

Hull, C. L. Stimulus-intensity dynamism (V) and stimulus generalization. *Psychol. Rev.*, 1949, **56**, 67–76.

Humphreys, L. G. Generalization as a function of method of reinforcement. *J. exp. Psychol.*, 1939, **25**, 361–372.

Jung, R. Neuronal integration in the visual cortex and its significance for visual information. In W. A. Rosenblith (Ed.), *Sensory Communication*. Cambridge, Mass.: M.I.T. Press, 1961. Pp. 627–674.

Konorski, J. *Conditioned Reflexes and Neuron Organization*. London: Cambridge Univer. Press, 1948.

Lashley, K. S., and Wade, M. The Pavlovian theory of generalization. *Psychol. Rev.*, 1946, **53**, 72–87.

Lettvin, J. Y., Maturana, H. R., Pitts, W. H., and McCulloch, W. S. Two remarks on the visual system of the frog. In W. A. Rosenblith (Ed.), *Sensory Communication*. Cambridge, Mass.: M.I.T. Press, 1961. Pp. 757–776.

Lindsley, D. B. The reticular system and perceptual discrimination. In H. H. Jasper (Ed.), *Reticular formation of the brain*. Boston: Little, Brown, 1958. Pp. 513–534.

Littman, R. A. Conditioned generalization of the galvanic skin response to tones. *J. exp. Psychol.*, 1949, **39**, 868–882.

Loucks, R. B. Studies of neural structures essential for learning: II. The conditioning of salivary and striped-muscle responses to faradization of cortical sensory elements, and the action of sleep upon such mechanisms. *J. comp. Psychol.*, 1938, **25**, 315–332.

Mednick, S. A., and Freedman, J. L. Stimulus generalization, *Psychol. Bull.*, 1960, **57**, 169–200.

Meyer, D. R., and Woolsey, C. N. Effects of localized cortical destruction on auditory discriminative conditioning in cat. *J. Neurophysiol.*, 1952, **15**, 149–162.

Morrell, F., and Jasper, H. H. Electrographic studies of the formation of temporary connections in the brain. *EEG clin. Neurophysiol.*, 1956, **8**, 201–215.

Moruzzi, G., and Magoun, H. W. Brain stem reticular formation and activation of the EEG. *EEG clin. Neurophysiol.*, 1949, **1**, 455–473.

Mountcastle, V. B. Modality and topographic properties of single neurons of cat's somatic sensory cortex. *J. Neurophysiol.*, 1957, **20**, 408–434.

Mountcastle, V. B., Poggio, B. F., and Werner, G. The relation of thalamic cell response to peripheral stimuli varied over an intensive continuum. *J. Neurophysiol.*, 1963, **26**, 807–834.

Pavlov, I. P. *Conditioned reflexes*. London: Oxford Univer. Press, 1927.

Penfield, W., and Rasmussen, T. *The cerebral cortex of man: A clinical study of localization of function*. New York: Macmillan, 1950.

Prokasy, W. F., and Hall, J. F. Primary stimulus generalization. *Psychol. Rev.*, 1963, **70**, 310–322.

Razran, G. H. S. Stimulus generalization of conditioned responses. *Psychol. Bull.*, 1949, **46**, 337–365.

Sharpless, S., and Jasper, H. H. Habituation of the arousal reaction. *Brain*, 1956, **79**, 655–680.

Spence, K. W. The differential response in animals to stimuli varying within a single dimension. *Psychol. Rev.*, 1937, **44**, 430–444.

Stevens, S. S. On the psychophysical law. *Psychol. Rev.*, 1957, **64**, 153–181.

Thompson, R. F. Primary stimulus generalization as a function of acquisition level in the cat. *J. comp. physiol. Psychol.*, 1958, **51**, 601–606.

Thompson, R. F. Effect of acquisition level upon the magnitude of stimulus generalization across sensory modality. *J. comp. physiol. Psychol.*, 1959, **52**, 183–185.

Thompson, R. F. Function of auditory cortex of cat in frequency discrimination. *J. Neurophysiol.*, 1960, **23**, 321–334.

Thompson, R. F. Role of the cerebral cortex in stimulus generalization. *J. comp. physiol. Psychol.*, 1962(a), **55**, 279–287.

Thompson, R. F. Thalamocortical organization of association responses to auditory, tactile and visual stimuli in cat. *XXII Inter. Congress of Physiol. Sci.*, Leiden. Series No. 48, 1057, 1962(b).

Thompson, R. F. Role of cortical association fields in auditory frequency discrimination. *J. comp. physiol. Psychol.*, 1964, **57**, 335–339.

Thompson, R. F., and Sindberg, R. M. Auditory response fields in association and motor cortex of cat. *J. Neurophysiol.*, 1960, **23**, 87–105.

Thompson, R. F., Johnson, R. H., and Hoopes, J. J. Organization of auditory, somatic sensory, and visual projection to association fields of cerebral cortex in cat. *J. Neurophysiol.*, 1963, **26**, 343–364.

Thompson, R. F., Smith, H. E., and Bliss, D. Auditory, somatic, and visual-response interactions and interrelations in association and primary cortical fields of cat. *J. Neurophysiol.*, 1963, **26**, 365–378.

Tunturi, A. R. A difference in the representation of auditory signals for the left and right ears in the iso-frequency contours of the right middle ectosylvian cortex of the dog. *Amer. J. Physiol.*, 1952, **168**, 712–727.

Wolpe, J. Primary stimulus generalization: A neuro-physiological view. *Psychol. Rev.*, 1952, **59**, 8–10.

Woolsey, C. N. Organization of somatic sensory and motor areas of the cerebral cortex. In H. F. Harlow and C. N. Woolsey (Eds.), *Biological and biochemical bases of behavior*. Madison: Univer. of Wisconsin Press, 1958. Pp. 63–81.

Woolsey, C. N. Organization of cortical auditory system: A review and a synthesis. In G. L. Rasmussen and W. F. Windle (Eds.), *Neural mechanisms of the auditory and vestibular systems*. Springfield, Ill.: Thomas, 1961. Pp. 165–180.

13. Stimulus Generalization in the Goldfish

Matthew Yarczower, *University of Maryland*

M. E. Bitterman, *Bryn Mawr College*

These experiments with the goldfish are part of a larger program of research on species differences in learning (Bitterman, 1960). Experiments I and II are concerned with wavelength generalization and wavelength discriminability, and with the relation between them. Experiments III and IV are concerned with the effects of stimulus intensity. The results should be of interest both to students of learning and to students of sensory function.

Experiments I and II

After working with the pigeon and finding no correspondence between the gradients of wavelength generalization they obtained and a wavelength discriminability function plotted earlier by Hamilton and Coleman (1933), Guttman and Kalish (1956) were led to question the old assumption—which goes back, in fact, to Thorndike (1898)—that generalization is inversely related to discriminability. When working with human subjects a few years later, Kalish (1958) did find evidence of such a relation, although he did not measure generalization in the usual sense of the term; his gradients of "generalization" were derived from ratings of similarity. In a recent experiment with the monkey, Ganz (1962) found generalization gradients that were perfectly flat to begin with, but that reflected the discriminability function after some discriminative training. More recently, Haber and Kalish (1963), working again with the pigeon, found an inverse relation between the difference in frequency of response to two wavelengths in generalization tests made after single-stimulus training and the number of differentially reinforced training trials subsequently required to establish a discrimination between them.

In our opinion, there is little reason to doubt that discriminability (in

This research was supported by Grant MH-02857 from the National Institute of Mental Health. It was done at Bryn Mawr College during the first-named author's tenure of a Special Research Fellowship awarded by the same Institute. We are indebted to Dr. H. G. Wagner and Dr. M. L. Wolbarsht of the Naval Medical Research Institute, Bethesda, Md., who made the optical equipment available.

the sense of resolving power) is an important factor in generalization. It must be admitted, at the very least, that the slope of a generalization gradient is limited by the resolving power of the animal. Certainly we cannot conceive of a generalization test that would yield a gradient of non-zero slope over a range of stimuli which are, in any meaningful sense of the term, non-discriminable. To say that discriminability is an important factor in generalization is not, however, to say that it is the only factor—that the discriminative capacity of an animal must inevitably be reflected in any generalization gradient we plot for it. When a given gradient fails to reflect discriminative capacity, we do not deny a relation between generalization and discriminability, but look for factors that operate to mask the relation.

The present experiments, which were intended primarily to provide some data on wavelength generalization and wavelength discriminability in the goldfish, afford an opportunity to examine the relation between generalization and discriminability in yet another species. Although the most satisfactory procedure for this purpose would have been first to obtain data on discriminability, and then to choose training and test stimuli for the generalization measurements on the basis of the discriminability function, the reverse procedure was used in the interest of obtaining both sets of data from the same subjects. The training stimuli were selected on the assumption that the discriminability function for the goldfish would not deviate substantially from the functions for the pigeon (Hamilton and Coleman, 1933), the monkey (Grether, 1939), and man (Wright, 1947), all of which are quite similar. After the tests for generalization were completed, some measurements of discriminability were made.

No effort was made in these exploratory experiments to equate the various stimuli for brightness. Since there were no dependable data on which to base the equation of brightness, it seemed reasonable first to work with stimuli that might be different in brightness as well as in hue, and later to attempt to estimate the contribution of variation in brightness to the results. There is no reason to suspect that the inverse relation between generalization and discriminability will appear less readily in work with multidimensional stimuli than in work with stimuli varying only in a single dimension, as long as the several dimensions are not weighted differently in single-stimulus training than in training with differential reinforcement. It is interesting to note that Blough (1961), who controlled for brightness in his work with the pigeon, found no more indication of the inverse relation than Guttman and Kalish (1956), who did not control for brightness.

The two experiments now to be described differed in two main respects: First, in Experiment I, generalization gradients were plotted in terms of latency, but in Experiment II, a technique was used that permitted the measurement of response frequency as well as response latency. Second, measurements of discriminability were made only in Experiment I.

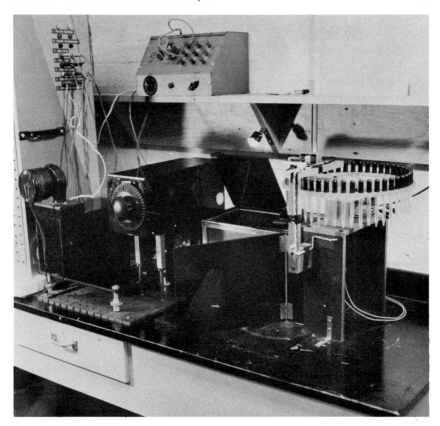

FIG. 1. The apparatus.

Method

Subjects. The subjects were 24 goldfish (*Carassius auratus*) about 4 in. long, obtained from a local dealer.

Apparatus. The main components of the apparatus, which is shown in Fig. 1, were the following: (1) a darkened enclosure of black Plexiglas to which each fish was brought in its individual 2-gal. aquarium;[1] (2) a target at which the fish was trained to strike—a thin diffusing disk of Plexiglas, 1.25 in. in diameter, suspended on a brass rod from the lid of the enclosure in such a way that it was lowered into the water of the aquarium as the lid was brought down; (3) a Farrand grating monochromator and associated optical equipment for projecting monochromatic light onto the target; (4) a live-worm dispenser for reinforcement (Longo and Bitterman, 1963); (5) equipment for programming discrete-trials experiments of several different kinds—the only feature of the training that was not

[1] Plexiglas is manufactured by Rohm and Haas, Philadelphia, Pa.

automated was the setting of the monochromator dial; and (6) equipment for measuring latencies and frequencies of response—specifically, a multivibrator-driven printing counter that registered latencies and an event recorder that registered responses to the target. The lamp that served as the source of illumination was a G.E. microscope illuminator, No. 18A/-T10/2P-6V, its ribbon filament imaged on the entrance slit of the monochromator. The entrance and exit slits of the monochromator were both set at the width of 0.5 mm., yielding a bandwidth of 5 mμ. The dial of the monochromator was calibrated in steps of 10 mμ. Response detection was accomplished by an amplifier into which was fed the output of a crystal phonograph mounted on the lid of the enclosure. The needle-holder of the cartridge contained the brass rod from which the target was suspended. The technique has been described elsewhere (Longo and Bitterman, 1959).

Preliminary training. After being accustomed to taking Tubifex worms given in the colony area, the animals were magazine-trained. Each animal was brought to the apparatus in its individual 2-gal. aquarium, which was placed in the Plexiglas enclosure. Then, at variable intervals, the feeder was operated, discharging a worm into the water at the rear of the aquarium (the end opposite the target). When the feeder operation was in operation, the inner rear wall of the enclosure (a piece of milk-white Plexiglas) was illuminated from behind for 6 sec. by a small white lamp; this light signaled the delivery of a worm and permitted the fish to find it. When the worms were being taken readily, target training was begun. At first, a baited target made of wire mesh was used. For twelve of the animals (seven in the first experiment and five in the second), it was illuminated with light of 550 mμ; for the remaining twelve animals (seven and five in the two experiments, respectively), with light of 580 mμ. Each contact with the target turned off the target light and produced a reinforcement, which was followed by a 5-sec. inter-trial interval in darkness. The amount of bait on the target was reduced gradually until the animals were responding to an unbaited target, after which the formal Plexiglas target was substituted for the wire mesh.

Single-stimulus training. Each animal was given from 70 to 140 reinforced trials with the Plexiglas target at the rate of 10 trials per day. The total number of trials varied from animal to animal because some progressed more rapidly than others. These trials were followed by one day of FR 2 training (that is, the second response on each trial was reinforced) and six days of FR 3 training. On each of the last two days of single-stimulus training, each animal had 5 FR 3 trials and 5 FR 1 trials in Gellermann orders. The inter-trial interval was 10 sec. (as it was in all subsequent phases of the work), and a 30-sec. time limit was introduced (that is, the animal had only 30 sec. in which to earn a reinforcement). If the animal did not make the required number of responses in 30 sec., the trial terminated, but the session continued until ten reinforcements had been earned.

Inter-trial responding was reduced almost to zero by having each inter-trial response reset the inter-trial interval timer and so postpone the start of the next trial. The target light for each animal was of the same wavelength in single-stimulus training as it was in the preliminary training.

Tests for generalization (Experiment I). There followed four days of generalization testing, on each of which there were 5 FR 1 trials with the training stimulus, a first set of 7 test trials, a second set of 7 test trials, and 5 more FR 1 trials with the training stimulus. The stimuli used on the test trials were (for animals trained at 550 mμ) 490, 510, 530, 550, 570, 590, and 610 mμ, or (for animals trained at 580 mμ), 520, 540, 560, 580, 600, 620, and 640 mμ. The seven stimuli in each set were presented in accordance with an Orders × Subjects Latin-square design. These trials were terminated by response, or, if there was no response, after 30 sec.; responses were not reinforced.

Tests for generalization (Experiment II). There were two differences between the testing procedures of the first and the second experiments. One was that in the second experiment, each stimulus was presented for 30 sec. regardless of whether the animal responded to it, thus permitting the measurement of frequency as well as latency of response. In addition, the test stimuli of the second experiment were presented in random order rather than in accordance with a Latin-square design.

Discriminative training (Experiment I). When the generalization tests were finished, discriminative training began. Each animal had 30 trials per day, 15 with a positive stimulus (S^D) and 15 with a negative stimulus (S^d) presented in Gellermann orders. Response to S^D was reinforced on the FR 3 schedule with a 30-sec time limit; S^d was presented for 30 sec., regardless of whether there was any response to it. Animals previously reinforced for responses to 550 mμ were trained with 550 mμ as S^D and 600 mμ as S^d; animals previously reinforced for responses to 580 mμ were trained with 580 mμ as S^D and 630 mμ as S^d. The training of each animal was continued until the mean latencies of its responses to the two stimuli differed significantly at the 5 per cent level on two of three successive days. In the next stage of training, each animal had 40 trials per day, and the wavelength of S^d was decreased in 10-mμ steps until the difference between S^D and S^d was no longer discriminable.

For example, a given subject might first have had 30 trials per day with 550 mμ positive and 600 mμ negative, the training being continued until there was a significant difference between the latencies of response to each stimulus on two of three successive days. Trials on the next day were given in the following order: trials 1–10 with 550 mμ as S^D and 600 mμ as S^d; trials 11–20 with 550 mμ as S^D and 590 mμ as S^d; trials 21–30 with 550 mμ as S^D and 580 mμ as S^d; trials 31–40 with 550 mμ as S^D and 570 mμ as S^d. The smallest difference between S^D and S^d that produced a significant difference (by Wilcoxon's test for unpaired replicates) was then used on the following day. For example, if the smallest difference that had been discriminated was 40 mμ (550 mμ vs. 590 mμ), then the order of presentation in the next stage was: trials 1–10, 550 mμ as S^D and 590 mμ as S^d; trials 11–30, 550 mμ as S^D and 580 mμ as S^d; trials 31–40, 550 mμ as S^D and 590 mμ as S^d. If the response latencies to 550 mμ and 580 mμ were significantly different, then on the following day 570 mμ was presented in counterbalanced order with 580 mμ (both negative) and 550 mμ (positive). The computation of the difference limen (DL) was based on the mid-point of the interval between the shortest wavelength that could be discriminated from S^D and the longest wavelength that could not be; if an animal could discriminate between 550 mμ and 590 mμ, but not between 550 mμ and 580 mμ, its DL at 550 mμ was taken as 35 mμ. After the DL at 550 mμ was determined for each animal trained at 550 mμ, its DL at 580 mμ was determined in the same manner as for the animals trained originally at 580 mμ. Similarly, after the DL determination at 580 mμ was made for each animal trained at 580 mμ, a second DL determination was made with 550 mμ as the standard.

Finally, exploratory DL determinations were made at six other spectral points: 450, 470, 490, 530, 610, and 630 mμ. Not all of the determinations were made with all of the animals, and the order of determinations was balanced over animals only very roughly. In each case, the standard was differentially reinforced, and in each case, except at 630 mμ, the variable stimuli were longer in wavelength than the standard.

Results

Generalization gradients based on the latency data of the two experiments are plotted in Fig. 2. (Note the inversion of the ordinate scale to

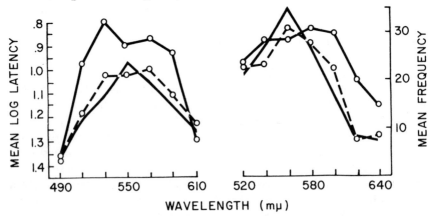

FIG. 2. Generalization gradients about 550 and 580 mμ in Experiments I and II. The open circles on the unbroken line represent the latency gradients of Experiment I; the open circles on the broken line, the latency gradients of Experiment II; and the simple line, the frequency gradients of Experiment II.

make the curves comparable to the frequency curves usually presented.) The two functions appear to be quite comparable; in fact, the correlation between the two sets of latency data is on the order of 0.90. Generalization gradients based on the frequency data of Experiment II, which also are plotted in Fig. 2, show a marked similarity to the latency gradients; the correlation between latency and frequency for Experiment II is on the order of 0.90. In general, the gradients about 550 mμ are much more symmetrical than the gradients about 580, which show a marked asymmetry.

Statistical analysis shows the latency gradient for the seven subjects trained at 580 mμ in Experiment I to be significantly asymmetrical in two respects. First, the latency of response to wavelengths shorter than the training stimulus is less than the latency of response to wavelengths longer than the training stimulus ($F = 4.91$, df $= 1/18$, $P < .05$). Second, there is a significant interaction between the magnitude of the deviation of test stimulus from training stimulus and the direction of the deviation ($F = 3.75$, df $= 2/18$, $P < .05$). (The pooled homogeneous sources of variance are taken as the error term in this analysis.) The latency gradient for six of the seven subjects trained at 550 mμ in Experiment I (the seventh was lost in the course of the experiment) does not show a significant departure from symmetry in terms of level ($F < 1$), although the interaction approaches significance ($F = 2.26$, df $= 2/10$, $P > .10$). A separate analysis shows no significant change with repeated measurements either in the shapes or in the levels of the gradients.

Statistical analysis of the latency data for the five 550-mμ and five 580-mμ animals of Experiment II on which complete data were obtained shows some asymmetry in both gradients. The gradient about 580 mμ is significantly asymmetrical with respect to level ($F = 20.75$, df $= 1/4$, $P < .05$), as is the gradient about 550 mμ ($F = 10.47$, df $= 1/4$, $P < .05$), although neither is significantly asymmetrical with respect to the interaction ($F < 1$). Both frequency gradients also show asymmetry with respect to level (F for 580 mμ $= 23.64$, df $= 1/4$, $P < .05$; F for 550 mμ $= 22.85$, df $= 1/4$, $P < .05$), but not with respect to the interaction ($F < 1$).

On the assumption that the discriminability function for the goldfish is like that for the pigeon, the monkey, and man, and that generalization is inversely related to discriminability, somewhat different gradients than those shown in Fig. 2 might have been expected. The gradient about 580 mμ should have been symmetrical rather than asymmetrical, while the gradient about 550 mμ should have been asymmetrical in a direction opposite from that shown. The results suggest either that the inverse relation has been masked or that the discriminability function for the goldfish is different in important respects from those for the other species.

The discriminability function obtained in Experiment I is shown in Fig. 3. It bears a substantial resemblance to those for the other species,

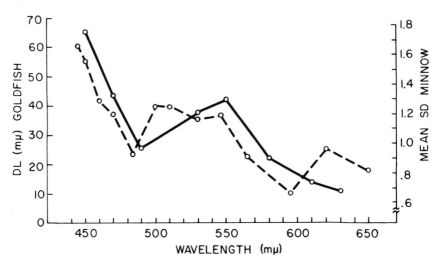

FIG. 3. Wavelength-discriminability functions for two species of fish. The unbroken line represents the data obtained for the goldfish in Experiment I; the broken line, the data for the European mudminnow from Wolff (1925).

particularly in the region 450–580 mμ. In the region of the longer wavelength, however, discriminability improves for the goldfish while it declines for the other species. As Fig. 3 shows, the discriminability function for the goldfish is also quite similar to a function based on choice measures plotted for the European mudminnow (*Phoxinus laevis*) by Wolff (1925). A recent biochemical study of goldfish cones by Marks and MacNichol (1963) also has yielded data consistent with the behavioral data obtained for the goldfish in Experiment I, at least over the 450–600 mμ range.

On the assumption of an inverse relation between generalization and discriminability, the asymmetry of the generalization gradients about 580 mμ shown in Fig. 2 is just what would be expected from the discriminability function of Fig. 3. The relative symmetry of the gradient about 550 mμ obtained in Experiment I also would be expected, but not the asymmetry of the gradient about 550 mμ obtained in Experiment II; while a certain amount of asymmetry about 550 mμ might be expected, the direction of the asymmetry in the gradients of Experiment II would not.

It should be noted, however, that the discriminability function of Fig. 3 is based on DL determinations made only at widely separated points, and, furthermore, that for the determinations at 550 and 580 mμ—the reinforced points in the generalization plots—only the longer wavelengths were used as comparison stimuli. In view of these procedural restrictions, only a quite restricted test of the relation between generalization and discriminability is really justified. We can, however, predict that if the upper DL is 40 at

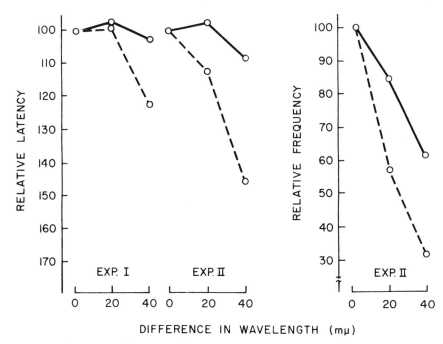

FIG. 4. Relative generalization gradients in the region of 40 mμ above the training stimulus (Experiments I and II). The unbroken line represents training at 550 mμ; the broken line, training at 580 mμ.

550 mμ, but only 20 at 580 mμ, then the generalization gradient should be less steep in the 40-mμ region above 550 (550–590 mμ) than in the 40-mμ region above 580 (580–620 mμ). Relative latency and frequency gradients for groups trained at 550 and 580 mμ over a range of 40 mμ above the training stimulus are shown in Fig. 4. The 580-mμ gradients are, in fact, steeper than the 550-mμ gradients, a result that is in accord with the inverse hypothesis. Type I analyses of the log-latency data and the frequency data on which these relative gradients are based were performed out of interest in the interaction terms, which provided tests of the significance of the differences in slope. The following results were obtained: For Experiment I (latency), $F = 1.18$, df $= 2/22$, $P > .20$. For Experiment II (latency), $F = 3.14$, df $= 2/15$, $.10 > P > .05$. (From the product of the two P-values, it may be estimated that the interaction in the pooled data of the two experiments is significant beyond the 5 per cent level.) For Experiment II (frequency), $F < 1$. In general, then, the tests do not provide unambiguous evidence of the inverse relation, although the general pattern of results obtained in these small-N experiments suggests that the relation might appear more clearly with further replication.

Experiments III and IV

As has already been noted, the generalization gradients about 580 mμ are higher on the side of the shorter wavelengths. While this asymmetry might be expected from the discriminability function, the peaking of the frequency gradient at 560 mμ indicates the operation of a factor other than discriminability. This peaking, which has some corollaries in the pigeon data (Honig, 1962), is a highly reliable effect, appearing in the gradients for each of the subjects of Experiment II. The asymmetry of the gradients about 550 mμ also contradicts predictions from the discriminability function and indicates the operation of another factor. The results for both training stimuli taken together suggest that there may be a preference for wavelengths in the region of 550–580 mμ, or an intensity dynamism favoring response to wavelengths in that region. One purpose of Experiment III was to evaluate this possibility; the non-differential reinforcement of a variety of wavelengths at three different levels of intensity made it possible to look for wavelength preferences and intensity effects. In Experiment IV, the role of intensity was studied in a generalization design. It is of interest that Blough (1959), working along similar lines with the pigeon, found intensity preferences but no evidence of dynamism.

Method

Subjects. The subjects were 19 goldfish about 4 in. long, obtained from a local dealer.

Apparatus. The apparatus was the same as that used in Experiments I and II, with one exception: A circular density wedge was positioned beyond the exit slit of the monochromator to permit variation in the intensity of the monochromatic light. A compensating wedge was not used, since the wedge was so close to the exit slit.

Procedure (Experiment III). Eight of the subjects were magazine trained in the same way as in the earlier experiments. On each day of the subsequent target training, there were 14 reinforced trials, two at each of the seven wavelengths used (450, 490, 530, 570, 590, 630, and 650 mμ); the density wedge was set at zero, which means that the intensity of stimulation was the same as was used in the earlier experiments. The animals were trained first with a baited mesh target and then shifted to the unbaited Plexiglas target. In the experimental training proper, four of the animals were given six cycles of FR 1 training per day for five days. Each cycle consisted of the successive presentation of the seven wavelengths at any one of three different levels of relative intensity (0, −1.6, or −3.2 log units); the seven wavelengths were presented in random orders. Of the six daily cycles, there were two at each of the three levels of intensity again in random orders. After the five days of FR 1 training, the schedule was changed to FR 3 for five more days. The four other subjects were treated in identical fashion, except that they were trained first at FR 3 and then shifted to FR 1. Since each of the seven wavelengths was presented twice each day at each of three intensities, there were 42 reinforced trials per day. Latency of response was measured as before.

Procedure (Experiment IV). Two groups of goldfish, one of six and the other of five animals, were magazine trained and then target trained. The wavelength of the light on the target was 550 mμ for the first group and 580 mμ for the second; the relative intensity was −.9 log units. Both groups were given 10 reinforcements per day on a variable-interval (VI) 30-sec. schedule until their performance stabilized, after which there were four days of generalization testing. On each testing day, there were 14 unreinforced presentations of the training wavelength, two at each of seven levels of intensity (0, −.3, −.6, −.9, −1.2, −1.5, and −1.8 log units). The testing procedure was the same as that used in Experiment II: each stimulus was presented for 30 sec., with a 10-sec. inter-trial interval, and frequency and latency of response were recorded on each trial. Each day's tests were preceded and followed by five presentations of the training stimulus reinforced on a VI 30-sec. schedule.

Results

The results of Experiment III are summarized in Fig. 5. Analysis of variance shows a significant inverse relation between latency and intensity ($F = 13.33$, df.$= 2/14$, $P < .01$), but no significant effect of wavelength ($F < 1$). Although Fig. 5 suggests that variation in intensity is particu-

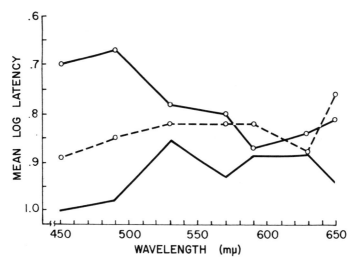

FIG. 5. Latency as a function of wavelength at each of three levels of intensity (Experiment III). The open circles on the unbroken line represent reference level; the open circles on the broken line, −1.6 log units; and the simple line, −3.2 log units.

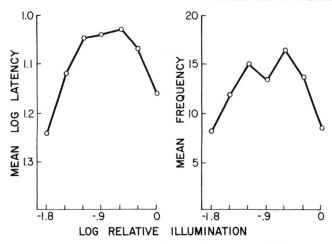

F I G. 6. Intensity generalization (Experiment IV).

larly effective at the shorter wavelengths, the interaction of intensity and wavelength does not reach significance ($F = 1.39$, df $= 12/84$, $P > .05$). The interaction of Subjects $\times$ Schedules is significant ($F = 6.33$, df $= 7/84$, $P < .01$), which presumably reflects the orders in which the different subgroups encountered the two schedules. None of the other interactions approaches significance.

Intensity-generalization gradients for the animals trained at 580 mμ in Experiment IV are plotted in Fig. 6. Analysis of variance shows no significant intensity dynamism, either in terms of a difference in level of response to stimuli brighter and dimmer than the training stimulus or in terms of an interaction between the magnitude and the direction of the difference in intensity. For frequency, F (direction of change) $= 1.41$, df $= 1/4$, $P > .05$; F (interaction) < 1. For latency, F (direction) $= 1.47$, df $= 1/4$, $P > .05$; F (interaction) < 1.

The data for the animals trained at 550 mμ are not presented, because the level of response in five of the six was extremely low; they showed rapid extinction in the first series of tests, from which they made no subsequent recovery. It seems likely that the difference between their performance and that of the animals trained at 580 mμ is to be attributed not to the wavelength of the training stimulus but to the vagaries of subject sampling.

The results of Experiment III give no evidence of a wavelength preference. A significant intensity dynamism appears, but the variation in latency of response with intensity is quite small relative to the variation shown in the wavelength-generalization gradients of Experiments I and II; over the range of 530–650 mμ, in fact, the effect of intensity is minute. It seems, then, that differences in brightness confounded with differences in wavelength could not have played a very significant role in determining the shapes of the wavelength-generalization gradients plotted in Experiments I and II. It is possible, of course, that the non-differential reinforcement of a variety of wavelengths and intensities in Experiment III minimized an intensity dynamism, which might well play a greater role in generalization tests made after single-stimulus training, and it is true that after single-stimulus training in Experiment IV, smaller differences in intensity than those used in Experiment II were found to produce even larger differences in latency of response. The effect of intensity in Experiment IV is not, however, a dynamism, but a generalization effect, and therefore in no way contradicts the assumption that confounded differences in intensity had a negligible influence on the shape of the wavelength-generalization gradients obtained in the first two experiments.

Summary

In Experiment I, wavelength-generalization gradients about 550 and 580 mμ were plotted in terms of latency of response for two groups of goldfish, after which measurements of wavelength discriminability at various spectral points were made with the same subjects. In Experiment II, wavelength-generalization gradients about 550 and 580 mμ were plotted in terms both of latency and frequency of response for two new groups of fish. Substantial evidence of an inverse relation between generalization and discriminability appeared in the data, but there were certain features of the generalization gradients that could not be explained in terms of discriminability and that suggested the operation of a wavelength preference or an intensity dynamism in the 550–580 mμ region. In Experiment III, latency of response to seven wavelengths presented at three different levels of intensity (all reinforced) was measured. In Experiment IV, intensity-generalization gradients were plotted in terms of latency and frequency. The results suggested that differences in intensity that might have been confounded with differences in wavelength contributed little to the shapes of the wavelength-generalization gradients plotted in the first two experiments.

REFERENCES

Bitterman, M. E. Toward a comparative psychology of learning. *Amer. Psychol.*, 1960, **15**, 704–712.

Blough, D. S. Generalization and preference on a stimulus-intensity continuum. *J. exp. Anal. Behav.*, 1959, **2**, 307–317.

Blough, D. S. The shape of some wavelength generalization gradients. *J. exp. Anal. Behav.*, 1961, **4**, 31–40.

Ganz, L. Hue generalization and hue discriminability in *Macaca mulatta. J. exp. Psychol.*, 1962, **64**, 142–150.

Grether, W. F. Color vision and color blindness in monkeys. *Comp. Psychol. Monogr.*, 1939, **15**, 1–38.

Guttman, N., and Kalish, H. I. Discriminability and stimulus generalization. *J. exp. Psychol.*, 1956, **51**, 79–88.

Haber, Audrey, and Kalish, H. I. Prediction of discrimination from generalization after variations in schedule of reinforcement. *Science*, 1963, **142**, 412–413.

Hamilton, W. F., and Coleman, T. B. Trichromatic vision in the pigeon as illustrated by the spectral hue discrimination curve. *J. comp. Psychol.*, 1933, **15**, 183–191.

Honig, W. K. Prediction of preference, transposition, and transposition-reversal from the generalization gradient. *J. exp. Psychol.*, 1962, **64**, 239–248.

Kalish, H. I. The relationship between discriminability and generalization: A reevaluation. *J. exp. Psychol.*, 1958, **55**, 637–644.

Longo, N., and Bitterman, M. E. Improved apparatus for the study of learning in fish. *Amer. J. Psychol.*, 1959, **53**, 616–620.

Longo, N., and Bitterman, M. E. An improved live-worm dispenser. *J. exp. Anal. Behav.*, 1963, **6**, 279–280.

Marks, W. B., and MacNichol, E. F., Jr. Difference spectra of single goldfish cones. *Fed. Proc.*, 1963, **22**, 519.

Thorndike, E. L. Animal intelligence: An experimental study of the associative processes in animals. *Psychol. Rev. Monogr. Suppl.*, 1898, **2**, 1–109.

Wolff, H. Das farbenunterscheidungsvermögen der Ellritze. *Zeit. f. Wiss. Biol.*, 1925, **3**, 279–329.

Wright, W. D. *Researches on Normal and Defective Colour Vision*. St. Louis: C. V. Mosby, 1947.

14. Stimulus Generalization in an Operant: A Historical Note

B. F. Skinner, *Harvard University*

During World War II, with the support of General Mills, Inc., and the Office of Scientific Research and Development, the use of living organisms to guide missiles was investigated. Pigeons were trained to peck a translucent plate upon which an image of a target area was projected through a lens system in the nose of the missile. Signals indicating the location of the image were taken from the plate for control purposes. A report of the project, "Pigeons in a Pelican" (*American Psychologist*, January 1960), refers to a "serious study of the pigeon's behavior" as it might affect performance in the missile. Some of this research was concerned with stimulus generalization. A report prepared in March 1944 contains the following material, which is unchanged in content except for the addition of explanatory material in square brackets.

Visual Properties that Acquire Control through Simple Conditioning

Punchboard Technique

Our standard method of setting up the pecking response is to condition the bird to break through paper to get food. A green cardboard matrix (Fig. 1) is cut to expose small areas (in this case, triangles) of white paper. The cardboard and paper are fastened to a slab of wood containing recesses filled with grain. The exposed areas lie just above the grain. When one of these "punchboards" is placed in a cage, the bird quickly learns to break the triangular areas. This pecking response transfers readily to a white triangle projected upon a screen, and the usual reinforcement can then be given. [If we begin by using tissue paper and slightly cutting open some of the exposed areas, the bird can be quickly conditioned to break open the rest. Progressively tougher papers can then be used.]

Keller Breland, Marian Breland, W. K. Estes, and Norman Guttman were associated with the author on the project and participated in the experiments described.

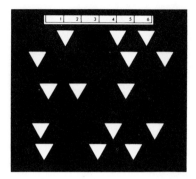

FIG. 1. Training Punchboard A
(scale is 6 in.).

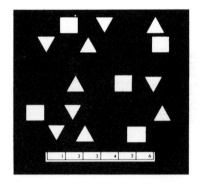

FIG. 2. Test Punchboard A
(scale is 6 in.).

The visual pattern of Fig. 1 has, of course, many properties: color, saturation, and brightness of background and of the figures; size of figures; shape; position, etc. Our present question is: Which of these properties are important in controlling the pecking response? How much induction will be shown to a pattern that differs with respect to any one property?

In the "punchboard technique" for studying induction, the strength of response to a changed pattern is estimated from records obtained with carbon paper. A solid slab of wood is covered with a record sheet, a carbon paper, a paper determining the color of the figures, and a matrix. The bird extinguishes the pecking response against this solid board, and a record is obtained of preferences for the forms cut in the test matrix.

Figure 14 shows the type of mark left by the bird. It is sometimes difficult to count the responses when many are made. The following data are for discernible minimums.

Induction between triangle, inverted triangle, and square. Eight birds were trained on Training Punchboard A (Fig. 1). Each bird broke, on the average, 55 triangles. The group was then extinguished for 20 min. on

Test Punchboard A (Fig. 2), where some triangles are inverted and small squares are included. The percentage distribution of pecks is shown in Fig. 3. The frequency for the squares is partly due to their greater area. A slight preference for the original position (triangle with apex down) is evident.

Two other birds, which were also trained on the punchboard of Fig. 1, had additional training on a triangle projected on a screen. [The birds were held at a 45° angle, head down, in cloth jackets. A 4-in. circular field, perpendicular to the bird's axis, was within pecking reach. Visual targets were projected on the disk from the rear.] Reinforcement was given with the usual movable food magazine [which brought food to the center of the illuminated disk for a few seconds] at low ratios for about 10 min. on each of twelve days. The triangle was white against a green background and about half the linear size of those in Fig. 1. The percentage distribution (Fig. 4) shows the emerging importance of both form and position. There is a very limited induction to the square and only a moderate induction to the inverted triangle.

A gradual increase in the relative strength of the "correct" response under prolonged reinforcement is a well-known phenomenon. It should be noted that it takes place without differential reinforcement (see later). Our training procedure can be expected to build up a tendency not only to respond but to respond correctly in the presence of conflicting patterns. However, this experiment does not suggest that shape is naturally a strong determiner of response.

A considerably greater dependence upon form can be shown if the test forms differ fairly widely. Four fresh birds were each allowed to break about 55 square areas in Training Punchboard B (Fig. 5). They were then

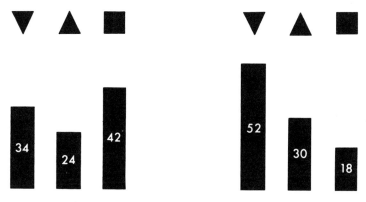

FIG. 3. Percentage distribution of first group on Test Punchboard A.

FIG. 4. Percentage distribution of second group on Test Punchboard A.

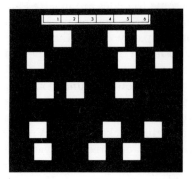

FIG. 5. Training Punchboard B
(scale is 6 in.)

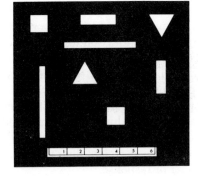

FIG. 6. Test Punchboard B
(scale is 6 in.)

extinguished for 20 min. on Test Punchboard B (Fig. 6). The areas of all test figures were in this case the same. The result is shown in Fig. 7.

A clear preference for the original form is shown in this experiment. There is a moderate induction to the triangle, but very little to the other figures. One interesting fact, the significance of which will be noted later, is that the birds tended to strike, if at all, near the ends of the bar-shaped figures.

Induction between triangles of different colors. In the first part of the preceding experiment the exposed areas on either the right or the left side of the test board were colored. [All areas on the training board were white.] Pale colors were used in order to maintain the original brightness contrast so far as possible. The position of the colored areas was changed from bird to bird to avoid interference with the previous result. By breaking down the same data according to color, some indication of color induction was obtained.

The result is shown in Fig. 8. There is a marked preference for white as against both light red and yellow. A comparison with Fig. 3 (the same

birds) suggests that, as a determining property, color is much more important than shape (at least for the shapes and colors used). The result for
pale green is not so clear. It may be significant that the background was
dark green in all these experiments.

Induction to triangles of different sizes. Eight newly trained birds were
allowed to break about 45 triangles on Training Punchboard A and were
then extinguished for 20 min. on Test Punchboard C (Fig. 9), containing
triangles of six sizes. The areas were .22, .43, .86, 1.3, 1.73, and 2.16 sq. in.
The area of the triangle on the training board was the same as the second
smallest of these—.43 sq. in.

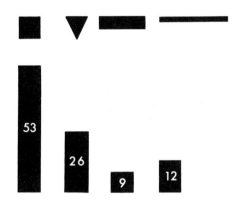

FIG. 7. Percentage distribution of responses on Test Punchboard B.

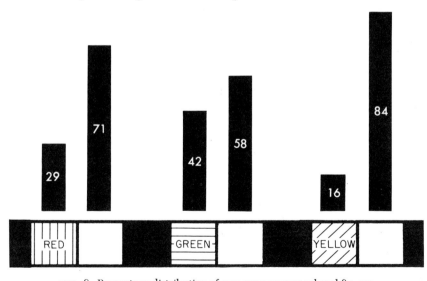

FIG. 8. Percentage distribution of responses among colored figures.

F I G. 9. Test Punchboard C (scale is 6 in.).

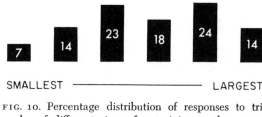

SMALLEST ——————————————— LARGEST

F I G. 10. Percentage distribution of responses to triangles of different sizes after training to the second
smallest size.

The result (Fig. 10) shows a clear tendency to strike larger triangles.
The size used in training received only 14 per cent and the single smaller
area only 7 per cent of the responses. Since the largest size did not, however, receive a proportional percentage, the inductive spread in that direction is perhaps limited.

A stronger preference for the training size can be set up with prolonged
conditioning. A fresh group of four birds which, like those in Fig. 4, had
also had training on a small projected image gave the percentages shown
in Fig. 11. The drift toward larger triangles has been stopped by the
longer training, or by the smaller training triangle in the case of the projected image, or both.

The tendency to prefer larger areas cannot be attributed merely to con-
spicuousness or availability, for evidence to be presented later indicates
that there is a genuine barrier to induction in the direction of smaller sizes,
and much of the responding to larger sizes is explained on other grounds
in the following section. Nevertheless, it is apparent that size of target is
relatively unimportant in controlling the response. A relatively free induction to adjacent sizes takes place.

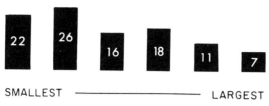

SMALLEST ——————————————— LARGEST

FIG. 11. Percentage distribution of responses to triangles of different sizes after longer training and training to a smaller size.

FIG. 12. Test Punchboard D (scale is 6 in.).

Nature of induction to larger triangles. In the carbon records obtained
in the experiments [above], the birds' responses were not equally distributed over the large triangles but, instead, tended to fall in the vertices.
A direct study of this effect was made. Four freshly trained birds were
trained on Training Punchboard A and extinguished on Test Punchboard
D (Fig. 12). There was a heavier concentration of responses than [before]
because all triangles were large, and the crowding of responses into the
corners emerged very clearly. Two representative carbons are reproduced
in Fig. 14. An attempt was made to record the distribution quantitatively.
The "vertices" were marked off by arcs with radii equal to one-third the
side of the triangle, and the discernible minima of responses in these areas
were counted. (The ratio of the area of the "center" to the total of the
vertices is roughly 1.25 : 1.00.) A group of four birds with the usual training on Punchboard A gave the percentage distribution shown in Figure
13*a*. A group of four with additional training on the smaller projected
image showed the stronger preference of Figure 13*b*. One of the latter
birds gave the records in Fig. 14.

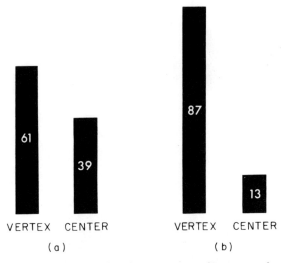

FIG. 13. Percentage distribution in parts of large triangle.

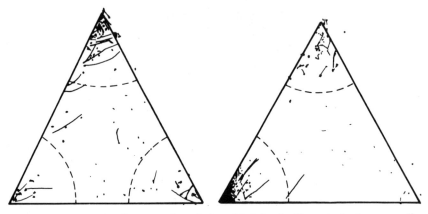

FIG. 14. Photostat of carbon record made by a bird that had been trained on a smaller triangle.

The induction to a large triangle is, then, very largely to the vertices, and is probably not genuine induction along the dimension of size. The corner of a large triangle is like a small (similar) triangle, and does not necessarily differ from it in size at all. The same similarity holds for certain other kinds of figures. It was noted [above] that after training to a square, the bird tended to respond to the *end* of a rectangular bar, which might be regarded as at least three-quarters of a square. We should have to use figures in which the smaller could not be found as part of the larger in order to evaluate the effect of size alone.

The "Periodic Reinforcement" Method

If the prevailing rate under periodic reinforcement is recorded as a baseline in the presence of a standard (usually quite complex) stimulus S^D, the inductive tendency to respond to any other stimulus S^Δ without further reinforcement can be determined from the rate after a change to S^Δ. In all the experiments to be discussed in this section, the birds had developed the rather sharp discrimination set up in the punchboard method of original conditioning. The punchboard consisted of a green background with white triangles. In the experimental apparatus, in which the birds had a long history, any part of the 4-in. circular screen could be struck to produce the reinforcement according to schedule. The screen was green and bore a white triangle in the center, but it was not necessary to strike the triangle. With only one exception in sixteen cases, the response remained localized within the triangle.

The procedure for measuring induction [was as follows]. Responses were recorded under periodic reinforcement, and when a suitable baseline had been established, the experimental chamber was darkened. The bird immediately stopped responding. A lighted chamber is not essential to the physical execution of the response. (It was later found possible to obtain a fairly high rate in the dark.) The cessation was due to the change in S^D. The visual stimulation from the plate and surrounding apparatus had acquired nearly complete control over the response, and (at least at the level of strength then prevailing) there was little or no induction to the tactual and auditory stimuli that remained after the chamber was darkened.

Induction to field with figure removed. Four birds were periodically reinforced [on a 1-min. fixed-interval schedule] for responding to any part of a green field containing a white triangle (⅞ in. on each edge) during 15 min. each day for several weeks. On the first day of the present experiment the triangle was removed from the field for 4 min. in the middle of the period, with the result shown in Fig. 15, where the horizontal bars mark the absence of the triangle. Four birds gave the same result: the response was still under the complete control of the triangle, even though responses to other parts of the screen would have been as readily reinforced.

On the following two days considerably longer exposures to the plain field were given, but with no change in the result (Fig. 16). On the second day of prolonged exposure, the birds remained in the presence of a plain field without responding for 30 and 55 min., respectively. Responses appeared immediately when the triangle was again restored.

In a repetition of this experiment with eight other birds, one bird was discovered to have shifted its response to the lower part of the field (near

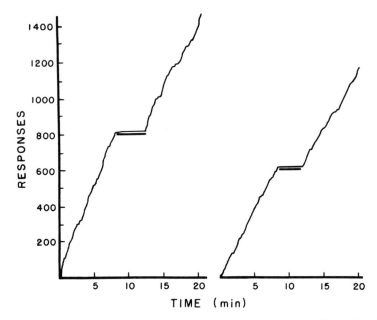

FIG. 15. Complete cessation of response when the triangle is removed from the field.

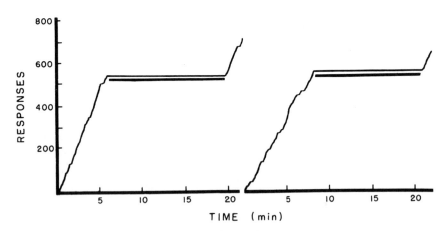

FIG. 16. Prolonged exposure to a plain field with no responses emerging.

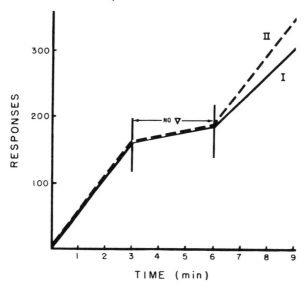

FIG. 17. Mean curves for eight birds, showing effect of removing the triangle upon the rate under periodic reinforcement.

the entrance of the food magazine). This bird continued to respond when the triangle was removed. Mean curves showing the slopes for 3 min. before, during, and after removal of the triangle on two days (I and II) are given in Fig. 17. The responding during the absence of the triangle is due almost entirely to the one exception just noted.

Induction to a plain field the color of the figure. How much of the lack of induction ... is due to the absence of triangularity, and how much to the absence of whiteness? This question can be answered experimentally. Three birds from the first experiment of Fig. 15 were tested on a fourth day. After a 4-min. period of no responding in the absence of the triangle, the entire field was made white. No responses were reinforced under this stimulus. Two representative records (for the same birds as Figs. 15 and 16) are in Fig. 18. A small amount of extinction to the white field is evident. When the white triangle on a green field is again presented, the usual rate is resumed. "Absence of triangle" can therefore be broken up into "absence of triangularity" and "absence of whiteness." Some of the strength is available under "whiteness" alone.

Induction to a larger figure. Induction to figures of different size is of practical importance since it determines the need for special training on pictures of the target from various distances.

Four birds with a long history of responding to a white triangle ⅞ in. on each edge against a green field were tested for induction to a white triangle 2 in. on each edge. The size was changed abruptly, and the smaller

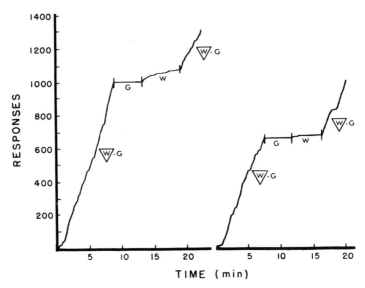

FIG. 18. Cessation of response after removal of figure and subsequent slight extinction when the field takes the color of the former figure (W: white, G: green).

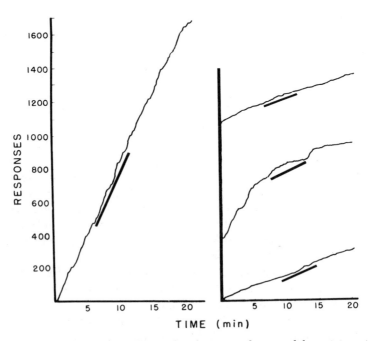

FIG. 19. Induction to a triangle of more than four times the area of the training triangle.

triangle was again presented after 5 min. All four records are shown in Fig. 19. One bird, with an unsatisfactory baseline, may have felt some effect, but it is obvious that the increase in size is of little importance. This agrees with the result from the punchboard experiment and is perhaps explained in the same way. If the large triangle is regarded as three small triangles with a connecting area, the induction to a field containing three triangles described below is relevant.

Induction to a smaller figure. The effect of a smaller triangle is quite different, as we should expect from the punchboard experiments. The experiment resembled that of [the preceding experiment], except that the new triangle measured only ⅛ in. on each side. Two typical records are shown in Fig. 20. (Note that, for reasons unrelated to this experiment, the units on the abscissa have been changed.) In the figure, "M" indicates the presence of the usual ⅞-in. triangle, "S" the small ⅛-in. triangle. An almost complete cessation of response is seen. This may be related to the practical behavior required in the training punchboard (though several weeks of responding to the solid green intervened), since a ⅛-in. hole would be too small to admit the bird's beak. Whatever the explanation, the lack of induction to a small figure dictates certain requirements of our training procedure. It will be necessary to give special training to the smallest image of the target that can possibly appear on the screen in the vehicle.

Conditioning to a smaller triangle. Some notion of the reconditioning necessary to equalize the rate under triangles of different size was supplied by a further experiment. The procedure of Fig. 20 was repeated for five days, except that responses were periodically reinforced on the same

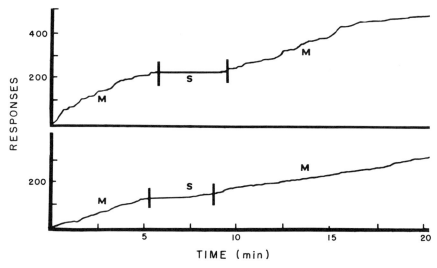

F I G. 20. Effect of a small triangle ("S") which replaces the usual size ("M").

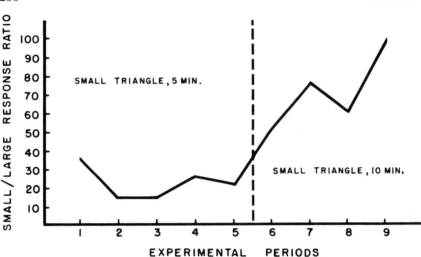

F IG. 21. Reinforcement of responses in the presence of a small triangle and the resulting increase in rate.

schedule in the presence of the small triangle. The rates during presentations of the small triangle are expressed as percentages of the rates in the presence of the larger triangle in the first five points of Fig. 21. No increase is apparent. The small triangle was then presented for a longer period of 10 min., as the first half of each experimental period. This was done for three days; on a fourth day the order of triangles was reversed. The rates, expressed as percentages of the rates in the presence of the larger triangle, appear in Fig. 21. There is an obvious conditioning of the response to the new stimulus, and the rate nearly reaches the rate in response to the standard triangle. The process is, however, rather a slow one, and appears to derive little support from the preceding conditioning to the larger triangle.

Abiding size preferences. After considerable training to larger and smaller sizes, the original (medium) size maintains some superiority. For four days following the experiment just described, the birds were periodically reinforced in the presence of all three sizes in a rough order of rotation. Each figure was presented for 5 min., and four presentations comprised a daily period. A typical result is shown in Fig. 22. Each curve is the average of the six records that had the same schedule of rotation. In every case the slope in the presence of the medium triangle is greater than adjacent slopes to other sizes.

The reduced rate in response to the larger triangle is, of course, not in agreement with the result reported [above]. It will be remembered, how-

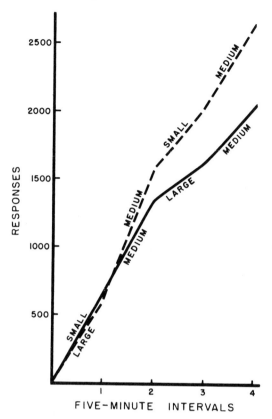

RESPONSES

FIVE−MINUTE INTERVALS

F I G. 22. Slopes maintained in response to triangles of three sizes after extensive conditioning.

ever, that considerable reinforcement in the presence of the small (⅛-in.) triangle has intervened. As in the case of Fig. 11, this training is effective in breaking down the "natural" spread in the direction of larger sizes.

The very considerable impartial reinforcement of three sizes during four daily periods makes no progress toward a full equalization of rates. The mean responses per 5-min. period were Large—384, Medium—618, and Small—521. The fact that the medium triangle was originally used in conditioning the birds may contribute to the results. Further experiments are needed to clarify the point, but a plausible explanation can be generated from some simple assumptions concerning inductive spread. If we assume an induction of 50 per cent to an adjacent size and a lesser spread—say, of 10 per cent, to a next adjacent, then the equal reinforcement of all three sizes will contribute strength in arbitrary units as follows:

	Large	Medium	Small
Reinforcing Large	10	5	1
Reinforcing Medium	5	10	5
Reinforcing Small	1	5	10
	16	20	16

which shows a superior strength for the medium triangle.

Induction to multiple figures. The addition of other figures to the field might be expected to leave no effect at all, or by creating a slightly novel S^Δ to reduce the rate, or by enlarging the opportunity of response to increase it. An actual test in which additional triangles of standard (medium) size were placed in the upper right and upper left quadrants of the field showed little effect. The four records from an experiment following the usual procedure are given in Fig. 23. It was determined by direct observation that the birds struck all three triangles with only moderate preference

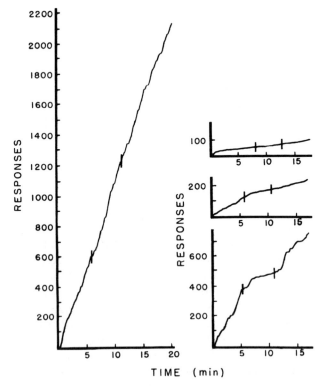

FIG. 23. The effect of placing additional figures in the field (between the vertical strokes).

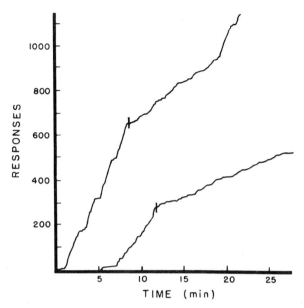

F IG. 24. Effect of changing the field from green to red, the figure remaining unchanged.

for the central standard position. Yet this topographical subdivision of response did not affect the rate, with the possible exception of one bird (lower right) that characteristically gave a rough baseline.

Induction to a field of different color. The part played by the color of the field (the white triangle remaining the same) was investigated by changing the color midway in the course of a daily experiment while continuing with periodic reinforcement. The typical result is shown in Fig. 24. In each case the experiment begins with the standard green background. At the vertical dashes this was changed to red. The first effect was a sharp reduction in rate, from which the bird gradually recovered under continued periodic reinforcement. Almost no recovery has occurred in the lower record before the end of the period, but all birds showed conditioning to the new background on the following days. The mean rates in responses per minute for four birds on the first day were Green Field—38, Red Field—18. A repetition with the same birds on a second day gave Green Field—47, Red Field—29. On a third day the red field was presented first. A mean rate of 25 responses per minute was obtained. Upon changing to a green field the rate remained about the same.

15. Effects of Discrimination Formation on Generalization Measured from a Positive-Rate Baseline

Norman Guttman, *Duke University*

The well-known findings of Hanson (1959) offer perhaps the clearest available picture of the changes in stimulus generalization which result from training a discrimination between two stimuli that differ in one dimension, on the continuum of the subsequent generalization test. Hanson's data demonstrate that following a wavelength discrimination the most effective stimulus is not that wavelength specifically reinforced, but some other wavelength systematically displaced beyond the positive stimulus in the direction away from the negative. This fact gives rise to the following question: What, then, is the least effective stimulus in the region of S— ? Is the least effective stimulus typically S— itself, or does the positive peak-shift have a negative analogue, so that there exists another stimulus value which is less effective than S— and is displaced away from S+ ?

The question, and the allied conjecture, cannot be readily dealt with under the conditions of Hanson's experiment because a whole range of test stimuli in the region of S— yields zero rates of responding, and one cannot discriminate among them. However, the possibility arises that if one were able to raise the baseline of responding rather uniformly above zero prior to discrimination training, one might then be able to see differences in the region of interest. Such was the strategy of the present experiment. The method was to reinforce key-pecking in the pigeon to all wavelengths later to be tested, to impose a discrimination between two selected wavelengths, and finally to test for wavelength generalization.

The experiment is a delicate one, and its outcome hinges upon the appropriate selection of training parameters. All test stimuli in the region of concern must elicit above-zero rates in the initial stages of the extinction test. This condition can be achieved when the parameters of both phases

This experiment was conducted with the valuable assistance of Robert Barrett, John Dalhouse, Peter Van Ryzin, and Mary M. Wheeler. The work was supported by Grant M-3917 from the National Institute of Health, U.S. Public Health Service.

of training permit a proper balance of excitatory and inhibitory effects. We selected the training conditions of the present study after training a few pigeons in preliminary studies which suggested suitable values and which also indicated in a rough way the plausibility of "negative peak-shift" hypothesis. We settled in favor of conducting a rather prolonged routine of variable-interval (VI) reinforcement of the test stimuli (rather than continuous reinforcement), and of carrying the discrimination training to a criterion of an S−/S+ rate ratio of approximately 1/3. These procedures, as will be seen, produced a final state that lay within the required range and permitted the relevant observations.

Method

The apparatus was a standard key-pecking apparatus in which the key could be illuminated by a Bausch and Lomb diffraction-grating monochromator. The intensities of the various monochromatic key-lights were those produced by the monochromator without adjustment of luminosity or radiant energy.

The subjects were six experimentally naïve white Carneau pigeons, whose body weights were reduced by food deprivation to 80 per cent of normal. After preliminary adaptation to the apparatus and training to eat in a completely darkened box from the food magazine, the subjects were trained to key-peck by the method of successive approximations. During this phase, the key was illuminated by a white light produced by a 7½-watt lamp. The subjects were permitted to obtain 25 continuous reinforcements during each of four experimental periods. Following this phase, fifteen daily sessions of VI reinforcement were conducted. During each session, each of nineteen different monochromatic lights was presented for two 30-sec. intervals. The work intervals were separated by 10-sec. blackouts, and the various wavelengths were presented in random orders. The nineteen reinforced wavelengths ranged from 510 to 600 mμ by steps of 5 mμ. The mean interval between programmed food reinforcements was approximately 40 sec.

Following training to all these wavelengths, successive discrimination training was carried out between 550 mμ and 560 mμ. Four subjects were run with 550 mμ reinforced (on the same VI schedule as previously used) along with no reinforcement for 560 mμ; two subjects were trained with 560 mμ reinforced and 550 mμ extinguished. These two wavelengths, as may be seen in Table 1, were the ninth and eleventh in the previous set of nineteen. Beyond each of them lay eight other previously reinforced wavelengths, and between them was another wavelength, the center one of the series. During discrimination training S+ and S− were presented in random alternation, and each was exposed fifteen times per daily training schedule. As before, each exposure lasted for 30 sec., and there were 10-sec.

TABLE 1

Total Responses in Five Minutes of Generalization Testing

Stimulus	Wave-length (mμ)	550+, 560— Subjects				Wave-length (mμ)	550+, 560— Subjects		
		B-13	B-23	B-24	B-28		B-26	B-27	Total
1	510	84	68	295	497	600	455	213	1612
3	520	98	102	257	497	590	532	329	1815
5	530	185	93	152	548	580	475	362	1815
6	535	172	140	194	566	575	527	240	1839
7	540	143	100	158	540	570	482	272	1695
8	545	180	104	219	492	565	476	367	1838
9 (S+)	550	116	100	72	11	560	274	140	713
10	555	170	50	81	3	555	45	65	414
11 (S—)	560	80	25	60	4	550	168	96	433
12	565	49	21	22	2	545	73	99	266
13	570	39	23	0	0	540	73	75	210
14	575	12	19	15	4	535	74	69	193
15	580	80	9	80	90	530	166	82	507
17	590	70	32	27	242	520	541	168	1080
19	600	74	66	150	558	510	629	175	1652

blackouts between exposures. As discrimination proceeded, and as the rate of responding to S— began to fall, a quick calculation of the S—/S+ rate ratio was made during the tenth and twentieth blackout intervals. If the ratio fell to at least 1/3 for the preceding block of five S+ and five S— intervals, discrimination training was terminated. The mean ratio actually achieved was 1/4.2, with a range from 1/3.07 to 1/6.04.

On the day following the achievement of discrimination to the foregoing criterion, each subject was carried through a test for wavelength generalization under extinction. The test series consisted of fifteen of the nineteen previously reinforced wavelengths; the second, fourth, sixteenth, and eighteenth stimuli were dropped out of the series to shorten the test. The remaining stimuli were presented ten times each in ten different random orders. The prior schedule of 30-sec. exposure intervals and 10-sec. blackout intervals was maintained.

Results

During VI reinforcement of responding to the test stimuli, the mean rate of responding rose to about 112 responses per minute (Fig. 1). This value is probably not asymptotic for such training conditions, but in all likelihood is not far below asymptote. The course of the first three sessions of discrimination training is shown in Fig. 2. At the start, the level of responding to S— is actually above that for S+, but presumably not for systematic reasons. By the end of the third session, the discrimination is well underway, and it subsequently follows a course we cannot conveniently depict since some animals drop out during the fourth session. The number of training sessions required ranged from four to seven.

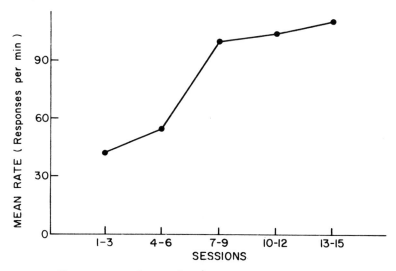

FIG. 1. Changes in rate of responding during VI training to all wavelengths.

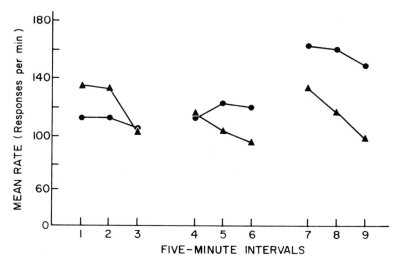

FIG. 2. Changes in rate of responding to S+ (circles) and S− (triangles) during first three sessions of wavelength discrimination.

The main finding of the study is presented in Fig. 3, which shows the mean number of responses in five minutes of extinction as a function of wavelength. The stimulus which on the average evokes the lowest level of activity is displaced 15 mμ from S− in the direction away from S+. This general pattern is supported by the records of individual subjects (Table 1). All four birds trained with 560 mμ as S− show a minimum in the range from 570 to 580 mμ. The two birds trained with 550 mμ as S− show a

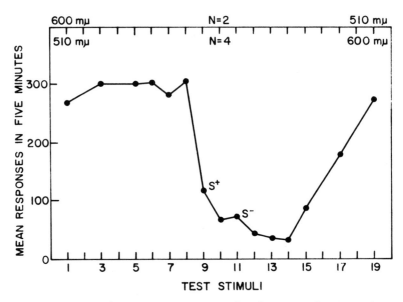

F I G. 3. Mean total responses to various wavelengths in generalization testing.

minimum between S− and S+, but also some other value in the range of
wavelengths shorter than S− for which the rate is less than the S− rate.
Because these individual minima occupy a range of values on the wavelength scale, the averaged curve shows a less pronounced minimum than
is characteristic of individual records; on the other hand, the averaged
curve is not markedly more systematic (in the sense of number of departures from a smooth function) than are the individual records.

The averaged curve is characterized by a displacement of the maximum
to a broad region located in the direction away from S−. For all subjects
the rate to S+ is markedly less than the rate to some wavelength (and
typically many wavelengths) in this region.

The magnitude of the effects of discrimination training upon the response baseline may be seen in Fig. 4, which compares the rates to various
test stimuli in the first minute of testing with the mean rates to various
reinforced wavelengths during the last five minutes of VI training. Whereas
the baseline varies irregularly over a range of about ±10 per cent of its
mean values, the factor of variation in the postdiscrimination gradient,
comparing peak and trough, is about eight. The initial rate to S+ in testing is below the VI baseline and very considerably below the mean rate
to S+ (139 responses per min.) in the last 5-min. unit of discrimination
training. No further account of this somewhat unexpected finding will be
attempted, but it is especially difficult to understand in view of the finding
of Friedman and Guttman (this vol., pp. 255–267) that a close correspon-

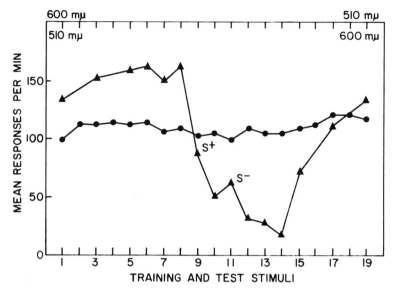

F IG. 4. Comparison of rates in first min. of generalization testing (triangles) with rates during last 5 min. of VI training (circles).

dence exists between S+ training level and S+ testing level in other discrimination-generalization experiments. Clearly, the effects of extinction to S− are very powerful under the present conditions. More important, however, is the indication that in the initial stages of extinction, certain stimuli elicit higher rates than were ever achieved in training to S+ (by about 19 per cent), and these are presumably analogous to the stimuli at the peak of the ordinary post-discrimination gradient.

Discussion

The findings offer support for a phenomenon of "negative peak-shift." The data available are as yet not as convincing as those which establish the positive peak-shift phenomenon and define some of the factors which contribute to that state of affairs. Yet it may be conjectured that the two phenomena are equally real, and that they may be inseparable facets of a single process. Findings such as those presented here are compatible with Spence's model (1937) of discrimination formation and generalization, which states that it is possible to construct arbitrary hypothetical inhibition and excitation curves of independent origin that would sum to the outline of the present curve, or practically any curve. However, we wish to note that in general the Spence model does not predict a shift of the generalization minimum, and that such an outcome would be a special case rather than the rule. Without exploring all the cases for which the Spence model would predict shifts in both maximum and minimum from

S+ to S— values, we may note only that such a pattern cannot result from any combination of linear underlying curves and that it cannot result from combining concave curves of equal slope, but that it can be derived from combining hypothetical convex curves of various relative slopes and heights. We are not in a position to question whether the third of these theoretical accounts can be applied to the present data. However, it does not seem unreasonable to conjecture about alternative possibilities, since it is not *a priori* very likely that this study has managed to achieve, without intending to do so, one of those cases in which a subtractive model involving convex curves can be correctly applied.

The alternative we offer is less specific than the Spence theory, and consists merely of the suggestion that a negative peak-shift may be looked for in all those situations where a positive peak-shift is definitely the rule. A positive peak-shift is by no means uniformly found in all available post-discrimination gradients (e.g., neither Jenkins and Harrison's [1960] data for pitch generalization in the pigeon nor unpublished data we obtained at Duke University for pitch generalization in the cat suggest this characteristic); yet it may be the case that those circumstances which produce the positive effect also produce the negative counterpart. It need hardly be added that the total of available data and analysis of this problem affords a very scanty basis for hypothesizing broad principles of any sort.

One change in technique that is being considered for the further study of this problem is continuous variation of the wavelength of the key illumination during preliminary training. This procedure might improve the stability of the baseline, provided that wavelength were sometimes also held fixed for short intervals. A somewhat different method for testing for the effect would be to return to intermittent reinforcement of all wavelengths after discrimination training. This procedure was tried with the present subjects, and the contour of the VI baseline transiently resembled the post-discrimination gradient obtained under extinction (Fig. 4). If the sort of phenomenon obtained in this study is a real one, it should be possible to obtain and measure it in a variety of ways.

It might well be profitable to pursue the entire problem of peak-shift along lines of thought that are closely determined by the nature of particular stimulus domains rather than to follow more abstract ideas that ignore the features of specific sensory systems. It cannot be overlooked that the only direct empirical evidence for the peak-shift phenomenon comes from wavelength-generalization experiments, apart from which peak-shift exists only as a theoretical (or—more accurately—a graphical) possibility in Spence's analysis of transposition. The color domain has two characteristics that are not typical of other systems.

Colors have opponent colors, as is indicated by such facts as complementarity, simultaneous contrast, successive contrast, and negative after-images. In addition, any monochromatic stimulus simultaneously excites two or more systems of receptive elements, so that one is required to regard any wavelength presentation as having a component nature. If peak-shift toward shorter wavelengths is observed after training to a positive yellowish-green stimulus (550 mμ) vs. a negative greenish-yellow stimulus (570 mμ), this result may be regarded as either an enhancement of the opponent of yellow (blue) or the enhancement of the green component of the two presentations, along with the inhibition (if negative peak-shift is real) of a longer wavelength system, yellow or red. Both types of processes—those dependent on the opponent nature of the system and those dependent on the component nature of the stimulations—could be at work, but it does not seem parsimonious or probable that both features would actually be involved in the establishment of associative connections. If they were, the mechanism of learning in reference to wavelengths would be handicapped by an ambiguity, by two levels of internal processing so to speak.

If one may hazard a guess about the plausibility of the alternatives, the more likely hypothesis would revolve around the component nature of the stimulus, if only because the enhancement of complements would on the average constitute a misrepresentation of the environment, a failure to respond to the information contained in the specific stimuli available, and a maladaptive form of organization. The opponent aspect of the color system is excellent for spatial and temporal pattern perception but not for learning to associate colors of objects with rewards.

The intriguing phenomenon of peak-shift may, in sum, prove a useful device for exploring associative processes, but it need not be regarded at this stage as the basis for a general principle to be extended from color to other continua of discrimination and generalization. It is unlikely that a fuller understanding and a quantitative analysis of wavelength-generalization phenomena in the pigeon can be developed on the premise that wavelength makes available a unidimensional continuum. As we already know, such stimulation produces an effect with several components, each of which can function as a conditioned stimulus, and it may well turn out that the results obtained with wavelength will be more readily generalizable to multidimensional stimulus situations than to unidimensional cases.

REFERENCES

Hanson, H. M. Effects of discrimination training on stimulus generalization. *J. exp. Psychol.*, 1959, **58**, 321–334.

Jenkins, H. M., and Harrison, R. H. Effect of discrimination training on auditory generalization. *J. exp. Psychol.*, 1960, **58**, 246–253.

Spence, K. The differential response in animals to stimuli varying in a single dimension. *Psychol. Rev.*, 1937, **44**, 435–444.

16. Discrimination, Generalization, and Transfer on the Basis of Stimulus Differences

Werner K. Honig, *Dalhousie University*

The purpose of this paper is to describe a series of studies on the control of behavior on the basis of stimulus differences. In order to clarify this exposition, certain terms will be defined at the outset. In all the studies, the stimuli lay either on the spectral continuum or on the intensity continuum. Values on the former are specified as millimicrons of wavelength (mμ), and on the latter as neutral-density (ND) values used to reduce the intensity emanating from the light source. We will distinguish between *specific stimulus values* that are physically specified, such as 520 mμ or ND 1.5, and *difference values*, which are defined as the difference between two simultaneously displayed specific values, or a *stimulus pair*. A given difference value can usually be obtained from a number of specific stimulus pairs. For example, the pairs 520, 540 mμ; 540, 560 mμ; and 600, 620 mμ are all instances of the difference value of 20 mμ. Similarly, the intensity pairs ND 0.5, 1.0, and ND 2.0, 2.5 are both instances of the difference value ND 0.5. The set of difference values derived from the specific stimuli on a continuum comprises a *stimulus-difference dimension*.

The present research focused on the acquisition, generalization, and transfer of discriminations between various difference values. Such discriminations will be called *stimulus-difference discriminations*, or SDD's. An SDD may contrast a small-difference value such as 20 mμ with a large-difference value such as 80 mμ, or identical stimuli such as ND difference 0.0 with a given difference value such as ND difference 1.5. We will refer to the two aspects of the SDD as the two "halves" of the discrimination. In the preceding example, the "identity half" would consist of those trials in which the ND difference 0.0 was displayed, and the "difference half" of the trials in which the ND difference 1.5 was displayed.

The research reported here was supported by Grant No. M-02414 from the U.S. Public Health Service, National Institute of Mental Health, while the author was at Denison University. This work would not have been accomplished without the help of a number of co-workers and assistants, including Roberta Williams Day, Ellen Kraft, Kirsten Werrenrath, Chryssanthos Vostandjoglou, Greg Gibson, and Dewey Slough. Study 2 has been published in brief form by Honig and Day (1962).

A final distinction to be observed is that between *stimulus pairs,* which are instances of a difference value without regard to the position of the stimuli as they are presented to the subject, and *stimulus combinations,* in which the position of the stimuli is specified. Thus, the pair 500, 560 mμ is an instance of the difference value of 60 mμ, and can be represented by one combination in which 500 mμ appears at the left key and a second in which it appears at the right.

In establishing SDD's, it was necessary to develop a strategy that avoided control by specific stimulus values. The training procedure was arranged so that all specific stimulus values were displayed (and reinforced) equally often in the presentation of both halves of an SDD. Typically, a set of specific stimulus values was used in training and testing. These values were paired in such a way that all the possible combinations representing a given difference value were displayed equally often.

Although this general strategy could be employed with a number of specific training methods, the present report will be confined to studies in which the difference value provided the relevant cue for a left-right discrimination between response keys. The key correct for the identity half of an SDD will be called the "identity" key; the key correct for the difference half is called the "difference" key. The terms "small-difference key" and "large-difference key" will be used in a corresponding fashion for small- vs. large-difference discriminations. Once the SDD's were established, the relevant stimulus-difference dimension was investigated by means of generalization tests in which difference values were presented between and beyond those used in discrimination training. The obtained generalization gradients were in the form of orderly control over key preference as a function of the difference value being displayed.

One aspect of this kind of discrimination that sets it apart from specific stimulus discriminations is worth noting here: such SDD's can, at least in principle, transfer directly between any sets of stimuli in the same modality, since the degree of difference is a dimension that can be abstracted from stimuli lying on any physical continuum. With most specific stimulus discriminations, questions of direct transfer can be asked only in a very restricted manner. It makes no sense, for example, to ask how a discrimination between a large and a small stimulus will transfer to two different hues. But it does make sense to ask how an SDD based on a size dimension will transfer to differences in hue. There may of course be *indirect transfer* from a discrimination between two specific stimulus values on one continuum to a specific discrimination on another, in that the acquisition of the first may speed the acquisition of the second.

But *direct transfer*—that is, the possibility of solving a new discrimination without errors—can be obtained across continua only with training on an abstract dimension, such as stimulus difference. Direct transfer between specific stimulus discriminations is obtained only when both the training and the transfer stimuli are on the same continuum, in which case such transfer is known as transposition, or when irrelevant aspects of the discriminative stimulus are altered, such as a change in the size of stimuli that are discriminated on the basis of hue. Aside from the interest intrinsic in the SDD's as a behavioral process, the possibility of direct transfer may give such discriminations a significant role to play in the study of perception and concept attainment.

Study 1

Spectral Stimulus Differences as a "Natural" Stimulus Dimension

The first study was a preliminary investigation to determine whether a stimulus-difference dimension can function as a "natural" dimension for stimulus control without explicit discrimination training. Pigeons were trained to respond in the presence of a difference value of 40 mμ. Other difference values were presented during a generalization test to determine whether the difference dimension exerted any control over behavior. This study was based on the original work by Guttman and Kalish (1956), who studied generalization gradients obtained after simple acquisition of an operant with specific spectral values. In this way, generalization on the fundamental dimension of spectral value and the derived dimension of spectral differences could be compared.

Method

Subjects. The subjects were three experimentally naïve White King pigeons, maintained at about 75 per cent of their free-feeding body weight.

Apparatus. A two-key operant behavior box was used. The keys were located 7½ in. above the floor and were 2 in. apart, center to center. Collimated white light was passed through Bausch and Lomb monochromatic interference filters to provide various pure spectral values. Additional yellow filters were used in conjunction with values greater than 570 mμ in order to eliminate contamination from the second-order spectrum. The various values were equated for brightness by a human observer, since Blough's work (1957) indicates that the spectral sensitivity function of the pigeon is very similar to that of man. The light on the keys provided the only illumination in the box except for the magazine light, which came on during reinforcement periods. Reinforcement consisted of the presentation of mixed grain for 4-sec. periods.

Procedure

Preliminary training. The pigeons were first taught to eat from the grain magazine whenever food was presented. Then they were taught by successive approximation to peck at the right key illuminated by 530 mμ. After 20 continuous reinforcements were obtained with this value, 590, 630, and 490 mμ were presented in succession, and 20 further reinforcements were given for responding to each of these. On the next day, five continuous reinforcements could be obtained for responding to each of the 15 stimulus values ranging from 490 to 630 mμ inclusive in 10 mμ steps. These 15 values were presented in random order, and the position of the illuminated key was randomized. This procedure was repeated on successive days, except that a fixed ratio (FR) 5 requirement was instituted on the second day, and a variable interval (VI) 30-sec. schedule was in effect thereafter, with the stimuli displayed for 3-min. periods until the bird responded reliably to the illuminated key.

VI training. During this phase, both keys were illuminated by two spectral values in such a way that the difference value was always 40 mμ. When stimuli in the range of 490–630 mμ were used, 11 different stimulus pairs were available (see Table 1). The values from 490–520 mμ and from 600–630 mμ each appeared in one stimulus pair, whereas those from 530–590 mμ each appeared in two pairs. Each of these 11 pairs was presented once in a block of trials, and each training session consisted of three randomized blocks. Each trial was 60 sec. long, and was followed by a blackout period of 10 sec., during which reinforcement was not available. During each presentation of each stimulus pair, one of the wavelength values was randomly selected as "correct"; each value within a pair was "correct" in this manner on half the trials. The key (right or left) at which reinforcement would be available was also randomized, and this, in conjunction with the randomization of the correct wavelength, determined for each trial which stimulus combination of the pair in question would be presented.

With the presentation of a variety of stimulus values, and the random assignment of reinforcement to each value and to each key, the only specific aspect of the stimulus situation that was systematically related to reinforcement was that the values from 530–590 mμ were reinforced twice as often as the others because these were each used in two stimulus pairs. The constant stimulus feature of interest for this study was the 40 mμ difference between the simultaneously displayed stimuli.

TABLE 1

STIMULUS PAIRS USED FOR VARIABLE-INTERVAL TRAINING IN STUDY 1
(Stimulus values used in two training pairs are italicized)

490, *530* mμ	550, *590* mμ
500, *540*	*560*, 600
510, *550*	*570*, 610
520, *560*	*580*, 620
530, 570	*590*, 630
540, 580	

For the first six sessions of this training, a VI 30-sec. schedule was in effect. For sessions 7–12, the mean inter-reinforcement was increased to 75 sec. At the end of this training period, the birds were responding at reliable and consistent rates.

Generalization tests. The generalization test was designed so that a variety of difference values from 0 to 80 mμ was presented by means of appropriate pairs of the spectral values used in VI training. For example, 15 pairs could provide no difference: 490, 490 mμ; 500, 500 mμ; ... 630, 630 mμ. Fourteen pairs provided 10 mμ differences: 490, 500 mμ; 500, 510 mμ; etc. In like manner, 13 pairs could be used to provide a 20 mμ difference value, and so on, through seven pairs available with a difference value of 80 mμ. Of the various available pairs, seven were chosen at random to represent each difference value for each subject during the generalization test. Each of these was presented once during each of two test sessions run on successive days. Each test session contained seven blocks of nine test periods each. During each block, one instance of each difference value was presented with order randomized. For example, during the first block, the difference value of 60 mμ might be represented by 490, 550 mμ; during the second block by 560, 620 mμ; and so forth. The two combinations derived from each pair were presented on successive days. The tests were run in extinction, and each test trial was 30 sec. long. The first test session was preceded by one block of training trials with the VI 75-sec. reinforcement schedule in effect.

Results

The question of interest is whether there was any systematic relationship between the rate of responding in the generalization test and the various difference values. The relevant data can be seen in Fig. 1, in which all the stimulus combinations representing a given difference value have been combined to provide the mean data for each value of the independent variable. It is clear from the line representing all test periods that there is very little difference between the number of responses emitted in the presence of the training value of 40 mμ and the various other test values. In other words, the dimension of stimulus difference appears to have had no control over response rate. A Treatments × Subjects analysis of variance confirms this impression, in that the F ratio for the treatments effect (between difference values) was less than 1.00.

The fact that responding to stimulus values in the middle of the range (530–590 mμ) was reinforced during training twice as often as responding to the other values may have led to stimulus control by specific stimulus values that could have obscured the effect of stimulus differences. In order to assess this possibility, the test periods were divided into three sets, and the mean total response rate to both keys was obtained for all the periods

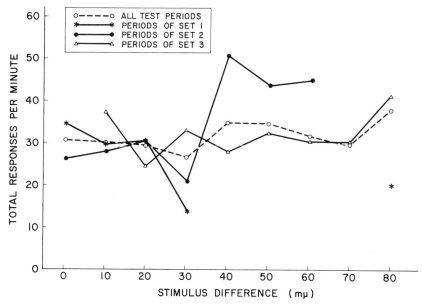

FIG. 1. Mean total response rates to both members of stimulus pairs in the generalization test of Study 1.

in each set. The first set consisted of those periods in which both of the stimuli had previously been used in only one training combination (i.e., 490–520 mμ and 600–630 mμ); the mean response rate was 29.0 responses per min. The second set consisted of those periods in which both the stimuli had been used in two training pairs (i.e., 530–590 mμ); the mean response rate was 32.4. The third set consisted of those periods in which one stimulus had been used in one training pair and the other in two; the mean rate was 31.8. From this result, it appears that the effect of differing frequencies of reinforcement with specific stimulus values was very small.

This analysis was carried one step further by subdividing the sets of test periods just described according to the difference value displayed in each period. In this way, generalization "gradients" were obtained for each set of periods, controlling for the different frequencies of reinforcement associated with specific stimulus values. These are plotted in Fig. 1 in addition to the over-all gradient. There is still rather little systematic effect of stimulus difference. The only major difference is that for stimuli of the second set, there appears to be a greater response rate for larger than for smaller difference values. This difference is probably not reliable, however, since the sample of periods with the large difference values in this group was rather small; there are only a few ways of obtaining 40, 50, and 60 mμ differences in the range from 530–590 mμ.

Discussion

These data indicate that even when a given difference value is a constant feature of an environment in which a response has been acquired, it does not function as a "natural" dimension of stimulus control for pigeons. In this way, the stimulus-difference dimension does not differ from certain primary dimensions such as auditory frequency, where Jenkins and Harrison (1960) have shown that without preliminary discrimination training, the generalization gradient is almost flat. Gradients for spectral value (Guttman and Kalish, 1956) and intensity (Blough, 1959) can be obtained without explicit training, but the possibility remains that even in such cases discrimination training takes place simply in the acquisition of the operant behavior, i.e., the animal must learn to locate the illuminated key, responding may be extinguished during time-out periods, etc.

The next step, therefore, appeared to be an attempt to produce stimulus control on the stimulus-difference dimension through explicit discrimination training. Following the traditional procedure for such efforts, one difference value (40 mμ) was made positive, and another value (0 mμ) was made negative. The same subjects were used, and the 40 mμ difference pairs used in the original training were continued as positive values. One-minute presentations of these were intermixed randomly with periods during which the 15 stimulus values in question were presented identically on both keys. Responding during these periods was not reinforced. The animals showed little tendency toward extinction during the negative periods, even though the mean inter-reinforcement interval during the positive periods was reduced to 30 sec.

STUDY 2

Discrimination and Generalization on the Basis of
Stimulus Differences

The failure to obtain a discrimination with the procedure just described may have been due to the nature of the response indicator required for the discrimination. To evaluate the difference value the animal must look at both keys, and there was nothing in the successive discrimination ("go, no-go") procedure to force him to do so. With this in mind, another and more successful technique was devised. Difference values provided the cues for a left-right discrimination between the response keys, the principal response measure being the proportion of the total responses made to each key.

Method

Four White King pigeons reduced to 70 per cent of their free-feeding weight were used in this study. The apparatus described in Study 1 was used, with the addition of a circuit that could be used to initiate blackout periods whenever reinforcements were presented. Preliminary training was similar to Study 1, but was restricted to a smaller range of stimulus values.

Discrimination training. The general aim was to make pigeons discriminate between 0 and 40 mμ difference values by making one key (the "identity key") correct with the display of 0 mμ differences and the other key (the "difference key") correct with the display of 40 mμ differences. For two birds, the identity key was always on the left and the difference key on the right; this procedure was reversed for the other two.

The training pairs were drawn from the stimulus values ranging from 500 to 570 mμ inclusive, in 10 mμ steps. The identity and difference combinations are shown in Table 2. Eight specific combinations comprised the "identity half" of the problem, and eight other combinations the "difference half." Not only were the same specific values used equally for both halves of the problem, but within each of these, all stimulus values were displayed on the correct key equally often.

The sixteen stimulus combinations used in training and shown in Table 2 were each presented once in a randomized order in a block of training trials. Three or four blocks of trials were presented during each session. Not more than three combinations from either half were allowed to occur in succession.

During training, each trial was terminated with a reinforcement. Correct responses were reinforced only if they followed an incorrect response by 4 sec. or more. This error-delay contingency prevented chaining of errors. A blackout period of 15 sec. at the end of each trial allowed us to record data and change stimuli. Initially, the problem was made as easy as possible by reinforcing the first or second correct response on each trial that occurred outside the error-delay contingency. This procedure provided a

TABLE 2

STIMULUS COMBINATIONS USED FOR THE TRAINING PROCEDURES OF STUDY 2

Identity Group		Difference Group	
Left Key	Right Key	Left Key	Right Key
500 mμ	500 mμ	500 mμ	540 mμ
510	510	540	500
520	520	510	550
530	530	550	510
540	540	520	560
550	550	560	520
560	560	530	570
570	570	570	530

quasi crf (continuous reinforcement) schedule for correct responses. After 12 sessions a VI schedule was introduced, in which each period started with the beginning of an inter-reinforcement interval and terminated with a re-inforcement. Thus, each trial had a minimum length determined by the schedule, but this could be extended (and reinforcement delayed) by errors. For 18 sessions the mean minimum trial length was 20 sec. During the last four training sessions, the mean minimum period was 37.5 sec.

The termination of each trial with a reinforcement has two advantages. It rules out the possibility that a reinforcement in the middle of the trial might signal which key is correct during the rest of the trial. Thus the animal cannot respond randomly to the two keys until he is reinforced, and then stay with the key at which he was reinforced. More important, the reinforcement is obtained equally often for all stimulus combinations. If trials were of fixed duration, an animal with a strong side preference could simply be reinforced on half the trials—those in which the preferred key was correct. The variable length of trials has the disadvantage that total response output is not comparable between trials unless trial length is also recorded; the primary dependent variable therefore is the percentage of the total responses emitted to the correct key.

Generalization tests. After 34 training sessions, all the animals were re-sponding close to 80 per cent correct on both the identity and the difference discriminations. To prepare the subjects for generalization testing, two further training sessions were given in which the trials lasted for 60 sec. regardless of reinforcements. This precaution did not affect accuracy. It was omitted in later studies. The generalization tests were administered in two sessions consisting of both training and test trials. All trials were 30 sec. long and followed by 10 sec. of blackout. Each session began with one block of 16 consecutive training trials. After this, two further blocks of training trials were randomly alternated with test periods. The test trials consisted of each possible pair of stimuli drawn from the range of 500 to 570 mμ. This provided stimulus differences ranging from 0 to 70 mμ with the number of instances decreasing as a function of size, as in Study 1. The order of the various pairs was randomized. One combination from each pair was presented in the first session, and the other during the second session. Each difference value was represented at least four times in each test session, thus necessitating the repetition of some of the combinations involving the larger differences. (For example, the 70 mμ difference could be obtained only with 500, 570 mμ and 570, 500 mμ. Therefore, each of these combinations was presented twice in each session.)

Results

Discrimination training. Accuracy of performance was assessed by av-eraging the per cent correct responses for the problems in each training session in which a VI reinforcement schedule was in effect. The benefits of the first 12 sessions (under a quasi-crf schedule for correct responses) were evident at the beginning of VI discrimination training, in that all animals started with an accuracy between 60 and 70 per cent. This rose gradually, and after 20 sessions of VI training, all animals were responding close to 80 per cent correct. Accuracy was not affected by changes in the details of the training procedure in the two sessions before testing, when all trials were made 60 sec. long, nor by the random alternation of test and training trials in the generalization test itself.

In discrimination training subsequent to the generalization tests in this study, still higher levels of accuracy were reached; the asymptote appears to be around 90 per cent. Discrimination-training data will be presented graphically for Study 3, in which the subjects were trained entirely on a VI schedule, so that a complete picture of the course of improvement can be seen.

Generalization tests. The results for the generalization test are presented in Fig. 2 for the four individual subjects. All the stimulus combinations representing a given difference value were combined to provide the data for each value of the independent variable. At the left side of the figure are curves representing the per cent of the total responses for each difference value to the identity key. At the right is the total response rate to both keys for each difference value. Whereas the combined response rate to both keys is very stable for the various difference values, there is a

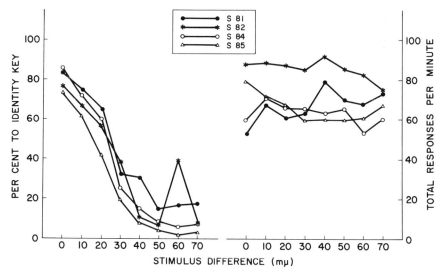

F I G. 2. Stimulus-difference gradients of key preference and total response rate from the generalization test in Study 2. Data are presented for individual subjects.

clear, orderly, and progressive shift between 0 and 40 mμ difference values in the distribution of responses between identity and difference keys. For each subject, the discrimination appropriate to the 40 mμ difference was transferred with improvement to 50, 60, and 70 mμ differences with the single exception of subject 82 at 60 mμ.

Discussion

We can see clearly that behavior was controlled by a dimension based on stimulus differences. That the birds could have based their key preference on any other cue appears out of the question. Since the same spectral values were used for both identity and difference pairs in training, and only the combinations of these values differed, this was the only available cue. Furthermore, the tests indicate that the birds did not learn merely 16 individual problems, since new combinations involving 50, 60, and 70 mμ differences show improvement over the 40 mμ difference, and since the rest of the differences show such a finely graded control over choice behavior.

The shift in preference was not accompanied by a decrement in total response rate to stimulus differences intermediate to, or greater than, those used in training. This result differs from parallel studies in which cues for a left-right discrimination were specific spectral values displayed identically on both keys (Honig and Shaw, 1962). In such cases, the presentation of intermediate spectral values in testing (but not during training) was accompanied by a marked decline in total response rate as well as an appropriate shift in preference. In the present case, the specific values in training and testing were of course the same, and all values were presented (and reinforced) equally often in training. Therefore, the absolute response rate appears to be governed by the specific values, and not by the relation between them. Only preference is governed by the dimension used as the basis for the trained discrimination.

The formation of SDD's and the production of the resulting gradients suggested various areas for further research. Transfer of the discriminations to new stimulus values was chosen as the most interesting line of investigation. As pointed out earlier, this question of direct transfer can be asked of SDD's where it cannot be asked of discriminations between specific stimulus values. Furthermore, the problem of transfer is central to the use of SDD's for research on perception and concept attainment. The studies on transfer that will be reported here involve three kinds of stimulus changes: (1) the presentation of new stimulus values on the continuum used in original training (in our case, new spectral values), (2) the alteration of an irrelevant aspect of the original training values (a reduction of the intensity of the spectral stimuli), and (3) the presentation of difference values on a new primary stimulus continuum (differences in intensity).

STUDY 3

The Small- vs. the Large-Difference Discrimination and
Its Transfer to New Spectral Values

One of the problems involved in research on transfer is that the animals may show specific stimulus preferences for certain transfer values over others, owing to the specific stimuli involved rather than to the degree of difference between them. To cite an example based on the research reported in the previous section: The birds that had been trained on an SDD using the range 500–570 mμ were presented with various difference values made up from stimuli in the range 590–630 mμ. They demonstrated a consistent preference for the values closer to the original training range (i.e., the shorter wavelengths). This result overrode any transfer of the SDD except where identical values were displayed, when some preference for the identity key became evident. To circumvent this kind of difficulty, it is necessary to equate the attractiveness of the specific stimulus values in advance. One way to do this is to present stimuli lying between the training stimuli, so that all the transfer stimuli are equidistant from the training values. This strategy was used in Study 3. A secondary question of interest was, Could the pigeons learn an SDD between a large- and a small-difference value, and, if so, would the small-difference discrimination transfer to still smaller stimulus differences, just as the (large-) difference discrimination had, in the previous study, transferred to still larger stimulus differences?

Method

Four new subjects were used for this study. The general procedure was much the same as that used for the first study, except that the quasi-crf sessions at the beginning of discrimination training were omitted.

Discrimination training. The training pairs were made up of values ranging from 500 to 640 mμ in 20 mμ steps. Combinations providing differences of 20 mμ (small difference) were to be discriminated from those providing 80 mμ differences (large difference). The small-difference key was on the right for two birds and on the left for the other two. The training combinations used in the small-difference and large-difference problems are presented in Table 3. Since there were fourteen small-difference combinations based on seven stimulus pairs but only eight large-difference combinations based on four stimulus pairs, the large-difference combinations were presented more often in order to let each key be correct on about half the trials. In the course of one session, three randomized blocks of 80 mμ difference trials (24 in all) were combined with two randomized blocks of 20 mμ difference trials (28 in all) in random order. Trials terminated with reinforcements. Trial length was determined by a VI schedule

TABLE 3

STIMULUS COMBINATIONS USED FOR THE TRAINING PROCEDURES OF STUDY 3

Small-Difference Group		Large-Difference Group	
Left Key	Right Key	Left Key	Right Key
500 mμ	520 mμ	500 mμ	580 mμ
520	500	580	500
520	540	520	600
540	520	600	520
540	560	540	620
560	540	620	540
560	580	560	640
580	560	640	560
580	600		
600	580		
600	620		
620	600		
620	640		
640	620		

throughout training. All animals started with a mean minimum trial length of 20 sec., but were transferred to the 37.5-sec. schedule in the course of training.

Generalization tests. This phase of the study is best viewed as the concurrent administration of two generalization tests. In one test, to be called the "training test," the training stimuli (500, 520, 540, . . . 640 mμ) were presented in various combinations to provide difference values of 0, 20, 40, 60, 80, and 100 mμ. In the second test, to be called the "transfer test," the stimuli 510, 530, 550, . . . 630 mμ were combined to provide the same difference values. These specific values, of course, lay between those used in training, and had not been presented previously. Within both the training and the transfer tests, all possible combinations representing the difference values from 0 to 100 mμ were presented at least once, and, as in Study 2, each difference value was represented at least eight times in the course of two test sessions. The order of specific combinations was randomized.

Training trials equivalent to one training session were mixed with training-test trials and transfer-test trials during each test session. These three kinds of trials alternated in random order except for a "warmup" sequence of 18 training trials at the beginning of each session. All trials were 30 sec. long. One animal was tested twice with retraining in between because of poor responding on the first test. The results have been averaged for the two tests for this subject.

Results

Discrimination training. The training data are presented in Fig. 3 in terms of mean percentage of correct responses, mostly over blocks of five sessions. The last point before the break in each curve represents the ac-

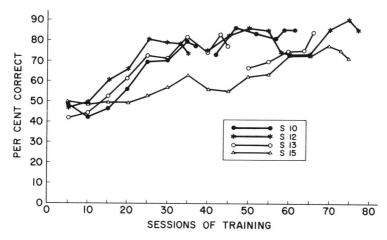

FIG. 3. The acquisition of the small- vs. the large-difference discrimination in Study 3.

curacy on training periods scheduled during the generalization test; this demonstrates that the discrimination was well maintained during these periods. For all animals except subject 15, who learned most slowly, data from additional training up to a second generalization test (described below) are presented after the break in the curve. Several weeks elapsed between the first test and the continuation of training. For two birds, there was little loss in accuracy, but one (subject 13) suffered a severe drop. Accuracy appears to level off at between 80 and 90 per cent, although, with continued training, levels above 90 per cent have been achieved. It should be noted that the first portion of each curve shows little or no improvement for several sessions, ranging from about 10 sessions for subject 12 to about 25 sessions for subject 15. The difficulty of the present discrimination is manifested here; most pigeons can learn left-right discrimination in which two specific spectral stimuli provide the relevant cue within the time it took these birds to demonstrate any improvement over the chance level.

Generalization tests. The data obtained from the training set will be called the "training gradient"; those obtained from the transfer test will be called the "transfer gradient." The results are presented for these gradients for individual animals in Fig. 4 in terms of the per cent of total responses to the small-difference key. There appear to be no systematic differences between gradients; for some animals, the training gradients look more orderly; for others, the transfer gradients. This impression is confirmed by the group results found in Fig. 5, in which the curves at the left indicate per cent of total responses to the small-difference key, and the curves on the right represent the mean total response rate to the stimulus pairs that provided the various difference values. Clearly, there is very little difference between the training gradients and the transfer gradients. The large-

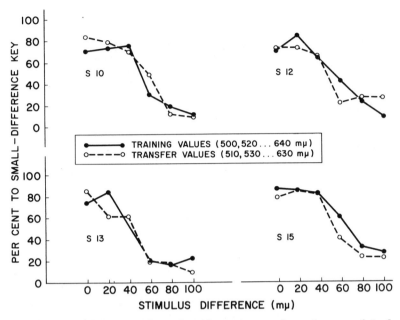

FIG. 4. Stimulus-difference gradients from the training and transfer tests of Study 3, compared for individual subjects.

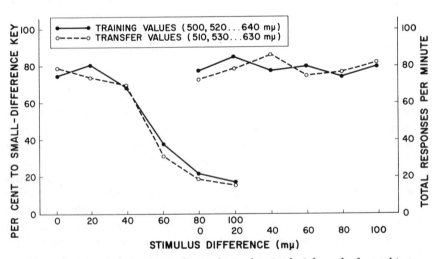

FIG. 5. Training and transfer gradients obtained in Study 3 from the four subjects.

difference discrimination is maintained at 100 mμ difference, with slight improvement; the small-difference discrimination is maintained at 0 mμ difference, although improvement is doubtful.

Discussion

Initially, we have obtained excellent transfer of the SDD to a new set of stimulus values, admittedly a set close enough to the training values so that response rate was not reduced when they were presented. Perhaps transfer in such a situation does not seem remarkable; nevertheless, the finding is important in that it establishes that complete transfer can occur, and it provides a standard against which other transfer studies may be compared. Furthermore, the phenomenon of transfer erases any lingering doubt that the original SDD's and resulting gradients may have been caused by some artifact associated with the specific values used in that study. In addition to providing data on transfer, this study confirms in a general way the findings of Study 2: The gradients are of the same mildly ogive shape, and there is no decrement in total response rate to both keys when new degrees of stimulus differences are presented.

STUDIES 4.1, 4.2, 4.3

The Effect of a Reduction in Intensity upon Spectral Difference Discriminations

One difficulty noted above with regard to transfer studies is that certain transfer stimuli may be more attractive than others, and that such preferences would tend to override an SDD, particularly if certain of the transfer stimuli are physically closer to the set of original training values than others. One way to avoid this problem is to alter the training stimuli so that changes are orthogonal to the original training dimension. In the present case, a reduction (or increase) in the intensity of the spectral values provided such a change, since the spectral values themselves were all matched for apparent brightness. Although such a change does not involve the presentation of a new stimulus dimension, and thus does not test for the limits of transfer of SDD's, the study of the effect of such an orthogonal change in the original training values appeared to be interesting and worthwhile.

Study 4.1: Method

Two of the birds used in Study 3 were used here. A third one of that group died, and the fourth was still trying to learn the original problem while this study was run. First, the birds were retrained on their original small-difference vs. large-difference problem according to the procedure

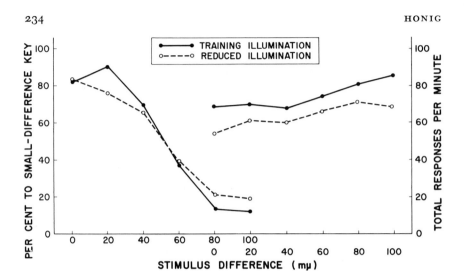

FIG. 6. Training and transfer gradients obtained in Study 4.1, representing the data from both tests and from both subjects.

described previously. When they reached a satisfactory level of performance, further generalization and transfer tests were administered.

The testing procedure can again be considered as the concurrent administration of continued training, a training test, and a transfer test. The training test consisted as before of training values (500, 520, 540, . . . 640 mμ) paired to provide difference values from 0 to 100 mμ. In the transfer test, the *same* values were presented while the light beam was masked to reduce intensity. This reduction was approximately equal to the insertion of an ND 0.5 filter. Owing to technical limitations of the apparatus, the insertion and removal of these masks took longer than our 10-sec. blackout period allowed, and the testing procedure had to be modified. The 30-sec. trials were divided into blocks of six. Each block was followed by a blank trial period during which the masks could be inserted or removed if necessary. Alternate blocks were training trials with reinforcements scheduled normally. On the other blocks, either six training test trials were presented with the training illumination, or six transfer test trials with reduced illumination. Each of the six trials in such a block provided one degree of stimulus difference—0 mμ, 20 mμ, 40 mμ, 60 mμ, 80 mμ, or 100 mμ. In all, eight training-test blocks and eight transfer-test blocks were presented in the course of two sessions of testing. Thus each degree of stimulus difference was presented eight times each under training and transfer conditions. The specific stimulus combinations providing the different degrees of stimulus difference were randomly assigned, but all possible combinations providing a particular difference value were exhausted before any of them was repeated. Each animal was tested twice in this fashion, with retraining on the discrimination in between.

Study 4.1: Results

The results for both training and transfer tests are shown in Fig. 6. Orderly gradients are evident both under training illumination and reduced illumination. The transfer gradient, however, is flatter, and the total-response rate, as indicated on the right side of the graph, is lower than on the training gradient by an average of about 11 responses per min. Orderly as these results look, it was evident from inspection of the individual data that each bird gave one "good" generalization test and one "poor" test. In the good test, the discrimination was well maintained throughout the training periods occurring during testing, the over-all response level was high, and there was little difference in rate between training and transfer conditions. This good test was the first one for one of the birds and the second one for the other. In the poor test, just the opposite was the case— the discrimination was poorly maintained and response rates were lower, with a large difference between the training and transfer conditions.

The results for both the poor tests and the good tests are presented separately in Figs. 7 and 8, respectively. On the poor tests, the transfer gradient is considerably flatter than the training gradient, and the difference in response rate is about 20 responses per min. On the good tests, both sets of curves look identical; the discrimination gradients cross five times in the course of six points. The over-all response rate is much higher for both the training and the transfer gradients. This analysis indicates that it is possible for perfect transfer to occur when an irrelevant aspect of the stimulus situation is changed. This finding was obtained when the response rate to the transfer stimuli was at a high level and equal to the response rate for the training stimuli.

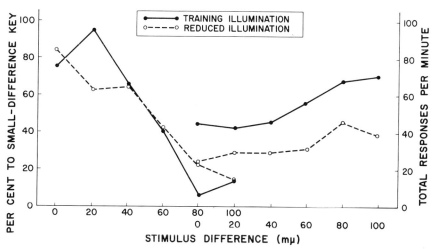

FIG. 7. Training and transfer gradients from the "poor" test obtained from both subjects in Study 4.1.

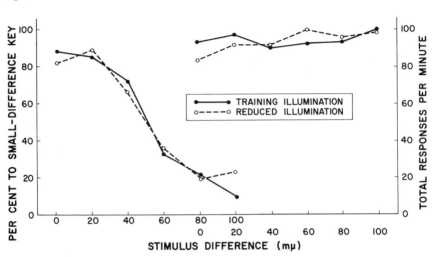

F IG. 8. Training and transfer gradients from the "good" test obtained from both subjects in Study 4.1.

Along with a lower response rate on the poor tests, we found a considerable difference in rate between the test and the training values. Since these differences between the results of the tests are confounded, the conditions responsible for the differences in slope between the preference gradients cannot be determined with certainty. It is attractive to hypothesize that if the animal does not "notice" the difference between training and test stimuli to a degree that will lead to a difference in absolute response rate to these sets of stimuli, the stimulus-difference gradient will be unaffected in the transfer condition. This conclusion is put in doubt, however, by the results from similar studies with our other group of animals.

Study 4.2: Method

The subjects were the four pigeons used in Study 2. Their discrimination between difference values of 0 and 40 mμ was maintained before the test series in this study was begun. The testing procedure was very similar to that provided in Study 4.1. Masks were inserted into the light beam of the projectors to produce transfer-test trials under reduced intensities. The difference values presented in the tests were 0 mμ, 10 mμ, 20 mμ, 30 mμ, 40 mμ, and 50 mμ. The birds were tested twice, with retraining preceding each test.

Study 4.2: Results

First test. The gradients obtained from the first test are shown in Fig. 9. Clearly, the transfer gradient is flatter than the training gradient, and it is also less orderly in that responses to the identity key are greater for 10 and

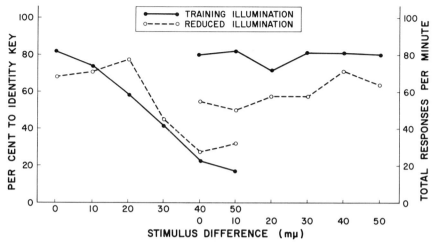

F I G. 9. Training and transfer gradients from the first test obtained from the four subjects in Study 4.2.

20 mμ differences than for the 0 mμ difference. Although this shift toward the identity key may merely represent a loss of stimulus control and the emergence of a position preference, it is conceivable that the animals were rendering a psychophysical judgment, namely, that under reduced illumination, the apparent difference between two spectral values is reduced. This seems reasonable in view of the fact that as light intensity is reduced, colors become less saturated and eventually only achromatic shades are visible.

Second test. In order to check the reliability of these results, a second test was administered after retraining. The results (Fig. 10) are similar to those obtained on the first test. The transfer gradient is flatter, and the flattening is due entirely to a shift toward the identity key. There is a marked difference in total rate between training illumination and reduced illumination. To check the hypothesis that the shift to the identity key represented a true psychophysical judgment of the change in similarity, it would have been useful to increase as well as reduce illumination, since an increase should lead to a shift in the opposite direction. Unfortunately, the optical system did not permit this.

In the meantime, we had obtained the results from Study 4.1. They indicated that slope differences between training and transfer gradients disappeared when response rates under training and reduced illumination were equal. In the present study, response rates were generally lower for all subjects under reduced illumination, so a direct comparison with the results of Study 4.1 was not possible. Instead, the transfer gradients from the two tests for each animal were compared in terms of the degree of re-

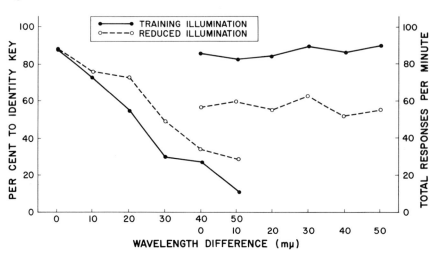

F I G. 10. Training and transfer gradients from the second test obtained from the four subjects in Study 4.2.

duction of response rate under reduced illumination. There appeared to be no tendency for gradients to be flatter with a greater reduction. However, the differences in the amount of reduction were relatively small. The next step in this analysis was to try to equate response rates under training and transfer conditions experimentally in advance of a third transfer test, in order to see whether this would equate the slopes of the corresponding gradients.

Study 4.3: Method
A procedure called "special training" was instituted in order to equate rates under reduced and training illumination without presenting the former in actual discrimination training, as that would contaminate test results. Only one key was illuminated at a time, alternating randomly between left and right. During each special training session, each stimulus value (ranging from 500 mμ to 570 mμ inclusive, in 10 mμ steps) was presented for 1-min. periods five times in randomized blocks. For the first, third, and fifth blocks, the masks reducing illumination were inserted; for the second and fourth, they were omitted. The same reinforcement schedule (VI 37.5 sec.) was used for all blocks. Regular training sessions with standard illumination alternated with special training on successive days. After seven sessions of special training for two subjects, and after fourteen sessions for a third, another generalization and transfer test was administered under regular and reduced illumination in the manner described for Studies 4.1 and 4.2. The fourth animal developed a dreadful position habit during retraining and was not tested in this series.

Study 4.3: Results

The results are presented in Fig. 11. In addition to training and transfer gradients, the points from the second transfer gradient of the previous study (4.2) are plotted as x's. The transfer gradient, while handsome, is flatter than the training gradient and the previous transfer gradient, and crosses the training gradient between 10 and 20 mμ of stimulus difference. The shift toward the identity key is thus not maintained. Although the difference in rate between training and reduced illumination was reduced by the special training from 33 responses per min. to 12 responses per min., the transfer gradient did not become steeper. If anything, it is flatter. These results indicate that there is a genuine loss of stimulus control under these conditions of reduced illumination, rather than a psychophysical judgment of greater similarity among stimuli. Furthermore, the results show that equating response rates between training and transfer stimuli is not a sufficient condition (though it may be necessary) for obtaining gradients of similar slope.

It may be, of course, that the special training procedure, involving the presentation of single stimuli, resulted in flattening of the gradient. Even with the other key blacked out, haphazard presentation (and thus reinforcement) on either key may have served to reduce any tendency toward discrimination with the transfer values. On the other hand, the training values were presented in the same manner, and there was no tendency toward flattening of the training gradient. There was no evidence during the discrimination sessions alternating with special training that the latter appreciably affected accuracy.

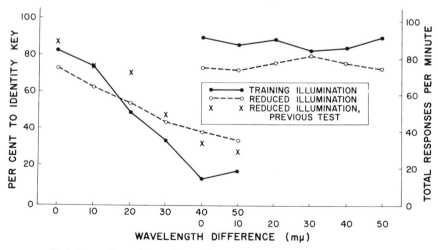

FIG. 11. Training and transfer gradients obtained from three subjects after special training in Study 4.3.

At any rate, the special training procedures necessary to produce equal response rates to transfer and training stimuli pose special technical problems. Perhaps the best solution is to have a three-key apparatus in which two keys are used for regular discrimination training and a third is used for special training. Furthermore, single-stimulus training should be carried out with both training and transfer values from the beginning of the experiment.

STUDIES 5.1, 5.2, 5.3, 5.4

Transfer of Stimulus-Difference Discriminations from Spectral Values to Differences in Intensity

Transfer of SDD's across continua would represent a very sophisticated performance and would indicate considerable generality of the control of behavior by such discriminations, once they become established. This is probably the most interesting and the most problematic of the transfer problems that we attacked in this series of studies. Differences in intensity were produced by a series of achromatic neutral-density (ND) filters. We were faced with the problem, familiar from previous work, that those transfer stimuli which were closest to the brightness of the spectral values would be preferred to the others. Furthermore, it was impossible to tell in advance what ND difference value would correspond psychologically to a given spectral difference value. The only "anchor" available was that identical ND values presumably correspond to identical spectral values.

Study 5.1: Method

Subjects. The four subjects used in Studies 2 and 4 were used in the present series.

Apparatus. A set of Kodak ND filters was used in place of the usual monochromatic interference filters. These had been cemented between two pieces of "B" glass. The reference density (nominal zero) was provided by two such pieces of B glass without any filter. The other densities were 0.5, 1.0, 1.5, 2.0, and 2.5. Six different intensity values were therefore available. Density is the negative logarithm of the proportion of incident light that is transmitted by the filter. Thus a filter with a density of 1.0 transmits $\frac{1}{10}$ of the incident light, a filter with a density of 2.0 transmits $\frac{1}{100}$, etc. For the human observer, the spectral values used in these studies were matched most closely in brightness by an ND value of 1.5.

Procedure. First, the subjects were retrained on their original SDD of 0 vs. 40 mµ, using the original stimulus range of 500 to 570 mµ. Satisfactory performance was rapidly attained, and a transfer test with ND values was administered without any previous exposure to these values. As in previous transfer tests, this one consisted of two sessions composed of three different

TABLE 4

STIMULUS COMBINATIONS USED FOR TESTING IN STUDY 5.1 AND TRAINING IN STUDY 5.3

Identity Group		Difference Group	
Left Key	Right Key	Left Key	Right Key
ND 0.0	ND 0.0	ND 0.0	ND 1.5
0.5	0.5	1.5	0.0
1.0	1.0	0.5	2.0
1.5	1.5	2.0	0.5
2.0	2.0	1.0	2.5
2.5	2.5	2.5	1.0

kinds of periods presented in randomized order (except for a block of discrimination warmup trials at the beginning of each session): training periods with monochromatic values, training-test periods with spectral values, and transfer-test periods with ND values. The training-test periods essentially duplicated the training periods in that only 0 and 40 mμ differences were presented (16 of each in each session), except that reinforcement was not available. The transfer test consisted of identity pairs, in which the six ND values were presented identically on both keys, and of difference pairs, in which these values were combined to provide intensity differences of ND 1.5. The specific pairs are listed in Table 4. Each of the twelve combinations was presented twice during each test session.

Study 5.1: Results

The results for the transfer test are shown in Fig. 12. The abscissa differs from those in most of the preceding figures in that specific ND stimulus

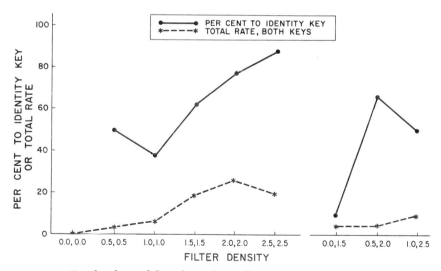

FIG. 12. Results obtained from four subjects from the transfer test in Study 5.1.

pairs rather than difference values are represented. Total response rate and per cent to the identity key are represented by separate curves. The identity pairs are at the left, the ND 1.5 difference pairs at the right.

The response rate for the ND identity pairs is quite low. Appreciable responding was found only with the dimmer values (ND 1.5, 2.0, and 2.5). An increase in the percentage of responses to the identity key accompanies the increase in rate. This preference rises from 50 per cent at ND 0.5 to 87 per cent at ND 2.5. (Only one response was made in the presence of ND 0.0, and the 100 per cent obtained for that point is spurious.)

The response rate for the ND 1.5 difference pairs was even lower than that for the identity pairs. If the SDD had transferred to these combinations, there would have been little responding to the identity key. This is clearly not the case except for the pair 0, 1.5, and even in that case the preference for the difference key is probably spurious owing to low rates. Inspection of the raw data showed that the dimmer value was preferred in all the pairs, a preference that overrode any discrimination based on stimulus differences. This is to be expected from the higher rates obtained from the dimmer values when identical values were presented. Across all pairs and all subjects, the preference for the dimmer key amounts to 79 per cent of the total responses emitted during the ND difference periods. It should be recalled that the spectral values on which the animals had previously been trained were close to the ND 1.5 stimulus in brightness, and that the spectral values used during training and testing with reduced illumination (Studies 4.2 and 4.3) were even dimmer. Therefore, the preference for the dimmer ND values was not surprising.

The results obtained on the training-test trials with monochromatic values are not shown in Fig. 12. These results were entirely consistent with previous tests. The preference for the identity key was 80 per cent for the 0 mμ difference trials and 18 per cent for the 40 mμ difference trials. The mean total response rate on both sets of trials was 90 responses per min.

Study 5.1: Discussion

This finding indicates that despite the problems involved in testing for transfer of the SDD from one set of stimulus values to another, it is possible to obtain transfer at least for the "identity half" of such an SDD. With the presentation of different stimuli during the transfer test, specific stimulus preferences are likely to override preferences cued by stimulus differences. When identical transfer values are displayed, such a contamination is at least avoided, and a genuine preference for the identity key can be shown, provided that the over-all response rate is reasonably high. It should be noted that the preference shown for the identity key, with ND values of 2.0 and 2.5 displayed on both keys, was equal to or greater than the same preference demonstrated when identical spectral values were displayed during the training-test periods.

We should consider the possibility that the density difference value of 1.5 presented in the transfer test was relatively small compared with the 40 mμ difference value on which the animals had been trained on the spectral dimension, and that this prevented the occurrence of transfer with the ND difference pairs. Three considerations argue against this. First, the ND 1.5 difference is psychologically (i.e., subjectively) considerably *larger* for the human observer than the 40 mμ spectral difference; in fact, it was chosen as a transfer-test value partly with this problem in mind. Second, the subjects showed that they could discriminate clearly between the two values presented in the ND difference trials by choosing the dimmer of the two quite consistently. Third, the ease with which they later learned the discrimination between ND 0.0 and ND 1.5 difference values (see Study 5.3 below) clearly indicates that the ND 1.5 difference was quite marked.

Study 5.2

Although this study was a failure, it is noted here in the interest of historical continuity and as a basis for subsequent research. The reasoning behind the study was this: in order to study transfer between the spectral and intensity continua, it was necessary to raise response rates to the ND values. The presentation of the latter on one key only might actually impede such transfer (see Study 4.3). It was therefore decided to present identical ND values on both keys, and to reinforce responding to the identity key only—i.e., to train the birds to the identity half of the SDD with ND values. The complete spectral SDD was independently maintained by presenting appropriate training sessions in alternation with the ND sessions. After the birds had learned this problem, intensity differences of 0.0, 1.0, and 2.0 were presented in a generalization test in the hope that the "difference half" of the SDD would transfer to the ND values from the spectral SDD when intensity differences were displayed. This hope was not confirmed; there was only a slight decrease in the preference to the identity key when these intensity differences were presented. To obtain SDD's on the intensity continuum, therefore, it seemed necessary to proceed with explicit training and testing of the sort presented originally for the spectral values in Study 2.

Study 5.3: Method

Discrimination training. The training procedure used originally (with the same subjects) in Study 2 was modified only to the extent that ND values rather than spectral stimuli were presented. The identity and difference pairs are listed in Table 4; they had also been used as test pairs in

Study 5.1. These pairs were randomized within blocks of twelve trials, and three such blocks were presented during each training session. As in previous training, each period ended with a reinforcement, which was scheduled on a VI 37.5-sec. schedule. A 4-sec. changeover-delay contingency was used to prevent chaining of errors.

Generalization tests. The tests consisted of two sessions in which ND differences ranging from 0 to 2.5 were presented in the test periods. These periods were randomly intermixed with training periods following one warmup block of training trials. Six blocks of six test periods were presented during each session, and during each block each of the six intensity difference values was presented once. The specific stimulus combination representing each value was chosen at random, but all suitable combinations were exhausted before any of them was repeated. Each difference value was thus represented on 12 test trials in the course of both test sessions.

Study 5.3: Results

Discrimination training. Compared with original learning of the spectral SDD, the acquisition of the intensity SDD was quite rapid. Three animals reached a stable over-all performance of 80 per cent correct by the ninth training session, and were run for a total of 12 or 13 sessions before the generalization test was administered. The fourth animal (subject 85) did not reach 80 per cent correct until the 24th session, and was tested shortly thereafter. All animals started on the first training session with good accuracy on the "identity problem," and with poor performance on the "difference" problem, thus confirming the findings obtained in Studies 5.1 and 5.2. When they were reinforced for responding to the difference key during the presence of the ND values, the accuracy on the "identity" problem fell at first and then recovered in the course of training.

Generalization tests. The test results for individual subjects are shown in Fig. 13, in which percentages are plotted at the left and total response rates at the right. The similarity between these findings and those from Study 2 is quite striking. There is a clear and orderly change in the preference for the identity key as a function of stimulus difference, whereas the total rate for both keys remains approximately constant. For three of the animals, the "difference problem" transfers from the ND training difference of 1.5 to the greater ND stimulus differences of 2.0 and 2.5 with some improvement, although little improvement was actually possible owing to the high over-all accuracy. It may be of some interest that the gradient is relatively flat between ND differences of 0.0 and 0.5 and drops precipitously thereafter. The indifference point—at which the animals would emit 50 per cent of their responses to each key—is closer to the ND difference value of 1.5 than to 0.0, which indicates that the psychophysical

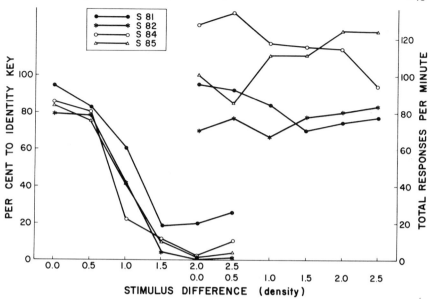

FIG. 13. Stimulus-difference gradients of key preference and total response rate from the generalization test in Study 5.3. Data are presented for individual subjects.

function relating intensity differences to behavior is not quite logarithmic.

This study demonstrates that the results originally obtained with the spectral dimension can essentially be duplicated on a different dimension. The rapid acquisition and high accuracy of the new discrimination indicate that indirect transfer from the spectral to the intensity SDD may have occurred. This is by no means certain, however, because the intensity SDD may have been easier than the spectral SDD. As indicated above, the ND 1.5 difference was subjectively greater for the human observer than the 40 mμ spectral difference. Since both of these had to be discriminated from pairs of identical stimuli, the ND discrimination may well have been easier to learn. To assess the transfer effect, it would be necessary to run an independent group on the intensity SDD without previous training. Nevertheless, it is my impression that an independent group would not have learned the problem as rapidly. Quite aside from the lack of any transfer of the discrimination per se, such a group would have had to eliminate the "error factors" (Harlow, 1959) that retard initial learning in a difficult discrimination.

Since the animals had acquired SDD's with two different sets of stimuli, it appeared of interest to combine stimuli from each set on test trials. To this end, we designed "mixed pairs" tests in which a spectral value was displayed together with an ND value on each trial. In such tests, the usual problems of presenting new stimuli in a transfer situation could presumably be avoided, and a perceptual "assessment" of the similarity between stimuli might therefore be obtained which could be compared with the apparent similarity attributed to the same pairs by human observers.

Twelve mixed pairs were presented by combining each of four spectral values—520, 540, 560, and 580 mμ—with ND values of 0.5, 1.5, and 2.5. These values were chosen from the eight spectral and six intensity values used in training, since the number of possible combinations would have been far too great for a test series. The spectral values decrease in saturation from 520 to 580 mμ, going from bluish-green to a rather washed-out yellow. Thus, they increased in similarity to the ND values as a function of wavelength, and preference for the identity key might be expected to increase accordingly. (It should be noted that the 580 mμ value had not been used as a training value with the animals. It was included because it was less saturated than 570 mμ, but its use proved to be unwise.) As indicated previously, the ND 1.5 value was closest to the spectral series in brightness, with the 0.5 value clearly brighter and the 2.5 value considerably dimmer. We could therefore expect the preference for the identity key to be greatest for pairs involving the intermediate intensity value.

Study 5.4: Method

Further training was given on the spectral and intensity SDD's for one or two sessions on each. All subjects had to perform satisfactorily on the SDD's before taking the "mixed pairs" test. The 12 pairs used in this test provided 24 combinations, each of which was presented once in random order during each of two test sessions. Two blocks of training trials on both forms of the SDD were intermixed with the test trials on each session. We could therefore concurrently assess performance on the spectral SDD, the intensity SDD, and the various mixed pairs.

Study 5.4: Results

The results from the "mixed pairs" test can be seen in Fig. 14. Data from the training periods are represented at the left of the figure. It is clear that the SDD's on both continua were well maintained during the test sessions. The data from the test periods are represented as groups of curves where the spectral value of the pair is indicated on the abscissa, and the ND value is indicated by the parameter of the curve. Preference for the identity key is represented in the center, and total rate to both keys is represented at the right. Median values for four animals were used for the former and mean values for the latter.

There is a clear preference for the identity key with the pairs involving ND 1.5, no strong preference for those with the ND 2.5 value, and a preference for the difference key when the ND 0.5 value is presented. This ordering corresponds to the expectations derived from subjective estimates

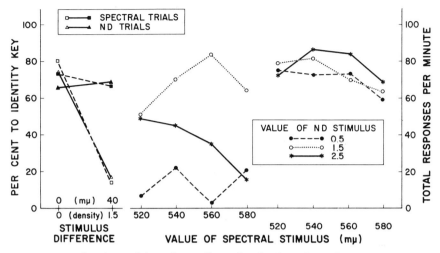

FIG. 14. Results obtained from four subjects for the "mixed-pairs" test of Study 5.4. Data from training trials are presented at the left, from test periods in the center and at right. The composition of each test pair is indicated by the combination of the abscissa value (spectral member) and the parameter of the curve (ND member).

by human observers, and is consistent with the response rates for ND values obtained in the first instance by stimulus generalization from the spectral values (Study 5.1). For the spectral values, there is an increase in preference for the identity key as a function of wavelength only for those pairs also involving the ND 1.5 value. For the others, no clear trend is apparent. The pairs involving 580 mμ are not consistent with either obtained or expected trends, and there is a slight but consistent decrease in total response rate for these pairs in contrast to the stability in response rate shown with the other values. It appears wise, therefore, to question the results obtained when the 580 mμ value was presented. Perhaps the animals really cannot be trusted to respond reliably on the basis of stimulus difference when there is any deviation whatsoever from the training series.

Apparently, although the intensity variable was an important factor in determining key preference, the spectral values made a difference only when paired with the intensity value closest to them in brightness. It should be remembered that the various spectral values were used to provide differences in saturation rather than differences in hue.

Study 5.4: Discussion

Let us try to interpret these data in a rather subjective and speculative manner. First, let us assume that the similarity between the keys was the only systematic factor determining key preference. Second, let us view the stimuli as providing points on two orthogonal dimensions, brightness and

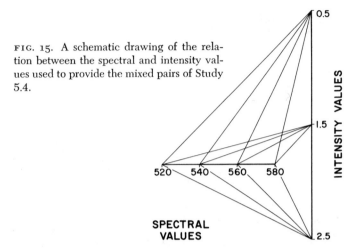

FIG. 15. A schematic drawing of the relation between the spectral and intensity values used to provide the mixed pairs of Study 5.4.

saturation, as shown in Fig. 15 (which assumes that the brightness of the spectral values was constant). Third, let us assume that the similarity between two stimuli is indicated by the length of the diagonal connecting them on that figure. Furthermore, let us assume that the differences in brightness that are determined by the intensity levels are relatively large compared with the saturation differences provided by the spectral values. Now it is clear from the figure that increments in the length of the diagonal due to spectral value are relatively great when the spectral value is paired with the intermediate intensity (1.5), and relatively small when it is paired with the greater or lesser intensity. Therefore it is understandable that the effect of spectral value in Study 5.4 should be relatively large with a small intensity difference, but small with a large intensity difference.

Although an extended analysis, based on a complex set of assumptions, may not be warranted by either the quantity or the quality of the data gathered in this particular study, I feel that such an analysis might profitably be applied to more extensive research on this kind of problem. In the present case, it would have been desirable (1) to have obtained more data to improve reliability, (2) to have used smaller intensity differences including ND values 1.0 and 2.0 in the stimulus series, and (3) to have paired ND values with wavelengths between 580 and 640 mμ, a series for which saturation increases, just as it decreases between 520 and 580 mμ. For the latter purpose, the birds trained on the 20 vs. 80 mμ difference discrimination (Studies 3 and 4.1) would have been suitable. Unfortunately, these birds were occupied with other work. With this sort of extension to the research effort described here, the kind of analysis presented above might again be applied, and perhaps with greater profit.

GENERAL DISCUSSION

Specific points of discussion have been presented in connection with each of the studies described above. It remains for me to present a few general considerations arising from the research. They are by no means exhaustive, and merely represent those lines of thought that I consider fruitful in the development of future research. Four topics will be discussed: (1) extensions of the method, (2) stimulus dimensions based on stimulus differences, (3) the opportunities for transfer, and (4) use of SDD's for the study of perception and scaling.

Extensions of the Method

A left-right differentiation proved to be a useful response indicator for this research, perhaps because a discrimination of position forces the animal to look at both keys. But it has some disadvantages. First, a side preference can be confused with a genuine indication of greater or lesser degrees of stimulus difference. Second, various stimulus differences have to be presented successively, which may retard learning. Third, a well-learned discrimination leaves little room for improvement, making indications of differences greater or lesser than those used in training hard to obtain.

It would therefore be useful to develop methods in which the response indicator is a rate difference under the control of successively or simultaneously presented difference values, which would serve as positive and negative stimuli. With successive presentation, a "go, no-go" discrimination would eliminate the first of the above disadvantages and partly eliminate the third, since response rates can usually increase over the rate to the positive value, although a decrease in a zero rate to the negative value is harder to accomplish. So far, our attempts to achieve the successive form of the SDD have been unsuccessful, although we used two birds that had previously learned the SDD on the conditional basis. Whether this failure stems from the fact that the stimuli were not close enough together, or whether response rate is for some reason locked in its control to specific stimulus values, is something that still needs to be determined.

In the simultaneous SDD, two groups of two values would be presented at once, with the animal learning to choose the more (or less) different of the two pairs in the manner described by Robinson (1955). The oddity problem could also be used. With the position of the correct pair randomized, the first and second of the above disadvantages could be eliminated, and a direct comparison between stimulus pairs would be possible.

Stimulus Dimensions Based on Stimulus Differences

The present work has been based on previous research on generalization and discrimination between specific values, much of it in the tradition of the original experiments of Guttman and Kalish (1956). We can ask whether a derived dimension of stimulus differences controls behavior in the same way as the primary dimension on which it is based. The appropriate comparisons are not yet available, because most of the previous work has used absolute response rate as the response indicator. (This is another argument for developing SDD's based on rate differences.) The closest comparison I know is a study on the bisection of spectral intervals by pigeons (Honig and Shaw, 1962). In this study, the animals were taught the conditional left-right discrimination with specific stimulus values as the relevant cues. The left-right preference gradients obtained from intermediate stimuli were quite similar to those obtained with SDD's, but, as mentioned above, there was also a great decrease in response rate when such values were presented. And the discrimination was acquired more rapidly. But interesting comparisons of phenomena such as "peak-shift" (Hanson, 1959) and transposition (Honig, 1962) following specific discriminations and SDD's cannot be made until the appropriate studies are carried out.

In one respect we do have a comparison between stimulus-difference dimensions and primary stimulus dimensions. Certain of the latter, such as the spectral dimension for pigeons, appear to be "natural" dimensions of stimulus control, in that generalization gradients are obtained without explicit discrimination training on the dimension. This is very unlikely to occur with a dimension of stimulus differences. Study 1 points in this direction. For difference dimensions, therefore, the generation of stimulus control can be studied from the outset, which is difficult to do for specific dimensions. Studies controlling the previous history of the subjects have shown that exposure to stimuli on the dimensions involved is critical in the generation of "natural" stimulus control (see the relevant discussion by Baron and Ganz in Chapters 6 and 9 of this volume). The common laboratory subject is hardly naïve in this respect. But the conditions necessary to produce "natural" stimulus control with primary dimensions, even when they are part of the experimental situation, such as learning to peck at an illuminated key, do not appear to generate stimulus control on corresponding difference dimensions.

The Opportunities for Transfer

Since stimulus difference values are abstractions, the issue of transfer is of particular interest. As pointed out earlier, most specific stimulus discriminations are not suitable for studies of direct transfer (zero-trial learning). The acquisition of learning sets depends on an abstraction of contingencies that are consistent among specific problems used in training, namely, that a stimulus designated as "correct" on one trial will remain correct for the rest of the problem. This abstraction of "rules of procedure" by the animal may occur entirely through the systematic elimination of error factors (Harlow, 1959). Such a theory is hardly surprising when the occurrence of errors is an essential cue for learning the rules, even when a correct guess on the first trial eliminates errors from the particular problem in question. But a more direct perception of the relationships and contingencies may be one of the processes involved, and could be observed when reduction in errors is not the primary characteristic of inter-problem transfer. With SDD's, the opportunity for a correct solution of problems without errors is at least available owing to the direct transfer that can occur. Although the elimination of error factors will probably be important in speeding the acquisition of new SDD's, a situation is presented where inter-problem transfer can be evaluated quite independently of the course of acquisition of the discrimination, and the discernment of relationships by the animal can be observed directly with an appropriate indicator response.

Direct transfer would provide insights into the formation of concepts as consistent forms of responding to characteristics of stimuli that are abstracted from different instances. The specific discriminations that are usually used for concept attainment are not entirely redundant, since various negative instances are usually necessary, and one or more stimulus variables tend to be confounded with the relevant cues in a single problem. If "triangle" is to be acquired as a concept, the negative instances must be varied, and in each case such factors as area, perimeter, occurrence of specific angles, and position must be controlled for by the suitable presentation of instances. The psychological importance of the presentation of partly redundant instances is therefore hard to assess. With SDD's, a single instance is sufficient for the acquisition of the concept of stimulus difference, since confounding factors, such as specific stimulus value and stimulus position, are controlled for in the acquisition of the SDD.

We can therefore ask how the display of redundant instances in the form of a number of sub-problems will affect the acquisition of a concept, both with regard to the speed of original learning and to transfer to new instances of the concept. In the present research, we always used several sub-problems in each half of an SDD. We did so in order to reinforce equally a range of specific stimulus values, so that we could make up new difference values from stimulus pairs which were unbiased with regard to specific preferences for one or the other member. A proper comparison between single-instance and multiple-instance SDD's still needs to be made.

The Use of SDD's for the Study of Perception and Scaling

Traditionally, animal research in the area of perception has used two methods: stimulus discrimination and stimulus equivalence. The discrimination method, used primarily to study difference thresholds, tells us what an animal can discriminate, but little about the perceptual characteristics of the stimuli involved. In the stimulus-equivalence method, a learned or unlearned response observed in one stimulus situation is elicited or emitted in a different situation, and the strength of this transfer is usually taken as an index of similarity between the situations. Among many examples, we may cite the investigation of generalization slope by Guttman and Kalish (1956), the use of equivalent responses to below-threshold and zero-intensity stimuli by Blough (1958), and the comparison by a monkey of actual expansion of a circle with the apparent expansion due to aftereffect of movement (Scott and Powell, 1963).

This general approach, while informative, has limitations, since the function relating response strength to subjective stimulus distance is not known, and comparisons of stimulus distance must be made on an ordinal rather than an interval basis. (See Blough's relevant discussion of generalization slope in Chapter 3 of this volume.) Furthermore, comparisons of stimulus intervals that are non-adjacent or on different dimensions are out of the question. In the SDD, however, the response indicator is controlled directly by stimulus differences defining a stimulus interval. This discrimination may therefore serve a perceptual scaling function.

If we could be certain that a given disposition (i.e., strength or preference) of the indicator response indicates a given psychological interval, we could take a major step toward comparing non-adjacent stimulus intervals on the same or different dimensions. This "if," however, is a thorny one, since an animal may be attaining the concept of stimulus difference at the same time that difference discriminations are being used for perceptual assessments. The transfer of the SDD that would make such assessments possible must remain an assumption unless we can find an index of the goodness of transfer that is independent of the perceptual assessment for which it is essential. But before giving up hope, let us consider three possible strategies for obtaining perceptual assessments aside from the strategy exemplified in connection with Study 5.4. To simplify the exposition, let us assume that the problem is to equate small and large stimulus intervals between an original training dimension and a new transfer dimension.

Transfer used as an indicator. The first strategy would be to make the best of a bad situation and use the degree of transfer itself as an indicator, much as the transfer of a response is used in the method of stimulus equivalence. The better the transfer, the more similar the original and new values. On this basis, Studies 3 and 4 indicate that 500, 520, 540, . . . 640 mμ are more similar to 510, 530, . . . 630 mμ than they are to 500, 520, . . . 640 mμ under reduced illumination. This method adds little to the equivalence method, except that it might be possible to ascertain the relative similarity of stimulus *dimensions* by comparing transfer from a training dimension to each of two other dimensions. But the actual equation of stimulus intervals could not be attacked in this way.

Absolute assessment of similarity. Ekman (1961) has described a method of magnitude estimation for the scaling of similarity in which human subjects assign numbers to various degrees of stimulus difference. A comparable measure with animals would be some disposition of the indicator response obtained under the control of stimulus differences. The main problem here is the assumption of good transfer. If this were solved, stimulus intervals on the transfer dimension would be equated to intervals on the training dimension when the indicator response is the same for both. This approach does not seem very promising at this time with pigeons, but the use of suitable methods with a more advanced species might make such a method feasible.

Relative assessment of similarity. This approach would employ an animal equivalent of the "method of cartwheels" (Dember, 1960, Ch. 3), in which two simultaneously present stimulus intervals are compared. After discrimination training with large and small differences on the original dimension, stimulus intervals on the transfer dimension could be presented together with one of the original pairs, and an equal-preference point between the two could be ascertained, at which the intervals are presumably equal. Again, specific preferences for values on one or the other dimension would have to be avoided. This method provides some internal checks and converging operations. For example, a variety of stimulus differences on the second dimension could be displayed together with a fixed difference value on the first dimension. Only if there were a clear ordering of preference between the varying and the constant stimulus differences could one look on the equation of the two difference values with some confidence. Furthermore, if two indifference points could be found, one equated to the small and the other to the large stimulus difference on the original dimension, then these points could be paired, and the preference of the "positive" over the "negative" difference on the new dimension should be equal to the corresponding preference on the original one.

REFERENCES

Blough, D. S. Spectral sensitivity in the pigeon. *J. opt. Soc. Amer.*, 1957, **47**, 827–833.

Blough, D. S. A method for obtaining psychophysical thresholds from the pigeon. *J. exp. Anal. Behav.*, 1958, **1**, 31–43.

Blough, D. S. Generalization and preference on a stimulus-intensity continuum. *J. exp. Anal. Behav.*, 1959, **2**, 307–317.

Dember, W. N. *The psychology of perception.* New York: Holt, 1960.

Ekman, G. Some aspects of psychophysical research. In W. A. Rosenblith (Ed.), *Sensory communication.* New York: Wiley, 1961.

Guttman, N., and Kalish, H. I. Discriminability and stimulus generalization. *J. exp. Psychol.*, 1956, **51**, 79–88.

Hanson, H. M. Effects of discrimination training on stimulus generalization. *J. exp. Psychol.*, 1959, **58**, 321–334.

Harlow, H. F. Learning set and error factor theory. In S. Koch (Ed.), *Psychology: A study of a science*. Vol. 2. New York: McGraw-Hill, 1959.

Honig, W. K. Prediction of preference, transposition, and transposition-reversal from the generalization gradient. *J. exp. Psychol.*, 1962, **64**, 239–248.

Honig, W. K., and Day, Roberta W. Discrimination and generalization on a dimension of stimulus difference. *Science*, 1962, **138**, 29–31.

Honig, W. K., and Shaw, Joyce. The bisection of spectral intervals by pigeons: A first attempt. Unpublished paper read at the Eastern Psychological Ass., 1962.

Jenkins, H. M., and Harrison, R. H. Effect of discrimination training on auditory generalization. *J. exp. Psychol.*, 1960, **59**, 246–253.

Robinson, J. The sameness-difference discrimination problem in chimpanzee. *J. comp. physiol. Psychol.*, 1955, **48**, 195–197.

Scott, T. R., and Powell, D. A. Measurement of a visual motion aftereffect in the rhesus monkey. *Science*, 1963, **140**, 57–59.

17. Further Analysis of the Various Effects of Discrimination Training on Stimulus Generalization Gradients

Herbert Friedman and Norman Guttman, *Duke University*

The experiments reported here were aimed at a more complete experimental analysis of the ways in which the wavelength-generalization gradient of the pigeon is affected by discrimination training. In addition, we examine, in somewhat greater detail than heretofore, generalization-test data obtained at various stages of extinction. However, this depiction of the changes in generalization performance during testing is secondary to the intention to clarify the modification of generalization accomplished by discrimination procedures.

The main point of departure is the well-known study by Hanson (1959), which exhibited that training of a discrimination between two successively presented monochromatic stimuli has the following effects. First, the maximum rate of responding to the subsequently obtained wavelength gradient (post-discrimination gradient = PDG) is systematically displaced away from the positive stimulus in the direction opposite to the location of the negative stimulus. Second, the PDG is narrowed rather symmetrically around its shifted peak when compared with the gradient obtained without explicit wavelength training. Third, the PDG's obtained by Hanson were unexpectedly high in comparison with the generalization gradient for a control group that obtained somewhat fewer reinforcements.

The height, slope, and position of such a PDG have to be regarded as the consequence of the whole set of changes that occur when variable-interval (VI) training on a single stimulus is replaced by a discrimination routine—a multiple schedule, in the terms of Ferster and Skinner (1957). The prevailing VI schedule gives way to a condition wherein half of the reinforced intervals are replaced by extinction periods in the presence of a new stimulus. In addition to the introduction of the second stimulus, the over-all mean interval between reinforcements is doubled, and the

This research was supported by Grant MH-3917 from the National Institute of Mental Health, United States Public Health Service. Herbert Friedman is now at the College of William and Mary.

total number of reinforcements per session is halved. During training the effects of these manipulations are seen as the gradual elimination of responding to S− and, typically, as a marked increase in rate of responding to S+. The latter effect was shown not only by Hanson (1959) but also by Smith and Hoy (1954), Jenkins (1961), and Reynolds (1961a, 1961b). Any of the foregoing manipulations and their manifest behavioral effects (not to mention implicit effects) could be related to the various features of the PDG. The present set of experiments is based on the fact (already observed by Reynolds [1961a, 1961b]) that these changes can to some extent be experimentally separated and their relation to aspects of the PDG determined.

Reynolds places emphasis on the observed rate increase to S+ during training, and appears to suggest that this phenomenon is sufficient to account for both the height of the PDG at S+ and the displaced peak. (The term "behavioral contrast" is employed by Reynolds in this connection, although it is not clear whether the term denotes just the observed S+ rate increase associated with the introduction of a multiple schedule or certain implicit changes in disposition as well.) However, an important point is that the S+ rate increase as delineated by Reynolds (1961a) occurs independently of the nature of the S− that is introduced in training. It will be convenient to employ the term "general effects" to refer to those manifest and implicit consequences of discrimination training (such as S+ rate increase and any possible enhancement of discriminative stimulus control over-all) that are not a function of the character of the discriminative stimuli or of the S+/S− difference. We may speak of other results (including, presumably, the amount of peak-shift) as "specific effects." In the usual operant discrimination situation, the development of these general effects coincides with the extinction of responding to a specific S−, and there is little evidence concerning the interaction of the two sorts of effects and little opportunity to make a separation.

The main technique used here as a step toward separating the general from the specific effects was to train a discrimination between two spatial patterns of monochromatic stimulation. The positive stimulus was the ordinary round key illuminated by 550 mµ, and the negative stimulus consisted of the shadow of a cross superimposed upon the key illuminated by the same wavelength. The outcome of such a discrimination can readily be compared with the generalization pattern resulting from a wavelength discrimination involving the same wavelength as a positive stimulus. The effective features of the negative pattern in the present pattern discrimination are presumably off the wavelength (or hue) continuum; this stimulus may thus be considered equidistant from all points in the continuum so that it will not distort the pattern of wavelength generalization. The approach embodied in this procedure resembles that of Jenkins and Harrison (1962), who used white noise or silence as the stimulus condition equidistant from the auditory frequency continuum, and also the method of Honig, Boneau, Burstein, and Pennypacker (1963), who used a blank key as a stimulus presentation functionally orthogonal to the continuum of line-tilt, in combination with either a reinforced or a non-reinforced vertical line segment.

Experiment I: Interaction of Pattern and Wavelength Discrimination

The first study was designed to determine how the general effects of a prior discrimination will combine with the specific effects of a wavelength discrimination to produce a typical PDG. The procedure explores the results of successive effects rather than simultaneous combination of general and specific effects. The experimental group (Pattern-Wavelength) was first trained on 550 mμ, then trained to discriminate between 550 mμ with and without a superimposed pattern, and finally trained to discriminate between 550 mμ as S+ and 570 mμ as S−. A control group (Pattern) was trained first at 550 mμ and then on the pattern discrimination only.

Method. The subjects were sixteen experimentally naïve white Carneau pigeons maintained at 80 per cent of ad libitum body weight and run after 23 hr. of deprivation. Ten birds were randomly assigned to the Pattern group and six to the Pattern-Wavelength group. The apparatus was two identically constructed Skinner boxes. The key illumination in one box, used for training and testing, was a Bausch and Lomb diffraction monochromator, but in the other box (used for training only) monochromatic key illumination was obtained by the use of two Bausch and Lomb interference filters on a swinging mount. Neutral filters were used to match the intensity of the filter-produced light to the monochromator output. Directly behind the key in each box was a sheet-metal cross, which could be inserted into the light beam by means of a small motor. When it was swung into position, the cross produced a shadow whose bars were about a fourth of the key-diameter in breadth. White noise was constantly present in the box, but there was no illumination except for the key light and food-magazine light.

The procedure began with training the pigeons to eat from the food magazine and giving them 60 continuous reinforcements for key-pecking over two days. All birds then received five daily sessions of VI reinforcement for key-pecking to 550 mμ, the stimulus that was present during continuous reinforcement. The mean reinforcement interval was 1 min. (VI 1′), and 60-sec. stimulus presentations were alternated with 10-sec. blackout intervals. Thirty stimulus presentations were given on each day of VI 1′ training. Then all birds were given pattern-discrimination training consisting of fifteen presentations of 550 mμ reinforced on a VI 1′

schedule randomly alternated with fifteen unreinforced 1-min. presentations of the shadow of the cross superimposed on 550 mμ. The Pattern group was continued on the discrimination until a session occurred in which the rate of responding to the cross pattern reached zero for five successive minutes, or until ten sessions of training were completed. All birds in the Pattern-Wavelength group were given ten daily sessions of pattern training, and on the eleventh day 570 mμ was substituted for the cross pattern as an unreinforced stimulus. The 550 vs. 570 mμ training was continued until a session occurred in which no responses to 570 mμ were observed for five successive minutes.

The Pattern group was given a wavelength-generalization test following the completion of pattern training. The Pattern-Wavelength group was given an identical test following the completion of the wavelength problem. The test session began with a warmup period of 2 min. of VI 1′ training to 550 mμ. The generalization test consisted of ten unreinforced presentations, each of 30-sec. duration, of each of the thirteen wavelengths from 480 to 620 mμ in ten mμ intervals, omitting 490 and 610 mμ. The set of wavelengths was presented each time in a different random order, and a 10-sec. blackout was interposed between successive exposures of the test stimuli. On the day following the first test, an identical second generalization test was given, but without a warmup period.

Results. As shown in Table 1, the rate to S+ (550 mμ) for both groups approximately doubled during the training of the pattern discrimination. The entire course of training for the Pattern-Wavelength group is presented in Fig. 1, which shows that when the negative pattern was replaced by a negative wavelength, there was a slight but temporary drop in rate of responding to S+. The second discrimination produces no appreciable rate increase to S+, but the generalization gradient that results (Fig. 2) is very similar to that obtained by Hanson for the same wavelengths as discriminative stimuli. The PDG shows a clear peak-shift, and is also some-

TABLE 1

Responses to 550 mμ (S+) per Min.

Group	N	Last Session VI Training	Last Session of Training	First Presentation in Testing
Exp. I: Pattern-Wavelength	6	42.4	87.8	86.7
Exp. I: Pattern	9	34.9	79.6	81.6
Exp. II: S− Extinction	10	30.7	80.7	28.2
Exp. II: Control	10	37.5	78.1	88.2
Exp. III: S− Extinction	4	30.3	63.8	18.3
Exp. III: Control	6	38.2	74.8	64.6
Exp. IV	4	34.6	71.2	81.0

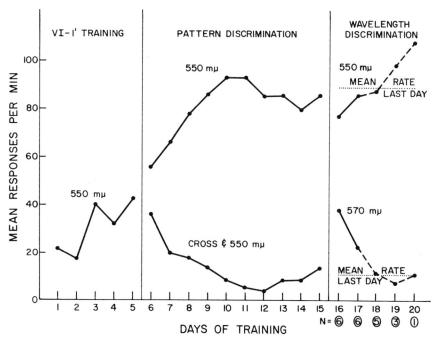

FIG. 1. Course of training of Pattern-Wavelength group, Exp. I.

what higher than the one reported by Hanson. The gradient for the Pattern group had its maximum at S+ (Fig. 5); this gradient will be discussed subsequently.

In analyzing responding to various wavelengths at the start of testing, it was found that the initial rate to 550 mμ (S+) was virtually identical to the terminal training rate for both groups (Table 1). However, the initial rate to 540 mμ for the Pattern-Wavelength group was higher than to 550 mμ (92.0 vs. 86.7 responses per min.), and the rate to 540 mμ remained higher during most of the course of testing. The initial rate to 540 mμ for the group that received pattern training only was lower than for 550 mμ, as is consistent with the shape of the gradient for the entire test. It seems clear that the introduction of 570 mμ during training of the Pattern-Wavelength group, which resulted in no increase in response rate to S+, did result in an increase in rate to 540 mμ during testing. The height of the shifted peak of the PDG, which is above that to be expected on the basis of the S+ training rate, appears to be the unique and specific result of training with an S− close to S+ on the test continuum. Furthermore, it is indicated that certain general effects of a pattern discrimination will combine with specific effects of a subsequent wavelength discrimination to produce a typical PDG.

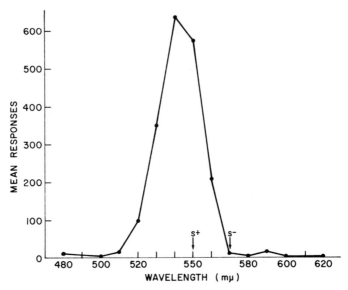

FIG. 2. Mean generalization gradient of Pattern-Wavelength group, Exp. I.

Experiment II: Separate Wavelength Extinction
after Pattern Discrimination

If the PDG is the composite product of some general effects and some wavelength-specific effects, then one may hypothesize that a shifted peak in the wavelength PDG may be obtained by separate extinction of a generalized wavelength after the training of a pattern discrimination. This hypothesis is based in part upon the finding of Honig, Thomas, and Guttman (1959) that separate extinction of a generalized wavelength following training to a single wavelength does not result in peak-shift; the main effect of such extinction is simply to lower the over-all level of responding in generalization testing, not the production of a PDG of the Hanson type. However, it is plausible that the general effects of virtually any discrimination may provide the sufficient condition for separate extinction to produce a peak-shift.

Method. To test this possibility, two groups of ten pigeons were trained in the same manner as the Pattern group of Experiment I: five days of VI 1' training to 550 mμ, followed by ten days of discrimination training with 550 mμ as S+ and the superimposed cross as S−. The experimental group was then subjected to a 40-min. period of extinction to 570 mμ on the day before the first generalization test. The control group was not given this extinction treatment. The generalization tests for both groups were the same as those in Experiment I, with the important exception that no further reinforcement of 550 mμ was carried out at the beginning of the tests.

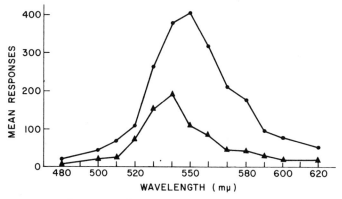

FIG. 3. Mean generalization gradients in Exp. II of experimental group (triangles) given separate extinction after pattern discrimination and control group (circles).

Results. The mean wavelength-generalization gradients for the two groups are shown in Fig. 3. It is apparent that the effect of extinction at 570 mμ is not simply an over-all reduction in the gradient, but a relatively greater reduction in the region of S—. Whereas the reduction in terms of absolute numbers of responses is greatest at S+, the greatest percentage of reduction is at 570 mμ (78.1 per cent). The per cent reduction for the longer wavelengths (560 to 620 mμ) is 73.5 per cent, while the corresponding reduction for the shorter wavelengths (480 to 540 mμ) is 47.2 per cent. Furthermore, the mean of the control gradient is found at 552.1 mμ, while the mean of the experimental group curve is located at 545.9 mμ, indicating that the extinction at 570 mμ has shifted the response distribution some six mμ toward shorter wavelengths. The greatest mean shift obtained by Honig *et al.* (1959) was 1.7 mμ. Thus it would seem that the discriminative control exerted by the key stimuli is greater after pattern discrimination than after training to one stimulus, and it may be suggested that the formation of virtually any discrimination produces, rather generally, a state of susceptibility to the specific extinctive effects associated with an unrelated stimulus.

Experiment III: Effects of Time-Out Periods

In the preceding experiment, pattern-discrimination training was used to produce an S+ rate increase during training and a peak-shift after separate extinction to a wavelength S—. However, it is known (Reynolds, 1961a) that time-out periods (no key light and the box completely dark) used in place of S— in a discrimination situation prohibit responding and result in a rate increase to S+. Thus it is possible that the sufficient condition for separate extinction of a wavelength to produce a peak-shift is merely the temporal patterning of stimulus presentations and distribu-

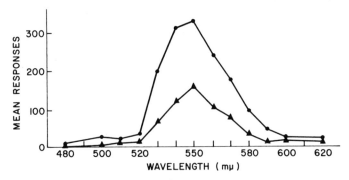

F I G . 4. Mean generalization gradients in Exp. III for an experimental group (triangles) given separate extinction after time-out training and a control group (circles).

tion of responding and reinforcements common to time-out and successive discrimination training. To test this possibility, Experiment II was repeated with the substitution of time-out periods for presentations of the cross-pattern previously employed as a negative stimulus. An experimental group of four pigeons was given separate extinction on 570 mμ prior to generalization testing, and a control group of six pigeons was tested for generalization without such treatment.

The results of time-out training (Table 1) replicate the finding of Reynolds (1961a) that such a schedule produces an increase in rate to the reinforced stimulus. In the present experiment, this increase is not an immediate effect of the institution of time-out periods; although there is virtually a complete elimination of responding during such intervals at once, the rate to 550 mμ did not increase during the first training period. However, even with the increase ultimately obtained, there is no evident difference in the form of the gradients yielded by the control and experimental groups (Fig. 4). The mean for the experimental group is located at 553.7 mμ, while the mean for the control group is 551.6 mμ. This slight difference is indeed in the opposite direction from what might be expected if it were the case that time-out training involved the formation of an unobserved discrimination. It is evident that, although a general effect of discrimination training is to produce an S+ rate increase, this change is not per se sufficient to sensitize the subject to the separate extinction of S− and yield a peak-shift.

Experiment IV: Pattern Discrimination and Slope
of Generalization Gradient

The wavelength generalization gradient for the group given pattern discrimination training only of Experiment I is considerably sharper than the gradients ordinarily obtained after VI training. Indeed, it closely re-

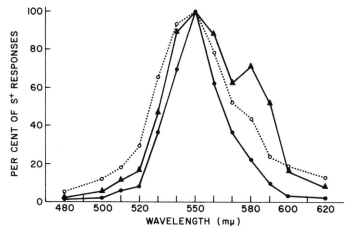

F I G. 5. Mean generalization gradients after pattern training in Exp. I (filled circles), Exp. II (triangles), and Exp. IV (open circles).

sembles in slope the PDG's reported by Hanson (1959). Such a finding would appear to indicate that discrimination training along one dimension increases the sharpness of the generalization gradient on another dimension, in accord with the findings of Reinhold and Perkins (1955). However, this finding is not replicated in the case of the comparable group in Experiment II (Fig. 5). There were two differences between the conditions for these groups. In Experiment I the pattern discrimination was carried to a criterion of non-responding to the negative pattern (mean number of training days was 6.1), and the generalization test was preceded by a 2-min. warmup period; in Experiment II discrimination training was carried out for ten days, and no warmup preceded testing.

In order to test whether the difference in gradients in Experiments I and II is due to the use of warmup before testing in Experiment I and not to the difference in amount of pattern-discrimination training, a group was trained as in Experiment I to a criterion of non-responding, and tested as in Experiment II without warmup. The mean gradient for the four pigeons so treated is shown in Fig. 5. The curve has a rounded peak with small differences among the three center test stimuli; it is very similar to the curve for the comparable group in Experiment II. The omission of a warmup period before testing thus seems to lead to a broader gradient. The results are in agreement with the finding of Thomas and Lopez (1962) that a period of delay between training and generalization testing results in a broader gradient; but in view of the role played by this variable, it does not appear possible from the present data to draw a satisfactory conclusion concerning the effects of pattern-discrimination training on the slope of the wavelength gradient.

Changes in the Generalization Gradient during Extinction

It is of interest to examine the alterations in the form of the generalization gradient as extinction progresses in testing. When the data for the
first twelve test series of Experiment I are employed to plot four successive averaged curves, representing test series 1 to 3, 4 to 6, 7 to 9, and
10 to 12, no systematic changes are seen in the form of the curves for either
group; the differences are essentially multiplicative, in accord with the
picture presented by Kalish and Guttman (1957). However, since individual subjects extinguish at various rates, an averaging method that is
independent of time and based instead upon total responses may be more
appropriate. Using the total set of 20 test series, the series for each bird
were divided into four groups which represented as closely as possible
the successive quarters of total responses. The mean gradients based upon
quarters of responses for the two groups of Experiment I are shown in
Figs. 6 and 7, in which each curve represents a nearly equal number of
responses. There is a clear and appreciable shift during extinction toward
a greater concentration of responding to the peak stimulus (shifted or
not), although the location of the gradient remains the same. Graphically
extrapolated peaks for the final three PDG's of Fig. 7 are within a range
of one mμ. The sharpening of the curves is easily seen in the gradients
of individual subjects, but the locations of the peaks are not as stable as
in the group curves.

The same analysis was carried out with the control gradient of Experiment II, as shown in Fig. 8. Here, too, the sharpening occurs, but the

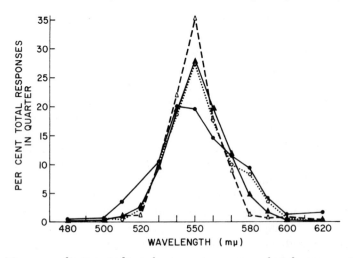

FIG. 6. Mean generalization gradients for successive quarters of total responses, Pattern
group, Exp. I. First quarter, filled circles; second quarter, open circles; third quarter,
filled triangles; fourth quarter, open triangles.

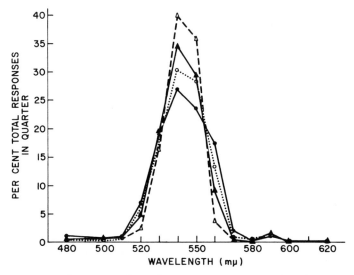

FIG. 7. Mean generalization gradients for successive quarters of total responses, Pattern-Wavelength group, Exp. 1. First quarter, filled circles; second quarter, open circles; third quarter, filled triangles; fourth quarter, open triangles.

gradient for the first quarter is very flat compared with the curves for the remainder of the test. A comparison of the Experiment II and Experiment I curves indicates that the main differences are to be found at the start of testing, which tends to support the view that a warmup procedure affects the gradient form.

The present analysis reveals effects which are consistent with the observation of Jenkins and Harrison (1960) that auditory generalization sharpens during testing, with the finding of Smith and Hoy (1954) that

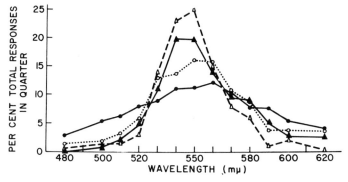

FIG. 8. Mean generalization gradients for successive quarters of total responses, Control group, Exp. II. First quarter, filled circles; second quarter, open circles; third quarter, filled triangles; fourth quarter, open triangles.

266   FRIEDMAN AND GUTTMAN

discrimination is enhanced during the course of extinction, and with the
re-analysis by Kalish and Haber (1963) of the Guttman and Kalish (1956)
data, which show an increasing proportion of responses to the training
stimulus over successive test series. In view of the extant data, one must
discard the assumption that the generalization gradients obtained at various stages of extinction are simply multiples of one another, even though
it may still be useful to compare generalization curves for different groups
by relying upon a multiplicative premise. The location of the gradient on
the test continuum does not appear to change in extinction, but the stimuli
remote from the maximum of the curve lose their effectiveness more rapidly than do the stimuli at the center.

Conclusions

The following conclusions can be drawn from the present series of experiments:

1. The initial rate of responding to S+ during generalization testing
following training to a single stimulus and a variety of discrimination procedures corresponds numerically to the S+ rate during training.

2. The initial rate to the peak stimuli of the wavelength PDG is in ex-
cess of the rate to S+.

3. Training on a wavelength discrimination without an S+ increase will
yield a shifted PDG when the S+ rate increase has been accomplished on
a prior pattern discrimination.

4. Training on pattern discrimination provides a sufficient basis for separate extinction to a wavelength S− to result in a shifted gradient, with
the maximum effect of extinction in the region about S−.

5. Time-out training leads to a large S+ rate increase but without explicit discrimination training and without its implicit effects. The location
and shape of the gradient after such training is unaffected by separate
extinction with another wavelength. Therefore, some effect of discrimination training in addition to S+ rate increase is involved in the shifted gradient after separate extinction.

6. The use of a warmup period before generalization testing affects the
shape of the gradient. A broader gradient is obtained when no warmup
period is used.

7. During generalization testing in extinction, the gradient becomes
sharper though the location of the gradient on the test continuum remains
the same.

Ferster, C. B., and Skinner, B. F. *Schedules of reinforcement.* New York: Appleton-Century-Crofts, 1957.
Guttman, N. Generalization gradients around stimuli associated with different
reinforcement schedules. *J. exp. Psychol.,* 1959, **58,** 335–340.

Guttman, N. and Kalish, H. I. Discriminability and stimulus generalization. *J. exp. Psychol.*, 1956, **51**, 79–88.

Hanson, H. M. The effects of discrimination training on stimulus generalization. *J. exp. Psychol.*, 1959, **58**, 321–334.

Honig, W. K., Thomas, D. R., and Guttman, N. Differential effects of continuous extinction and discrimination training on the generalization gradient. *J. exp. Psychol.*, 1959, **58**, 141–152.

Honig, W. K., Boneau, C. A., Burstein, K. R., and Pennypacker, H. S. Positive and negative generalization gradients obtained after equivalent training conditions. *J. comp. physiol. Psychol.*, 1960, **56**, 111–116.

Jenkins, H. M. The effect of discrimination training on extinction. *J. exp. Psychol.*, 1961, **61**, 111–121.

Jenkins, H. M., and Harrison, R. H. Effect of discrimination training on auditory generalization. *J. exp. Psychol.*, 1960, **59**, 246–253.

Jenkins, H. M., and Harrison, R. H. Generalization gradients of inhibition following auditory discrimination learning. *J. exp. Anal. Behav.*, 1962, **4**, 435–442.

Kalish, H. I., and Guttman, N. Stimulus generalization after equal training on two stimuli. *J. exp. Psychol.*, 1957, **53**, 139–144.

Kalish, H. I., Haber, A. Generalization: I. Generalization gradients from single and multiple stimulus points. II. Generalization of inhibition. *J. exp. Psychol.*, 1963, **65**, 182–189.

Reinhold, D. B., and Perkins, C. C., Jr. Stimulus generalization following different methods of training. *J. exp. Psychol.*, 1955, **49**, 423–427.

Reynolds, G. S. Behavioral contrast. *J. exp. Anal. Behav.*, 1961, **4**, 57–71. (a)

Reynolds, G. S. Contrast, generalization, and the process of discrimination. *J. exp. Anal. Behav.*, 1961, **4**, 284–294. (b)

Smith, M. H. Jr., and Hoy, W. J. Rate of response during operant discrimination. *J. exp. Psychol.*, 1954, **48**, 257–264.

Thomas, D. R., and Lopez, L. J. The effects of delayed testing on generalization slope. *J. comp. physiol. Psychol.*, 1962, **55**, 541–544.

18. Stimulus Generalization of a Positive Conditioned Reinforcer

David R. Thomas, *Kent State University*

Stimulus generalization is commonly said to have occurred when an organism responds to stimuli that are similar to, but not identical with, the stimulus used in training. Such a definition implies that the function of the stimulus is to elicit an involuntary response (eliciting function) or to set the occasion for a voluntary one (discriminative function). In either case, the response that is measured is directly contingent upon and follows or is contemporaneous with the stimulus in question.

As Skinner (1938) has pointed out, however, stimuli may have still other functions. For example, a stimulus may have an emotional effect whereby it facilitates or inhibits ongoing behavior. An electric shock or a tone that has been associated with an electric shock are examples of such emotional stimuli. Stimuli may also have a reinforcing function whereby they strengthen the behaviors that precede their presentation. Such stimuli include food (a primary reinforcer) and any neutral stimulus that has been associated with food (a secondary or conditioned reinforcer).

Examples of the generalization of eliciting and discriminative functions abound in the literature. Recent evidence (e.g., Ray and Stein, 1959; Hoffman and Fleshler, 1961; Hoffman, this vol., pp. 356–372) indicates that the emotional (inhibiting) function may generalize as well. Studies performed in our laboratory suggest that the (conditioned) reinforcing properties of a stimulus also generalize to similar stimuli. Some of these studies will be described here, and their implications for theory and for further research will be explored.

In an experiment reported by Thomas and Williams (1963), 40 experimentally naïve homing pigeons were reduced to 75 per cent of their ad libitum weight and trained to peck at a translucent, unlighted key in a dimly illuminated Skinner box. Initially, each pecking response produced a 2-sec. exposure of a light of 550 mµ on the pecking key, followed immediately by 3 sec. of access to food. The pigeons were not required to peck at the key *when it was illuminated* to receive reinforcement. Next, they were subjected to various fixed-ratio schedules (FR 15, FR 25, and FR 50) to build up their response rates. Finally, they were given 10 days of variable-interval reinforcement training (the inter-reinforcement period averaging 30 sec.) for half-hour sessions each day. As before, all reinforcements were preceded by 2-sec. exposures of the 550 mμ light on the otherwise unlighted pecking key.

At the completion of this variable-interval (VI) ½ training, four groups of pigeons were tested for resistance to extinction with 2-sec. exposures of lights of 550 mμ, 530 mμ, 510 mμ, or no light on the key, respectively. During the test no food reinforcement was given, but the stimulus exposures were presented according to the same VI schedule used in training. Testing of individual pigeons was continued until an extinction criterion of no responding for a period of 5 minutes was met. On the day after this test, each pigeon was retrained with 550 mμ exposures followed by reinforcement. Daily training sessions continued until response totals met a stability criterion of less than 20 per cent fluctuation on three consecutive days. At this time the pigeons were retested in extinction using a stimulus condition, during exposures, other than the one used on the first test. Retraining and retesting were continued until all the pigeons had received four tests, one with each stimulus condition. The order of presentation of these stimuli was randomized among the pigeons to control for extinction effects.

The reinforcement contingency used in this experiment was such that the pigeon was not required to respond to the 550 mμ stimulus to receive a reward. When food reinforcement was programmed, a peck at the blank key produced the 550 mμ stimulus followed 2 sec. later by food regardless of the pigeon's intervening behavior. Nevertheless, all the pigeons developed "superstitious" responding (Skinner, 1948) to the 550 mμ stimulus during its 2-sec. presentations. These responses, as opposed to those given to the blank key, are not indicative of the reinforcing function, but rather of the discriminative function of the stimulus. For this reason these responses, when they occurred during the extinction tests, were recorded separately from the responses to the blank key. This made it possible for us to study the generalization of "superstitious" responding to the monochromatic stimulus while we were investigating the generalization of the conditioned reinforcing property of the same stimulus.

In order to obtain a gradient of conditioned reinforcement, the response totals to the blank key for all pigeons on all tests were used. Thus, all 40 pigeons contributed to the mean values for each stimulus condition in the upper curve in Fig. 1. It was found that the greatest number of responses was given to the blank key when aperiodic exposures of a light of 550 mμ, the positive conditioned reinforcer, were presented. Furthermore, the number of test responses decreased for stimulus values of increasing distance from 550 mμ, producing the typical generalization gradient. Analysis of

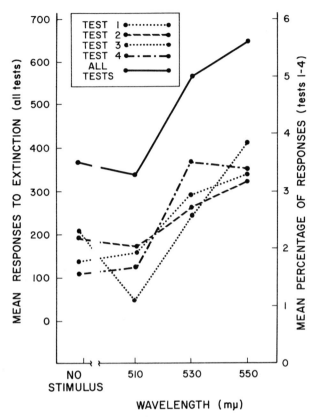

FIG. 1. Generalization gradients of conditioned reinforcement: responses to extinction measure.

variance indicates that the differences between means in this over-all (pooled across tests) gradient are significant: $F (3/117) = 5.27, P < .01$.

Randomization of the sequence of experimental treatments among the pigeons controlled for the extinction effect in the sense that there was no bias in favor of a particular stimulus condition. However, this does not negate the possibility that a change in generalization occurred, possibly as a function of discrimination learning, during successive retraining and retesting sessions. Whether there was such a change can be detected by comparing generalization gradients obtained on each of the four separate extinction tests. If it were true that discrimination learning had taken place, we should observe a progressive steepening of the generalization gradients with each retest.

To make the slopes of the obtained generalization gradients of the four tests directly comparable (i.e., to adjust for differences in the level of responding), the number of responses of each pigeon on Tests 1, 2, 3, and

4 was transformed into a percentage of total response output for each particular test to form what may be called gradients of relative generalization. More specifically, conversions were done in the following manner: For extinction Test 1, for example, the number of responses given by individual pigeons for each of the stimulus values was divided by the total number of responses made by all pigeons for all the stimulus values on Test 1. These decimals were transformed to percentages by multiplying them by 100. Then these individual percentages were summed for the various test stimuli and divided by the number of pigeons tested with each of these stimuli. This yielded the mean percentage of responses for the different test stimuli on Test 1. A similar procedure was used with the remaining extinction tests.

The four test gradients, in terms of the mean percentage of total responses, are also presented in Fig. 1. Despite considerable variability, all of the tests demonstrated generalization of the conditioned reinforcer. Only the gradient obtained in Test 3 showed significant differences attributable to stimuli: $F\ (3/36) = 5.18, P < .01$. However, there is no evidence of a progressive steepening of the gradient with successive retesting. Thus, the failure of more than one of the individual test gradients to achieve statistical significance must be attributed to the great variability in intersubject performance. The generalization gradient for scores pooled across tests is significant because the increased n in each stimulus condition serves to reduce the error variance sufficiently to yield an acceptable level of confidence.

The other measure of performance studied in the Thomas and Williams (1963) experiment was the time to extinction under each stimulus condition. As with number of responses, all times were corrected to include only the number of minutes that were spent responding to the blank key, thereby producing the test stimuli. This correction was made by subtracting from the total number of minutes to extinction for each pigeon the amount of time during which the key was illuminated by the test values. The mean number of minutes to extinction spent responding to produce the various stimulus values, pooled over all four tests, is plotted in Fig. 2. An analysis of variance showed that the differences between means in this gradient are significant: $F\ (3/117) = 6.31, P < .01$.

Again, to test the hypothesis that discrimination learning may have occurred with repeated retesting and contaminated the over-all gradient shown in Fig. 2, the separate test gradients of time to extinction were compared. In order to control for the differences in response strength on each of the four tests, all times were converted to percentages of the total amount of time spent by all pigeons for each test regardless of the stimulus values. The computational procedure used to obtain these percentages is similar to that described previously for converting the number of re-

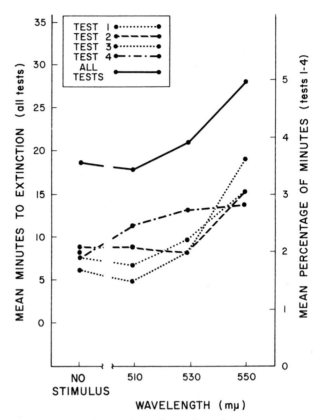

FIG. 2. Generalization gradients of conditioned reinforcement: time to extinction measure.

sponses into percentages. The resulting gradients of the mean percentages of time on the four tests for each of the stimulus values are also presented in Fig. 2. It will be observed that generalization gradients were received from each of the four tests. Only the gradient produced in Test 3 showed significant differences attributable to stimuli: F $(3/36) = 6.00$, $P < .01$. However, inspection reveals no progressive steepening of the gradients with successive retraining and retesting.

As mentioned earlier, the "superstitious" responses, made while the monochromatic stimulus was exposed on the pecking key, were analyzed to investigate the discriminative function possessed by the training stimulus light of 550 mμ. Since the time to extinction was greater for responding to produce the 550 mμ light than to produce the other test values, the 550 mμ value was presented more often than the others during the extinction tests. For this reason, the mean number of responses *per minute* during exposures was employed to compare responding to the different test stim-

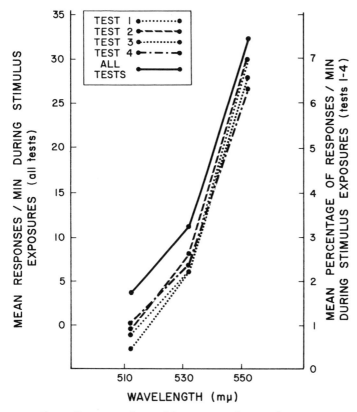

FIG. 3. Generalization gradients of "superstitious" responding in extinction.

uli. The generalization gradient of these responses, obtained by pooling the data received on the four separate tests, is shown in Fig. 3. Because these responses were made during the actual presence of the stimulus values, this gradient reflects the discriminative function, as opposed to the reinforcing function of the 550 mμ stimulus. Analysis of variance indicates that differences between means in this across-tests gradient are highly significant: F $(2/78) = 28.92$, $P < .01$. Furthermore, steep generalization gradients were obtained on each of the four separate tests, as also shown in Fig. 3. Analysis of variance showed significant differences $(P < .01)$ in the case of each of these gradients.

The findings of Thomas and Williams (1963) with regard to "superstitious" behavior are tangential to the theme of this paper and may be dealt with briefly. This was not the first study to demonstrate that stimuli may exert control over behavior that is only adventitiously correlated with reinforcement. In a paper by Morse and Skinner (1957), it was reported that when a stimulus was presented for brief periods during a VI session, pigeons developed different rates of responding in the presence of that stimulus and in its absence. In the Thomas and Williams (1963) study, the discriminative cue for superstitious responding was systematically manipulated, and a gradient of generalization was the result.

Of primary concern to us here is the data relevant to conditioned reinforcement. The Thomas and Williams (1963) experiment demonstrated a reliable generalization gradient for responding which produced the conditioned reinforcer. Subsequent work in our laboratory has extended their procedure, testing with stimuli of both longer and shorter wavelength than the original and testing each value more than once in an effort to obtain reliable gradients of conditioned reinforcement from individual organisms. Although statistically reliable bi-directional gradients have been obtained from subjects tested in this way, they lacked the requisite stability and uniformity to be useful as a baseline for further study. In addition to the fact that it requires a considerable expenditure of time and effort, this procedure lacks the many advantages of the Guttman and Kalish (1956) technique in which each subject is tested with many repetitions of a wide range of stimuli administered during a single test session. With this latter procedure, inter-test fluctuations in age, temperature, time of day, etc., are completely eliminated.

Thomas and Caronite (1964) have performed an experiment employing a modification of the Guttman and Kalish (1956) test procedure appropriate to the conditioned-reinforcement situation. A secondary purpose of their study was to examine the influence of successive discrimination training on the gradient of conditioned reinforcement thus obtained.

The subjects were 24 experimentally naïve homing pigeons, reduced to 75 per cent of their ad libitum weight by food deprivation and maintained at this level throughout the experiment. The apparatus and training procedure (for the 12 control subjects) were the same as that used by Thomas and Williams (1963). After conditioning and FR training, the pigeons in both experimental and control conditions were given half-hour sessions of VI ½ on 3 consecutive days. Then, while the control group had 10 additional daily half-hour sessions of VI ½, the experimental group received 10 daily sessions of discrimination training consisting of the concurrent scheduling of VI 1 with 550 mμ presentations always followed by food and VI 1 with 570 mμ presentations never followed by food.

Generalization testing for all subjects was carried out in the following manner: Immediately following the last training session there was a blackout (the overhead light was turned off) for 30 sec. while the counter was reset to zero and the conditions were changed to extinction and to a schedule of continuous conditioned reinforcement. Then the overhead light was turned on and the test began. The first peck started a clock for 30 sec. and also produced a 2-sec. presentation of a given monochromatic stimulus on the pecking key. Each peck at the blank key during the next 30 sec. produced another 2-sec. presentation of that stimulus, and during this 30 sec. both the number of pecks at the blank key that produced the stimulus and the number of pecks during the 2-sec. presentations of the stimulus were separately recorded. Each 2-sec. monochromatic stimulus presentation was followed by a momentary (1 sec.) blackout to prevent responses initiated in the presence of that stimulus from being recorded as having been made to the blank key, thereby producing the next presentation of the monochromatic stimulus, etc. At the end of the 30 sec. there was a blackout for 10 sec. while the monochromatic interference filter was changed. The first peck after the termination of this blackout produced a different monochromatic stimulus and signaled the start of a 30-sec. test period with that stimulus available. The 5 test stimuli (510, 530, 550, 570, and 590 mμ) were ordered in many random sequences (a different random sequence for each pigeon), and each test was continued until the pigeon failed to respond at the blank key for a period of 5 min. following the completion of the preceding sequence of all 5 stimuli. Thus, although the pigeons differed in the number of test series administered, each one was tested equally often with each of the 5 test stimuli. The first response to the blank key in each 30-sec. test period was not included in the analysis, since the response merely served to inform the pigeon of the reinforcement condition that prevailed during the next 30 sec. and the pigeon had no basis for anticipating the consequences of the response before the response was made.

The generalization gradients of both the experimental and the control groups for responses to the blank key are presented in Fig. 4. For each

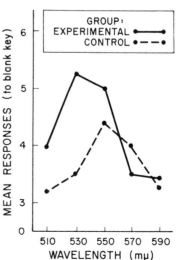

FIG. 4. Generalization gradients of conditioned reinforcement, with and without previous discrimination training.

pigeon the total number of responses to obtain each stimulus was divided by the number of 30-sec. test periods during which that stimulus was available to obtain the mean number of responses per 30-sec. period. The values reported in Fig. 4 are the group means of these individual mean scores. The gradient for the control group shows a peak (mode) at the original stimulus value and a greater decrement toward shorter than toward longer test wavelengths. This asymmetry following training with a stimulus of 550 mμ has typically been obtained in studies of generalization of the discriminative function of this stimulus (cf. Guttman and Kalish, 1956; Honig, 1961; Thomas and King, 1959; etc.). The stability of individual performance is reflected in the fact that of the 12 pigeons in the control group, 8 showed a peak of responding to obtain the 550 mμ stimulus, 3 peaked at 570 mμ, and 1 peaked at 530.

The gradient for the experimental group shows an elevation and a displacement of the gradient parallel to that which occurs with the generalization of the discriminative function following successive discrimination training. Clearly, the negative stimulus value of 570 mμ shows a depression in responding, whereas the 530 and 510 values are enhanced. Of the 12 pigeons in the experimental group, 6 peaked at 550 mμ, 5 peaked at 530 mμ, and 1 responded equally to 550 and 530.

The reliability of the elevation of the gradient of conditioned reinforcement following discrimination training was analyzed as follows. On the basis of past evidence, we would predict that the 530 value for the experimental group would show an enhancement as a result of discrimination training with 550 mμ as positive and 570 mμ as negative. We therefore performed a t test between mean responses to 530 mμ in the two groups to see whether the enhancement observed in Fig. 4 is statistically reliable. The result was a t of 2.81, 22 df, which is significant at the .02 level.

The displacement of the post-discrimination gradient was analyzed in the following manner. For each pigeon the generalization gradient was treated as a grouped frequency distribution with the wavelengths as scores on the abscissa and the number of responses as f on the ordinate, and the mean of this distribution was then computed. The mean of these individual means was 547.52 in the experimental group as opposed to 550.85 in the control, yielding a $t = 4.57$, 22 df, $P < .01$.

Responses made during the 2-sec. exposures of the monochromatic stimuli are "superstitious" in the sense that food reinforcement occurred, when programmed, independently of the pigeon's behavior during the stimulus presentations. Because the pigeons responded in the physical presence of these stimuli, this responding may be said to reflect the discriminative function of the stimulus, as opposed to its reinforcing function. For each pigeon the number of responses in the presence of each of the monochromatic stimuli was divided by the number of stimulus presentations to ob-

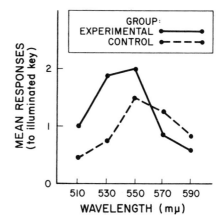

FIG. 5. Generalization gradients of "superstitious" responding, with and without previous discrimination training.

tain the mean number of responses per 2-sec. presentation period. The values presented in Fig. 5 are the group means of these individual mean scores.

The gradients in Fig. 5 are essentially similar to those of the same two groups presented in Fig. 4 except that they are even more stable. On a relative basis the discriminative gradient of the control group is steeper than its reinforcing gradient; in Fig. 4 less than 24 per cent of the control group's total responses were made to produce the 550 mµ stimulus, and in Fig. 5 the comparable figure is over 30 per cent. Also reflecting this greater stability is the fact that of the 12 pigeons in the control group, 9 peaked at 550 mµ, 2 peaked at 570 mµ, and the remaining 1 responded equally to 530 and 570.

The two gradients of superstitious responding were statistically compared in a manner parallel to that used with the data in Fig. 4. The greater level of responding in the experimental group at 530 mµ is significant, ($t = 2.40$, 22 df, $P < .05$). The displacement of the gradient of the experimental group is also significant. The mean of the control group means is 554.79 vs. 543.06 for the experimental group ($t = 6.10$, 22 df, $P < .01$). Seven of the pigeons in the experimental group peaked at 550 mµ and 5 at 530 mµ.

Although studies employing the method of demonstrating conditioned-reinforcement effects through the prolonging of responding in extinction appear frequently in the conditioned-reinforcement literature, the validity of this procedure has been questioned on a number of bases. Various alternative interpretations of increased responding in extinction in conditioned reinforcement studies have been offered. In a recent monograph by Kelleher and Gollub (1962), these hypotheses have been critically evaluated and evidence inconsistent with them convincingly presented. The interested reader should refer to their paper for a more detailed discussion.

In this paper we will be concerned with the relevance of these alternatives to the concept of conditioned reinforcement to the program of studies reported here.

The "discrimination hypothesis" (cf. Bitterman, Fedderson, and Tyler, 1953) points out that the resistance to extinction of a response is inversely related to the similarity between conditions during extinction and conditions during training. This fact brings into question some studies in which the presence of a "conditioned reinforcer" following responding in extinction leads to more responding to extinction. In a control group the absence of the "conditioned reinforcer" makes the extinction condition more readily discriminable from the training condition, and may result in decreased responding on this basis alone.

The intermittent reinforcement training condition used in the Thomas and Williams (1963) and Thomas and Caronite (1964) studies makes the applicability of a discrimination interpretation questionable. The great majority of emitted responses, even during training, were followed· by neither primary nor conditioned reinforcement. Furthermore, in these studies the measurement of responding said to reflect conditioned reinforcement was taken when the key was blank, and thus the overt stimulating conditions at the time of this measurement were the same regardless of the stimulus that was presented during the reinforcement periods.

Bugelski (1956), who introduced the resistance-to-extinction technique in his famous (1938) study, has offered an "elicitation" interpretation of his earlier data. He feels that the "conditioned reinforcer" is a cue that elicits a chain of behavior (e.g., approach to the food magazine, feeding, return from the magazine, etc.) which eventually leads to another response. The absence of this cue in the typical "control group" interrupts this chain (more drastically than does merely the absence of the feeding component), thereby reducing the probability of additional responding. Considerable evidence inconsistent with the elicitation hypothesis has been reported in the paper by Kelleher and Gollub (1962) noted earlier. They point out, for example, that in fixed-interval (FI) or differential enforcement of low-rate (DRL) schedules the delivery of reinforcement results in a subsequent zero rate rather than a rate increase. In a study by Kelleher (1961) a similar effect was observed during extinction with FI and DRL scheduling of the conditioned reinforcer, the magazine click in a pigeon Skinner box. There is no reason to doubt that a parallel finding could be obtained with a visual conditioned reinforcer such as that used in our laboratory, and the study should be done. Clearly, the facts of reinforcement scheduling contraindicate an elicitation interpretation.

The "facilitation hypothesis" (cf. Wyckoff, Sidowski, and Chambliss, 1958) suggests that the "conditioned reinforcing stimulus" serves as a cue for subsequent behavior (e.g., "random activity," an instrumental or a consummatory response) which transfers positively to (facilitates) the response used to reflect conditioned reinforcement. For example, if in a rat Skinner box the food cup is located close to the bar, a response to the magazine sound (magazine approach) would keep the rat in the vicinity of the bar, thereby increasing the probability of additional responding.

A facilitation interpretation may be applied to both resistance to extinction and new-learning procedures. With both of these procedures a possible control group consists of subjects for whom the "conditioned reinforcer" is not response-contingent. With such a design Wyckoff *et al.* (1958) found no evidence for a reinforcing effect separate from the facilitating effect of the stimulus. On the other hand, a series of studies by Crowder and associates (1959) found that such a distinction is indeed possible. Research is currently underway involving the use of yoked controls in a study similar to that of Thomas and Williams (1963), but data sufficient for reporting are not yet available. It may be noted, however, that studies involving the scheduling of the conditioned reinforcer such as that by Kelleher (1961) are inconsistent with facilitation as well as elicitation interpretations.

Because the new-learning technique for demonstrating conditioned reinforcement is not subject to discrimination and elicitation interpretations, an experiment was performed by Caronite and Thomas (1964) to examine the generalization of conditioned reinforcement in such a situation. As will be indicated later, certain aspects of the design tend to rule out a facilitation interpretation as well.

The subjects were 30 homing pigeons, of which 15 were naïve and 15 had been used in a previous study involving key pecking. All subjects were maintained at approximately 70 per cent of ad libitum weight throughout the experiment. Each pigeon was given 10 days of VI ½ training with the key always illuminated with a light of 550 mμ. During this training a 1¾ in. × 4⅛ in. treadle was attached to the grid floor near the right side of the experimental chamber, but the treadle was inoperative. On the day following the tenth day of VI training, the pigeons were divided into 3 groups of 10 each (5 naïve and 5 experienced). On this test day the key was not illuminated. Each press of the treadle produced a 2-sec. exposure on the key of a light of 550 mμ (Group 1), 530 mμ (Group 2) or 510 mμ (Group 3), but no food. During testing the key was inoperative.

Three different measures of the acquisition of treadle pressing were taken: Latency between the first and second responses, total responses to extinction, and total time to an extinction criterion of 5 min. without responding. The results indicate generalization gradients with all three of these measures. A Kruskal-Wallace analysis of variance indicates a signifi-

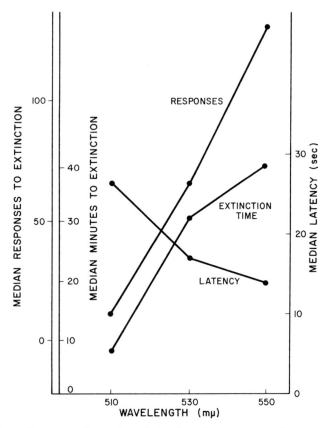

F I G. 6. Generalization gradients of conditioned reinforcement: new-learning procedure.

cant difference ($P < .05$) attributable to stimuli with both responses and time to extinction. The gradient for latency, while not significant, indicated the same trend. These gradients are presented in Fig. 6.

In the design of the experimental chamber in this study we took into consideration the work of Wyckoff *et al.* (1958). The location of the treadle was such that the response to the key when illuminated (approach and peck) would remove the pigeon from the vicinity of the treadle, thereby reducing the probability of additional responding. The positive finding in spite of this spatial arrangement argues strongly against a facilitation interpretation.

Although the key light clearly has a discriminative (cue) function in this study (for key pecking), particularly at the beginning of treadle-press training, this function drops out long before the pigeon stops responding to the treadle. This observation parallels one made in a study by Ratner (1956) with rats and a magazine click as the conditioned reinforcer. It indicates that reinforcing and discriminative functions of stimuli are differentiable also on the basis of differences in resistance to extinction.

The elicitation hypothesis of Bugelski (1956) is inapplicable to a new-learning situation and need not concern us here. The response chain established in training (from the key to the feeder back to the key) is not elicited in the test situation. Instead, a new component (treadle press) is added to the chain, and later members are either extinguished or allowed to drop out. The discrimination hypothesis (Bitterman *et al.*, 1953) is equally inapplicable to a new-learning task. Thus it appears justifiable to conclude that in this study the key light did serve as a conditioned reinforcer, and that this reinforcing property generalized lawfully to other stimuli.

The experiments reported in this paper and others currently under way in our laboratory have attempted to separate the reinforcing from the discriminative functions of a stimulus so that its control over behavior in both of these relationships can be independently assessed. Clearly, we differ with Wyckoff *et al.* (1958) in our contention that these stimulus functions are separable. Although the evidence on this point is not yet all in and research on this problem is continuing, we feel that the majority of the data support our position. The study by Thomas and Caronite (1964) further indicates that the effect of discrimination training on generalization of the reinforcing function parallels its effect on the generalization of the discriminative function. Discrimination training was selected as a variable to investigate because its effect on the discriminative function of the stimulus is so highly predictable. The results of their study suggest that the same principles governing generalization of the discriminative function apply also to reinforcing and perhaps to other still unexplored stimulus functions as well. This generalization about generalization is of course subject to empirical verification, and we trust that the appropriate studies will be performed.

Although earlier work in the area of stimulus generalization (from this laboratory and most others) concentrated on the eliciting or discriminative functions of the stimulus, the work reported in this paper represents an application of familiar procedures to the study of more complex stimulus-response relationships. Several other papers in this volume report programs of research directed toward this same general goal. The work of Hoffman (this vol., pp. 356–372) is a good case in point. In his research on conditioned suppression, the generalization of an emotional or motivational effect of a stimulus is systematically explored. In the work of Honig (this vol., pp. 218–254), the generalization of responding based on concepts of equality and difference is examined. Cumming and Berryman (this vol., pp. 284–330) have begun to investigate stimulus control in complex learning situations involving matching to sample, oddity, and related problems.

It may be predicted with some confidence that one main line of future development in generalization research will be the further application of techniques and principles derived from the study of eliciting and discriminative functions to increasingly complex situations involving other functions of stimuli.

In conclusion, we suggest that the textbook definition of stimulus generalization is in need of modification. It means more than the fact that the organism responds to stimuli that are similar to, but not identical with, the stimulus used in training. Stimulus generalization refers rather to the fact that an S-R relationship (of any sort) tends to be maintained despite a change in the S component. By achieving a better understanding of the role played by the stimulus component in that relationship, we will progress in the direction of more thoroughly understanding and more successfully predicting and controlling that behavior.

REFERENCES

Bitterman, M. E., Fedderson, W. E., and Tyler, D. W. Secondary reinforcement and the discrimination hypothesis. *Amer. J. Psychol.*, 1953, **66**, 456–464.

Bugelski, R. Extinction with and without sub-goal reinforcement. *J. comp. Psychol.*, 1938, **26**, 121–134.

Bugelski, R. *The psychology of learning.* New York: Holt, 1956.

Caronite, S. C., and Thomas, D. R. Generalization of a positive conditioned reinforcer as measured by the "new learning" technique. Paper presented at Midwest Psychol. Ass., St. Louis, 1964.

Crowder, W. F., Gay, B. R., Bright, M. G., and Lee, M. F. Secondary reinforcement or response facilitation?: III. Reconditioning. *J. Psychol.*, 1959, **48**, 307–310.

Crowder, W. F., Gay, B. R., Fleming, W. C., and Hurst, R. W. Secondary reinforcement or response facilitation?: IV. The retention method. *J. Psychol.*, 1959, **48**, 311–314.

Crowder, W. F., Gill, K. Jr., Hodge, C. C., and Nash, F. A. Jr. Secondary reinforcement or response facilitation?: II. Response acquisition. *J. Psychol.*, 1959, **48**, 303–306.

Crowder, W. F., Morris, J. B., and McDaniel, M. H. Secondary reinforcement or response facilitation?: I. Resistance to extinction. *J. Psychol.*, 1959, **48**, 299–302.

Guttman, N., and Kalish, H. I., Discriminability and stimulus generalization. *J. exp. Psychol.*, 1956, **51**, 79–88.

Hoffman, H. S., and Fleshler, M. Stimulus factors in aversive controls: The generalization of conditioned suppression. *J. exp. Anal. Behav.*, 1961, **4**, 371–378.

Honig, W. K. Prediction of preference, transposition, and transposition-reversal from the generalization gradient. *J. exp. Psychol.*, 1962, **64**, 239–248.

Kelleher, R. T. Schedules of conditioned reinforcement in experimental extinction. *J. exp. Anal. Behav.*, 1961, **4**, 1–5.

Kelleher, R. T., and Gollub, L. R. A review of positive conditioned reinforcement. *J. exp. Anal. Behav.*, 1962, **5** (suppl.), 543–597.

Morse, W. H., and Skinner, B. F. A second type of superstition in the pigeon. *Amer. J. Psychol.*, 1957, **70**, 308–311.

Ratner, S. C. Reinforcing and discriminative properties of the click in a Skinner box. *Psychol. Reps.*, 1956, **2**, 332.

Ray, O. S., and Stein, L. Generalization of conditioned suppression. *J. exp. Anal. Behav.*, 1959, **2**, 357–361.

Skinner, B. F. *The behavior of organisms.* New York: Appleton-Century-Crofts, 1938.

Skinner, B. F. Superstition in the pigeon. *J. exp. Psychol.*, 1948, 38, 168–172.

Thomas, D. R., and Caronite, S. C. Stimulus generalization of a positive conditioned reinforcer: II. The effects of discrimination training. *J. exp. Psychol.* (in press).

Thomas, D. R., and King, R. A. Stimulus generalization as a function of the level of motivation. *J. exp. Psychol.*, 1959, **57**, 323–328.

Thomas, D. R., and Williams, J. L. Stimulus generalization of a positive conditioned reinforcer. *Science*, 1963, **141**, 172–173.

Wyckoff, L. B., Sidowski, J., and Chambliss, D. J. An experimental study of the relationship between secondary reinforcing and cue effects of a stimulus. *J. comp. physiol. Psychol.*, 1958, **51**, 103–109.

19. The Complex Discriminated Operant: Studies of Matching-to-Sample and Related Problems

William W. Cumming, *Columbia University*

Robert Berryman, *Hunter College*

Most experiments on operant generalization and discrimination have concentrated on the ways in which stimuli act to control the rate of emission of relatively simple responses, i.e., the generalization of the "discriminative function" of the stimulus. This concept, first introduced by Skinner (1938), has freed psychology from many of the more rigid and restrictive aspects of Pavlovian and Watsonian behaviorism. Stimuli are no longer considered to have only an elicitative function, but may, at times, play different roles in the control of behavior. We speak, for example, of the reinforcing function of a stimulus, whether primary or secondary, positive or negative.

When the term "stimulus generalization" is applied to the discriminative aspect of a stimulus, it denotes the observation that behavior, conditioned in the presence of a particular stimulus, continues to be emitted even though the properties of the stimulus have changed. The term "stimulus discrimination" denotes the restriction of the reinforcement contingencies to some specifiable aspect of stimulation, so that behavior comes to be controlled by the presence or absence of that stimulus aspect. The power and precision of this form of stimulus control are surely by now an experimental commonplace.

An examination of the complex discrimination situation suggests that stimuli may well exercise an additional function. For several years we have been involved in the experimental analysis of a number of related types of complex discriminative behavior. Our concern has centered on what Lashley (1938) called "conditional" discriminations, as well as on similar problems in the more recent experimental literature. Initially, our interest lay in issues involving the principle of stimulus generalization as it applies to the complex case. That interest has survived the necessity

The work reported here was supported by the National Institute of Mental Health, U.S. Public Health Service, under Research Grant MH-03673. The authors are indebted to many individuals, but particularly to John A. Nevin, who has contributed substantially to the research reported here.

to map out, in a prolonged set of "pilot" studies, the rough features of a terrain inadequately explored by earlier investigators.

We have taken the "matching-to-sample" problem as a representative conditional discrimination. The studies thus far undertaken have, we believe, finally brought our experimental program to the point at which it can begin to deal with the several generalization problems peculiar to complex discrimination procedures.

In simple successive or simultaneous discriminations, the discriminative stimuli have an invariant relation to reinforcement and extinction— thus, the presentation of S^D is an occasion for reinforcement of the specified response, while the presentation of S^Δ is an occasion for some other behavior. Here, the function of the discriminative stimuli is the control of specific responses. However, in more complex types of discriminative situations, a stimulus may function as a selector of discriminations, rather than of individual responses. We refer to the conditional discrimination (Lashley, 1938), in which the significance of a discriminative stimulus is not invariant, but changes in relation to the stimulus context in which it appears. Thus, the correct response cannot be made solely on the basis of a single stimulus, but must be based on the properties of two or more stimuli. This point can perhaps be made clearer by an example. The simple successive discrimination in which an organism is reinforced (S^R) for responding to a red key and extinguished (X) for responding to a green key can be schematized:

$$S^D_{\text{red}} \cdot R \rightarrow S^R \ \text{ or } \ S^\Delta_{\text{green}} \cdot R \rightarrow X ,$$

while the simultaneous case can be diagrammed:

$$\begin{bmatrix} S^D_{\text{red}} \cdot R \rightarrow S^R \\ S^\Delta_{\text{green}} \cdot R \rightarrow X . \end{bmatrix}$$

The bracket indicates that both contingencies are present.

A conditional discrimination, such as matching-to-sample, in which the subject must first respond to a red or green standard stimulus (ST) to produce red and green comparison stimuli (CO), with responses to the CO of matching hue reinforced and responses to the CO of non-matching hue extinguished, would be diagrammed:

$$ST_{\text{red}} \cdot R \longrightarrow \begin{bmatrix} CO^\Delta_{\text{green}} \cdot R \rightarrow X \\ ST_{\text{red}} \cdot R \rightarrow 0 \\ CO^D_{\text{red}} \cdot R \rightarrow S^R , \end{bmatrix}$$

Or, on other trials:

$$ST_{\text{green}} \cdot R \longrightarrow \begin{bmatrix} CO^D_{\text{green}} \cdot R \rightarrow S^R \\ ST_{\text{green}} \cdot R \rightarrow 0 \\ CO^\Delta_{\text{red}} \cdot R \rightarrow X , \end{bmatrix}$$

where $R \rightarrow 0$ indicates that a response has no effect.

In these cases, reinforcement is contingent upon the relation between the ST and the CO's. Two alternative views are possible of the role of the ST: (a) the ST's and CO's form a stimulus compound that functions as a unitary discriminative stimulus, and (b) the ST is exhibiting a "selective" or "instruction" function that momentarily strengthens a particular discrimination. The answer to the question of which view is preferable lies in examining some of the detailed properties of behavior in the conditional discrimination situation. We shall return to this problem later, following the review of experimental results.

In our experimental situation, the subject is faced with a standard (ST) or sample stimulus. A response to this stimulus produces several comparison (CO) stimuli. Responses to the CO's are reinforced or extinguished according to some predetermined rule. The example given above illustrates the simplest case, in which the subject is reinforced for selecting the CO that "matches," i.e., has the same physical properties as the standard. An examination of an expanded diagram for the basic procedure will reveal the many relations it bears to traditional psychological problems:

$$ST_i \cdot R \longrightarrow \begin{cases} CO_m \cdot R \rightarrow S^R \rightarrow \text{Inter-trial interval} \\ ST_i \cdot R \rightarrow 0 \\ CO_n \cdot R \rightarrow X \rightarrow \text{Inter-trial interval} \,. \end{cases}$$

In this diagram, ST_i represents one of a set of standard stimuli, and CO_m and CO_n two members of a set of comparison stimuli.

This diagram represents a trial-by-trial, non-correction procedure. For the moment, we omit consideration of such procedural details as randomization of the sequence of presentation of stimuli and their spatial modes of appearance, etc.

The major parameters of this situation include (1) *interrelations of the ST and CO sets,* both in terms of the number of stimuli involved and of their specific stimulus properties; (2) *temporal relations* between the ST and the presentation of the CO's; and (3) *reinforcement contingencies* governing the effects of responses to either ST or CO. We will next describe some of the types of procedure that emerge when these parameters are varied.

Interrelations of the ST and CO Sets

If the number of ST and CO stimuli is made large, the paradigm encroaches upon the problem area of learning to learn, or *learning sets*. If sets of stimuli are defined such that every member of the set possesses some common property, while differing in other aspects, the procedure can be adapted to the study of *concept formation* by reinforcing responses to CO's sharing some common property with the ST. If the CO's do not necessarily match the standard but lie on the same continuum, we get something akin to *psychophysical scaling*. Obviously, the nature of the reinforcement contingencies for responses to the *CO*'s poses a considerable problem in such a case. Later, we will have an opportunity to examine some of the alternative means available for dealing with this issue.

Temporal Relations

In the diagrammed case, the *ST* and the *CO*'s are all simultaneously present. Obviously, delay intervals can be interposed between the response to the *ST* and the presentation of the *CO*'s, ranging from zero (the *ST*'s disappearing and the *CO*'s simultaneously appearing) through delays of greater length. In this way the situation becomes equivalent to what has traditionally been called *delayed reaction*.

Reinforcement Contingencies

In the *matching-to-sample procedure,* the subjects are reinforced for responding to the *CO* with the same physical properties as the *ST*. By altering the contingencies so that the *CO* most different from the *ST* is specified as "correct," the *oddity* problem is generated. If the *CO*'s lie on the same continuum as the *ST* but have only an arbitrary relation to it, or lie on another continuum altogether, *symbolic matching* and *oddity* are defined. In symbolic matching, *ST* specifies S^D, and in symbolic oddity, *ST* specifies S^Δ. Finally, it is possible to study the effects of *schedules of reinforcement* on both responding to *ST* and responding to *CO*.

This examination of the basic paradigm and its variations leads us to the problem of generalization among the various stimulus elements. In terms of the types of situations we have been discussing, three possible interactions exist: (1) generalization among the *ST* stimuli, (2) generalization among the *CO* stimuli, and (3) generalization from *ST* to *CO* stimuli. These relations, and some of their implications, can be represented diagrammatically. At first, we look at the case in which there are two *ST*'s and two *CO*'s (Fig. 1). Both the *ST*'s and the *CO*'s are assumed to lie on the same continuum. On the upper line, labeled "*ST*," the dots represent

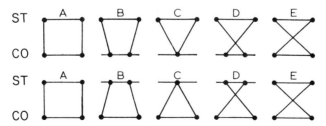

FIG. 1. Diagram of generalizations among *ST* and *CO* stimuli under various stimulus separations in the matching-to-sample procedure.

the position of the two ST's on the continuum. The lower line gives the same information for the CO's. A line connecting a given ST-CO pair indicates the reinforcing contingency. Finally, the upper row shows the case where the physical properties of the ST's are held constant, while those of the CO's are permitted to vary; the lower row represents the reverse instance. In all cases, each variable stimulus is represented as moving from one end of the continuum to the other.

In the upper row of diagrams, Case A is the standard matching-to-sample procedure and Case E is oddity. Cases B and D are close to the matching and oddity situations, respectively, and can be thought of as representing generalized matching and oddity. Case C appears as a degenerate instance; however, cases where either the ST or CO stimuli are highly similar, but not identical, should be of great interest.

Comparison of Case B in the upper row with the homonymous case in the lower row suggests that there are no differences in the total amount of stimulus generalization. The same is true for Case D. If the ST is exercising a different function from the CO's, however, it might be expected that there would nonetheless be differences in behavior in these two situations. Diagrams for three-stimulus matching and oddity have a similar implication. Here, in the oddity case, the amount of generalization from the matching (incorrect) CO is greater for the intermediate ST than for the ST's lying at the ends of the continuum. Further examination of these situations will be needed to determine the heuristic value of this particular system of schematic representation.

REVIEW OF EXPERIMENTAL WORK

Since the experiments described below are either already published, in press, or in preparation, we will omit many specific procedural and substantive details. A brief review of experimental results seems, however, to be worth undertaking, since it shows not only the past and present directions of our research, but also the empirical bases for our discussion of the nature of stimulus functions within the conditional discrimination situation.

Some of the variables we have studied may be identified as follows: (1) The formal relations, as outlined above, between the ST and CO stimuli. The experiments here have dealt with the acquisition of matching, oddity, and arbitrary matching. (2) The temporal relations between the ST and CO stimuli. Studies here have contrasted acquisition and stable-state performances for simultaneous matching, zero delay, variable delay, and titrating delay. (3) The effects of schedules of reinforcement for correctly selecting the S^D on each matching trial. Experiments have provided information comparing fixed-ratio (FR 1, FR 3, FR 6, FR 10) and VR 3 performances. (4) The effects of various drive manipulations on matching performance in the delay case. (5) The effects of such drugs as sodium pentobarbital, lysergic acid diethylamide, and chlorpromazine on both simultaneous and delayed matching performances.

In this paper we will attempt to summarize some of the effects uncovered by this series of studies and will, in addition, try to point up some implications and questions they raise for the concept of stimulus control over complex discriminative behavior.

General Procedures

Before starting a review of the experimental findings, it seems economical to describe those general aspects of procedure that were constant throughout the program.

Subjects. In all experiments the subjects were white Carneaux pigeons, ranging from 1 to 14 years in age, obtained from the Palmetto Pigeon Plant, Sumter, S.C. On arrival, the wings and tails of the birds were clipped, and they were then housed in individual cages. After giving the birds free access to a grain mixture of 50 per cent Kaffir, 40 per cent vetch, and 10 per cent hemp (occasionally alternated with maple peas) for ten days to two weeks, we took the mean of the last five days' weighings as the ad libitum weight. The birds were then reduced to 80 per cent of this weight by feeding them about 5 gm. daily. Grit and water were continuously available in the home cages. Experimental sessions were scheduled only if a bird's weight was within 15 gm. of the 80 per cent ad libitum weight.

In experiments involving hues as stimuli, the pecking response was differentiated to the center key in a three-key chamber. During this time the center key was transilluminated with one of the colors used. After the response was shaped, the birds were given about ten reinforcements (on FR 1) for pecking each of the three keys when they were illuminated with the three hues used, for a total of approximately ten reinforcements per color per key. In experiments using geometrical forms as stimuli, the birds were magazine trained in the experimental three-key chamber, and then placed in a separate one-key chamber and differentiated to a white key. One hundred regular reinforcements were then given. In both cases, the birds were introduced directly to the main experimental procedures after completion of the preliminary shaping process.

Apparatus. Two response chambers were used, one equipped for the presentation of hues, the other for geometric forms.

The *hue chamber* was in the form of an isosceles right triangle, about $24 \times 24 \times 35$ in., with three keys and a grain hopper mounted on one wall. Diffuse general illumination was provided by incandescent ceiling lamps, and each key could be individually transilluminated with any one of three Christmas-tree bulbs.

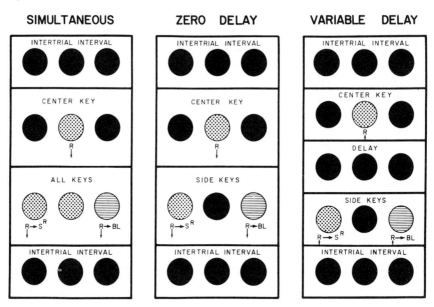

FIG. 2. Schematic representation of the basic matching procedures. R = responses, S^R = reinforcement, BL = blackout.

The *form chamber* was of trapezoidal form, 12 in. deep, 10 in. across the front, and 5 in. across the back. Three transparent keys and a grain magazine were mounted on the front panel. In-line display units could project equilateral triangles, circles, and squares on a screen immediately behind the keys. Incandescent lamps provided over-all illumination.

All aspects of the experimental procedure were programmed automatically by circuitry located in a separate control room.

Experimental procedure. The schematized procedure for our experiments is shown in Fig. 2. The three major types of experimental condition, simultaneous, zero-delay, and variable-delay, refer to the temporal relations between ST and CO. In all cases a trial is begun by presenting ST (either hues or geometric forms) on the center key. In the simultaneous condition, a response to ST results in the presentation of CO on the side keys while ST remains on, with the result that the response to CO is made with ST present. In the zero-delay condition, a response to ST both terminates this stimulus and produces CO. In the variable-delay condition, a response terminates ST, and a variable-delay interval elapses before the presentation of CO. During this interval all responses are without effect.

Responses to the side key that has been specified as "correct" are followed by 3-sec. of grain presentation. Responses to the "incorrect" key produce a blackout, usually of 3-sec. duration, during which all illumination in the chamber is off. A 25-sec. inter-trial interval follows either reinforcement or blackout; on its termination, the next trial is presented. It should be noted that this is a non-correction procedure.

Stimulus sequences, and the side key on which the correct *CO* appeared, were randomized throughout.

Acquisition of Simultaneous Matching[1]

An obvious point of departure is an examination of the acquisition of the simultaneous matching performance. Three birds were committed to this study. The stimuli used were red, green, and blue lights. All subjects were given 140 trials per day; the first 10 and the last 10 trials were excluded from data analysis. Each day the sequence of stimulus conditions shown in Table 1 was randomized in a block of 12, which was repeated until 140 trials had been presented. Order within the block of 12 was changed to a new random permutation each day.

TABLE 1

STIMULUS CONDITIONS

Condition	Left Key	Center Key	Right Key
1	Blue	Red	Red*
2	Red*	Red	Blue
3	Green	Red	Red*
4	Red*	Red	Green
5	Red	Blue	Blue*
6	Blue*	Blue	Red
7	Green	Blue	Blue*
8	Blue*	Blue	Green
9	Red	Green	Green*
10	Green*	Green	Red
11	Blue	Green	Green*
12	Green*	Green	Blue

* Response reinforced.

Acquisition of matching follows a very predictable sequence. For the first three or four sessions, the animals' performance remains at a chance level; that is, the animal is correct on 50 per cent of the trials. Thereafter performance rapidly improved until after 10 to 15 days' exposure, the animal is being reinforced on almost 100 per cent of the trials. Typical performances of three birds on this procedure are shown in Fig. 3. The early portion of the experiment, in which the animals remain at chance levels of matching, is characterized by an almost complete position habit (Fig. 4), although different birds take up this habit on either the right or the left keys.

These basic features of the acquisition of simultaneous matching have

[1] Cumming and Berryman (1961).

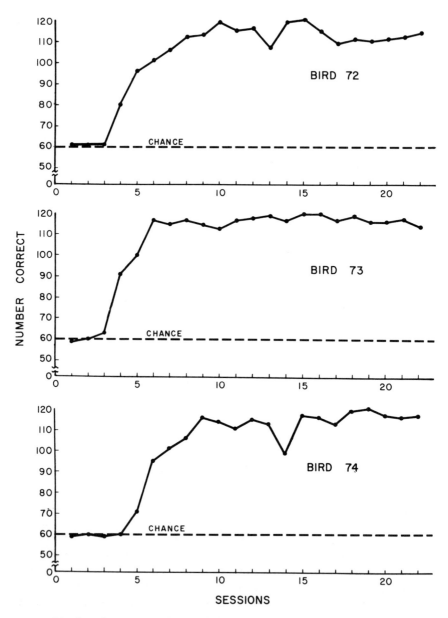

FIG. 3. Number of correct matches (out of a possible 120) for the first 22 experimental sessions.

292

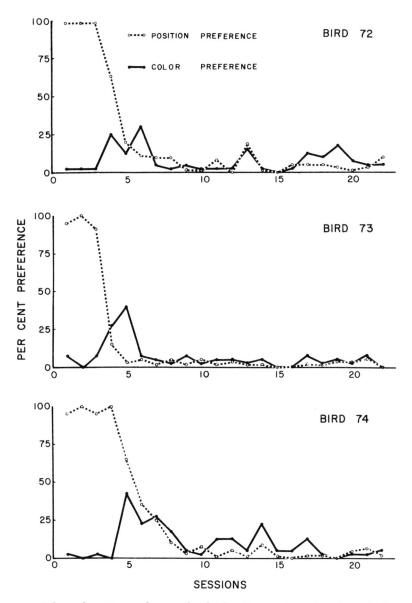

FIG. 4. Color and position preferences for the first 22 experimental sessions. Preference indices were constructed by considering chance performance as 0 per cent preference, and the maximum possible deviation from chance as 100 per cent preference.

been repeatedly observed. For example, the experiment on variable-delay matching, reported below, also involved the acquisition of simultaneous matching. The seven birds in this latter study required a mean of 705 trials to reach a criterion of 75 per cent correct matching, as compared with the mean of 700 trials for the three birds shown in Fig. 3. Comparable position habits were also observed.

Generalization of Matching to a Novel Stimulus

After a 22-day exposure to the procedure described above, in which three pigeons acquired simultaneous matching, yellow Christmas-tree bulbs were substituted in the apparatus for the blue bulbs that had been used previously. This meant that on any trial in which a blue light was scheduled to be presented on either the center or the side keys, a yellow light appeared. As before, responses to side keys of matching hue were reinforced, regardless of whether the match was required to yellow, to green, or to red. Figure 5 shows the per cent correct matching for each of the three subjects for each of the center key hues. The first column in the figure presents the performance on the final (22nd) day of the matching procedure with the blue light. The middle column shows that on the first day with the yellow light substituted, all birds dropped to approximately chance when the hue to be matched was yellow. However, matching behavior was maintained when the center key hue was green or red. Instead of matching the yellow hue, subjects reverted to a position preference whenever the ST was yellow. On the second day with the yellow light substituted for the blue (the final column in Fig. 5), considerable acquisition of yellow matching was shown for all birds.

The inability of the birds to match yellow demonstrated that matching performance per se does not generalize to a novel stimulus, at least when the small amount of training given here precedes the introduction of that stimulus. It is interesting to note that the birds in this experiment did not systematically avoid yellow by responding to hues for which they had previously been reinforced. Nor did they show any preference for the yellow. Their behavior was simply that of reverting to a position habit when the yellow key was the ST.

On the other hand, it seems likely that a small alteration in the physical characteristics of one of the stimuli would not have resulted in such an extreme decrement in performance as shown here. Certainly, some generalization of the previously trained matching performance could be expected to similar stimuli. The fact that on the second day of exposure to the yellow light some acquisition is shown by all birds does not necessarily mean that some sort of "learning to learn" behavior is being displayed. In fact, in this case, the bird is learning to match only one hue, whereas in the earlier training it had been required to learn to match three hues concurrently.

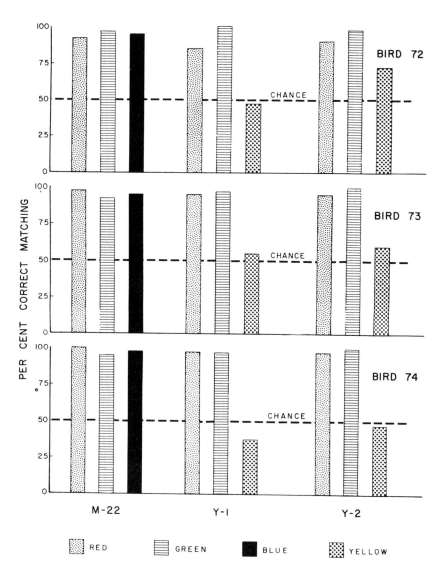

F IG. 5. Per cent correct matching for the 22nd experimental session, and for the two sessions in which a novel yellow *ST* was substituted for the blue. Matching of each *ST* is separately presented.

Acquisition of Simultaneous Oddity

It is tempting to suppose that the requirement that the birds select the comparison key of the same hue as the standard has no special status. As experimenters we may set the experiment up in this way largely because of our own history in matching stimuli. Skinner (1950), in discussing the acquisition of matching, said, "Choosing the opposite is also easily set up. The discriminative response of striking-red-after-being-stimulated-by-red is apparently no easier to establish than striking-red-after-being-stimulated-by-green." Ginsburg (1957), on the other hand, found that oddity—or, as he called it, "non-matching"—was acquired significantly faster than matching. In terms of the number of trials necessary to reach a criterion of 80 per cent correct, birds on a matching procedure required a mean of 897 trials, while birds under an oddity procedure required an average of only 119 trials. In the face of these contradictory findings, we decided to perform an experiment replicating our earlier study of simultaneous matching acquisition but changing the procedure only to the extent that birds were reinforced for selecting the odd hue on the side key rather than the matching hue. Six birds were exposed to this procedure for a total of twenty sessions.

The acquisition functions for these subjects are shown in Fig. 6. Five of the six birds in this study began at levels well above the chance performance. Only one of these subjects, Bird 341, shows an acquisition curve resembling that found in simultaneous matching in that it begins at a chance level and proceeds rapidly toward a high level of performance. Four of the six subjects, on the other hand, begin at approximately 70 per cent correct but acquire the oddity performance only very slowly. In order to compare the acquisition of oddity more directly with the acquisition

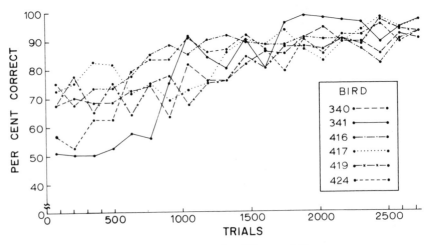

FIG. 6. Per cent correct in oddity acquisition.

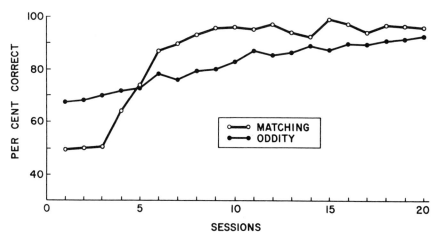

FIG. 7. Comparison of matching and oddity acquisition.

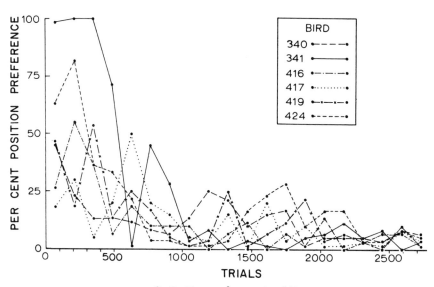

FIG. 8. Position preference in oddity.

of matching, we have averaged the performance of the three birds from our first study and of the five birds that show a non-matching-like performance in this study and have presented the result in Fig. 7. This figure shows clearly the very slow acquisition characteristic of oddity as compared with matching and the large difference in initial levels of performance. It is not clear whether these two curves would eventually converge.

Another striking difference between acquisition of oddity and acquisition of matching is shown in Fig. 8, in which position preferences under the oddity procedure have been plotted. Only Bird 341,.the bird with a matching-like performance in the per cent correct function, shows an initial complete position habit such as that characteristic of acquisition of matching. For this subject the correct performance emerges as the position habit drops out, as was the case for birds acquiring matching. Other subjects in this study show a much lower level of position habit initially, and the elimination of the position habit does not appear to be correlated with the acquisition of oddity.

It is clear that our conclusions about learning of oddity and matching differ from those of Ginsburg (1957) in that we find very slow acquisition of oddity and rapid acquisition of matching. The conclusions one might reach concerning the relative difficulty of the two performances will depend crucially upon the criterion of learning used. Gingsburg (1957) defined acquisition as a 20-trial session in which the animals got 16 correct. Any such per cent criterion, if suitably chosen, could alter the conclusions from either study. If the acquisition criterion is placed very close to the initial level of performance, the chances of meeting the criterion early are, of course, enhanced.

The interpretation of Ginsburg's (1957) data is made difficult by ambiguity in his paper about the number of stimuli employed. While four stimuli were available in his apparatus, the possibility exists that he used only two of these in the experimental situation, while in our study, three alternative stimuli were used. Our analysis indicates that the difficulty of the oddity situation, as well as of the matching situation, increases with increasing numbers of alternative stimuli.

Generalization of Oddity to a Novel Stimulus

On Day 21, following the first 20 days of acquisition of oddity described above, yellow lights were substituted for the blue lights, as had been done in the earlier study of simultaneous matching. To describe the results of this operation, three different types of trials must be differentiated: (1) trials identical to those used in the acquisition phase of the experiment, i.e., those in which red and green served as ST's and as both of the CO's; (2) trials in which the ST was yellow, while red or green appeared as a CO; (3) trials in which yellow appeared only as a CO. When both the ST's and the CO's were red or green, type (1) above, the birds averaged 88.0 per cent, a value little different from their final performance on oddity. When the ST is red or green, and yellow is one of the CO's, type (3) above, accuracy falls to 61.6 per cent. This level is (a) considerably lower than the last day of oddity acquisition, (b) only slightly lower than performance on initial exposure to oddity, and (c) substantially higher than the level of performance under the novel stimulus achieved by the simultaneous matching animals. This suggests that when a novel stimulus is introduced as the correct CO, animals revert to the type of performance they displayed at the beginning of acquisition. For trials on which yellow is the ST, type (2) above, accuracy is at 77.9 per cent, an intermediate value.

These data imply that the function of the ST is not to tell the animal which stimulus is incorrect, but rather to signal which stimuli are to be selected. In other words, the bird has not learned that, for example, when red is the ST he should avoid red. Rather, he has learned that when red is ST he should select either blue or green. If both of these stimuli are unavailable, as when yellow is the alternative CO, he can only revert to the unconditioned performance. It is possible to devise an experiment that might provide a clearer analysis of this situation. We might speculate that if red were the ST, and the CO's blue and yellow, the bird should have little difficulty in picking the "odd" CO, even though the situation is different from any to which he has been previously exposed. If the results of this experiment were to substantiate the prediction, they would suggest that it may be economical to regard the ST as a "selector of discrimination" or as exercising an "instructional" function, rather than as simply forming a compound with the CO's.

Acquisition of Simultaneous Symbolic Matching

The matching and oddity procedures contrast in that, in the former, the ST is identical with the correct CO, while in the latter it is identical with the incorrect CO. This could be taken to mean that the ST indicates the S^D in matching but the S^Δ in the oddity situation. The results of the generalization phase of the oddity experiment, however, suggested that the ST was in fact indicating an alternative pair of S^D's, rather than simply S^Δ. (This may well account for the slowness of oddity acquisition.) In the light of these considerations, it seemed necessary to investigate further the relations between ST and the correct CO.

As has been indicated, there is no reason to assume that oddity and matching represent the only possible types of relations between ST's and CO's; in fact, such a relation can be purely arbitrary, or "symbolic." To investigate the behavioral consequences of such relations, an experiment in symbolic matching was undertaken. Under the experimental regime established, a blue ST specified responses to a green CO as correct, a red ST specified a blue CO, and a green ST specified red. This is apparently similar in some respects to what Ginsburg (1957) termed "amatching."

Five birds were exposed to this procedure for a total of 30 days. Acquisition of this performance is shown in Fig. 9. The birds begin slightly above chance. The records appear to be intermediate between the acquisition of matching and the acquisition of oddity. Position habits comparable to those seen in matching acquisition were not observed in this case. Nonetheless, there appeared to be a slightly greater tendency for the animals to take up position preferences than with oddity.

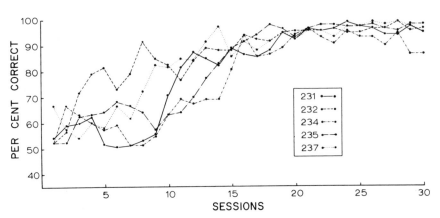

FIG. 9. Per cent correct for five subjects during the first 30 sessions of exposure to symbolic matching.

Some consideration of the possible stimulus combinations in this case (the transformations imposed upon Table 1 by the symbolic matching contingencies) reveals that when the symbolic standards are substituted for the matching standards, half of the trials consist of heterogeneous stimulus combinations, in which all three stimuli are different, and half consist of trials identical with those used in oddity. The paradox is that symbolic matching is one-half oddity, and the other half not matching! Conversely, symbolic oddity would consist of trials that are divided equally between heterogeneous stimulus combinations and matching. (A study of this latter case is currently in progress.)

Our finding that the symbolic case is intermediate, as well as Ginsburg's (1957) finding that "amatching" is intermediate between "matching" and "non-matching," combined with the observation that this situation includes oddity trials, leads us to analyze separately the heterogeneous trials. The acquisition of both types of trials is compared in Fig. 10. Initially, oddity performance is superior, as might be expected from the earlier data. After about one week, however, both performances become and remain comparable until the end of the experiment. Acquisition on the heterogeneous trials does not follow the same course as simultaneous matching. This may show that symbolic matching is an inherently different performance, or the effect may be due to the interspersed oddity trials. Obviously, however, the intuitive notion that symbolic matching is an exceedingly difficult task is not borne out by these data. Accuracy levels reached at comparable stages in acquisition, although perhaps slightly worse than simultaneous matching, are nonetheless better than those observed under oddity. Therefore, the idea that situations in which the ST and the correct CO are identical are fundamentally easier is open to considerable doubt.

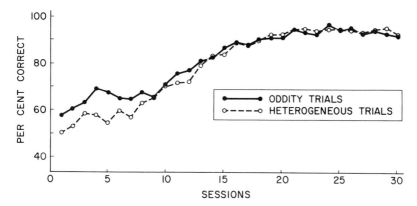

FIG. 10. Per cent correct on heterogeneous and oddity trials during 30 sessions of exposure to symbolic matching. Heterogeneous trials are those in which neither CO is a physical match for ST; oddity trials are those in which the incorrect CO is a physical match for ST. Data are means for all five subjects.

Acquisition of Delayed Matching[2]

The major intent of this study was to determine acquisition functions for the delayed matching case. The vast majority, if not all, of the studies of delayed responding involve progressive lengthening of the delay interval. This results in a situation in which the amount of training on each of the different delay intervals is left uncontrolled. For this reason we undertook an experiment in which the birds were exposed not only to the simultaneous and zero-delay cases but also to a number of variable delays from the very beginning of acquisition. Following initial shaping, the birds were placed directly on this experimental procedure, which exposed them to the simultaneous condition, the zero-delay condition, and five variable delays of 1, 2, 4, 10, and 24 seconds, or seven different experimental conditions in all. Since each hue must appear equally often on the left and right side keys and in combination with the alternative hues, there is a total of 12 different stimulus conditions. Each stimulus condition appears with each delay condition, thus defining a total of 84 possible combinations. In order to increase exposure to the center key ST, a fixed ratio of 5 to this stimulus was required rather than a single response.

After 9 daily sessions consisting of 23 practice or warm-up trials and 168 experimental trials, none of the seven birds showed any tendency to acquire the matching performance. In fact, on two-thirds of the experimental sessions performance was below the chance level, suggesting that in this situation in which the reinforcement contingencies were only marginally effective, the birds frequently selected the odd hue. With the ex-

[2] Berryman, Cumming, and Nevin (1963).

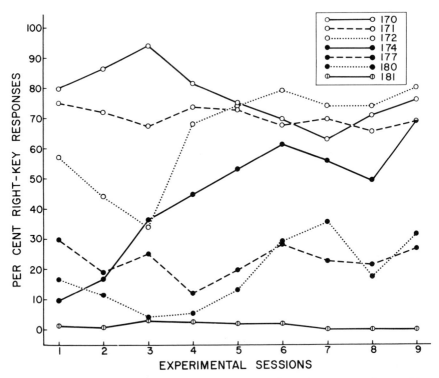

FIG. 11. Per cent right-key responses during the first 9 days of exposure to the variable-delay procedure. The 50 per cent level represents equal responding to the left and right keys.

ception of one bird that maintained throughout a total left-key position preference, the other birds did not show the position habits which have been characteristic of the earlier studies in acquisition of matching. The pattern of position preference (given in Fig. 11) displayed by the other six birds is of some interest. Following some initial fluctuations, the per cent of right-key responses began to cluster around either the 25 or the 75 per cent point, indicating that the animals were making 75 per cent of their responses to one key or the other. The basis of this behavior is entirely unclear, but obviously cannot be derived from probability-matching formulations such as those reviewed by Estes (1959) and Woodworth (1958).

Since the birds had shown no sign of acquiring the performance under the randomized presentation of all 7 experimental conditions after 1,719 trials, it was decided to revert to the simultaneous-matching condition. All birds were therefore exposed to the simultaneous-matching condition. As the results shown in Fig. 12 indicate, the course of acquisition for these birds was very much the same as it had been for the birds in the previous

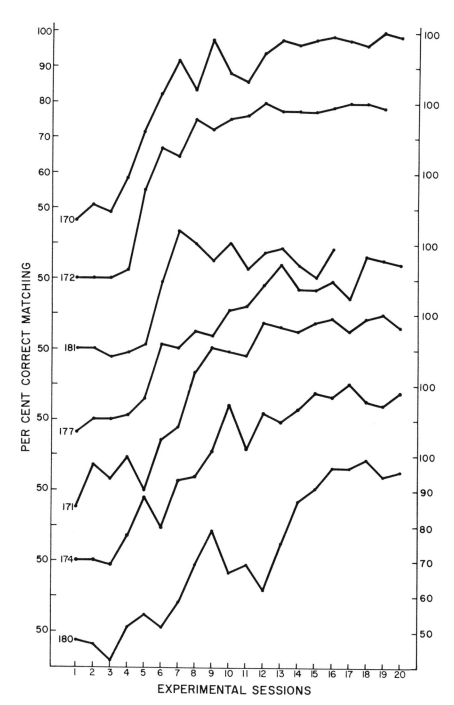

FIG. 12. Acquisition of simultaneous matching following 9 days' exposure to the variable-delay procedure. The curves for individual subjects are nested in an arbitrary order; each curve has been displaced upward 20% from the one immediately below it.

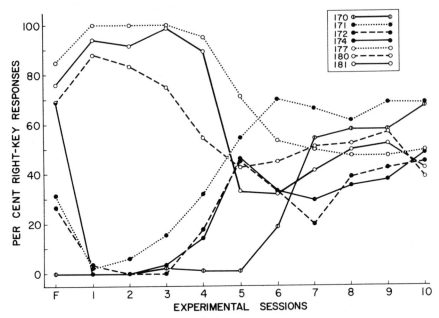

FIG. 13. Per cent right-key responding during the first 10 days' exposure to simultaneous matching. Data from the final day of exposure to the variable-delay procedure are represented as experimental session "F."

study of the acquisition of simultaneous matching. Prior exposure to some 234 trials on the simultaneous condition of course imbedded in 1,485 delay trials seems to have resulted in no transfer whatsoever.

An interesting point concerns the effects of the introduction of the simultaneous-matching procedure on the position preferences. On the first session of exposure to this procedure all animals took up and maintained a systematic position preference (Fig. 13). Another similarity to the performances shown in Fig. 3 is evident in that as the strength of this position preference declined, the correct simultaneous-matching performance emerged.

After 20 experimental sessions on simultaneous matching, the subjects were returned to the variable-delay procedure. Performances under this condition are shown in Fig. 14. Although exposure to the variable-delay procedure resulted in no generalization to the simultaneous situation, it is clear that the converse was not the case. Simultaneous matching began at a high level which was maintained throughout the 60 sessions, while performance on the zero-, 1-, and 2-sec. delays appears to be significantly above chance for all subjects. By the end of the 60th session the performance level for all subjects was ranked in the order of simultaneous, zero, 1, 2, 4, 10, and 24 seconds. This of course suggests that the order of experi-

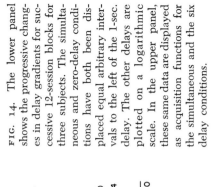

FIG. 14. The lower panel shows the progressive changes in delay gradients for successive 12-session blocks for three subjects. The simultaneous and zero-delay conditions have both been displaced equal arbitrary intervals to the left of the 1-sec. delay. The other delays are plotted on a logarithmic scale. In the upper panel, these same data are displayed as acquisition functions for the simultaneous and the six delay conditions.

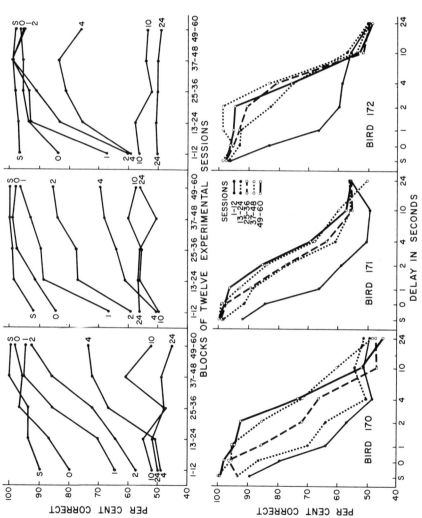

mental conditions does in fact represent an order of increasing difficulty of performance.

Blough (1959) observed that pigeons in the matching situation tend to develop specific superstitious chains which are correlated with the ST's. Even after repeated observation, we were unable to identify any such superstitious chains in our animals. This may, of course, be due to procedural differences between our experiment and Blough's, including the facts that we used 3 standard stimuli instead of 2, and did not systematically increase the delay interval. Although we were unable to observe stimulus-specific superstitious chains mediating the delay interval, we did observe that behavior during the delay interval was discriminably different from behavior during the inter-trial interval, even though these two intervals do not differ in terms of their immediate stimulus properties. The delay interval was usually occupied by agitated pacing back and forth in front of the response panel. During the inter-trial interval the birds typically slowly circled the experimental chamber.

If there are differential chains mediating the delay interval, such chains must start with the presentation of the sample stimulus. It is therefore likely that their presence can be revealed by inspection of quantitative measures of behavior on the center key FR 5 during the presentation of the ST. Examination of the time required to complete this ratio revealed that temporal differences in behavior could be correlated with different key colors. Such differences were found. Birds 170 and 172, for example, showed consistent differences, although in opposite directions, between latency to the green key and latencies to the other two hues. Other measures such as measures of magnitude and topography might reveal similar differential characteristics.

Motivation and Delayed Matching

The availability of three well-trained subjects on the delayed-matching problem made it possible to investigate the effects of some motivational variables upon this delayed performance. Each of the birds was given a total of 4 experimental sessions in which it was permitted to continue the delayed-matching problem until satiated. Satiation was defined as a break of 10 min. or more in which no responses occurred. Such satiation sessions were typically very long. For one of the birds, for example, the range in number of trials to satiation on the 4 sessions of exposure was from 616 to 771, representing over 6 hr. of experimental time. The weight gain during such a session was very large. It often required 4 or 5 days of subsequent deprivation before the bird had been returned to its 80 per cent weight. It was then possible to compare the early trials in such sessions to the late trials. These data are shown in Fig. 15, in which the stippled bars represent the mean per cent correct for each experimental condition dur-

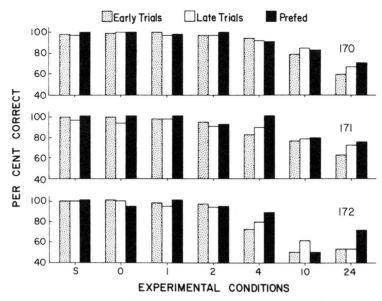

FIG. 15. Per cent correct matching within the variable-delay procedure in relation to motivational variables.

ing the first 126 trials of each session and the white bars represent per cent correct for the last 126 trials of each session. The satiation operation has very little effect upon delayed matching, although there is some suggestion that performance at long delays may be slightly improved as the drive is reduced. This effect is, of course, confounded by the fact that by the last 126 trials of a session birds had been exposed during that experimental session for many "warm-up" trials.

In order to control for this possible contamination, sessions were run in which the birds were fed prior to the experimental session, so that a low drive level could be achieved without exposure to the experimental procedure during satiation. After some preliminary investigation, it was found that a substantial reduction in the number of trials to satiation could be achieved by prefeeding the birds 10 per cent of their body weight two hours before the start of experimentation. Data from sessions in which the birds were pre-fed are shown in Fig. 15 as black bars. The conclusions are substantially the same as those derived from the satiation sessions. There is even some suggestion that performance at long delays may be further improved by this procedure. It can therefore be concluded that such changes as are seen are in fact due to manipulation of the drive variable rather than to a warm-up, or practice, effect.

It seems clear that motivational variables play a very small role in this complex discriminative performance. If the slight improvement at long delays is a real phenomenon, it would be accounted for by differences in the bird's behavior during the delay interval. The possibility exists that a high drive level may result in behavior during the delay interval which breaks up superstitious chains. Such behavior, for example, as going to the food magazine and searching the floor for grain is broadly incompatible with the stimulus-specific behavior required by the mediating-chain hypothesis.

Titrating Delayed Matching

It is obvious that there are a number of alternative procedures for the investigation of delayed matching. Some investigations have been conducted in our laboratory on a procedure that we call "titrating delayed matching."

In this procedure the delay intervening between the center-key response and the presentation of the side keys was variable and depended upon the bird's performance. Two successive correct matches resulted in an increment to the delay interval on the next trial of approximately ½ sec. Each error shortened the delay period on the succeeding trial also by approximately ½ sec. This means that while the bird is doing well, the delay progressively lengthens until he reaches an interval that will permit him to be correct on two-thirds of the trials. The delay interval tends to remain at such a level since he is at that point decreasing the delay as frequently as he is increasing it.

The delay interval was controlled by a recording attenuator that also provided a continuous record of the interval at which the bird was working. A record typical of that obtained with several birds under this procedure is shown in Fig. 16. It shows that Bird 172 began the experimental session at a minimal delay of approximately ½ sec. and then progressively lengthened the interval until during the latter portion of the session the delay remained at around 10 sec. This delay interval is consistent with this particular animal's performance under the variable-delay procedure. This suggests that delayed-matching performance does not require the presence of simultaneous-matching trials, and is unaffected by the absence of delays other than those at which the bird can successfully work. This

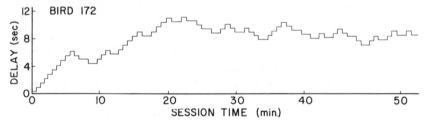

FIG. 16. A selected titrating delay record for Bird 172.

titrating schedule has obvious advantages for work with psychopharmacological agents, motivational variables, and so on, since it provides an immediate and continuous record of the bird's capability for sustaining a delay.

Acquisition of Zero-Delay Matching

The failure to find any signs of acquisition when birds were initially exposed to the variable-delay procedure suggested that within our situation the simultaneous presence of both the ST and the CO's was a necessary condition for learning. Since other investigators (e.g., Blough [1959]) have reported successful acquisition of zero-delay matching, we considered it important to study this problem in order to be able to compare our findings with those of other laboratories, and to contrast acquisition of zero-delay with acquisition in the simultaneous-matching, oddity, and symbolic-matching conditions.

In all respects the procedure was a replication of the simultaneous-matching experiment, except that the ST went off as the CO's came on, and a total of 42 sessions was run with each of 6 birds. (Three additional birds were started in the experiment, but were dropped later because of procedural errors.)

The individual acquisition functions are shown in Fig. 17. The data are in striking contrast to those obtained under other procedures in that most of the birds show major reversals, and all of the functions are exceedingly ragged. The 75 per cent accuracy criterion was met only after 2,562 trials, compared with approximately 700 for the simultaneous condition.

On the first day one bird is at chance but the other five are below chance, and the mean accuracy is 44.1 per cent. The birds do not have heavy position preferences in all cases. Of the nine birds started, only one had a position preference approaching those characteristic of simultaneous matching. The mean position habit on the first day was 38.7 per cent, contrasted with about 97 per cent for simultaneous matching. It is interesting to note that the position preference increased for each bird prior to the acquisition of matching. In some animals, simple hypotheses other than position preference appeared during the first few days. For instance, Bird 337 always picked the blue or green CO. When both of these CO's were present, the animal responded to whichever was on the right (100 per cent on Day 4).

Even after 42 days of exposure, the birds were only averaging 92 per cent correct, compared with the 97 per cent correct the three simultaneous-matching animals achieved after 22 days.

Obviously, the simultaneous presence of the ST and CO's is not required for learning. However, the zero-delay case does represent an exceptionally difficult problem.

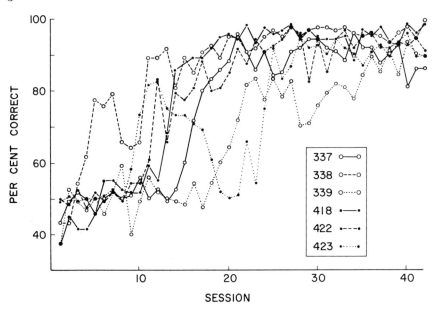

F I G. 17. Per cent correct during acquisition of zero delay.

Ratio Reinforcement of Matching Behavior[3]

In all of the preceding experiments each correct response has been followed by reinforcement. Ferster (1960) found improvement of performance when a number of matches were required for reinforcement, and we have attempted to replicate these results. Cage and other details of the experimental procedure remained as in the earlier studies, except that the inter-trial interval was reduced to one second, and each correct response, rather than resulting in reinforcement, simply advanced a stepping switch. When the prescribed number of correct responses had been emitted, reinforcement was delivered. Incorrect responses had no effect on the reinforcement stepper, although they of course advanced the trial stepper. As in our other study, a non-correction procedure was used. Fixed ratios of 1 (CRF), 3, 6, and 10 were used, as well as a variable ratio of 3.

Figure 18 shows the per cent correct matching under each of these ratio sizes. It was disturbing to find that our data did not replicate those of Ferster (1960), which are plotted in Fig. 18 for comparison. In our study the birds showed their best performance under fixed ratio 1, or continuous reinforcement. In Ferster's experiment accuracy of matching improved over the range of fixed ratios we studied. We are at a loss to account for this discrepancy in findings, although several procedural differences may

[3] Nevin, Cumming, and Berryman (1963).

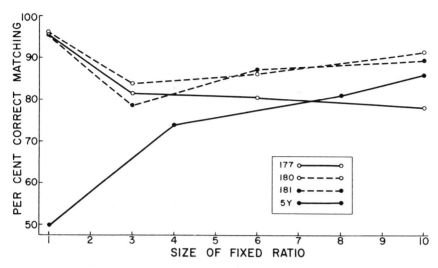

FIG. 18. The relation between accuracy of matching and size of the fixed ratio. Data from our subjects are means for the last five days' exposure to each schedule. Data from Ferster (1960) for his subject 5Y are plotted for comparison.

be implicated. Ferster employed a brief magazine-light reinforcement for each correct response within the ratio, as well as a brief blackout for errors within the ratio. In addition, he used only two alternative stimuli. His procedure was equivalent to what we have called zero-delay in that the ST was extinguished when CO's were presented. While we had a 1-sec. inter-trial interval, Ferster employed none. Perhaps most significant was the fact that Ferster employed a correction procedure in that errors resulted in the repetition of the trial until the correct response was made. Such a procedure, of course, breaks up any position habit the bird may develop, and permits it to form a discrimination that is not based upon the center key ST. (By switching key side after an incorrect response, the bird could "match" better than chance.) Nonetheless, Ferster reports that birds on CRF did no better than chance.

Ferster (1960) observes that exposure to ratio-matching schedules results in break-run behavior similar to that found under simple schedules of reinforcement, and this kind of performance was also observed in all three of our subjects.

In order to investigate the properties of this complex discriminative performance under a ratio schedule of reinforcement, we have examined the accuracy of the matching performance as a function of the ordinal trial number after reinforcement. These data are shown in Fig. 19, in which per cent correct matching is plotted as a function of the ordinal trial number after reinforcement with size of the fixed ratio as a parameter. As the

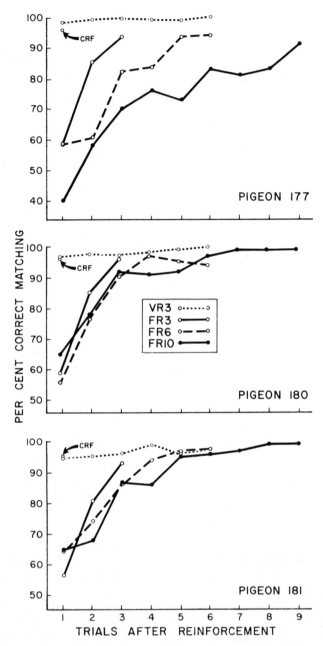

FIG. 19. Accuracy of matching as related to the ordinal number of the trial since reinforcement, for FR 3, FR 6, FR 10, and VR 3. CRF (FR 1) accuracy is plotted for comparison. All points are means for the last five days' exposure to each schedule.

bird advances in the ratio, accuracy improves, and there is some suggestion that this improvement is also a function of the size of the fixed ratio.
This means that immediately following a reinforced matching response,
when the bird has returned to the simple operant of key pecking, he is still
not "paying attention" to the *ST* in that this cue exerts little control over
his behavior. Since the increase in accuracy following a reinforcement
rises to an asymptote, and since this reduced-accuracy performance occupies a larger and larger fraction of the fixed ratio as the fixed ratio is
reduced, this explains the dip in our function at low fixed ratio values.

In order to demonstrate that this performance decrement is not due
to decrease in the density of reinforcement we exposed each animal to
a variable ratio 3, and the results of that operation are also plotted in
Fig. 19. It can be seen that in the case of variable-ratio reinforcement
of matching, no post-reinforcement decrement in accuracy is observable.
Birds perform just as well immediately after reinforcement as later in the
variable ratio.

The finding that behavior is weak immediately following reinforcement
on a fixed ratio schedule carries the implication that in the matching
situation discrimination may also be weak under similar schedule conditions. However, as we had noted, it is possible that the observing be-

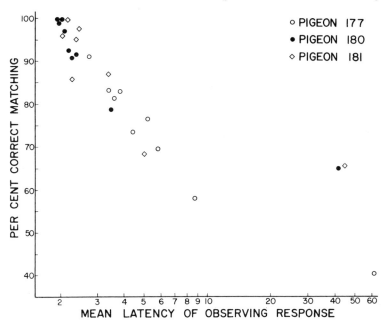

FIG. 20. The correlation between mean observing response latency in seconds (on a
logarithmic scale) and mean accuracy of the subsequent match, for each ordinal trial
number since reinforcement on Day 9 of exposure to FR 10.

havior on which the discrimination is based is itself weak. We examined this possibility by recording the time needed to complete a fixed ratio of 5 required on the center key. This center key, or observing reponse "latency," was recorded for each ordinal trial following reinforcement. As indicated in Fig. 20, as the ordinal trial number increases, the latency decreases, resulting in a high correlation when these measures are plotted against each other. Although latencies immediately after reinforcement clearly do not fall in the distribution, the other latencies, when plotted on a logarithmic scale, show a linear relation to accuracy, which is highly similar for all three subjects. Clearly, these latencies are measures of the strength of the birds' observing behavior, or the extent to which they are "paying attention" to the ST. Conversely, the increased exposure to ST, on occasions when latencies are long, is without beneficial effect.

Effects of Drugs

A number of studies of the effects of drugs on some of the previously described procedures have been carried out. This work has a twofold basis: (1) the effects of drug variables on complex discriminations is of general psychopharmacological interest, and (2) performance-specific drug effects are sometimes useful in suggesting possible qualitative differences in behavior.

Drugs and simultaneous matching. Birds used previously in the study of simultaneous hue matching were exposed to doses of 5 and 10 mg/kg sodium pentobarbital, 0.05 mg/kg lysergic acid diethylamide, and 10 and 20 mg/kg chlorpromazine, as well as 20 mg/kg chlorpromazine administered 3 hours before the experimental session.

The effects of these drugs on matching accuracy are exhibited in Fig. 21. Pentobarbital, at 5 mg/kg, did not appreciably affect accuracy; at 10 mg/kg, accuracy was initially well below the normal range, but returned to normal levels by the end of the 144-trial session. Lysergic acid produced an initial period of inactivity, during which the birds did not respond to the keys, followed by essentially normal performance. The chlorpromazine data showed such great variability, both within and across subjects, that no firm generalizations can be made.

Pentobarbital and delayed matching. Three birds, whose experimental careers have been described above in the variable-delay experiment, were once more stabilized on this procedure by retraining them for 18 days with randomized presentation of all 7 experimental conditions (simultaneous, zero delay, and delays of 1, 2, 4, 10, and 24 sec.) at 84 trials per day.

Next, three dose levels of sodium pentobarbital were introduced in the sequence: 10.0 mg/kg for 6 sessions; 5.0 mg/kg, 3 sessions; 7.5 mg/kg, 6 sessions; control, 6 sessions; 5.0 mg/kg, 3 sessions. All doses were in-

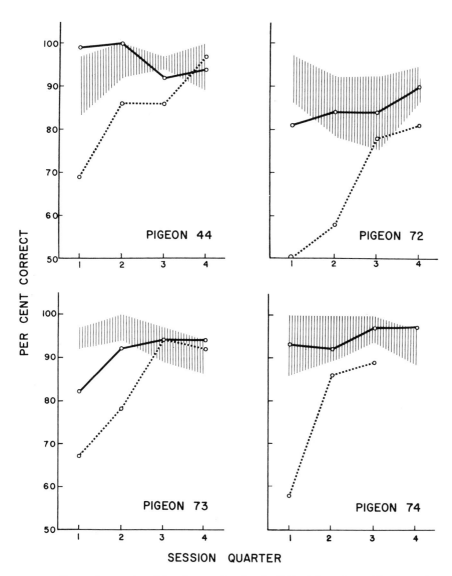

FIG. 21. Per cent correct matches by quarters for the 144-trial session, with 10 mg/kg of sodium pentobarbital and 0.05 mg/kg of lysergic acid diethylamide. The shaded area indicates the range of normal accuracy. Dotted lines show performance with pentobarbital, solid lines performance with lysergic acid.

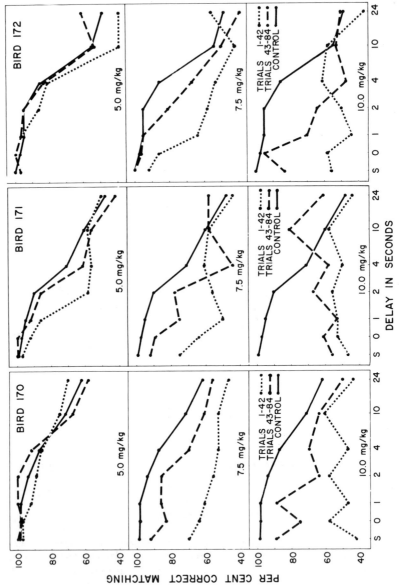

FIG. 22. Accuracy of performance on the variable-delay procedure for three dose levels of sodium pentobarbital.

jected into the pectoral muscle 10 minutes before each session. Control and drug days were alternated by running the birds 5 days a week, with drug administration scheduled only on Tuesdays and Thursdays.

Control and drug performances are shown in Fig. 22. Since the daily records showed that the control performance was virtually constant throughout the experiment, and unaffected either by antecedent drug administration or by the number of days between sessions, the mean values of the 18 control days were used to establish the control accuracy functions. Accuracy functions for drug performance were prepared for both the first and the last halves of the sessions.

The results show that 5 mg/kg has only a slight effect, while 7.5 and 10.0 mg/kg produce progressively larger decrements. At the two higher doses there is recovery in the second half of the session, but it does not return to the control level.

One pattern of behavior associated with the decreases in accuracy at the higher dose levels is the increasing tendency of the subjects to take up a position preference. This effect is shown in Fig. 23. Control and 5.0 mg/kg position preferences are substantially the same. While there are slight increases in control position preference as a function of delay length for Birds 170 and 171, Bird 172 shows a quite sharp increase beyond 2 sec., and rises to an almost total preference at 24 sec.

At doses greater than 5.0 mg/kg, position preference increases with increasing dose level up to 4 sec. Effects beyond this delay are unclear.

It should be noted that there is no forced correlation between accuracy and position preference. For example, at 10.0 mg/kg, Bird 171 is at chance both on short delays and at 24 sec., while position preference is high for the short delays and zero for the 24-sec. delay.

Effects of pentobarbital on zero-delay matching and on oddity. Six birds with histories of 42 sessions on the zero-delay procedure, and six birds with 40 to 50 sessions on simultaneous oddity served as subjects. Dose levels of 5.0, 7.5, 10.0, and 12.5 mg/kg were administered in random order until each bird had had three sessions at each level. As before, the drug was injected into the pectoral muscle 10 minutes before sessions. A single control session intervened between successive drug administrations.

Over-all accuracies for the zero-delay subjects are shown in Fig. 24. Each experimental point is based on the mean for three sessions at a given dose. The control points are means of 13 control sessions run during the course of the experiment.

These functions in general show a small effect at 5.0 mg/kg, followed by a consistent decrement in accuracy with increasing doses. One subject, Bird 337, showed some decrement in accuracy over the first 6 control days; this accounts for the fact that its control performance is appreciably lower than that for 5 mg/kg. The control performance recovered to its

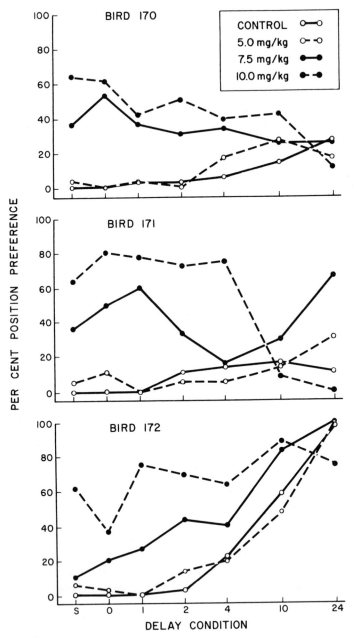

FIG. 23. Position preference in relation to delay condition for three dose levels of sodium pentobarbital.

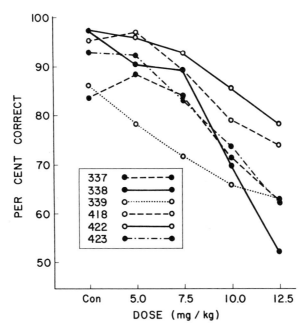

FIG. 24. Over-all accuracy as a function of pentobarbital dose level for zero delay.

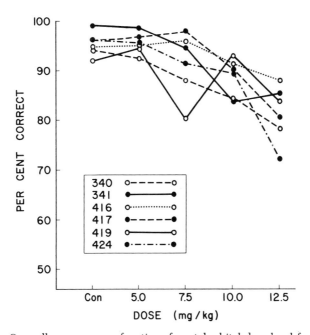

FIG. 25. Over-all accuracy as a function of pentobarbital dose level for oddity.

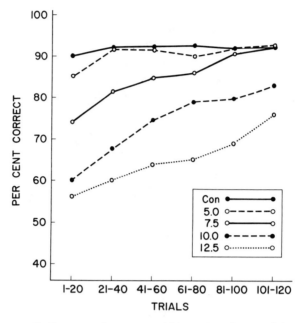

FIG. 26. Recovery of accuracy within sessions for zero delay.

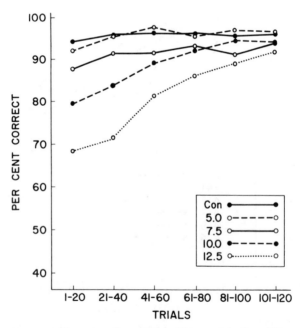

FIG. 27. Recovery of accuracy within sessions for oddity.

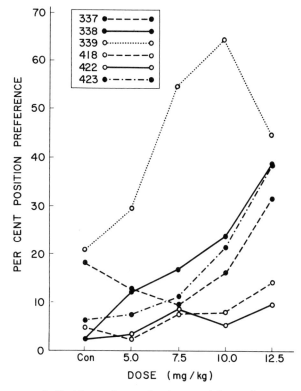

FIG. 28. Position preference for the zero-delay performance.

original level as the experiment progressed, however. The other 5 subjects maintained stable control performance throughout.

These data show that the effects of pentobarbital are closely similar to those observed for the simultaneous condition earlier. They are, however, in striking contrast to the oddity accuracy functions shown in Fig. 25. Obviously, the oddity performance is far less sensitive to the drug effect, with accuracy remaining high for all subjects even at the 12.5 mg/kg dose level.

Recovery functions are shown in Fig. 26 for zero delay and in Fig. 27 for oddity. Recovery for zero delay is very much like that found for the simultaneous condition. At the end of 120 trials, accuracy for the oddity performance has returned practically to the control level. The position-preference data are displayed in Figs. 28 and 29. Correlated with the decrements in accuracy is a tendency for position preferences to increase.

The finding that simultaneous matching and oddity are differentially affected by pentobarbital carries with it the suggestion that these two performances require qualitatively different types of behavior.

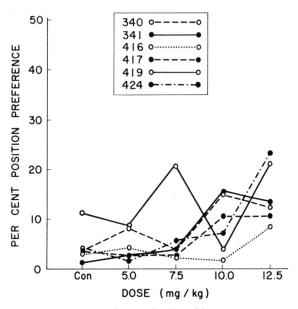

FIG. 29. Position preference for the oddity performance.

Hypotheses

One of the most striking features of data on matching acquisition is the extent to which the animals display what we have called preferences. Very frequently in the initial stage of acquisition of matching, animals display an almost complete preference for either the right or the left comparison stimulus. Other kinds of preference are often seen, such as preference for a particular hue as *CO*, or in other studies, preferences for particular geometric forms when presented as a comparison. These preferences are similar to the phenomena that other authors have referred to as "hypotheses," "means-end readinesses," or "strategies." Since the term hypotheses seems to be most widely used in this connection, we shall employ it here. However, we shall bear in mind what Tolman and Kreshevsky (1933) had to say in this connection: "... a 'means-end-readiness' or a 'hypothesis' (or 'desire' or 'conditioned-response connection' or whatnot) is also but a special value or form of the general relation obtaining between stimulus situations (together, of course, with the physiological condition of the animal) and given succeeding responses. That is, a hypothesis or a means-end-readiness (or the like) is the name for an observed relatively specific type of correlation, or equation, holding between stimulus situations and resultant response patterns."

In fact, we are not using the term hypothesis to indicate any special mode of problem solutions which the subject may bring to the experiment

TABLE 2

CONFORMITY TO SOME SELECTED HYPOTHESES IN THE 96-TRIAL SESSION
ON DEC. 1, 1962, FOR BIRD 421

Hypothesis	No. of Applicable Trials	No. of Conforming Trials	Per Cent Conformity
1. Right Preference	96	33	34.4
2. Circle Preference	64	28	43.8
3. Square Preference	64	25	39.1
4. Triangle Preference	64	43	67.2
✿ ✿ ✿			
5. Matching	96	71	74.0
6. Circle → Circle	32	21	65.6
7. Square → Square	32	19	59.4
8. Triangle → Triangle	32	31	96.9
✿ ✿ ✿			
9. Circle → Right	32	13	40.6
10. Square → Right	32	3	9.4
11. Triangle → Right	32	17	53.1
✿ ✿ ✿			
12. Circle → Square	16	6	37.5
13. Circle → Triangle	16	5	31.3
14. Square → Circle	16	6	37.5
15. Square → Triangle	16	7	43.8
16. Triangle → Circle	16	1	6.3
17. Triangle → Square	16	0	0.0

and "try out," but rather we intend, as will be obvious, to examine some of the natural history of hypotheses.

Table 2 contains an examination of a typical record in the acquisition of matching of geometric forms. (*ST* and *CO* were a circle, a square, or a triangle.) In the table, 17 separate hypotheses are examined. The data are taken from Bird 421 on December 1, 1962. This bird had had approximately 3 months of previous experience with matching and on the day in question was partially through the acquisition stage of the performance. (It should be noted that acquisition of form matching is much slower than acquisition of hue matching.) Such an intermediate level of performance has been selected because it serves best to display the phenomena we wish to examine. Matching was reinforced with 3 sec. of grain, and errors produced a 10-sec. blackout.

The first four hypotheses listed in the table are simple preferences, or hypotheses without regard for the stimulus presented on the center key. Thus, the first hypothesis, right preference, consists of a tally of the number of trials out of a possible 96 in which the bird might have pecked the right key. As can be seen from the table this occurred on 33 trials or 34.4 per cent of the total applicable trials. The second, third, and fourth hypotheses examine preferences for the individual geometric forms as the *CO*. Since there are three forms and only two are presented on any given trial, these preferences can be examined on only 64 of the total 96 trials. The fifth hypothesis consists of the "correct" one, that of matching or responding to the *CO* which has the same geometric form as the *ST*. As can be seen, on the day in question, Bird 421 made 74 per cent correct matches. Hypotheses 6, 7, and 8 divide the matching performance according to the cue on the center key. Here the question is, Does the bird match some stimuli better than others? Hypotheses 9, 10, and 11 examine the right position preference as a function of the cue on the center key. Hypotheses 12 through 17 examine the errors in matching. That is, when the center key was a circle (hypotheses 12 and 13), how often did the bird select a square on the side keys, and how often did he select a triangle on the side keys? These are, of course, the errors the bird made in matching the circle.

Since we have defined hypothesis as a correlation between a stimulus situation and the resultant response pattern, it is, of course, impossible to determine the correlation by observing a single isolated response. A single response might show a right preference, a circle preference, matching, circle matching, avoidance of squares, and so forth. It is only by examining the over-all proportions in which the animal divides his responses among these several hypotheses, that we may detect patterns of responding.

The most obvious thing to be found in Table 2 is that the animal was in fact matching the triangle to a much greater extent than the square or the circle. In fact, when the triangle was on the center key, the animal made only one error in matching, or 96.9 per cent correct. The performance is not entirely accounted for by this animal's preference for triangles on the comparison keys. Rather, the reverse is true. The 67.2 per cent triangle preference shown in hypothesis 4 is rather the result of the fact that the animal matches the triangle almost perfectly when it is on the center key. The next obvious conclusions from the data are that when a square is *ST*, the animal prefers the left comparison key about 90 per cent of the time. The bird is matching the circle on the center key about 15 per cent more than we would expect by chance, but shows no clear hypothesis in the presence of the circle.

We can therefore characterize the performance shown on this day as follows: When the square is *ST* the animal goes to the left, when the triangle is *ST* the animal matches, and when the circle is *ST* the animal distributes his responses somewhat at random according to the hypotheses we have examined, with the exception that some preference is shown for the matching performance. We have not, of course, examined all possible hypotheses. One thinks immediately of hypotheses that might be based upon the sequence of stimuli presented, or responses. While we have looked in a separate analysis at the distribution of response sequences within the experiment, and found no reliable sequential hypotheses emerging, it is possible, of course, that when the circle is on the center key the animal is actually basing his behavior upon some such sequential hypothesis. Such a stimulus-specific sequential hypothesis would be extremely difficult to tease out of a small sample of data like the present. However, sequential hypotheses are minimized in the present experiment by the inclusion of a 25-sec. inter-trial interval.

Now, the behavior shown in Table 2 is clearly a most remarkable performance and shows far more control by the ST than one would assume from simply observing that the animal made only 74 per cent correct matching responses. If we were to characterize this performance in terms of the schematic paradigm presented earlier, the situation would look something like the following:

$$ST_{triangle} \rightarrow [CO_{triangle} \rightarrow R],$$
$$ST_{square} \rightarrow [CO_{left} \rightarrow R],$$
$$ST_{circle} (\rightarrow) [CO_{circle} \rightarrow R].$$

Had we considered such a performance the "correct" one, Bird 421 would have been correct on 81 rather than 71 of the 96 trials, or, 84.4 per cent. In fact most of the errors would have occurred when the center key was a circle, and for that reason the low degree of observed correlation when the circle is ST has been indicated in the above paradigm by placing the arrow in parentheses.

It is tempting to consider that the bird is playing a somewhat different game than we are. That is, in spite of the programmed reinforcement for matching, the bird is in fact doing some things which are different. This suggests that his performance is independent of the programmed contingencies to a degree, but such a suggestion may be misleading. We have found in our data considerable suggestion that even when behavior appears not in accord with the programmed reinforcement contingencies, it is nevertheless true that the hypotheses displayed are a product of the programmed contingencies.

Examples of this phenomenon are not difficult to find. Thus, for example, when we have programmed reinforcement for simultaneous matching, the birds display an almost complete position preference. However, when the reinforcements are programmed for responses to the odd stimulus, no such substantial position habits emerge. An additional example is found in our data on delayed matching. When birds are placed on a variable-delay procedure in which a delay is introduced between the offset of the ST and the onset of CO's, birds show a position habit. However, the preference shown is 75 per cent for one side and 25 per cent for the other. When this procedure is switched to simultaneous matching, all subjects immediately shift toward a much more pronounced position habit. Although these hypotheses are not the "correct" ones (i.e., the behavior for which reinforcement is programmed), they nevertheless are quite clearly controlled by the reinforcement contingencies the experiment provides.

One aspect of hypothesis behavior has shown itself often enough in our data to deserve comment. It seems possible that some incorrect hypotheses more readily lead to learning the correct performance than others. We have pointed out that in all of the data on simultaneous matching, birds begin with an extremely pronounced position habit, while the matching performance remains at chance levels. This stage is followed by a rapid loss of the position habit during a period in which the matching is being speedily acquired. Birds exposed to the simultaneous oddity program, by contrast, begin with only a moderate position habit which is not maintained. At the same time, they make the correct oddity choices at much higher than chance levels. One might expect that since there is no interfering hypothesis, and since the correct performance is receiving more reinforcement during this early stage of acquisition, the improvement would be rapid. In fact, as we have seen, the reverse is true, and the oddity performance is acquired very slowly.

The data from Table 2 suggest another way in which this interesting relation between hypotheses and learning can be checked. While Bird 421 had acquired triangle matching, circle and square matching were only moderately above chance. A pronounced position habit was displayed, however, during the square-matching trials. The suggestion that a position habit may lead to more rapid acquisition predicts that Bird 421 should show more rapid learning of square matching than of circle matching. To check on this possibility, data for five 4-day blocks beginning with the day shown in Table 2 were examined, and the acquisition curves for circle and square matching are shown in Fig. 30. It is clear that at least in this small sample of data the prediction is confirmed. Should this suggestion prove to have a greater generality, we might be led to observe that a major difference between oddity and matching lies in the kinds of hypotheses each produces, and these in turn are responsible for the differential rates of acquisition under the two conditions.

The reasons for the superiority of learning under conditions of a position habit are certainly far from clear. It seems possible, however, to consider that the paradigm, in which an ST changes the probability of lower-order discriminations, places some requirements upon the way in which the

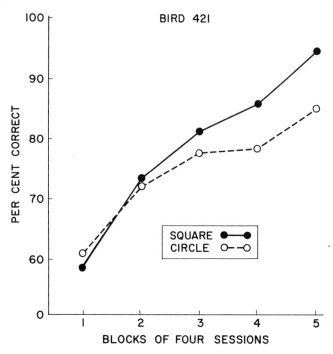

FIG. 30. Per cent correct for stimulus conditions in which *ST* is a circle or a square. Data are means for blocks of four sessions, following approximately three months of exposure to form matching.

more complex reflex is constructed. To be more explicit, the selected discrimination (the portion in brackets in our paradigm) is, in reality, more complex than we have indicated. It consists of two distinct units—selecting the proper *CO* when it is on the right, and selecting the same *CO* when it is on the left. These two sub-units must be made to act as a unit before this discrimination can come under the control of the *ST*. This concatenation of sub-units is facilitated under the conditions of position habit —when the bird is "paying attention" to the side on which the stimulus is presented.

We have observed cases in which only one of these positional sub-units was conditioned to the *ST*. A notable case was that of Bird 181. This animal was placed on the simultaneous-matching procedure following nine days of exposure to the randomized delayed-matching procedure described above. This bird displayed a systematic inability to match blue or green when they appeared as *CO*'s on the left key, although these hues were matched successfully when they appeared on the right. In all cases, ability to match red (either on the right or on the left) was normal. Other similar cases can be found in our data on acquisition of zero-delay matching. When the ST controls only one of the sub-units, an effective ceiling below 100 per cent is put on the performance level.

SOME SUMMARY REMARKS

Earlier in this paper, we entertained the notion that the ST in our experiments may have a function somewhat different from the discriminative function which the CO stimuli perform. Specifically, we have characterized the CO's as the S^D's of simple discriminations, and the ST as a selector of discriminations, or "instructional" stimulus. We leave open the possibility that ST's control is mediated through the presence of an "instructional response" such as that suggested by Schoenfeld and Cumming (1963). The argument for such a "selective" or "instructional" function might rest on at least three different grounds.

A. An "operational" distinction between ST and CO may be pointed out. The operational uniqueness of ST is inherent in our experimental procedure. It is presented first, and sometimes, without any overlap with the CO's. Reinforcement contingencies vary with changes in the ST's, but not with changes in the CO's. For a given pair of CO's, the behavior to be reinforced is determined by the antecedent ST. Although the operational distinction between the ST's and the CO's is clear, the argument that the ST's play a unique role in the control of behavior cannot be based solely on this difference. Rather, the validity of such an argument must be judged in relation to observed behavioral effects.

B. A number of effects which we and others have observed do indeed appear to support the notion that the ST is exercising a special stimulus function. For example: (1) In ratio matching we found that the degree of control over behavior exercised by ST was a function of its ordinal position within the fixed ratio. This would not be expected in simple concurrent discriminations (CONC FR EXT) where the animal either does not respond, or responds correctly. The discriminative function of a stimulus does not appear to vary when a fixed-ratio contingency is imposed, while such a contingency conspicuously alters the "instructional" or "selective" function. (2) The effects of sodium pentobarbital on performance indicate that simple discriminative stimulus control remains intact at dose levels that obliterate the instructional control of ST. That is, the animals execute the sequence of required responses, continue to discriminate the presence of hues on the keys, and can in fact discriminate one hue from another, as in shown by the maintenance of performance in oddity even at high dose levels. Thus, there is little reason to believe that a simple S^D-S^Δ discrimination would be affected at the dose levels employed. (3) Oddity performance was found to be strikingly different from matching. Yet, there is no reason to believe that the bird's ability to discriminate red, green, and blue differs from one situation to the other. Since simple discriminative behavior is the same in both of these situations, it is the relation of the *ST*'s to the *CO*'s that occasions the differences in performance. (4) The delayed-matching experiment demonstrated that the *ST* can control discriminations over a considerable interval of time. In this situation, the function of the *ST* is not the simple discriminative control of a response. The animal is not just being told to make a response after some time interval; he is being told which cues to use. (5) The data on generalization of oddity to a novel stimulus imply that a stimulus exercising an instructional function acts as a selector of S^D's rather than of S^Δ's. Since we did not condition a response to a yellow *CO* following a red or a green *ST*, the bird is unable to carry out the performance.

C. Evidence of this sort does not constitute incontrovertible proof of the existence of a separate stimulus function. The worth of this notion, as is the case with all such concepts, must ultimately be assessed in terms of its experimental and theoretical utility.

At present, considerable attention is being given to observations indicating that generalization not only depends upon the physical nature of the stimuli, but also has to do with the functional relation of the stimulus to the response. This is reflected in numerous studies of possible differences between excitatory and inhibitory gradients, and in the finding that generalization of secondary negative reinforcers does not mirror that of secondary positive reinforcers. We see no reason to expect that generalization of *ST*'s in our experiment would be the same as generalization of the *CO*'s. In addition, we have evidence of another dimension of the stimulus generalization problem in the complex case, in that we must consider generalization from *ST* to the correct *CO*, as an oddity.

Certain relations between *ST* and *CO* control the complex patterns of behavior, or hypotheses, exhibited by our subjects. We observed, for example, that Bird 421 in the form matching experiment developed a position habit when the *ST* was a square, but did not show this hypothesis when *ST* was a circle. The generalization of this position habit could be determined by varying the properties of the square. Generalization in such a case would be evidenced, not in variations in strength of specific single responses, but rather in changes of complex patterns of behavior, as they are related to changes in the *ST*. Studies of the function of *ST* in this situation should contribute to our understanding of stimulus generalization.

REFERENCES

Berryman, R., Jarvik, M. E., and Nevin, J. A. Effects of pentobarbital, lysergic acid diethylamide, and chlorpromazine on matching behavior in the pigeon. *Psychopharmacologia*, 1962, 3, 60–65.

Berryman, R., Cumming, W. W., and Nevin, J. A. Acquisition of delayed matching in the pigeon. *J. exp. Anal. Behav.*, 1963, **6**, 101–107.

Blough, D. S. Delayed matching in the pigeon. *J. exp. Anal. Behav.*, 1959, **2**, 151–160.

Cumming, W. W., and Berryman, R. Some data on matching behavior in the pigeon. *J. exp. Anal. Behav.*, 1961, **4**, 281–284.

Estes, W. K. The statistical approach to learning theory. In S. Koch (Ed.), *Psychology: A study of a science*, Vol. 2. New York: McGraw-Hill, 1959.

Ferster, C. B. Intermittent reinforcement of matching to sample in the pigeon. *J. exp. Anal. Behav.*, 1960, **3**, 259–272.

Ginsburg, N. Matching in pigeons. *J. comp. physiol. Psychol.*, 1957, **50**, 261–263.

Lashley, K. S. Conditional reactions in the rat. *J. Psychol.*, 1938, **6**, 311–324.

Nevin, J. A., Cumming, W. W., and Berryman, R. Ratio reinforcement of matching behavior. *J. exp. Anal. Behav.*, 1963, **6**, 149–154.

Schoenfeld, W. N., and Cumming, W. W. Perception and behavior. In S. Koch (Ed.), *Psychology: A study of a science*, Vol. 5. New York: McGraw-Hill, 1963.

Skinner, B. F. *The behavior of organisms.* New York: Appleton-Century, 1938.

Skinner, B. F. Are theories of learning necessary? *Psychol. Rev.*, 1950, **57**, 193–216.

Tolman, E. C., and Krechevsky, I. Means-end-readiness and hypothesis. A contribution to comparative psychology. *Psychol. Rev.*, 1933, **40**, 60–70.

Woodworth, R. S. *Dynamics of behavior.* New York: Holt, 1958.

20. Approach, Avoidance, and Stimulus Generalization

Eliot Hearst, *NIMH, Saint Elizabeths Hospital, Washington, D.C.*

A few years ago I was a member of a group that studied EEG responses in well-trained monkeys (Hearst *et al.*, 1960). One of our monkeys had to press a lever continuously in order to avoid shocks. Toward the end of the study we decided to disconnect the shock circuit and take out the lever, in order to see whether EEG patterns would change if lever pressing were prevented. We thought that removal of the lever was an easy way to prevent lever pressing, but it turned out that we were wrong; even after the lever had been removed, the monkey continued to respond at the same rate for hours, bouncing his hand up and down in the area where the lever had once been. With our realization that "phantom pressing"— as we called these vigorous depressions of an imaginary lever—left the monkey as free of punishments as when he was pounding on a real lever, we were able to control the disappointment that usually accompanies the failure of an experiment.

Whether or not this case history is a clear example of exaggerated stimulus generalization, it does illustrate some of the distinguishing properties of a continuous-avoidance response, for example, its relatively high resistance to extinction and its apparent dependence on non-exteroceptive stimuli. Some of these properties may prove important in accounting for the differences that we have observed between generalization gradients for certain types of appetitive and aversive behavior.

Although the general goal of our research has been to find out whether stimulus-generalization gradients for approach and avoidance behavior differ in any fundamental way, most of the completed work has involved a comparison of appetitive and aversive behavior in free-responding situations, as exemplified by variable-interval (VI) food-reward schedules and by Sidman-type avoidance (SAV) schedules. Relatively steady rates of

The assistance and suggestions of Minnie B. Koresko, Alice Torovsky, Peter Edmond, Roger Poppen, and Joe Whitley were invaluable in carrying out the experiments described here. This research has benefited from the critical comments of Peter Carlton and Murray Sidman, as well as from several suggestions made by Norman Guttman.

responding are obtained on both these procedures. Only recently have we begun work with discrete-trial situations and other kinds of free-operant food-reward schedules.

There are two prevalent but almost contradictory views regarding the nature of generalization gradients for approach and avoidance. Clinical reports, psychiatrists who talk in learning-theory terms, and several experimental studies (see Mednick and Freedman, 1960) have suggested an unusually large amount of stimulus generalization among neurotic and psychotic individuals, as well as among normal experimental subjects who are made more fearful than control subjects. Masserman (1950, p. 56), for example, has remarked that every clinician will recognize the "irrational generalization" of human neuroses whereby "anxiety and patterned defense begin to spread to other situations only remotely or 'symbolically' associated with the neurotigenic situation." This point of view seems to imply that aversively controlled behavior generalizes more extensively than other types of behavior.

In contrast to this view is the theoretical framework of Miller (1944, 1948). The assumption that "approach generalizes more widely than avoidance" serves as one of Miller's basic principles in analyzing conflict behavior and displacement. His predictions regarding the behavior of rats that are exposed to an approach-avoidance conflict in a runway are based in part on this assumption about differential generalization gradients. Miller (1959) and his associates have mustered a good deal of data in support of this hypothesis, and Miller (1959, 1961) has extended the approach-avoidance distinction to generalization gradients on dimensions other than the spatial one of the runway.

The experiments to be reported here indicate that the relative slopes of approach and avoidance gradients depend critically on the type of situation in which they are measured. As usual, things turn out to be much more complicated than we would have liked them to be.

Some Experimental Results

Initial Findings

Our first series of experiments involved the simultaneous comparison of appetitive and aversive generalization gradients in individual rhesus monkeys. A Primate Test Chamber (Foringer) was equipped with two response mechanisms, a chain that hung in the center of the chamber and a lever that projected from one wall. A 110 v AC house light, mounted above a milk-glass screen in the top of the chamber, served as a general illuminant during experimental sessions. The intensity of this light was varied during generalization testing.

Five subjects were first trained to press the lever to avoid shock on an SAV schedule (Sidman, 1953a) in which the response-shock (R-S) and

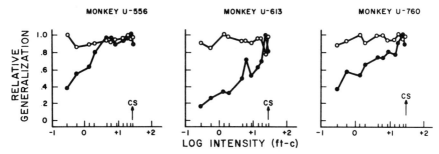

FIG. 1. Prediscrimination generalization gradients for concurrent approach and avoidance in three monkeys. All subjects were originally trained in the continuous presence of the brightest light intensity (indicated as the "CS"). ● Reward. ○ Avoidance.

the shock-shock (S-S) intervals were both equal to 10 sec.; by responding at least once every 10 sec., subjects could avoid shock entirely. After the monkeys had learned to avoid shock efficiently, the chain was inserted into the chamber and the monkeys were trained to pull it to obtain food pellets on a 2-min. VI schedule (Ferster and Skinner, 1957). From then on, the reward and avoidance schedules were always in effect simultaneously.

The subjects were given ten additional sessions of exposure to the concurrent schedules of reward and avoidance. Throughout all these training periods, the house light stayed on continuously at its maximum intensity.

During generalization tests, light of eleven different intensities was presented. The eleven intensities included the brightest, used during training, and ten others, all dimmer than the training stimulus. No rewards or punishments were possible during generalization tests. Further details of the training and testing procedures can be obtained from our previous reports (Hearst, 1960; 1962).

Separate generalization gradients for the two responses are shown in Fig. 1 for three of the monkeys.[1] Relative generalization (on the ordinates) was scaled by assigning the value of 1.00 to the peak of each gradient; all other response frequencies were expressed as decimal fractions of this maximum value.

For every monkey the reward gradient was much steeper than the avoidance gradient; the response controlled by shock avoidance generalized much more widely than the response controlled by food reward.

In order to find out whether a similar difference between gradients for approach and avoidance would occur even after discrimination training, we next gave these monkeys special training in the discrimination of two

[1] The other two monkeys (not included in the figures) showed similar differences between the appetitive and aversive gradients. These subjects are not included in the figures because illnesses later forced us to drop them from the study (i.e., before postdiscrimination gradients (Fig. 2) could be obtained).

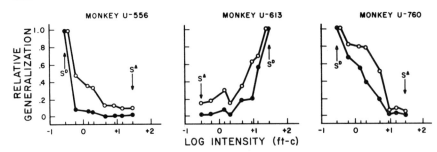

FIG. 2. Postdiscrimination generalization gradients for the three monkeys shown in Fig. 1. Two subjects had the dimmest test intensity as the S^D during discrimination training, whereas the third subject (U-613) had the brightest test intensity as the S^D. In all cases the S^Δ intensity was at the opposite end of the intensity continuum. • Reward. ○ Avoidance.

different house-light intensities. For two of the subjects a very dim light intensity (S^D) signaled the same concurrent schedules of food reward and shock avoidance as before; the former training stimulus (the brightest light) signaled a period (S^Δ) in which the monkey could obtain neither food nor shock. The third monkey continued in a situation in which the brightest light was S^D; when the dim intensity (S^Δ) was presented, neither food nor shock was possible.

All monkeys mastered the appetitive half of the discrimination within a few experimental hours, but it required many sessions and several procedural changes before discrimination indices for the avoidance response reached comparable levels. We tested for postdiscrimination gradients only after S^Δ rates for both responses were consistently less than 10 per cent of their S^D rates. Figure 2 shows these postdiscrimination gradients.

The steepness of both gradients increased markedly over their prediscrimination levels, and the differences between the two gradients were much smaller than before. Nevertheless, the same qualitative difference still existed between the two gradients: The avoidance gradient lay above the reward gradient for all subjects. The greater generalization of the avoidance response was particularly obvious for Monkeys U-556 and U-760 in the intensity region relatively near S^D.

Further Experiments

Although the amount of generalization was consistently greater for avoidance than for approach in this initial series of experiments, there are several confounding factors that must be eliminated before one can talk about the observed differences in a more fundamental way. Let us consider several of these factors and the evidence against their importance.

(1) *Differential response rates.* During training and testing sessions, all the monkeys pressed the avoidance lever more frequently than they pulled the chain. It is conceivable, therefore, that the differences between

the two generalization gradients could have resulted from the unequal response rates on the two manipulanda. This argument would predict, for example, that a flatter gradient would also be obtained for the stronger of two appetitively controlled responses.

There are, however, data from Guttman's laboratory (Guttman, 1956; Kalish and Guttman, 1957) which indicate that response rate itself does not have such an effect on gradients of relative generalization. Guttman (1956) found that groups of pigeons differing in over-all response output did not differ systematically in amount of relative generalization; response strength affected generalization gradients in a multiplicative way. Similarly, Sidman (1961) observed that gradients of relative generalization in individual monkeys were independent of avoidance-response rate. On the other hand, some of my own results with pigeons in a food-reward situation indicate that birds trained on short VI intervals do yield higher response rates during training and sharper gradients during testing than birds trained on long VI intervals; this of course is the opposite result from that predicted by the argument of the preceding paragraph.

Perhaps the most convincing answer to this argument regarding differential response rates lies in some of our other results. We have shown (Hearst, 1962) that rats trained to press a lever on VI schedules for food reward show much higher lever-pressing rates and sharper gradients along a light intensity continuum than rats trained to press a lever on SAV schedules. In these experiments approach gradients were sharper than avoidance gradients even though VI response rates were higher than avoidance rates. Also, those of our original monkeys (Figs. 1 and 2) whose avoidance and VI rates were most similar did not exhibit less of a difference between the two gradients than monkeys whose SAV and VI response rates were far apart.

(2) *The type of response.* Since chain pulling functioned as the food-producing response and lever pressing as the shock-avoiding response for all the original subjects, it is possible that (a) differences in the physical properties of the manipulanda, or (b) their relative position in the test chamber with respect to the source of the light stimuli, affected the results.

We were able to check on the importance of this factor in a subsequent experiment in which two groups of monkeys were trained to make only one response.[2] The first group learned to press a lever to avoid shock, and the second group learned to press a lever to obtain food pellets. The details of the training and testing procedures were essentially the same as in the prediscrimination phase of the earlier monkey work, except that a 1-min. VI reward schedule was used instead of the earlier 2-min. schedule, the R-S and S-S intervals were set at 20 sec. rather than 10 sec., and the food-

[2] This study examined possible effects of amygdalectomy on stimulus generalization and was done in collaboration with Karl Pribram.

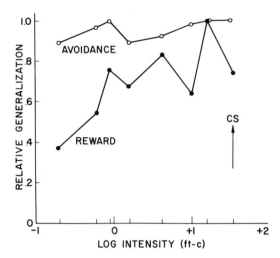

FIG. 3. Generalization gradients for two different groups of monkeys ($N = 4$ in each group). One group ("reward") pressed a lever for food pellets only, the other group ("avoidance") for shock avoidance only. The brightest test intensity served as the training stimulus (CS) for all subjects.

reward group had been deprived of food for 46 hr. instead of 22 hr. By choosing these particular values, we were able to obtain mean VI and SAV lever-pressing rates that did not differ so much as in the earlier experiments.

Figure 3 shows generalization gradients obtained under these conditions. The avoidance gradient was very flat whereas the reward gradient was relatively sharp. Statistical tests revealed no significant differences in response to the eight test stimuli on the avoidance gradient; on the other hand, there were significant differences in response to the test stimuli on the reward gradient. Once again, therefore, the approach gradient proved to be sharper than the avoidance gradient.

This result eliminates type and spatial location of the manipulanda as important factors in our initial results. Since each monkey performed only one response in this experiment, it is also improbable that the earlier results were due to (a) unknown response interactions (superstitious chaining) occurring in the two-response situation, or to (b) the order of training the approach and avoidance responses.

(3) *Relative drive levels.* Since other studies (Rosenbaum, 1953; Bersh, Notterman, and Schoenfeld, 1956; Jenkins, Pascal, and Walker, 1958; Thomas and King, 1959) have indicated that the slope of generalization gradients is an inverse function of drive level, one might argue that the relative slopes of the two gradients could be reversed if other drive levels for approach and avoidance were selected. This argument

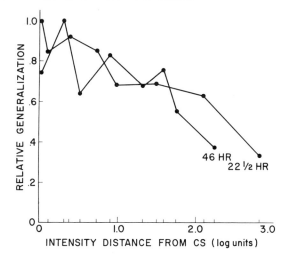

FIG. 4. Generalization gradients for two groups of monkeys ($N = 4$ in each group) trained and tested under either 22½- or 46-hr. food deprivation. A bright light served as the training stimulus for both groups, but its absolute intensity was different for the two groups.

suggests that the approach gradient would be flatter than the avoidance gradient if the hunger drive were very high and the shock level very low.

The reward gradient of Fig. 3 was obtained under an extremely high level of food deprivation (46 hr.), but its slope proved to be quite sharp in comparison with the avoidance gradient. Moreover, the reward gradient of Fig. 3 was not very different from the reward gradients of Fig. 1, which were obtained after 22 hr. of food deprivation.

In a later experiment we were able to compare some monkeys trained and tested under 22½-hr. food drive with the 46-hr. group shown in Fig. 3. Each of these groups was trained to press a lever for food reward only; there was no concurrent avoidance involved.[3] Figure 4 is a comparison of reward gradients under the two drive levels. Both gradients were comparatively sharp; neither was very similar to the flat gradients typically obtained after SAV training. In addition to the group results summarized in Figs. 3 and 4, almost all individual subjects showed relatively sharp appetitive gradients whether they were trained and tested under 22½-hr. deprivation or under 46-hr. deprivation.

[3] The 22½-hr. monkeys were trained in a new test chamber where the cage illumination during training was dimmer than in the 46-hr. group. Therefore, the gradients are plotted in terms of distance from the training stimulus, rather than in absolute intensity values. Because of this absolute intensity difference, caution should be observed in comparing the two gradients of Fig. 4. For our purposes it is necessary only to show that both gradients are much sharper than the typical SAV gradient.

These results strongly suggest that, even under very high hunger motivation, VI gradients are significantly sharper than the flat gradients obtained after SAV. Prior reports confirm this conclusion, too, since they have rarely, if ever, shown extremely flat VI gradients at high drive levels, e.g., 60 per cent of normal body weight (Thomas and King, 1959).

What about variations in the parameters of shock? Bersh et al. (1956) observed flatter auditory gradients with higher shock values in the classical conditioning of human heart rate. Would we have obtained sharper avoidance gradients in our operant situation if shock level during the training phases had been lower? I have not systematically examined this possibility, but our SAV monkeys ($N =$ approximately 20) required different shock levels during the initial shaping of avoidance behavior. Once each monkey had acquired the response, however, the shock intensity for all subjects was set at approximately 5 ma. (0.6-sec. duration). Almost all our SAV animals have shown flat gradients; thus there did not appear to be any relationship between the shock level used during initial training and the form of the generalization gradient.

A recent study by Sidman (1961) revealed that threefold changes in shock duration, although affecting response rate, had no effect on postdiscrimination gradients of relative generalization. Randall (this vol., pp. 134–153) has similarly noted that tetanizing shock levels, which produced obvious "emotional" effects in his cats, were no different from lower shock levels in their effect on equivalence behavior. These results support the view that variations in shock level may not be especially important insofar as generalization effects on avoidance schedules are concerned.

(4) *The stimulus dimension and the absolute value of CS.* Most of our work has been done along a continuum of light intensity, with the brightest available intensity as the training stimulus. The choice of this value was based mainly on practical reasons. It is very hard to shape an animal in lever pressing if the experimenter has trouble seeing the subject.

We have evidence that our choice of a bright training stimulus did not strongly bias the results. The postdiscrimination gradients of Fig. 2 showed greater generalization for avoidance than for approach, and two of the three monkeys had the dimmest intensity as S^D and the brightest as S^Δ. Also, in our rat work (Hearst, 1962) some subjects were given initial training in the presence of a very dim light, whereas others were trained in a very bright light. During generalization tests all the rats in the reward group showed peaks of response strength in the vicinity of the training stimulus, even though the individual gradients were considerably more irregular than those of the monkeys. Five of the six rats in the avoidance group showed very flat gradients, regardless of whether they were trained in the presence of the dimmest or the brightest stimulus. Differences between the slopes of approach and avoidance gradients in these rat studies

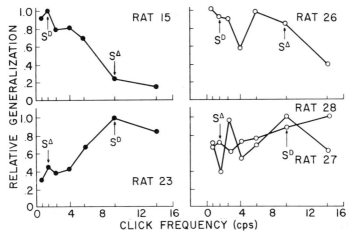

FIG. 5. Postdiscrimination generalization gradients (combined data for three generalization tests) along an auditory click-frequency continuum. Rats 15 and 23 were trained to press a lever to obtain food reward; rats 26, 27, and 28, to avoid shock. As noted on the figures, during discrimination training some rats had a high click frequency (9.3 cps.) as S^D and a low frequency (1.5 cps.) as S^Δ, whereas the others had the low frequency as S^D and the high as S^Δ. Mean S^Δ/S^D ratios were better for the appetitive discrimination (approximately 0.17) than for the avoidance discrimination (approximately 0.39) at the end of discrimination training, just before the generalization tests. • Reward. ○ Avoidance.

were statistically significant; as in our other work, the VI gradient proved sharper than the SAV gradient.

We have done some generalization work with monkeys and rats along an auditory dimension (click frequency), with some subjects trained in the continuous presence of a very rapid click frequency and others in the presence of a very slow click frequency. Interestingly enough, prediscrimination generalization gradients along this auditory dimension were rather flat for both avoidance (SAV) and approach (VI). This auditory continuum appears to be an irrelevant one, even for food-rewarded lever pressing, prior to specific discrimination training—a result similar to that of Jenkins and Harrison (1960). However, after appetitive or aversive discriminations had been established with one click frequency as S^D and another as S^Δ, subsequent tests yielded flatter generalization gradients for the avoidance response than for the appetitive response (Fig. 5).

Generalization Gradients During Discrimination Training.

Several workers (e.g., Appel, 1960a; Appel, 1960b; Hearst, 1962) have encountered serious difficulties in attempting to train avoidance discriminations in the free responding situation, especially when the physical properties of the controlling stimuli do not differ greatly. If SAV is programmed

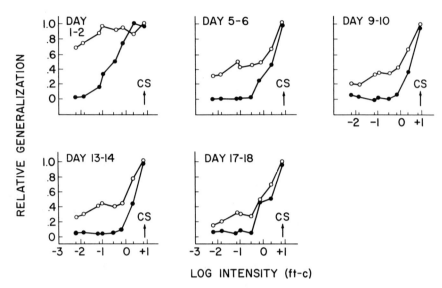

FIG. 6. Generalization gradients for concurrent approach and avoidance during successive stages of discrimination training for Monkey 179. The S^D (indicated as CS in the figures) was the brightest light intensity; the seven other intensities were S^Δ's for both approach and avoidance. • Reward. ○ Avoidance.

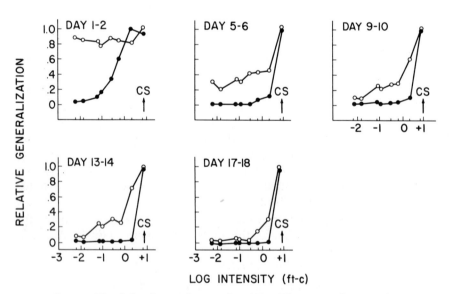

FIG. 7. Same as Fig. 6, but for another monkey (No. 70). • Reward. ○ Avoidance.

in the presence of one stimulus value and avoidance extinction is programmed at another stimulus value, special training procedures are often required to achieve a discrimination index as good as that obtained in the final stages of an appetitive discrimination. Our observation of the greater generalization of SAV prior to discrimination training would lead one to expect this kind of effect on subsequent discrimination learning. Such a result occurred in the experiments of Haber and Kalish (1963), who found in a food-reward situation that pigeons with initially flatter generalization gradients proved harder to train in a subsequent discrimination than subjects which had initially sharp gradients.

In some monkeys we have studied the formation of a concurrent approach-avoidance discrimination by a method that enabled us to obtain generalization gradients during each session of discrimination learning. These monkeys were trained in the presence of a bright light to press a lever, mounted about 1 ft. above the floor of the chamber, in order to obtain food pellets on a 1-min. VI schedule; concurrently, they had to press another lever, mounted about 1 ft. above the food lever, to avoid shock. The R-S and S-S intervals were both equal to 10 sec. After behavior on the two levers was reliable from day to day, we ran a prediscrimination generalization test and obtained results similar to those shown in Figs. 1 and 3; the avoidance gradient was flat and the reward gradient relatively sharp.

The subjects were next exposed to a discrimination-training procedure in which every one of the eight test intensities was presented daily, but food-lever responding was rewarded, and shock avoidance was necessary on the other lever, only in the presence of the brightest intensity. There was a mixed order of stimulus presentations. Each presentation lasted 2 min., and each of the eight stimuli was presented approximately 16 times during 4-hr. daily sessions.

This procedure was a combination of discrimination training and generalization testing, since subjects were presented with all the test stimuli during every experimental session. Consequently, generalization gradients could be plotted on each experimental day.

Figures 6 and 7 show the development of the concurrent appetitive and aversive discriminations over the course of 18 experimental days in two monkeys. On Days 1–2 the appetitive discrimination was already quite good, and after Days 5–6 it did not improve very much more. The avoidance discrimination, on the other hand, was quite poor on Days 1–2. Improvement in the avoidance discrimination continued throughout the 18 days shown.

Some Interpretations of These Results

Several factors seem to me important in explaining these differences between approach and avoidance generalization gradients. And one can speculate, I hope in a testable way, on possible applications of these results and arguments to other kinds of generalization gradients and to other types of approach and avoidance situations. The following interpretations are not incompatible with each other, and because of their interrelatedness it may be that we could have used fewer than four general categories to enumerate them.

Internal vs. External Cues

If someone were to obtain a flat gradient along a particular stimulus dimension, he would ordinarily conclude that he had been studying an "irrelevant" stimulus dimension. "Irrelevant for a specific response" is perhaps a more precise way of stating this conclusion. By applying such an analysis to our results, we could say that the dimension of cage illumination is simultaneously relevant for the food-rewarded response and irrelevant for the avoidance response. To characterize a dimension as "irrelevant" or "relevant," however, does not really do much more than restate our empirical observations regarding the form of the generalization gradient for that dimension. Nevertheless, if we can actually show by an independent argument that certain non-visual stimuli exert relatively more control over the SAV response than over the VI response, then an interpretation based on the relevance of various stimulus dimensions would have applicability to our results.

Theoretical discussions of avoidance behavior (Schoenfeld, 1950; Sidman, 1953b, 1954; Dinsmoor, 1954, 1955; Solomon and Brush, 1956; Hefferline, 1958, 1962; Mowrer, 1960; Anger, 1963) have frequently emphasized non-exteroceptive cues as the important ones controlling the avoidance response. Schoenfeld (1950) stresses the role of proprioceptive cues in "trace" avoidance conditioning, and has hypothesized that the termination of these cues is the major source of reinforcement for the avoidance response. Hefferline (1958, 1962) and his colleagues have lent experimental weight to this hypothesis by demonstrating striking correlations between certain movements of an avoidance subject and certain autonomic measures of "anxiety." Dinsmoor (1954, p. 39) argues that the "stimuli produced by the subject himself in making responses other than that prescribed by the experimenter are to some extent correlated with shock." These "other-responses" thus come to serve as warning stimuli for avoidance behavior, and their termination provides a basis for the reinforcement of the avoidance reaction.

Mowrer and Keehn (1958) and Mowrer (1960) discuss Schaefer's (1957) conjecture that (a) on SAV schedules only continued responding is "safe," and that (b) the situation-as-a-whole *without the correct response* is the real danger signal in SAV; the subject discriminates between the situation-plus-the-correct-response and the situation-without-the-correct-response. Mowrer accepts such an analysis as essentially accurate; however, he believes that another explanatory factor must be added to it: the concept of a buildup of fear throughout the R-S interval. On this latter point Mowrer stresses the temporal cues involved in SAV, an aspect of the situation that Anger (1963) also emphasizes in his theoretical treatment of SAV.

Sidman himself (1953b, 1954) analyzes the emergence and persistence of the avoidance response by pointing out that all behavior except lever pressing may produce shock; therefore non-avoidance behavior becomes dangerous to the subject and provides the cues for the avoidance response, which, by virtue of being incompatible with these other forms of behavior, automatically terminates the "danger signal." This of course is very similar to the analysis offered by Schoenfeld (1950), Dinsmoor (1954), and Hefferline (1958, 1962).

Despite differences in emphasis, these interpretations are in essential agreement concerning the cues important in avoidance situations that do not involve a discrete, response-terminated exteroceptive stimulus. Whether the stress is on the role of response-produced cues from non-avoidance behavior or on the power exerted by temporal and interoceptive "emotional" factors, these writers all suggest that internal cues constitute a large part of the stimulus complex which controls the avoidance response—probably a larger part than these non-exteroceptive cues play in the control of an appetitive response. Therefore, one would expect a flatter gradient for avoidance than for approach along an exteroceptive dimension such as cage illumination.

This explanation for the greater generalization of avoidance than of approach is very similar to the explanation that Miller (1944, 1948, 1959) offers to explain the opposite result. He hypothesizes that when an avoidance subject is tested with a generalization stimulus different from the CS, the specific responses involved in avoidance as well as the "fear motivating these responses" are both weakened. On the other hand, when a similar test is given to approach subjects, the variation of stimuli affects only the responses involved in approach, and not the hunger drive, which "is primarily dependent on internal physiological factors. Therefore, the gradient of approach should fall off less steeply than that of avoidance" (1959, p. 221). Thus, Miller postulates that it is the relative importance of internal cues in approach behavior that flattens the approach gradient relative to the avoidance gradient, whereas we consider it reasonable, at least for the Sidman-avoidance and trace-avoidance situations, to use an analogous argument to deduce the opposite effect.

Miller has left room in his framework for the possibility that under certain circumstances avoidance gradients may prove to be flatter than approach gradients. He states (1959, p. 222) that "if the drive motivating avoidance were elicited chiefly by internal cues, which remained relatively constant in different external stimulus contexts, whereas the drive motivating approach was primarily aroused by external cues which changed with the stimulus context," the gradient of approach should be steeper than that of avoidance. However, he believes that this type of situation is less common than the one he has studied. Therefore, Miller and I appear to disagree principally on the frequency with which flatter-avoidance-than-approach should occur; my opinion is that greater generalization for avoidance than for approach ought to be a relatively frequent occurrence. In addition, it seems to me that this result is more consistent with a number of clinical and experimental observations than the result Miller emphasizes.

As a consequence of this discussion, one might deduce that appetitive schedules which are relatively more dependent than VI on internal cues should exhibit flatter exteroceptive gradients than VI schedules do. Therefore, an experiment comparing gradients after training on a differential-reinforcement-of-low-rate (DRL) schedule (Ferster and Skinner, 1957) with VI gradients seemed worth doing. DRL, like SAV, appears more dependent than VI on temporal discriminations and on proprioceptive feedback from the subject's other behavior (see, for example, Anger's [1956, 1963] discussions of mediating behavior on DRL and SAV schedules).

Minnie Koresko, Roger Poppen, and I have recently completed such a comparison of visual generalization gradients after VI and DRL training.[4] The results strongly support the argument advanced in the preceding paragraph. Of 20 pigeons that provided line-tilt gradients after 1-min. VI training, 18 had a gradient peak at the CS and 12 showed extremely sharp gradients, as defined by a slope index (Hiss and Thomas, 1963) greater than 20 per cent (i.e., CS Test Responses/Total Test Responses to All Eight Stimuli > .20). Of 24 DRL pigeons (16 subjects tested on 6-sec. DRL and 8 subjects on 10-sec. DRL), only two subjects showed sharp gradients (index > .20), and only five subjects exhibited a gradient with its peak at the CS value. Thus, even within the appetitive realm itself, generalization gradients may be sharp or flat depending on the contingency between response and reinforcement during training.

These experiments suggest that exteroceptive generalization gradients may be useful as indicators of the extent to which internal cues play a role in interval, ratio, and other appetitive schedules. The relations between the type of behavioral baseline and stimulus generalization have not re-

---

[4] In a personal communication, Neal E. Miller independently suggested a comparison of VI and DRL gradients as a good test of the "internal-cues hypothesis" for approach-avoidance differences.

ceived much attention in the past; however, I think that such research deserves a place of some importance in the future. As a matter of fact, inattention to the details of the baseline behavior and its possible interactions with conditions during the generalization test (see the next section of this discussion) may have contributed to the wide variety of gradient slopes and forms that have been obtained in previous studies of stimulus generalization.

We have suggested in this section that certain types of avoidance gradients for exteroceptive stimuli are relatively flat because proprioceptive and other internal stimuli are the most important cues controlling the avoidance response. Another possible explanation for our results might state that cage illumination yields a flat SAV gradient because non-visual exteroceptive stimuli are much more powerful than visual cues in the control of SAV. For example, Brush *et al.* (1952) and Guttman (1963) suggest that a sharp aversive gradient and possibly a flat approach gradient might be obtained along the exteroceptive dimension of floor texture, the "source of the shock."

Differences in Resistance to Extinction

During performance of an approach response the delivery of food pellets is usually a frequent and clearly discriminable event for the subject. By providing feedback about the accuracy of behavior, the presentation of primary reinforcement helps to eliminate "unnecessary" or "incorrect" aspects of the response through the process of selective reinforcement.

On the other hand, once an SAV response has been acquired, shocks occur very infrequently, and subjects have no comparable feedback as to the accuracy or appropriateness of their responding. The relatively poor temporal discriminations observed on SAV, as compared, for example, with those on DRL and fixed interval (FI), are probably due to the lack of feedback in the form of a discriminable event like a pellet.[5] Because of the absence of such external feedback during conditioning, an avoidance response ought to persist for a long time even during extinction; conditions during SAV training are more similar to those during SAV extinction than is the case for VI training and extinction (see, for example, the arguments of Sheffield and Temmer [1950] and Jacobs [1963]). As Prokasy and Hall (1963) have pointed out, extinction may interact in complex ways with the variation of test stimuli during simultaneous generalization testing. Hiss and Thomas (1963) have provided data that can be used to support Prokasy and Hall's argument.

[5] Rats ordinarily show much better temporal discriminations on SAV than monkeys do (Anger, 1963). It is probably significant that rats characteristically receive many more shocks than monkeys do on this procedure.

Several studies (Humphreys, 1939; Wickens, Schroder, and Snide, 1954; see also Lewis, 1960, and Kimble, 1961) have in fact shown that variables (e.g., intermittent reinforcement) which increase resistance to extinction also tend to flatten generalization gradients. Therefore the broad gradients obtained here after SAV training could be related to the observation that SAV behavior is very resistant to extinction. Exactly why increased resistance to extinction goes hand in hand with flattening of generalization gradients is probably a theoretical question of no small importance.

The function of primary reinforcement as feedback, as a provider of "information" to the subject, seems important, too, in explaining the much slower acquisition of an avoidance discrimination than of an appetitive discrimination (Figs. 6 and 7). In an appetitive situation the discrimination is probably acquired rapidly because food rewards act discriminatively, as well as reinforcingly; rewards occur in one stimulus (S^D) and not in the other (S^Δ). A well-trained SAV subject, on the other hand, rarely receives a shock; when the discrimination procedure begins, therefore, it is extremely difficult for the subject to tell the difference between the contingencies in S^D and those in S^Δ.[6] Eventually, however, when a large enough number of shocks are received in S^D, the avoidance discrimination starts to improve. One might expect that if occasional "free shocks" were given in S^D throughout discrimination training, the avoidance discrimination would be learned much more quickly.

Operant-Respondent Interactions

Several theoretical treatments of avoidance behavior (e.g., Schoenfeld, 1950; Solomon and Wynne, 1954; Mowrer, 1960) have viewed the development of an avoidance response as a dual process. The first stage might be said to involve the classical conditioning of an anxiety response, as occurs in the Conditioned Emotional Response (CER) procedure of Estes and Skinner (1941) and Hunt and Brady (1951). This initial phase of avoidance conditioning sets the scene for the emergence of a response—the avoidance response—which terminates a stimulus complex that has become aversive through association with punishment.

Classical conditioning with respect to general apparatus cues probably takes place early in SAV training. These situational cues are paired with shock, and therefore the "experimental chamber" should function as the CS in the anxiety paradigm.[7] Classical conditioning with respect to gen-

---

[6] A related finding from human experiments may be that of Green, Sanders, and Squier (1959), who observed better discrimination learning with small fixed ratio (FR) schedules in S^D than with large FR's.

[7] See, for example, discussions of "apparatus fear" and stimulus generalization in McAllister and McAllister (1962, 1963) and experiments involving the incubation of anxiety in Saltz and Asdourian (1963).

eral apparatus cues probably occurs much less strongly in the instrumental approach situation, where primary reinforcement is produced only by a very specific response. These differences in amount and kind of classical conditioning may play a role in the greater generalization of avoidance than of approach observed in the present experiments.

The work of Fleshler and Hoffman (1961) and Hoffman (this vol., pp. 356–372) is relevant in this connection. Their experiments have shown that an auditory CER stimulus in pigeons generalizes very broadly to other tonal frequencies during the initial sessions of generalization testing, as measured by the extent to which generalization stimuli suppress ongoing behavior. The flat gradients exhibited by our SAV monkeys and rats could be partially due to a similar effect. If classically conditioned CER's do generalize broadly, then one would also expect wide generalization for the instrumental avoidance response, which is probably controlled to some extent by sensory feedback from these "emotional" responses (e.g., Hefferline, 1958; Soltysik and Kowalska, 1960; Jaworska and Soltysik, 1962). Thus the flat gradient for an operant SAV response could occur as an indirect result of a flat gradient for other, classically conditioned responses.

It is not obvious how a comparable effect could occur in the appetitive situation, where generalized apparatus cues do not appear to be specifically correlated with food reward, or at least not to the extent that shocks are correlated with apparatus cues in the avoidance situation. Also, classically conditioned appetitive responses may generally show sharper gradients than classically conditioned CER's; such a difference would have obvious applicability to our reported findings.

Novel Stimulus Effects

When a clearly discriminable, novel stimulus (e.g., a flashing light or a buzzer) is presented during ongoing appetitive behavior (e.g., lever pressing for VI food reward), it usually results in a depression of that behavior. When such a stimulus is presented during continuous-avoidance behavior (i.e., SAV), it often has a facilitating effect on responding. In my experience, apparatus failures that result in the occurrence of strange sounds or lights in the experimental chamber have frequently produced abrupt increases in the avoidance responding of monkeys; this has even happened after avoidance behavior had been extinguished (an effect reminiscent of Pavlovian "disinhibition"). Stone and MacLean (1963) have provided experimental evidence along the same lines. They found that an irrelevant auditory stimulus facilitated the SAV behavior of rats, and they suggested that "irrelevant exteroceptive stimulation may energize only aversively controlled behavior" (p. 264).

Sidman's finding (1958) that a CER stimulus will depress appetitive response rate and facilitate avoidance rate in monkeys may illustrate a related effect, if we assume that novel stimuli and CER stimuli elicit a similar pattern of emotional response (anxiety)—which[8] forms an important part of the stimulus compound that evokes the avoidance response. Soltysik, Jaworska, Kowalska and Radom (1961) have in fact shown (a) that a novel stimulus will lead to an acceleration of heart rate, just as does the standard CS used during Pavlovian defensive conditioning, and (b) that the avoidance response will usually occur whenever there is an increase in "defensive excitement," one indicant of which is accelerated heart rate (see also Soltysik and Kowalska, 1960).

In the appetitive situation the subject has never learned a specific instrumental response in the presence of these "emotional" cues; therefore, a variety of responses may compete with the lever response and lead to a depression, rather than a facilitation, of operant output.

In our situation the novel test stimuli (i.e., variations in cage illumination) may have elicited "emotional responses" that interfered with VI rate and, if anything, facilitated SAV response rate. Worth noting in this regard is the observation that several of our monkeys have shown slightly more responding at the dim end of the intensity continuum than at the bright training stimulus value (a reverse gradient).

Evaluation of Possibilities

A few explanations for our findings of generalization differences between VI and SAV have been proposed. In my opinion the "internal-cues hypothesis," which stresses the role played by proprioceptive and interoceptive stimuli in certain behavioral situations, seems the most worthy of serious consideration. It is hard to believe that "novel stimuli" would exert more than a transient effect; and the approach-avoidance differences were quite permanent, since they were observed both at the beginning and at the end of a given generalization test, as well as during subsequent generalization tests in the same subjects. Also not too cogent is the argument that the extremely flat avoidance gradients are mere reflections of the greater resistance to extinction of the avoidance response; the approach-avoidance differences were usually clear even on the first few trials of generalization testing, and were just as likely to occur in subjects whose SAV responses extinguished relatively rapidly.

If one accepts the internal-cues hypothesis, then it would appear an untenable oversimplification to interpret our gradient differences as resulting from "approach" vs. "avoidance." Each different behavioral situation presumably involves control by both exteroceptive and interoceptive

---

[8] That is, the sensory feedback of the physiological changes.

cues, and it may be the relative power exerted by each of these systems that determines the shape and slope of various exteroceptive generalization gradients. Since gradient steepness appears critically dependent on factors that cross the boundaries of appetitive and aversive behavior, a dichotomy based purely on approach vs. avoidance seems to me to have lost most of its attractiveness.

Relationship to Prior Studies

One factor in particular stands out when we attempt to compare our results to prior studies of approach, avoidance, and stimulus generalization, as exemplified by the work of Miller (1944, 1959), Hoffman and Fleshler (1963), and others who have used either a single appetitive response or a single avoidance response in studying generalization (see studies summarized in Mednick and Freedman, 1960). This factor is the amount of discrimination training given before generalization testing.

In Miller's runway situation, subjects had, for all practical purposes, received discrimination training along a spatial dimension before the conflict tests were given. During initial appetitive training the subjects had traversed the entire runway and had presumably learned to discriminate "distance" from the goal.

The experiments of Hoffman and Fleshler (1963) and others have almost all involved conditioning of avoidance or approach responses to a discrete, "delayed" exteroceptive CS. As Jenkins and Harrison (1960) have shown, differential training of this sort (where S^D is some value along the stimulus dimension, and S^Δ is the absence of S^D) is sufficient to sharpen gradients along that dimension, even though differential training to two different values on the dimension is never given. Therefore, good exteroceptive control of the avoidance response (and consequently a sharper gradient) is much more to be expected in situations involving a discrete, delayed CS than in situations that involve trace conditioning or a continuously maintained stimulus (as here).

In fact, Mowrer and Lamoreaux (1951) have observed that inter-trial responses occur much more often on a trace than on a delayed avoidance procedure. As these authors have aptly remarked, in the delayed procedures with an auditory CS the "situation-when-safe is always quiet and the situation-when-quiet is always safe," whereas on the trace procedure "the situation-when-safe is always quiet, but the situation-when-quiet is not always safe"; subjects on the trace procedure must learn to discriminate the inter-trial quiet periods from those following the momentary CS. The greater generalization (or "poorer discrimination") during trace conditioning may represent an effect intermediate between delayed-CS conditioning, where the avoidance response actually terminates the exteroceptive CS, and SAV conditioning, where there is no shock-correlated exteroceptive stimulus at all.[9]

This argument suggests that a comparison of approach and avoidance gradients after delayed-CS conditioning would lead to much less of a difference between the two types of gradients than was found here. The degree of exteroceptive control ought to be relatively good for both approach and avoidance on the delayed procedure, due to differential training of the sort pointed out by Jenkins and Harrison (1960). As a matter of fact, in their comparison of gradients after approach or avoidance training with a delayed CS, Hoffman and Fleshler (1963) eliminated all avoidance subjects that did not meet a high criterion of avoidance, i.e., did not show good exteroceptive control. It was necessary for them to follow this procedure in order to permit a fair comparison with the well-discriminated approach response, but this procedure effectively selected avoidance subjects that were particularly adept at the auditory discrimination. During initial generalization testing after this preliminary training, avoidance gradients were actually sharper than appetitive gradients.

Our data (Fig. 2) also show that discrimination training reduces the difference between approach and avoidance gradients. After even more extensive discrimination training than described here was given, differences between the two gradients eventually disappeared (Hearst, 1962).

In addition to prior discrimination training, there are several other procedural differences between our experiments and previous ones; and any one or a combination of these factors could have affected the approach-avoidance comparisons. Among these factors are group vs. individual data, the number of different generalization stimuli presented during testing, conflict and non-independence of the two responses, locomotor vs. manipulative behavior, the duration of generalization testing and its relation to extinction of the response, the reinforcement schedule during training, and the presence or absence of food or shocks during testing. At the present time it is hard to evaluate the relative importance of each of these factors.[10]

[9] Konorski (1961, p. 116) makes the following related comment: "A peculiar property of trace CR's is that they are very widely generalized: even the application of new stimuli, much different from the original CS, produces salivation at the appropriate moment after their cessation. . . . This property of trace CR's seems to suggest that they are formed not to the traces of the given exteroceptive stimulus itself, but rather to some of its consequences which are common for various sorts of stimuli. Since any external stimulus elicits an orientation reaction, it may be that the proprioceptive stimuli generated by this reaction form the true basis for elaboration and occurrence of trace CR's."

[10] In a recent article Solomon (1964) criticized the approach-avoidance comparisons of Miller and his collaborators and suggested that an unbiased test of the differential-steepness assumption would require the establishment of topographically symmetrical instrumental responses for approach and avoidance. In order to achieve this, Solomon proposed an experiment in which the avoidance "response" requires a long sequence of instrumental behavior, just as does the approach response in the runway.

Concluding Remarks

We can conclude from the results of our experiments and those of others that one can establish no simple rule about differences in stimulus generalization between approach and avoidance behavior. However, it does appear to be the case that Sidman-type avoidance situations lead to much flatter exteroceptive gradients than are normally obtained after most VI food-reward schedules. If the factors we have emphasized in analyzing this effect are actually the important factors, then one should frequently obtain broader gradients from avoidance subjects than from approach subjects. Miller's (1959) suggestion that a difference in this direction ought to be relatively infrequent is not supported by our results.

Although the research discussed in this report began as a comparison of approach and avoidance gradients, this original focus has (perhaps fortunately) receded into the background. More interesting, I think, are possible implications of these results for general problems in the field of stimulus generalization. If the type of behavioral baseline is so important in determining the slope and form of subsequent gradients, then one wonders exactly what a single stimulus-generalization gradient tells us. Are experimenters justified in using results from 1-min. VI to draw strong conclusions about systematic laws of stimulus generalization, or about specific relationships between "generalization" and "discrimination"?

Our initial experiments demonstrated that a subject may display a flat generalization gradient (avoidance) even while he is clearly "attending" to variations along that stimulus dimension (as evidenced by the simultaneously sharp approach gradient). In this volume other authors have suggested that a gradient may be flat because (1) the subject does not and never will have the physiological capacity to make discriminations along that dimension, (2) the subject has never previously had any exposure to or discrimination training along that particular dimension, and (3) for various other reasons the subject may not "attend" to variations along the dimension. To these possibilities must be added the case in which the subject possesses the physiological capacity, has been exposed previously to that stimulus dimension, and clearly attends to the stimulus, but nevertheless still displays a flat gradient. Apparently, as Cumming and Berryman point out (this vol., p. 329), "Generalization not only depends upon the physical nature of the stimuli, but also has to do with the functional relation of the stimulus to the response."

It is almost a truism that each response in an organism's repertoire, regardless of whether it is an approach response or an avoidance response, is controlled by a variety of stimuli. For some types of behavior one stimulus dimension (perhaps exteroceptive) may predominate, whereas for other types of behavior another stimulus dimension (perhaps interoceptive) may predominate. In addition, it is possible that different stimulus dimensions may predominate at different levels of acquisition, so that stimulus control of particular responses may eventually become "internalized" (see, for example, Hefferline, 1962), even though there was initially a high degree of exteroceptive control.

Our suggestion that punishment-controlled behavior frequently generalizes very broadly may have relevance to clinical findings of extreme stimulus generalization among neurotic or psychotic individuals, as illustrated, for example, in the spread of phobic, compulsive, or anxiety reactions to new stimulus situations. Certain behavioral patterns of such individuals seem to be remarkably persistent in the same way as are well-developed avoidance responses. There are many reasons why such behavior could generalize very broadly, but it is possible that variables analogous to those discussed here in analyzing SAV behavior are important. Internal, "emotional" cues and proprioceptive stimuli may exercise more than a normal amount of control over the behavior of such individuals, as compared to the control exerted by stimuli from the external environment. Therefore, these individuals appear "withdrawn from reality" and continue to press phantom levers as vigorously as our monkey that had no lever to press.

REFERENCES

Anger, D. The dependence of interresponse times upon the relative reinforcement of different interresponse times. *J. exp. Psychol.*, 1956, **52**, 145–161.

Anger, D. The role of temporal discriminations in the reinforcement of Sidman avoidance behavior. *J. exp. Anal. Behav.*, 1963, **6**, 477–506.

Appel, J. B. The aversive control of an operant discrimination. *J. exp. Anal. Behav.*, 1960, **3**, 35–47. (a)

Appel, J. B. Some schedules involving aversive control. *J. exp. Anal. Behav.*, 1960, **3**, 349–359. (b)

Bersh, P. J., Notterman, J. M., and Schoenfeld, W. N. Generalization to varying tone frequencies as a function of intensity of unconditioned stimulus. Air Univer., School of Aviation Medicine, U.S.A.F., Randolph AFB, Texas. Report No. 56–79, 1956. Pp. 1–4.

Brush, F. R., Bush, R. R., Jenkins, W. O., John, W. F., and Whiting, J. W. M. Stimulus generalization after extinction and punishment: An experimental study of displacement. *J. abnorm. soc. Psychol.*, 1952, **47**, 633–640.

Dinsmoor, J. A. Punishment: I. The avoidance hypothesis. *Psychol. Rev.*, 1954, **61**, 34–46.

Dinsmoor, J. A. Punishment: II. An interpretation of empirical findings. *Psychol. Rev.*, 1955, **62**, 96–105.

Estes, W. K., and Skinner, B. F. Some quantitative properties of anxiety. *J. exp. Psychol.*, 1941, **29**, 390–400.

Ferster, C. B., and Skinner, B. F. *Schedules of reinforcement.* New York: Appleton-Century-Crofts, 1957.

Fleshler, M., and Hoffman, H. Stimulus generalization of conditioned suppression. *Science*, 1961, **133**, 753–755.

Green, E. J., Sanders, R. M., and Squier, R. W. Schedules of reinforcement and discrimination learning. *J. exp. Anal. Behav.*, 1959, **2**, 293–299.

Guttman, N. The pigeon and the spectrum and other perplexities. *Psychol. Rep.*, 1956, **2**, 449–460.

Guttman, N. Laws of behavior and facts of perception. In S. Koch (Ed.), *Psychology: A study of a science*, Vol. 5. New York: McGraw-Hill, 1963. Pp. 114–178.

Guttman, N., and Kalish, H. I. Discriminability and stimulus generalization. *J. exp. Psychol.*, 1956, **51**, 79–88.

Haber, A., and Kalish, H. I. Prediction of discrimination from generalization after variations in schedule of reinforcement. *Science*, 1963, **142**, 412–413.

Hearst, E. Simultaneous generalization gradients for appetitive and aversive behavior. *Science*, 1960, **132**, 1769–1770.

Hearst, E. Concurrent generalization gradients for food-controlled and shock-controlled behavior. *J. exp. Anal. Behav.*, 1962, **5**, 19–31.

Hearst, E., Beer, B., Sheatz, G., and Galambos, R. Some electrophysiological correlates of conditioning in the monkey. *EEG clin. Neurophysiol.*, 1960, **12**, 137–152.

Hefferline, R. F. The role of proprioception in the control of behavior. *Ann. NY Acad. Sci.*, 1958, **20**, 739–764.

Hefferline, R. F. Learning theory and clinical psychology—an eventual symbiosis? In A. Bachrach (Ed.), *Experimental foundations of clinical psychology.* New York: Basic Books, 1962. Pp. 97–138.

Hiss, R. H., and Thomas, D. R. Stimulus generalization as a function of testing procedure and response measure. *J. exp. Psychol.*, 1963, **65**, 587–592.

Hoffman, H., and Fleshler, M. Discrimination and stimulus generalization of approach, of avoidance, and of approach and avoidance during conflict. *J. exp. Psychol.*, 1963, **65**, 280–291.

Humphreys, L. G. Generalization as a function of method of reinforcement. *J. exp. Psychol.*, 1939, **25**, 361–372.

Hunt, H. F., and Brady, J. V. Some effects of electroconvulsive shock on a conditioned emotional response ("anxiety"). *J. comp. physiol. Psychol.*, 1951, **44**, 88–98.

Jacobs, B. Repeated acquisition and extinction of an instrumental avoidance response. *J. comp. physiol. Psychol.*, 1963, **56**, 1017–1021.

Jaworska, K., and Soltysik, S. Studies on the aversive classical conditioning; 3. Cardiac responses to conditioned and unconditioned defensive (aversive) stimuli. *Acta. Biolog. exp.*, 1962, **22**, 193–214.

Jenkins, H. M., and Harrison, R. H. Effect of discrimination training on auditory generalization. *J. exp. Psychol.*, 1960, **59**, 246–253.

Jenkins, W. O., Pascal, G. R., and Walker, R. W. Deprivation and generalization. *J. exp. Psychol.*, 1958, **56**, 274–277.

Kalish, H. I., and Guttman, N. Stimulus generalization after equal training on two stimuli. *J. exp. Psychol.*, 1957, **53**, 139–144.

Kimble, G. *Hilgard and Marquis' conditioning and learning.* (Rev. Ed.) New York: Appleton-Century-Crofts, 1961.

Konorski, J. The physiological approach to the problem of recent memory. In

J. S. Delafresnaye (Ed.), *Brain mechanisms and learning*. Oxford: Blackwell Scientific Publications, 1961. Pp. 115–130.

Lewis, D. J. Partial reinforcement: a selective review of the literature since 1950. *Psychol. Bull.*, 1960, **57**, 1–28.

Masserman, J. H. A biodynamic psychoanalytic approach to the problems of feeling and emotions. In M. L. Reymert (Ed.), *Feelings and emotions*. New York: McGraw-Hill, 1950. Pp. 49–75.

McAllister, W. R., and McAllister, D. E. Role of the CS and of apparatus cues in the measurement of acquired fear. *Psychol. Rep.*, 1962, **11**, 749–756.

McAllister, W. R., and McAllister, D. E. Increase over time in the stimulus generalization of acquired fear. *J. exp. Psychol.*, 1963, **65**, 576–582.

Mednick, S., and Freedman, J. Stimulus generalization. *Psychol. Bull.*, 1960, **57**, 169–200.

Miller, N. E. Experimental studies of conflict. In J. McV. Hunt (Ed.), *Personality and the behavior disorders*. New York: Ronald Press, 1944. Pp. 431–465.

Miller, N. E. Theory and experiment relating psychoanalytic displacement to stimulus-response generalization. *J. abnorm. soc. Psychol.*, 1948, **43**, 155–178.

Miller, N. E. Liberalization of basic S-R concepts: Extensions to conflict behavior, motivation, and serial learning. In S. Koch (Ed.), *Psychology: A study of a science*, Vol. 2. New York: McGraw-Hill, 1959. Pp. 196–292.

Miller, N. E. Some recent studies of conflict behavior and drugs. *Amer. Psychologist*, 1961, **16**, 12–24.

Mowrer, O. H. *Learning theory and behavior*. New York: Wiley, 1960.

Mowrer, O. H., and Lamoreaux, R. R. Conditioning and conditionality (discrimination). *Psychol. Rev.*, 1951, **58**, 196–212.

Mowrer, O. H., and Keehn, J. D. How are intertrial "avoidance" responses reinforced? *Psychol. Rev.*, 1958, **65**, 209–221.

Prokasy, W. F., and Hall, J. F. Primary stimulus generalization. *Psychol. Rev.*, 1963, **70**, 310–322.

Rosenbaum, G. Stimulus generalization as a function of level of experimentally induced anxiety. *J. exp. Psychol.*, 1953, **45**, 35–43.

Saltz, E., and Asdourian, D. Incubation of anxiety as a function of cognitive differentiation. *J. exp. Psychol.*, 1963, **66**, 17–22.

Schaefer, V. H. Avoidance conditioning in the absence of external stimulation: Some experimental and genetic parameters. Unpublished doctoral dissertation, Univer. of Illinois, 1957.

Schoenfeld, W. N. An experimental approach to anxiety, escape and avoidance behavior. In P. H. Hoch and J. Zubin (Eds.), *Anxiety*. New York: Grune and Stratton, 1950. Pp. 70–99.

Sheffield, F. D., and Temmer, H. W. Relative resistance to extinction of escape training and avoidance training. *J. exp. Psychol.*, 1950, **40**, 287–298.

Sidman, M. Avoidance conditioning with brief shock and no exteroceptive warning signal. *Science*, 1953, **118**, 157–158. (a)

Sidman, M. Two temporal parameters of the maintenance of avoidance behavior by the white rat. *J. comp. physiol. Psychol.*, 1953, **46**, 253–261. (b)

Sidman, M. Delayed punishment effects mediated by competing behavior. *J. comp. physiol. Psychol.*, 1954, **47**, 145–147.

Sidman, M. By-products of aversive control. *J. exp. Anal. Behav.*, 1958, **1**, 265–280.

Sidman, M. Stimulus generalization in an avoidance situation. *J. exp. Anal. Behav.*, 1961, **4**, 157–169.

Solomon, R. L. Punishment. *Amer. Psychologist*, 1964, **19**, 239–253.

Solomon, R. L., and Brush, E. S. Experimentally derived conceptions of anxiety and aversion. In M. R. Jones (Ed.), *Nebraska symposium on motivation*, 1956. Lincoln: Univer. of Nebraska Press, 1956. Pp. 212–305.

Solomon, R. L., and Wynne, L. C. Traumatic avoidance learning: the principles of anxiety conservation and partial irreversibility. *Psychol. Rev.*, 1954, **61**, 353–385.

Soltysik, S., Jaworska, K., Kowalska, M., and Radom, S. Cardiac responses to simple acoustic stimuli in dogs. *Acta. Biolog. exp.*, 1961, **21**, 235–252.

Soltysik, S., and Kowalska, M. Studies on the avoidance conditioning. I. Relations between cardiac (type I) and motor (type II) effects in the avoidance reflex. *Acta. Biolog. exp.*, 1960, **20**, 157–170.

Stone, G. C., and MacLean, M. Increased rate of avoidance responding associated with non-contingent auditory stimulus. *Psychol. Rep.*, 1963, **13**, 259–265.

Thomas, D. R., and King, R. A. Stimulus generalization as a function of level of motivation. *J. exp. Psychol.*, 1959, **57**, 323–328.

Wickens, D. D., Schroder, H. M., and Snide, J. D. Primary stimulus generalization of the GSR under two conditions. *J. exp. Psychol.*, 1954, **47**, 52–56.

21. The Stimulus Generalization of Conditioned Suppression

Howard S. Hoffman, *Pennsylvania State University*

When a stimulus has typically preceded an unavoidable noxious event, subsequent presentations of that stimulus will often cause a reduction in the rate of ongoing hunger-motivated responses. This phenomenon (conditioned suppression) was initially investigated by Estes and Skinner (1941), and because of its relevance to the broad problem of learned anxiety, it has since been the subject of many experiments (see Brady and Hunt, 1955; Sidman, 1960).

For the past several years, a sizable portion of the work in our laboratory has been concerned with the manner in which conditioned suppression is mediated by stimuli that are like, but not identical to, the stimulus that was involved in the original training. This latter phenomenon, the stimulus generalization of conditioned suppression, commanded special attention because it represents one of the mechanisms by which aversive controls can affect large segments of an organism's behavior (Mednick, 1958).

Our general approach has been to employ pigeons as subjects and key pecking on a variable-interval (VI) schedule of food reinforcement as the baseline (ongoing) behavior. The choices were based upon practical considerations. Under appropriate circumstances, the key peck in pigeons can be a remarkably stable behavior. Moreover, substantial response rates can be readily generated. Both factors are obviously important when one seeks to establish a baseline for the assessment of suppression. Our initial work was concerned with stimulus generalization of conditioned suppression along the acoustic dimension of tonal frequency.

Experiment I

Method

Subjects. The subjects were six domestic White Carneaux pigeons. They were about 2 years old at the start of this work.

This research was supported by National Institute of Mental Health Grants M-2433 and MH-02433-05. Morton Fleshler collaborated in all phases of the work. Phillip Jensen collaborated in the last three experiments, which were conducted during a National Science Foundation summer program of research participation for college teachers at Pennsylvania State University.

F I G . 1. Pigeon chamber and wing-band arrangement. (The shock connector is shown to the right.)

Apparatus. The experimental chamber and the associated equipment have been fully described elsewhere (Hoffman and Fleshler, 1961). Briefly, they consisted of a Foringer pigeon chamber, equipment to program reinforcement and tones, cumulative recorders and counters to assess key pecking, and a special-purpose connection (Hoffman, 1960) to deliver electrical shock to the birds via a pair of permanently worn wing bands. The wing bands consisted of standard bead (¼″ diameter) chain which was wrapped twice around the base of each wing. Figure 1 shows the salient features of the chamber and connector.

The tones employed in this work were spaced at approximately equal intervals along a logarithmic scale (300, 450, 670, 1000, 1500, 2250, and 4500 cps). They were equated for intensity so that each produced a reading of 80 db spl on the C scale of a General Radio sound-survey meter when the microphone was placed in the position typically occupied by the bird's head.

Procedure. In the initial experiments (Fleshler and Hoffman, 1961; Hoffman and Fleshler, 1961) the pigeons were trained in a series of stages:

(1) Deprivation to 80 per cent of free-feeding weight and adaptation to the apparatus and to the wing bands and connector.

(2) Training to establish a base rate of pecking on a VI 2 schedule of reinforcement.

(3) Adaptation to the tone that was to be paired with shock (1000 cps).

(4) Adaptation to the six other tones.

Stages 3 and 4 of the procedure were included in order to mitigate suppression that might be produced by the presentation of novel stimuli (i.e., the six test tones) during the tests for stimulus generalization. It is of interest that although the 1000 cps tone produced some suppression during the early phase of stage 3, the effects of the adaptation achieved by the end of stage 3 generalized to all tones. Thus throughout stage 4, the birds' pecking behavior was unaffected by the presence or absence of tone, regardless of frequency.

(5) Shock at the end of the 1000 cps tone until all pecking ceased during the tone, but the rate was normal in the absence of the tone.

During stage 5, tones had a duration of 48 sec. and occurred on an average of once every 10 min. Shock was administered via the wing bands during the final 8 sec. of each tone.

The index of suppression used is expressed arithmetically as a ratio:

$$\frac{\text{Pre-tone } R\text{'s} - \text{Tone } R\text{'s}}{\text{Pre-tone } R\text{'s}},$$

where Pre-tone R's are equal to the number of responses in the 40 sec. before tone onset and Tone R's are equal to the number of responses during the 40 sec. of pre-shock tone.[1]

Observe that the ratio is one when there are no Tone R's (complete suppression), zero when Pre-tone R's are equal to Tone R's, and negative when Tone R's are greater than Pre-tone R's. This ratio serves as a control for differences in over-all response rates within sessions, among sessions, and among subjects, and it is equivalent to measures of relative suppression that have been used in several other experiments (Brady, 1955; Geller, 1960; Ray and Stein, 1959).

Figure 2 shows typical cumulative records at various points during the development of conditioned suppression. Records A and B, respectively, illustrate the moderate degree of suppression obtained to the tones at the onset of tone adaptation (stage 3) and the lack of suppression obtained by the sixth adaptation session. Records C, D, and E are samples of three progressive stages of the general course of the aversive conditioning. Record C shows the 30th tone-shock pairing. Pre-tone rate is stable and greater than tone rate. After tone-shock, responding is depressed but slowly accelerates to the pre-tone rate. Record D illustrates the effects of continued training. Behavior becomes somewhat less stable, tone suppression is increased, and behavior after tone-shock offset is markedly depressed for an extended period. Record E is an example of behavior that has reached the experimental criterion used in this study; the base rate is relatively stable, and suppression is complete during tone. The achievement of criterion was

---

[1] When reinforcement occurred, either during the tone or during the pre-tone period, the reinforcement time was subtracted from that period and the R's in the suppression ratio were expressed as rates, so as to correct for time spent feeding.

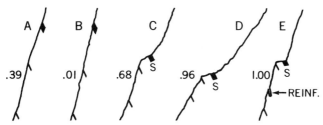

FIG. 2. Typical cumulative records taken from various points during training. The first vertical mark in each record indicates the beginning of the 40-sec. pre-tone period; the second indicates the onset of the 48-sec. tone. The broad solid mark indicates the final 8 sec. of the tone; an *s* appears next to this mark when shock occurs during that period. The value of the suppression ratio for each record is presented to the left of that record. (All records are from Bird 5.)

a very slow process for most birds. In general, it required approximately 600 trials administered over approximately 70 sessions.

(6) Upon reaching criterion, the use of shock was discontinued; and without altering the schedule of positive reinforcement, the generalization tests were conducted.

Throughout these and subsequent sessions, the subjects were always run with the shock connector in place, although no shocks were ever delivered. Each test session lasted approximately 1.5 hr. and had the following pattern: The pigeon was placed in the apparatus with all lights off and remained in this state for at least 30 sec. The session was started with the onset of the lights in the box. The bird was first given a 10-min. period in which to develop a more or less stable rate of pecking. The seven stimuli were then presented sequentially and in random order. Each stimulus had a duration of 40 sec., and a 9-min., 20-sec. interval of silence occurred between the tones. The sequence of the tones was varied from day to day. Each tone was presented, once in each session, with its position determined by one row of a set of Latin squares. The number of responses was recorded for each of the seven tone periods, and also for the seven 40-sec. pre-tone periods that ended with tone onset. At the end of the session, all lights were turned off and the pigeon was removed. Test sessions were continued until extinction of suppression was substantial to all but the test tone used in original training (1000 cps). Different birds received a total of from 14 to 25 test sessions. The only treatment difference between subjects was that two birds had their body weight lowered to 70 per cent during stage 5 and returned to 80 per cent after a few sessions of stage 6. Otherwise, the treatment was uniform. The procedural variations for two of the birds during steps 5 and 6 were included to enable us to assess the manner in which the motivation for the ongoing behavior affected the gradient of stimulus generalization.

Results

Figures 3 and 4 illustrate the results of this work. Figure 3 shows the gradients produced by a single subject (Bird 5) that was trained and tested at 80 per cent body weight. Each gradient is averaged across five successive sessions. At the beginning of testing, generalization of suppression was broad. As testing proceeded, however, the gradient narrowed severely. It will be recalled that no shocks occurred once testing began. Thus the observed differences in the gradients reflect changes in the suppressing capacities of the several tones during the extinction of suppression.

In one respect, the sharpening of the gradient during testing is a curious phenomenon in that it seems to represent the development of discriminated behavior without either previous or concurrent differential reinforcement. Although we can offer no simple explanation of this effect, it is noteworthy that a number of investigators have reported a similar phenomenon (Hovland, 1937a, 1937b, 1937c; Littman, 1949; Wickens, Schroder, and Snide, 1954; Brown, 1942; Jenkins and Harrison, 1960).

Figure 4 illustrates the kinds of gradients that were produced by manipulation of the birds' body weight. All gradients in Fig. 4 are from Bird 21.

The upper graph shows the gradients at the two different levels of body weight, and the lower one shows the continued performance at 80 per cent body weight. The 70 per cent body-weight gradient is fairly sharp, showing only a moderate degree of generalization. The first gradient produced after the body-weight increase is much broader. As noted in Fig. 3, the 70 per cent gradient represents the mean value for the first three sessions of testing, whereas the 80 per cent gradient is for sessions

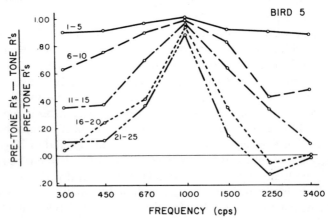

FIG. 3. Generalization gradients for Bird 5. The number spans (1–5, 6–10, etc.) of each gradient indicate the sessions included.

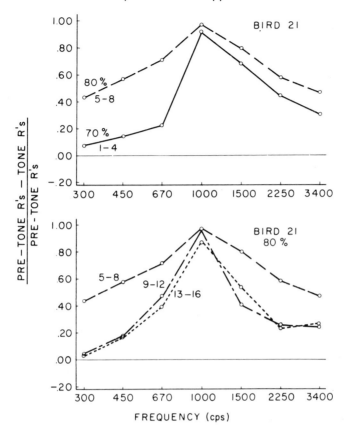

F I G. 4. Generalization gradient for Bird 21. The upper graph presents the gradient at 70 per cent body weight and the initial gradient at 80 per cent body weight. The lower graph presents the gradients obtained during continued testing at 80 per cent body weight (with the initial 80 per cent gradient repeated). The number spans (1–4, 5–8, etc.) of each gradient indicate the sessions included.

4–6. It should be recalled that no shock occurred once testing had begun. The right graph shows that with continued testing at 80 per cent, the gradient slowly sharpens in a manner similar to that of birds tested solely at 80 per cent body weight.

Since the broadening of the gradients with increased body weight was in a direction opposite to that which would be expected from continued extinction, it was concluded that the degree to which suppression generalized was an inverse function of the motivation for the ongoing, positively reinforced, behavior.

One effect of the changed deprivation level was a modification of the over-all rate of responding. The magnitude of this effect can be estimated by averaging the response rates during the pre-tone periods of test sessions conducted under the two different deprivation levels. For Bird 21, the average pre-tone response rate during test sessions 1–4 (70 per cent free-feeding weight) was 110 responses per min.; however, during sessions 5–8 (80 per cent free-feeding weight), the bird's average rate was 55 responses per min. In general, this finding is consistent with those of several other studies (e.g. Clark, 1958) in which VI rate was found to be an inverse function of percentage body weight. Because response rate changed with the modification in the percentage body weight, it could not be determined whether motivation level or its effects on response rate produced the change in the generalization gradient. Regardless of which factor is responsible for the change, however, the results of this phase of the work made it clear that the generalization of suppression is determined in part by variables which control ongoing behavior, and that manipulation of these variables can profoundly influence the magnitude of such generalization.

Experiment II

At the conclusion of the initial work, the birds were returned to their loft. After a period of approximately 2½ years, the five surviving birds were again adapted to individual cages and were thereafter maintained, by restricted feeding, at 80 per cent of their free-feeding weights. The birds were then run on a VI 2 schedule for ten sessions, each of which lasted approximately 2 hr. This was done in order to re-establish a stable base rate of pecking. No tones were presented during these sessions, and during these sessions as well as during the test sessions which followed, the shock connector was in place but no shocks were presented.

Tests for stimulus generalization were then begun. The procedures for these tests were identical to those employed in Experiment I.

Results

Figure 5 shows the final portion of the results of original experiments conducted almost three years previously (the dashed lines) and also shows the results of Experiment II (the solid lines). The gradients shown by dashed lines were obtained by working backwards from the final tests in Experiment I. Since different birds were tested for different numbers of sessions, the procedure of working backwards precludes showing the data from the first few sessions. Each point in the main body of Fig. 5 represents the mean suppression ratio for all five birds over a four-day period of testing. The curves in the inset show the data from a single bird (No. 21), and serve to illustrate the degree to which curves based on means correspond to the data from the individual organism.

As seen in the first of the dashed lines, during the stage of extinction shown, the gradient was relatively sharp but still exhibited some sup-

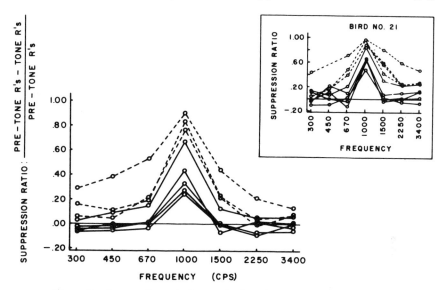

FIG. 5. Generalization gradients before and after the interpolated period. The solid lines show results of the present sequence of tests, whereas the dashed lines show the terminal gradients that were obtained more than two years previously.

pression on both wings. As the extinction progressed, however, the suppression controlled by stimuli on the wings of the gradient extinguished at a higher rate than the suppression controlled by the tone that had been used in training (1000 cps). The result was a further sharpening of the gradient.

In general, the 2½-year interruption had little, if any, observable effects. By the end of the earlier experiment, the extinction of the 1000 cps tone had progressed to the point where the mean suppression ratio for this stimulus was .68. The decrement of .09 that was found when 2½ years intervened between blocks of trials is only slightly larger than the previous decrement of .07, which was obtained just prior to the interruption. By the end of the initial experiments, the extinction of the stimuli on the wings of the gradient had advanced to the point where the mean suppression ratio for each of these tones was below .22. In the present study, this trend continued through the first block of trials. By the second block, the stimuli on the wings of the gradient exhibited almost no tendency to suppress pecking, i.e., no point showed a suppression ratio of over .02.

The experimenters were surprised to note that during later stages of this study, a large number of negative ratios were obtained for stimuli on the wings of the gradient. These reflect a condition in which the rate of response is increased during the presentation of a tone. It was decided to test this effect separately for each of the five birds. In general, the negative ratios tended to occur only toward the end of extinction. For this reason, each bird's record was divided into two sections. The dividing point used was the first session which, when averaged with the following three sessions, would yield a suppression ratio of below .50 for the 1000 cps tone. All trials beyond this point were included in the test of significance. For each occurrence of a 300, 450, 2250, and 3400 cps tone, the difference between the number of responses in the tone and pre-tone periods was found. On the basis of these differences a t test for related samples was run on each bird.

The results are found in Table 1. Four of the five birds show a significant increase in response rate when tones on the wings of the gradient were present during this section of extinction. The one bird whose results did not show this effect never dropped much below .45 for the 1000 cps tone at any time during extinction. It is possible to combine these separate t tests by the formula $\chi^2 = -2 \Sigma \log_e p$ (Winer, 1962, pp. 43–45). This yields an over-all χ^2 with 10 df of 59.94, which is significant beyond the .001 level.

Discussion. The facilitation that was observed during the late stages of testing is puzzling, and, at present, attempts at an explanation must be largely speculative. Ray and Stein (1959) have observed a similar phenomenon in the course of discrimination training on conditioned suppression. Toward the end of their training procedure, the S_Δ (a stimulus that was never paired with shock) tended to cause an elevation in response rate. They suggested that during discrimination training, the period in the absence of the warning signal is frequently terminated by the onset of the S_D (a stimulus which was consistently paired with shock). As a result, this period becomes somewhat aversive relative to the S_Δ period, which is never

TABLE 1

TESTS OF SIGNIFICANCE FOR DIFFERENCES BETWEEN NUMBER OF RESPONSES IN
PRE-TONE VS. TONE PERIODS FOR THE FOUR EXTREME STIMULI
DURING THE LATE STAGES OF EXTINCTION

(A negative t value indicates that response rate during tone exceeded the
response rate in the pre-tone period.)

Bird No.	t Value	df
10	.134	59
11	−3.06**	43
21	−3.66**	15
5	−2.72**	71
9	−2.51*	67

*$P < .05$ for a two-tailed test.
**$P < .01$ for a two-tailed test.

terminated by the onset of the S_D. Although no discrimination training was employed in the present study, the sharpening of the gradient is similar to the effects of such training, and it seems possible that during the period of a sharpened gradient, a mechanism such as the one described by Ray and Stein (1959) might have been operating.

A second possibility is that during the late stages of the extinction procedure, the tones were to some extent energizing the positively reinforced behavior. A facilitation of this sort is consistent with the proposition that mild levels of anxiety may augment the effects of deprivation to produce an increase in the rate of hunger-motivated responses (Brown, 1961, Chap. 5).

A third possibility is that the speed-up was a product of the interaction between the testing procedure and the baseline schedule. During the present study, key pecking was maintained on a VI schedule of reinforcement, and it is a property of this schedule that it locks up when a predetermined time has elapsed since a given reinforcement. Once the schedule locks up, however, the next peck, regardless of its time of occurrence, will yield a reinforcement. When the bird suppresses to a given tone, the rate of response is low, but because of the lock-up feature of the schedule, the probability of reinforcement per response is elevated. In general, this condition would tend to cause an increase in rate of response, and it seems possible that exposure to this condition during the extinction of suppression might have facilitating effects which would persist after the Conditioned Emotional Response to the warning signal had ceased to cause suppression.

The broad features of the retention data are perfectly clear-cut. When testing was resumed after a 2½-year interruption, the tones continued to cause suppression and the level of suppression for a given tone was inversely proportional to the frequency difference between that tone and the tone that had been used in training. Moreover, the level of suppression for each tone was approximately what one would expect, had testing proceeded without interruption. In short, the original aversive experience left effects that persisted (essentially without distortion) over a time span which encompassed approximately one-fifth of the life of the organism.

This finding is consistent with the results of Razran (1939) and Wendt (1937), which revealed that conditioned responses are retained over long periods. They are also consistent with those of Thomas, Ost, and Thomas (1937). Their work revealed that the gradient of stimulus generalization for behavior maintained under positive reinforcement exhibits negligible changes during a 21-day interpolated interval. In general, the present results extend the implications of previous work by simultaneously demonstrating the longevity and the specificity of the behavioral consequences of aversive controls.

Experiment III

By the end of Experiment II, the extinction process had progressed to a stage where the negative effects of the original aversive training were scarcely discernible in the behavior of the subjects. Only the 1000 cps tone caused any suppression at all, and the degree of suppression associated with this tone was not very substantial. It seemed possible, however, that in part these effects were deceptive. What, for example, would happen if the subjects were placed under emotional stress? Would the tones again cause substantial suppression, and, if so, how would the effects of the stress be distributed among them? The answers to these questions were of particular interest because of their relevance to problems associated with the clinical management of anxiety.

Method

The plan was to create a stressful situation by periodically administering electrical shock throughout an additional sequence of tests. The initial step was to establish an appropriate shock level for each bird. This was accomplished in a single short session (about 5 min. per bird), conducted on the day following the completion of Experiment II of the present sequence. Each subject was placed in a specially constructed Plexiglas chamber, and a series of brief shocks of increasing intensity was presented until a level was found that produced a marked, but not violent, reaction. The Plexiglas chamber was used to preclude the formation of a direct association between shock and the normal testing situation. In this session and in the test sessions that followed, shock was generated by an Applegate constant-current stimulator. The levels that were established in the fashion described above varied from bird to bird with a range of 1.25 ma. to 3.0 ma.

The tests for stimulus generalization were begun on the day following the determination of shock levels. These tests were similar to those in Experiment II except that periods of darkness (Time Out) occurred in the interval between presentations of tone and that a brief electrical shock was presented during each Time Out (TO). Since it is known that all pecking ceases during periods of darkness (Ferster and Skinner, 1957), the technique of administering shock during TO's would minimize the tendency for the birds to directly associate the shock with either the tones or the pecking behavior itself. Moreover, since the TO's with their associated shocks were to be evenly distributed throughout the sessions, the relationship of tone to shock would be uniform across tones.

The sequence of events in each session was as follows: The pigeon was placed in the chamber and the lights were turned on. After being given a 10-min. period in which to stabilize its response rate, the pigeon was placed in a condition of TO. During the TO the house lights and key light were turned off, and reinforcement was not available. The TO lasted 2 min.

Forty seconds after the beginning of the TO, the bird was administered a brief electrical shock (2 sec.) at the level that had been established previously. Six minutes and 40 sec. after the end of the TO, one of the seven tones was presented (without shock). As in Experiment II, the tone lasted 40 sec. Two minutes and 40 sec. after the termination of the tone, another TO with associated shock occurred. This pattern was repeated until the full series of seven stimuli had been presented. Then after 2 min. and 40 sec. the session ended. The sequence of stimuli was determined in the same manner as in the previous experiments. The subjects were run for eight sessions of testing on the shock condition.

Results

The effect of the introduction of shock on the baseline behavior varied somewhat from bird to bird. For several birds, it caused a temporary reduction in rate during the first minute or so following each TO. For other birds, it produced a slight speed-up during this period. In almost every instance, however, the rate returned to a level that was very nearly normal by the time each tone was introduced. For example, during the final four sessions of Experiment II, the average key-pecking rate across all birds in the several pre-tone periods was 74 responses per minute. During the first four sessions of Experiment III, the comparable average rate was 77 responses per minute.

Although the shocks did not cause a marked change in the base rate of pecking, they produced a dramatic modification in the subjects' response to the tones. Figure 6 shows the two gradients obtained during the eight "shock sessions," and for purposes of comparison also shows the final gradient from Experiment II of the present sequence. The inset shows the data from Bird 21. As shown in Fig. 6, there was a sudden and marked increase in the level of suppression to all seven stimuli. The rise was complete after two sessions in the shock condition and showed little change in the next six sessions. For the 1000 cps tone the mean suppression ratio across all birds increased from .24 to .65. Since all 40 of the suppression ratios obtained to the 1000 cps tone under this condition were higher than the last pre-shock ratios of the respective birds, it is obvious that the effect for this tone is statistically significant.

The effects of the shocks on the rest of the stimuli were analyzed in two separate tests. As seen in Fig. 6, the suppression to stimuli other than the 1000 cps tone was in general higher during the shock condition sessions than during the four sessions that preceded the introduction of shock. To evaluate the statistical significance of this effect, a non-parametric rank test for related groups was employed (Jonckheere, 1954). It contrasted the responses (suppression ratios) of a given subject to a given tone in the eight shock-condition sessions with those of the eight sessions prior to shock. The results for the six tones (the test tone exclusive of the training

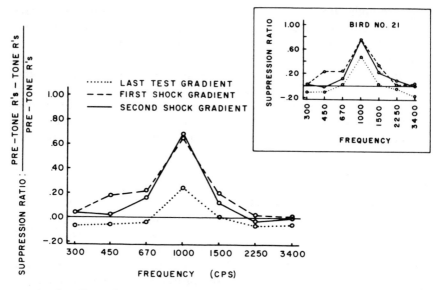

FIG. 6. The effects of emotional stress. The dotted line shows the final gradient from Experiment II of the present sequence. The solid and dashed lines show the gradients obtained during subsequent stress conditions. (The inset shows the comparable data from Bird 21.)

tone) and the five subjects were pooled. The test was highly significant: $Z = 6.52$, $P < .0001$.

It can also be seen in Fig. 6 that the effects of the stress condition were not evenly distributed among the tones, and, more specifically, that the suppression produced by a test stimulus was a function of the similarity of that stimulus to the training stimulus. To assess the significance of this finding, a non-parametric rank test for an ordered hypothesis involving related groups was conducted. A related group consisted of the responses to the three stimuli, on a given side of the gradient (e.g. 300, 450, 670), and the ordered hypothesis was that tones closer in frequency to the 1000 cps tone produce greater suppression (e.g. 670, 450, 300). For a given animal there are two comparison groups per session and thus sixteen comparison groups for the eight shock-condition sessions. The results for the five subjects were all in the predicted direction, and a test combining these results was significant at the .0001 level ($Z = 4.61$).

Discussion

The results of Experiment III provide an answer to the question of whether the negative effects of the aversive training administered three years previously were, in fact, permanently eliminated during the extinction procedures. They were not. When the subjects were placed under emotional stress, the tones again caused substantial suppression, and, moreover, the degree of suppression for a given tone was largely determined by the similarity between that tone and the one that had been employed in the original aversive training.

In the initial study with two of the present subjects, it was found that the degree to which suppression generalized was in part determined by variables that affect the ongoing behavior. In general, an increase in the motivation for the ongoing behavior produced a *reduction* in the breadth of the gradient. The present results supplement those of the initial study by revealing that the breadth of the gradient is *increased* by variables which enhance the emotional state of the subject.

Experiment IV

In Experiment III, the occurrence of shocks during the sessions led to an amplification of the suppression produced by the several tones. Experiment IV was conducted to determine whether this amplification, once initiated, would persist when shocks were no longer present.

Method

The use of TO's with shock was discontinued, and beginning on the day following the termination of Experiment III, the birds were run for eight additional sessions under the procedures that had been employed in Experiment II of the present sequence.

Results

The baseline behavior was insensitive to the removal of the TO's with shock. During Experiment IV the mean rate in the several pre-tone periods was 77 responses per minute, a value that is almost identical to the mean of the rates observed in Experiments II and III.

Figure 7 shows the two gradients obtained in Experiment IV and for purposes of comparison also shows the final gradients obtained in Experiments II and III. The inset shows the data from Bird 21. When the TO's with shocks were removed and normal testing conditions were reinstated, the suppression controlled by the tones showed an immediate drop; yet, even after several sessions, suppression to the 1000 cps tone did not drop to the level exhibited at the end of Experiment II.

Non-parametric rank tests were employed to evaluate the reliability of the observed differences between the results of Experiment IV and the other two levels of performance, i.e., Experiment III and the final level of Experiment II. The first of these tests (a related-groups analysis) concerned the effect of the removal of shock on the suppression to the 1000 cps tone. For each subject the suppression ratios produced by the 1000 cps tone during the eight sessions of Experiment IV were compared with the comparable data from Experiment III. The result for subjects combined was significant: $Z = 4.34, P < .0001$. The same test was used for the com-

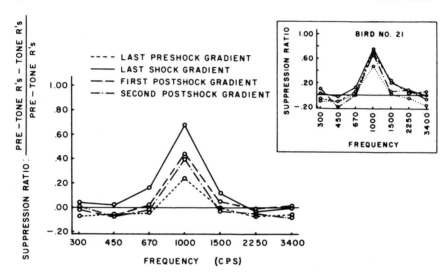

FIG. 7. The aftereffects of emotional stress. The solid line shows the final gradient from the stress condition. The dashed lines show the gradients obtained in the sessions following the termination of the stress condition. The dotted line shows the final gradient obtained prior to the initiation of the stress condition. (The inset shows the comparable data from Bird 21.)

parison of the suppression to the 1000 cps tone between Experiment IV and the final eight sessions of Experiment II. The result was again significant: $Z = 2.677, P < .01$.

Two tests were conducted on the six other tones. Their format was similar to the first of the tests reported in Experiment III. For a given subject, the eight suppression ratios to a given tone for either the eight final sessions of Experiment II or the eight sessions of Experiment III were contrasted with the comparable data from Experiment IV. It was found that the drop from Experiment III to Experiment IV was significant, $Z = 5.667, P < .0001$, but that the small observed difference between the levels in Experiment IV and Experiment II was not statistically significant: $Z = 1.33, P > .05$. Apparently, with the removal of the stress condition, all tones showed a reduction in their capacity to produce suppression. For the 1000 cps tone, however, the reduction was less than complete.

Discussion

The decline in suppression with the removal of the stress condition is consistent wtih expectations. The finding that all tendencies toward suppression did not immediately return to the pre-stress level, however, is surprising, and it appears that its explanation will require a far deeper understanding of aversive controls than currently exists. Perhaps this result depended upon some form of conditioning during the stress period.

If so, however, it is difficult to specify just what was conditioned and to see why the aftereffects of the stress were not distributed uniformly among the several tones. Perhaps the emotional by-products of the stress remained after the conditions that produced them were removed. If so, why did the baseline behavior fail to reflect these effects, and why did the effects persist throughout the eight sessions of Experiment IV? Finally, one may ask whether the occurrence of tone during the stress condition was a critical factor in producing the result. Clearly, much more work will be necessary if these and related questions are to be answered.

For the present, however, we can only note that these results seem to have numerous implications for our comprehension of problems associated with the clinical management of anxiety and its symptomatic manifestations. Not only does stress amplify the emotional response to stimuli with an aversive history, but, once amplified, these responses can continue to produce their negative effects (conditioned suppression) long after the source of stress has been removed.

General Conclusions

When viewed in the context of the previous history of these birds, the present results make it clear that aversive training can produce a profound effect upon behavior and, moreover, that the effects can persist through a significant portion of the subject's life. Exposure to a noxious event which is consistently preceded by a neutral stimulus endows that stimulus with the capacity to suppress behavior, and stimuli which are similar to it also exhibit this capacity. In general, the degree to which the suppression generalizes is an inverse function of the motivation for the ongoing behavior and a direct function of the physical similarity between that stimulus and the one involved in the original aversive training. The mere passage of time plays little, if any, role in these processes. Finally, when stimuli that have been employed in extinction procedures are presented during a period of emotional stress, they regain a part of their former capacity to suppress behavior, and the effect may persist long after the stress period has ended.

REFERENCES

Brady, J. V. Extinction of a conditioned fear response as a function of reinforcement schedules for the competing behavior. *Arch. Psychiat.*, 1955, **39**, 5–19.

Brady, J. V., and Hunt, H. F. An experimental approach to the analysis of emotional behavior. *J. Psychol.*, 1955, **40**, 313–324.

Brown, J. S. The generalization of approach responses as a function of stimulus intensity and strength of motivation. *J. comp. physiol. Psychol.*, 1942, **33**, 209–226.

Brown, J. S. *The motivation of behavior.* New York: McGraw-Hill, 1961.

Clark, F. C. The effect of deprivation and frequency of reinforcement on variable-interval responding. *J. exp. Anal. Behav.*, 1958, **1**, 221–228.

Estes, W. K., and Skinner, B. F. Some quantitative properties of anxiety. *J. exp. Psychol.*, 1941, **29**, 390–400.

Ferster, C. B., and Skinner, B. F. *Schedules of reinforcement.* New York: Appleton-Century-Crofts, 1957.

Fleshler, M., and Hoffman, H. S. Stimulus generalization of conditioned suppression. *Science*, 1961, **133**, 753–755.

Geller, I. The acquisition and extinction of conditioned suppression as a function of the baseline reinforcer. *J. comp. physiol. Psychol.*, 1960, **3**, 235–240.

Hoffman, H. S. A flexible connector for delivering shock to pigeons. *J. exp. Anal. Behav.*, 1960, **3**, 330.

Hoffman, H. S., and Fleshler, M. Stimulus factors in aversive control: The generalization of conditioned suppression. *J. exp. Anal. Behav.*, 1961, **4**, 371–378.

Hoffman, H. S., Fleshler, M., and Jensen, P. Stimulus aspects of aversive controls: The retention of conditioned suppression. *J. exp. Anal. Behav.*, 1963, **6**, 575–583.

Hovland, C. I. The generalization of conditioned responses: I. The sensory generalization of conditioned response with varying frequencies of tones. *J. exp. Psychol.*, 1937, **17**, 125–148. (a)

Hovland, C. I. The generalization of conditioned responses: III. Extinction, spontaneous recovery and disinhibition of conditioned and of generalized responses. *J. exp. Psychol.*, 1937, **21**, 47–62. (b)

Hovland, C. I. The generalization of conditioned responses: IV. The effects of varying amounts of reinforcement upon the degree of generalization of conditioned responses. *J. exp. Psychol.*, 1937, **21**, 261–276. (c)

Jenkins, H. M., and Harrison, R. H. Effect of discrimination training on auditory generalization. *J. exp. Psychol.*, 1960, **59**, 246–253.

Jonckheere, A. R. A test of significance for the relation between *m* rankings and *k* ranked categories. *Brit. J. Statist. Psychol.*, 1954, **7**, 93–100.

Littman, R. A. Conditioned generalization of the galvanic skin response to tones. *J. exp. Psychol.*, 1949, **39**, 868–882.

Mednick, S. A. A learning theory approach to research in schizophrenia. *Psychol. Bull.*, 1958, **55**, 316–327.

Ray, O., and Stein, L. Generalization of conditioned suppression. *J. exp. Anal. Behav.*, 1959, **2**, 357.

Razran, G. H. S. Studies in configural conditioning. VI. Comparative extinction and forgetting of pattern and of single-stimulus conditioning. *J. exp. Psychol.*, 1939, **24**, 432–438.

Sidman, M. Normal sources of pathological behavior. *Science*, 1960, **132**, 61–68.

Thomas, D. R., Ost, J., and Thomas, D. Stimulus generalization as a function of the time between training and testing procedures. *J. exp. Anal. Behav.*, 1960, **3**, 9–14.

Wendt, G. G. Two-and-one-half-year retention of a conditioned response. *J. gen. Psychol.*, 1937, **17**, 178–180.

Wickens, D. D., Schroder, H. M., and Snide, J. D. Primary stimulus generalization of the GSR under two conditions. *J. exp. Psychol.*, 1954, **47**, 52–56.

Winer, B. J. Statistical principles in experimental design. New York: McGraw-Hill, 1962.

22. Investigations of Response-Mediated Generalization

G. Robert Grice, *University of Illinois*

For several years we have been engaged in a program of research directed at the problem of mediated generalization. Our attack has been focused on the "response-produced–cue" theory, which has provided the basis for Guthrie's theory of stimulus generalization, Hull's principle of secondary generalization, and Miller and Dollard's principle of acquired stimulus equivalence, and has provided the basis for extensive theoretical discussion and research. As is well known, the theory states that responses serve as mediators because of their sensory consequences. If the same response is made to two stimuli, these stimuli are supposed to become more equivalent, and generalization of other responses should occur between them because of the common sensory elements introduced by the mediating response. Probably the most distinctive feature of our research in this area is that we utilize explicit, identifiable, and experimentally controlled responses as mediators. This is in contrast to the more usual practice of merely assuming that such responses occur and have stimulus consequences. All of the work to be reported here has been in human conditioning employing generalization of the conditioned eyelid response as evidence for mediational effects.

One basic experimental paradigm usually has been employed in this research. It utilizes a differential conditioning procedure in which three stimuli are presented. One of these is the conditioned stimulus that is always paired with an air-puff unconditioned stimulus. The other two are negative stimuli and are never reinforced by the air-puff. The three stimuli are presented in an irregular order on successive trials of the experiment. The subjects also make two instructed responses, manual or verbal, to the three stimuli. One of these responses is made in common to the conditioned stimulus and to one of the negative stimuli, on trials when either of these stimuli occurs. The other response is made to the second negative stimulus. There is always complete counterbalancing of the negative stimulus that has the response common to the conditioned stimulus,

The research reported here was supported by Grants G-4416 and G-14223 from the National Science Foundation.

and of the response that serves in common to the two stimuli. After counterbalancing, the negative stimuli may be identified as a "Same-Response Stimulus" and a "Different-Response Stimulus." Evidence for a mediational effect consists of an asymmetrical generalization function. According to mediation theory, there should be a larger number of generalized eyeblinks to the negative stimulus to which the mediating response is made in common with the conditioned stimulus than to the other negative stimulus, with the response not so associated.

In one such experiment, reported by Grice and Davis (1960), we used three tones that varied in frequency (240, 850, and 1900 cps) as stimuli. The middle tone was the conditioned stimulus, and the high and low tones were negative. The mediating responses were two lever-switch responses, one made with the first finger of the right hand and the other with the thumb of the left hand. In addition to the usual conditioning instructions, subjects were given discrimination-reaction–time instructions to respond quickly with one of these responses to the middle tone and to one of the others, and with the second manual response to the third tone. The airpuff always followed the middle tone at a ½-sec. inter-stimulus interval. A total of 100 trials were presented, the last 60 including 20 presentations

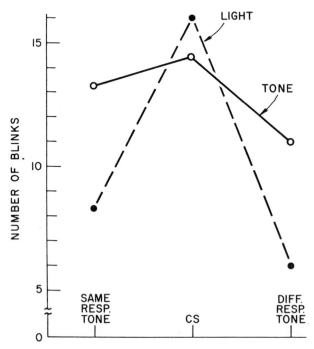

FIG. 1. Grice and Davis (1960) experiments. One-half sec. inter-stimulus interval.

of each tone. The number of blinks to each tone on these trials is indicated in Fig. 1 by the points connected by the solid lines. As may be seen, the predicted asymmetry was obtained, and it was statistically significant.

A second very similar experiment was conducted in which the middle tone was replaced by a light as the conditioned stimulus. Mediated generalization is supposed to depend entirely on the action of a mediating response, and, as far as the externally presented stimuli are concerned, it should occur across sensory modalities as well as within. The results of this experiment are indicated by the broken lines of Fig. 1. Again, the predicted asymmetry was obtained and was significant. The difference in the absolute levels of the functions is presumably due to the difference between within-modality and cross-modality primary generalization. The degree of asymmetry, however, which indicates the mediational effect, did not differ significantly between the two experiments.

In these experiments we were concerned with the possibility of artifacts' resulting from non-associative facilitative effects, which might occur if reaction time systematically varied between stimuli. However, covariance adjustments for variations in speed of the mediating responses did not reduce the degree of asymmetrical generalization.

Studies of Implicit Mediators

While the present program is primarily concerned with the effect of overt mediating responses, the literature frequently assumes that such responses may be implicit. Several of our experiments have been directed toward the problem of determining whether implicit representations of these same responses may be effective. In one experiment (Grice and Davis, 1958) similar to those above, subjects were instructed to make the manual reactions after the trial was over. Thus, during the inter-stimulus interval, the subject was presumably set to make the proper response. Although a very small degree of asymmerty in the predicted direction was obtained, it was not statistically significant. In a second experiment, an attempt was made to intensify this differential set to respond. Subjects were asked to make the switch response as a discrimination-reaction–time response to a click that occurred at the termination of the tones. This time there was no asymmetry at all. In a third experiment, after an initial practice period, subjects were asked just to "think about" and implicitly rehearse the proper response on each trial. Again, no evidence of mediated generalization was obtained. Of course, there are real difficulties with this experiment. We don't know for sure whether the proper "thoughts" did occur on each trial, and if they did, we don't know their latencies.

Another experiment proved to be one of this kind even though it was not originally planned for this purpose. It was designed to study the mediational effects of spoken words rather than the manual responses. The words "High" and "Low" replaced these responses. However, it turned out that the reaction times for the words were considerably slower than for the lever-switch responses, and they usually did not occur until after the end of the trial. The results of the experiment were completely negative so far as mediational effects were concerned. In summary, then, we have never obtained any evidence that implicit representations of mediating responses can serve as mediators, at least in the way a simple stimulus-response analysis of such things would seem to imply. Whenever we have obtained these effects, the mediating response has been overt, and the mediating and mediated responses have occurred very close together.

The Response-Unconditioned Stimulus Interval

If one conceives of mediated generalization as being dependent upon response-produced cues, a variable that becomes of immediate importance is the time interval between the mediating response and the unconditioned stimulus. This, of course, is because of the relation to the well-known facts about the inter-stimulus interval in conditioning. From this point of view, the Grice and Davis (1958, 1960) experiments that did yield positive results would hardly seem to represent a very efficient condition. There was a constant, ½-sec. inter-stimulus interval, with the mediating response occurring as a reaction-time response to the conditioned stimulus onset. Now reaction time is variable, and the result was that it frequently occurred late in the inter-stimulus interval, and often even after the unconditioned stimulus was over. Presumably, the proper arrangement would be for the mediating response always to take place *before* the unconditioned stimulus, at a favorable inter-stimulus interval.

A first attempt. The first experiment we conducted in an attempt to approximate this arrangement involved two presentations of the conditioned stimulus on each trial. The conditioned stimulus came on for a ½-sec., was off for 1 sec., and then came on for ½-sec. The negative stimuli were presented in the same way. The subjects made their discrimination-reaction–time responses to the first presentation; the puff occurred at the end of the second presentation of the conditioned stimulus. We then looked for conditioned responses during the second presentation. The logic of this experiment was, of course, that the mediating response took place before the unconditioned stimulus, and traces of cues produced by this response should be present in the scoring interval. The result of this experiment was completely negative. When we used the three-tone design, no asymmetry was obtained at all. This result is somewhat embarrassing to response-produced–cue theory. Although the experiment has its definite limitations, it certainly seems that it should have been a more favorable condition than the earlier experiments with the short inter-stimulus interval.

Experiments with response-produced unconditioned stimulus. One serious problem with the preceding experiments, and with this research in general, is the inherent variability of the reaction times of the mediating response. In the experiments reported so far, this introduced variable time relations between the mediating response and both the conditioned stimulus and the unconditioned stimulus. A technique that we have recently found promising eliminated one of these sources of variability. This technique is to arrange for the performance of the mediating reaction to deliver the air-puff. Miller and Cole (1936) reported a very interesting experiment in which pressing a telegraph key delivered the unconditioned stimulus, in their case a shock. This produced a very rapid and stable increase in the frequency of eyeblinks. However, the technique has never previously been used with any differential conditioning procedures. In the next two experiments, we used our same three-stimulus design with a light as the conditioned stimulus and the two tones as negative. When the mediating response was made to the light, it delivered the puff. Following Miller and Cole (1936), it occurred immediately, except for about a 60 ms lag in the air line. In the first of these experiments, the mediating responses were the two manual responses. In the second they were verbal—the words "One" and "Two." The results of these experiments in terms of anticipatory responses are presented in Fig. 2.

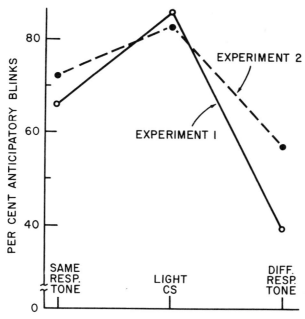

FIG. 2. Response-presented unconditioned stimulus. Experiment 1, manual mediating response; Experiment 2, verbal mediator.

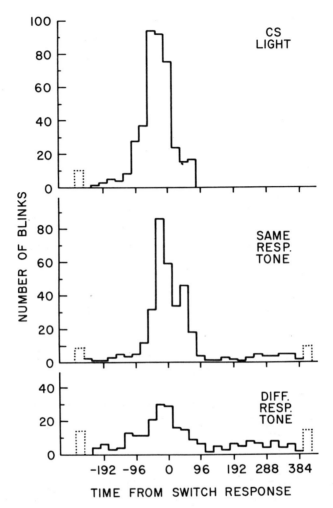

FIG. 3. Latency distributions. Immediate, response-presented unconditioned stimulus. Manual mediator. Units are milliseconds.

The solid lines labeled Exp. 1 are for the manual responses. Very clear-cut asymmetrical generalization was obtained in each experiment, and it was statistically significant. The effect was larger with the manual mediating responses than with the words. This condition represents the largest such effect we have yet obtained.

One thing that is essential to an understanding of these phenomena is a careful examination of the temporal relationships between the mediating and mediated responses. In conventional eyelid-conditioning experiments, it is common to plot the latency distribution of conditioned responses with respect to onset of the conditioned stimulus. Here, it makes more sense to plot the latency of the blinks with respect to the mediating response. This has been done, and the distributions for the manual-response experiment are plotted in Fig. 3.

The zero point on this figure is the moment of closure of the lever switch. In other words, it is approximately the completion of the rapid, switch-snapping response. Negative values precede this point, and positive values follow it. These data are quite remarkable for two reasons. The first is the extremely low variability they have for behavioral data. Of course, the distribution of blinks to the conditioned stimulus is attenuated by the time for unconditioned responses, but the interquartile range is only 55 ms. However, the distribution for the "Same Response Tone" is not so attenuated, and has an interquartile range of only 80 ms. Blinks to the "Different Response Tone" do not display such a pronounced mode, and have an interquartile range of 217 ms. Thus, the asymmetrical generalization is due to the difference in frequency of response within an extremely limited period of time.

The second remarkable thing about the data is the time at which the blinks occur. As may be seen, they are approximately synchronized with the completion of the switch response—half of them actually precede it. This is clearly not what the response-produced–cue theory would predict. The blinks should follow the mediating response by an interval equal to a reaction time. Of course, there is the travel time of the switch, which means that the mediating response actually began a bit earlier. But, even so, it appears clear that the latency of these responses with respect to the mediating response is less than conditioned-response latency. Thus, while the predicted asymmetry was obtained, the response-produced–cue theory appears unable to account for the details of the data.

Data from the experiment using words as mediators are presented in Fig. 4. These data are less precise, and the degree of asymmetry is also less. The blinks appear to occur even earlier with respect to the mediating response. However, we do not attach too much importance to this at the present time, since we are not sure at just what stage in the formation of the verbal response our voice-key was activated. At least the spoken word seems to work pretty much the way the manual response does, although why it is less precise and less effective we do not know.

Although the two preceding experiments eliminated variability in the interval between the mediating response and the unconditioned stimulus and yielded the predicted asymmetrical generalization, they still should not represent an optimum arrangement from the point of view of response-produced–cue theory. As stated earlier, if the stimulus consequence of a response is to be regarded as the essential mediating event, then the unconditioned stimulus should follow the mediating response at a favorable

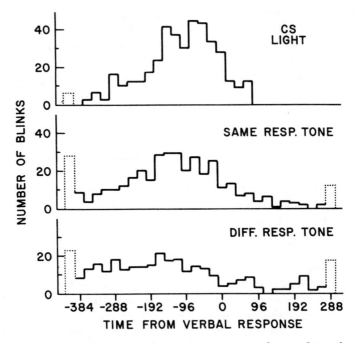

FIG. 4. Latency distributions. Immediate, response-presented unconditioned stimulus. Verbal mediator.

conditioning interval. In the next experiment, this was accomplished by introducing a delay, so that the puff followed the manual response to the conditioned stimulus by 0.5 seconds. The termination of the light-conditioned stimulus and of the negatives tones were also delayed until this time. Otherwise, the experiment was the same as the response-presented–puff experiment just described that used the manual mediators. In spite of the presumably favorable conditions, this experiment produced a negative finding. There was absolutely no evidence of asymmetrical generalization. In fact, the precision of the experiment was such that, on the basis of the .95 confidence limits, we may reject the hypothesis that a true difference in the predicted direction between the two tones is as large as 1.5 responses.

The latency distributions for this experiment are presented in Fig. 5. Looking first at the data for the conditioned stimulus, under this delayed-puff condition there is no evidence of a modal frequency of blinks synchronized with the manual response. There is a mode occurring within the ½-sec. delay interval. This looks very much like ordinary conditioning data if a conventional conditioning stimulus had occurred at the point of the manual response. In fact, these data are the only evidence we have yet obtained which suggest that a response can serve as a conditioned stimulus for eliciting the conditioned eyelid response. Turning to the negative stimuli, however, we see not only no asymmetry, but no evidence of a modal frequency to either stimulus. If the mediating response was serving as a conditioned stimulus when it was made to the light, it certainly did not act as one when it occurred in response to another stimulus. Now, according to response-produced–cue theory, this is precisely what is supposed to produce mediated generalization.

In summary, then, our results have produced almost no support for the response-produced–cue theory. When we have obtained the asymmetry suggesting response mediation, conditions have been unfavorable from the point of view of the theory. When conditions suggested by the theory have been favorable, we have not obtained the phenomenon. This does not mean that we may not yet obtain favorable evidence. There may be defects in our experiments that we can correct. But at least at the present time, it appears that the theory lacks the generality it is widely assumed to possess.

This leaves us with the task of attempting to explain our rather impressive positive instances of "response mediation," which involve the approximate synchrony of the mediating and mediated responses. One possibility is that some implicit or central mediator precedes and evokes both responses together. Perhaps this could be verbal. Yet it is a bit difficult to see why a ½-sec. delay of the puff should completely wipe out such a proc-

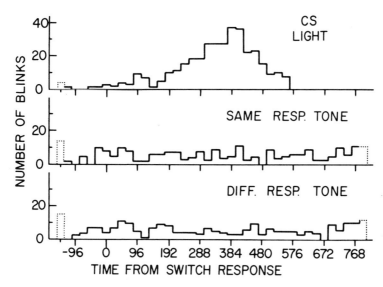

FIG. 5. Latency distributions. Response-presented unconditioned stimulus, delayed ½ sec. Manual mediator.

ess. Besides, our attempts to produce implicit mediators experimentally have never worked. We have also considered the possibility that there exists a principle of response integration by means of which separate responses become organized into coordinated acts. The extremely small variability between the responses suggests something like this. It has been suggested before that there may be response-response learning as well as the more widely publicized varieties. If something like this does exist, it is probably important, and we should study it.

REFERENCES

Grice, G. R., and Davis, J. D. Mediated stimulus equivalence and distinctiveness in human conditioning. *J. exp. Psychol.*, 1958, **35**, 565–571.

Grice, G. R., and Davis, J. D. Effect of concurrent responses on the evocation and generalization of the conditioned eyeblink. *J. exp. Psychol.*, 1960, **59**, 391–395.

Miller, J., and Cole, L. E. The influence of a "voluntary" reaction upon the development and the extinction of the conditioned eyelid reaction. *J. genet. Psychol.*, 1936, **48**, 405–440.

Index

abstraction, 250

acquisition: curves, 113–114; of cue distinctiveness, 132; reacquisition, 136; effect on generalization, 170; of matching behavior, 291–301 *passim*, 309; of oddity, 296–298; acquired stimulus equivalence, 373

adaptation, effect on saturation, 36–37

Ades, H. W., 141, 147

Albe-Fessard, A., 171

all-or-none response, 140

Allen, W. F., 171

Amassian, V. E., 171

Anger, D., 342f, 345n

Appel, J. B., 339

approach-avoidance generalization gradients, 331–336, 341, 351; and discrimination training, 340n; differences between, 351

Asdourian, D., 346n

association-response areas, ablation of, 173f

asymmetry of generalization function, 373–375, 379

Atkinson, R. C., 112

attending hierarchy, 62–70, 115

attention, 66, 82ff, 174

Attneave, F., 78, 109

attractiveness of stimulus situation, 39–44, 48, 51, 229, 233

auditory cortex: ablation of, 135, 139–143 *passim*, 149, 164, 171, 173; neural activity of, 160; spatial relations of, 163. *See also* cerebral cortex

auditory generalization, 57, 265

avoidance, 41, 331–351 *passim;* conditioned avoidance behavior, 134, 138, 141, 148; approach-avoidance generalization gradients, 331–336, 340f, 351; continuous-avoidance behavior, 331, 347

Baron, M. R., 4, 15, 115f

Barrera, E., 139

Bartley, S. H., 174–175

Bass, M. J., 166

Beckenbach, E., 82

behavioral contrast, 111

behavioral control, 76

behavioral coordinates, 74

Békésy, G., 27

Bellman, R., 82

Bergum, B. O., 44

Berryman, R., 4, 281, 301n

Bersh, P. J., 336, 338

"best frequency," 168

bidimensional gradients, 30

bidimensional stimuli, 81, 85, 106, 108

bidirectional gradients, 104, 274

Bilodeau, E. A., 4, 15

Bitterman, M. E., 112, 179, 278, 281

Blackwell, H. R., 167

Bliss, D., 171

Blough, D. S., 96–99, 112, 180, 188, 224, 252, 306, 309

Boneau, C., 46, 57, 257

Borenstein, P., 164

Boring, E. G., 27

Bowsher, D., 171

Brady, J. V., 346, 356, 358

brain damage, *see* auditory cortex; cerebral cortex

brightness, 34f, 62. *See also* intensity

Brogden, W. J., 157

Brown, J. S., 4, 15, 18, 27, 52, 157, 169f, 175, 360

Brown, T. S., 119

Bruner, J., 164

Brush, F. R., 342, 345

Bugelski, R., 278, 281

Burke, C. J., 112

Burstein, K. R., 57, 257

Buser, P., 164, 171